THE STORY OF

Lake City

COLORADO

And Its Surrounding Areas

Including the Tale of Alferd Packer—
The Colorado Cannibal

P. David Smith

WESTERN REFLECTIONS PUBLISHING COMPANY®

Lake City, Colorado

ISBN 978-1-937851-21-7

First Edition
Printed in the United States

Cover and text design by Laurie Casselberry
Laurie Goralka Design

Cover photo by Tricia Hartman

Western Reflections Publishing Company
P. O. Box 1149
951 N. Highway 149
Lake City, Colorado 81235
www.westernreflectionspublishing.com
(970) 944-0110

DEDICATION

*To my wife Jan, for always putting up with the times alone
while I have been writing my books, and for the many hours
that she spent helping me in editing, retyping,
and other tasks related to my being an author.*

*Thank you, and I still continue to love you more every day,
especially after fifty years of marriage.*

Oh Beautiful Lake City

Oh beautiful Lake City
Here is where I want to be,
Here with the mountains high above
Here with the folks that I love.

Oh beautiful Lake City
Here's where I want to be,
Here where the deer and trout abound
Wildflowers springing from the ground
Here with the sun's golden beams,
Here with the trees and mountain streams.

Condensed from the words of a song written by Alex Carey

TABLE OF CONTENTS

Acknowledgments

‎—⦿—

There are five main written sources that the author has relied upon heavily in writing this book. Two of them are his own books — *Exploring the San Juan Triangle* and *Ouray — Chief of the Utes*. The first of these books is a 2004 update of *Mountain Mysteries,* which was written in 1978 by this author and Marvin Gregory as the first historical trail and road guide to the western San Juans. The update, *Exploring the Historic San Juan Triangle,* expanded the book to a larger area and has a chapter on each of the major San Juan mountain towns, including Lake City. It is also a historical travel guide along all of the highways and most of the jeep trails of the San Juan Mountains. *Ouray — Chief of the Utes* is the story of Ute Chief Ouray, the only overall chief of the Utes (although the title was given to him by the U.S. government, it was accepted by the Utes), but also contains the story of the Ute people in historic times, much of which coincides with the lifetimes of Ouray and his beloved wife Chipeta. It further contains a chapter on the Alferd Packer event. Ouray was there to advise Packer and his companions to not make the trip across the San Juan Mountains in the winter of 1873-74, and he was coincidentally there when Packer showed up at the Ute agency on Cochetopa Pass in the spring of 1874; looking, according to Ouray, much too well off for a man who had undergone the hardships that he claimed he had endured.

The other three books used extensively for reference include a Masters' Thesis (later a book) by Thomas Gray Thompson entitled, *The Social and Cultural History of Lake City, Colorado, 1876 to 1900.* He does an extremely good job for the time (1961), but misses some of the discoveries made by historians since then. His book is especially good in trying to put the "Lake City Spirit" into words. Unfortunately, the work is out of print, but the thesis may be found at the Western State University Library in Gunnison and at the Hinsdale County Museum in Lake City. *Tiny Hinsdale of the Silvery San Juan* was written in 1964 by

9

lifelong residents Carolyn and Clarence Wright and has been reprinted by Western Reflections Publishing Company. It is based on oral and written history, family and personal experiences, and the events which the authors lived or shared. It also contains ninety-four photographs that are invaluable in themselves. The final book is *Geology and Ore Deposits Near Lake City, Colorado,* written by John Duer Irving and Howland Bancroft for the United States Geological Survey as *Bulletin 478* in 1911 (also reprinted by Western Reflections Publishing Co.). Although a geological book, the authors fortunately used plenty of words to describe the climate, topography, and history of Hinsdale County. Their book also describes the minerals that were being mined at each mine, and the particular troubles, needs, or techniques needed at those mines.

To these five sources has been added information on Lake City and Hinsdale County from over 100 other books. Some of this information involves only a paragraph or two, while some take up several chapters. In addition, dozens of pamphlets, newspapers, and articles supplement information from the five primary sources and other books. All source material may be found in the bibliography of this book and hopefully will be of value to anyone wishing information on a particular subject.

And last, but not least, the author is very indebted to several local residents who have reviewed this manuscript, especially Marty Priest for her fine job of editing; Burton and Nora Smith for local history and especially on Lake San Cristobal's and Lake City's early tourist history; Michelle Pierce for additional information on Alferd Packer; Linda Pavich, Hinsdale County Clerk, for help with courthouse research; Henry Woods for important historical input, Edna Mason for permission to use her beautiful nature photographs, and Lyn Lampert for local history, letting me use extensive quotes from his book *Lake City Serendipity,* and for his other thoughts on what makes Lake City special.

This satellite photo of the San Juans in the late spring shows the high country still covered with snow and makes the canyons, rivers, and large creeks very visible. Most of the spots without snow would have been good hunting areas for the Native Americans. (Courtesy of NASA Earth Observatory – 1973)

INTRODUCTION

⸺◉⸻

Lake City, Colorado and Hinsdale, its surrounding county, contain awesome scenic beauty, wonderful opportunities for outdoor sports, and charming people; yet it is one of the least known areas of Colorado. It is also one of the most isolated spots in the Continental United States and the least in density of population of any county in Colorado. After several booms and busts, Lake City was at one time officially pronounced to be "the most remote spot in the Continental United States" by the U.S.G.S. [1]

Hinsdale County lies in the southwestern part of Colorado and contains 621,440 acres (1,123 square miles). The altitude ranges from 8,500 feet, where the Lake Fork of the Gunnison River crosses the county's northern boundary into Gunnison County, to more than 14,000 feet at five major peaks in the county. Although Hinsdale County has in the past had some good economic times, it suffered from boom and bust cycles of its gold and silver mines from 1875 to 1910 — discoveries that burst on the scene and then petered out just as quickly. Irving and Bancroft, in their book *Geology and Ore Deposits Near Lake City, Colorado,* delicately called this phenomena "alternate periods of general excitement and (then) excessive activity," and they noted that although other mining camps went through the same stages that in "few places in Colorado have they been so pronounced as at Lake City." [2]

After 1910 its economy continued to decline through a half a century of depression. Today, Hinsdale County and the Town of Lake City still strive to overcome the problems of extreme remoteness, an amazing but very short tourist season, long winters, and not enough lasting business enterprises to keep all of the people who want to live in Lake City employed.

In the early boom days of San Juan mining, Lake City was considered the "Queen of the San Juans." During this time it quickly became the biggest and by far the most civilized and sophisticated of the early San

Juan towns; and, for a while, Lake City was called the "Metropolis of the San Juans." Unfortunately, the initial boom was soon over. Within five or six years Lake City started to decline, but to the credit of its inhabitants, Lake City never did become a ghost town, although all the other mining camps in Hinsdale County eventually did.

Out of these times of continual boom and bust, an attitude arose among the residents that stayed in Lake City — an attitude that has endured to some extent right up to present. Thomas Thompson wrote:

The social and cultural pattern set by the early leaders engendered a quality of endurance and faith in the future." [3]

This author would describe what happened as being like a queen, who was forced to step down from her throne, yet still kept her dignity, grace, refinement, and hopeful manner.

Thomas Thompson, who based his entire thesis on this theory, quoted old time resident M. K. Mott to support his thoughts on the matter in terms of the early prospectors:

I am like the miners, for I still believe that some "next spring" that wonderful gold vein will be found and that the beautiful mountain town of Lake City will once again be teeming with life. It is a wise Providence that arranged the gold and silver so that one generation does not get it all. [4]

In present times, over a thousand people come to Lake City and Hinsdale County to join the locals and stay for most of the summer in second homes or in recreational vehicles. It is as if they have found their "home" and don't need to go anywhere else in the summer. They usually return year after year, bringing their kids, and later in life, their grandchildren; but only about 450 hardy souls presently live in Lake City year-round. Part of the draw to the area has been the spectacular scenery and great fishing; but, as solitude becomes more precious in the hustle and bustle of our world, places like Lake City will become more and more important to many people. This quiet, slow way of life will probably not change much for Lake City in the near future. One reason is that 95.3% of all the land in the county is government land and there simply are not many places on private land to put people. Much of the public land in Hinsdale County is officially designated "Wilderness" by the United States government, and development opportunities are rarely present and motorized access is denied.

Most of the San Juan Mountains are high and rugged. This shot from the top of Engineer Mountain shows Engineer Pass in the foreground, American Flats (the light colored area) in the center left, and Wetterhorn and Matterhorn in the distance. (Bill Fries III Photo)

Tourism is the major industry of Hinsdale County at present, but some small scale mining is still carried on. Many of the year-round locals are employed in some form of governmental activity — city, county, state, or the school system. The population in the summer swells with tourists from Texas, Oklahoma, Louisiana, and many other states seeking relief from the heat in their part of the country, but the summer season is short. The town is at full capacity (about 2,000 to 3,000, including campers and those in recreational vehicles) for only two months (around June 15 to August 15); but there is also a month or so on each side of that peak season where tourism is respectable.

In the winter, after the tourists and most of the second homeowners have gone, the residents make their own entertainment, much of it of a kind that has not been seen in the United States for many years. Time is spent socializing around the fire or at the small local coffee shops. Winter activities include snowmobiling, ice skating, ice fishing, ice climbing, snow shoeing, or skiing at the local ski hill. Get-togethers are popular to play cards, or celebrate a birthday, or see a talent show at the town's small theater. The churches and bible study groups are also important.

As Duane Smith and Duane Vandenbusche put it on the first page of their book *A Land Alone*:

> *(Local residents of the San Juans) believe they have been sharpened and hardened by the numbing cold, heavy snow, high elevation, and rugged terrain of the region.*[5]

While this statement continues to be true even today, Lake City year-round residents revel amidst the harsh elements inherent with living in the San Juans; and they fiercely treasure the people, personalities, and the natural beauty that make up their unique community.

The history of Lake City and its surrounding area is important, because of its special contributions to Colorado's past and what it will certainly contribute to Colorado's future. There were many exciting events that happened in Lake City and Hinsdale County, even though the area was never as rough around the edges as most Colorado mining towns. It is important that we know and understand the local history as we progress into a crowded future that is certain to put pressure on a unique way of life that draws special people to Hinsdale County year after year. It is important that we preserve what is still physically left of the past; which, except for frequent fires, has been done very successfully right up to the present. But most importantly, the very diverse way of life that exists in Lake City and its surrounding area needs to be recognized, protected, and encouraged. If not, the present and past spirit of Lake City and Hinsdale County will cease to exist. Hopefully that will never happen.

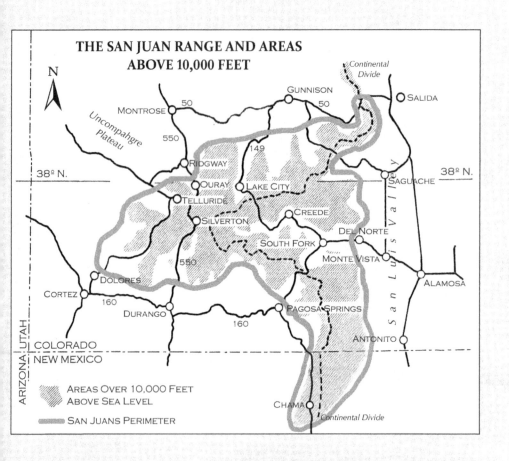

THE SAN JUAN RANGE AND AREAS ABOVE 10,000 FEET

Note the bulge to the west of the Continental Divide, which was caused by the San Juan Dome and shifted the Rio Grande River's headwaters much further west but still on the eastern side of the Continental Divide. It is a long story but this also put Lake City in Texas at one time. (Western Reflections Publishing Co. map)

CHAPTER 1

BEFORE THERE WAS A TOWN

T he future spot on planet Earth where Hinsdale County and the Town of Lake City, Colorado, would eventually be established is at the north central edge of today's San Juan Mountains and is almost in the exact center of the southwestern quarter of the State of Colorado. [6] Mountains have been formed, grown larger, and been worn down at this spot for eons, as the area is affected by the plate movements of the earth, as well as having had several episodes of extreme volcanic activity. In contrast, there have also been vast time periods when the area was covered by shallow seas. The present mountains were only beginning to develop about 30 to 35 million years ago (as opposed to the 4 ½ billion year history of the earth), when a great dome was formed by extensive volcanic activity.

Ash, lava, and the pushing up of the ground from below raised the highest elevation of what geologists now call "The San Juan Dome" to over 26,000 feet above sea level. The dome was so high that it shifted the location of the Continental Divide, moving it in a great bulge to the west along a north-south line from Cochetopa Pass all the way south to a spot slightly north of present-day Wolf Creek Pass. Famous early historian Hubert Bancroft wrote that "it was as if the great spinal cord of the continent had bent upon itself in some spasm of the earth."[7] The mountains that we see today are actually the remains of the San Juan Dome after it has been worn away by millions of years of erosion, mainly by glaciers. These glaciers grew and shrank about fifteen times during three major glacial episodes over the millennia until about 10,000 B.C., when most of the glaciers disappeared and the earth was well out of the Great Ice Age and into a warming trend that was even hotter than at present.[8] The San Juans are the largest range and have the highest average elevation of any mountains in the continental United States, and, at more than 10,000 square miles, is larger than some states.[9]

The warmer climate and melting glaciers meant that the rivers in the San Juan Mountains were at times much deeper and wider than at present. This was due to not only the melting of glacial ice, but also because the climate at that time had much more rain and snow than at present. The extra moisture meant that the land was not as arid as today, and great masses of vegetation grew below the glaciers and rivers, including tall grasses, huge shrubs, and massive trees. At that time, the San Juan Mountains were a very fertile land that attracted much greater numbers and much larger animals than the land supports today. These animals included mastodons, wooly mammoths, and saber tooth tigers.

As a result of all of this activity by fire and ice, the San Juan Mountains became very steep; and, because they are relatively new, geologically speaking, very rugged. When Hubert Bancroft published his *History of Nevada, Colorado, and Wyoming* in 1890, he declared the San Juan Mountains to be "the wildest and most inaccessible region in Colorado, if not all of North America."[10] Even after millions of years of erosion, fourteen of today's San Juan Mountains are still over 14,000 feet in elevation. Five of those "fourteeners" are in Hinsdale County (Uncompahgre - 14,309 feet, Wetterhorn -14,015 feet, Handies -14, 048 feet, Sunshine -14,034 feet, and Redcloud - 14, 034 feet), and hundreds of Hinsdale peaks are over 13,000 feet. All of the volcanic activity and plate shifting that formed these mountains also brought something else that became very important in the nineteenth century. Mineral waters and acids, as well as gas-based mineral solutions, were forced upwards into the San Juan Mountains through cracks and fissures in the earth. When the solutions cooled, they left behind valuable minerals locked in veins. Most of the major mines of the San Juan Mountains were developed along these veins and fault lines — although finding and following a vein could be a difficult job. In addition, a vein might vary from fabulously rich to extremely low grade within a matter of a few

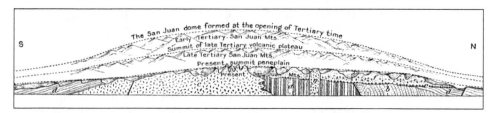

The San Juan Dome was 26,000 feet high and was reduced in size by erosion – mainly the action of glaciers. Now the highest peaks of the San Juans are a little over 14,000 feet, but the dome explains why the San Juan rivers run in four different directions (north in the northern San Juans, south in the southern San Juans, etc.). (Reprinted from U.S.G.S. Professional Paper 95B)

feet; or a vein might disappear altogether, only to reappear in almost any direction or at any distance. Very few valuable mineral deposits in the San Juans were found in placer deposits, such as were seen by early California prospectors, who twenty years earlier found gold lying as nuggets in California streams. A few small exceptions included rivers near present-day Ridgway, Telluride, and Rico.

Humans arrived late in the history of the formation of the San Juans, but plenty of evidence has been found in Hinsdale County that the area was inhabited by Native Americans for at least 11,000 years before American prospectors arrived. At one time, it was thought that the first inhabitants of Hinsdale County, the Paleo Indians, lived mainly at lower elevations on the plains and were not in the high Colorado mountains, except during a few summer hunting expeditions each year. However it is now known that as the Ice Age ended, the climate in North America became warmer, and the big animals like the mammoths and mastodons migrated south out of Alaska and Canada and were followed by Paleo man. By 10,000 B.C., the early Americans had followed their game south alongside the Rockies and then from the Colorado plains into the Colorado Rockies, including Hinsdale County.

Mike Pierce, an archeologist, reports that as a result of an amateur and professional survey in Gunnison and Hinsdale counties that over 1,100 Native American living sites were documented in those two counties. Many more sites may have been missed and have not been discovered yet. He also reported that Folsom, Agate Basin, and Goshen/Plainview points indicate that Native Americans had arrived in Hinsdale County by 9000 B.C.[11]

A major travel route for these early hunters, as well as their game, was nearby Cochetopa Pass. Relatively large numbers of Paleo Indians lived in the future Gunnison area and must have often traveled into what is now Hinsdale County in search of game. Despite finding their fire pits, fine spear and atlatyl points, and stone tools, we know very little about these people. One exception is at W Mountain near Gunnison, and only about twenty-five miles from Hinsdale County, where pit houses and artifacts show that these ancient people built living shelters and spent at least part of the winter in or at the edge of the San Juan Mountains. Hopefully, many other new discoveries of early American habitation will be made in the Hinsdale area as well as other promising parts of the San Juans.[12]

About 6500 B.C. the Paleo hunters were followed by the Archaic People, who lived in the Colorado mountain areas off and on for about 6,000 years. The Archaic people were not in the San Juans as often as the Paleo had been, probably because by that time the large animals of the mountains had died off from lack of huge plants for food or because they had been killed off to extinction by the early Native American hunters. Instead, the Archaic People hunted huge herds of ancient buffalo in the high mountain valleys like the San Luis Valley and South Park, as well as on the plains. These buffalo were much bigger than the buffalo of present time—some were seven feet tall at the shoulders. The Archaic People also gathered fruits, berries, and nuts to supplement their diet. Near the end of Archaic time (about 500 B.C.) some of the people started growing their own food instead of relying only on wild plants.

Although there are many opinions on the exact date of the arrival of the Ute Indians in the San Juan Mountains and the directions from which they came, they definitely arrived by 1300 A.D. The earliest theory of Ute arrival is that they evolved from the Archaic people and were therefore in the San Juans by 500 B.C. It is impossible to state that any of the later Native American tribes called the San Juans home because they were nomadic people, constantly moving with the change of seasons, and winter was always spent outside the San Juan Mountains.[13]

The early Utes led a fairly harsh life and probably only visited the fringes of what they called the "Shining Mountains" until they began to trade with and steal horses from the Spanish, who were settling in New Mexico Province by the 1600s. The early Spanish visited the eastern San Juan Mountains by following the Rio Grande River; which, if they went far enough, led them directly into today's Hinsdale County. The Utes were some of the first Native Americans to obtain and domesticate the horse from the Spanish, and it gave them a great advantage over other Western Native American tribes, both in trading advantages and during times of war. The Utes became so powerful by 1700 that they were the only people for the next 150 years that could truthfully claim any part of the "Shining Mountains" as part of their land.

The early Utes traveled in small bands, usually just a family unit or two, using hunter-gatherer techniques to obtain their food. They would join together in the winter with other Ute bands in the lower valleys surrounding the San Juan Mountains, and then in the summer they would split up and head back into the mountains. They used two main routes in or near the future Hinsdale County when traveling east-west through the San Juan Mountains from the San Luis Valley and one of their winter quarters near present-day Delta. One main trail was over what is now called Los Piños Pass from Cochetopa Pass and then along Cebolla ("little onion" in Spanish) Creek to the Gunnison River (called San Xavier by the Spanish).[14] The other trail was over Cochetopa Pass to the Gunnison River, which the Americans originally called the Grand. There were also many smaller Ute trails in the area, including one up the Lake Fork of the Gunnison. The Utes used a high north-south mountain summer trail near the Continental Divide that leads through today's Hinsdale County from Cochetopa to Weminuche Pass to the present-day Bayfield/Pagosa Springs area.[15] The Tabeguache, later called Uncompahgre Utes, were the subgroups of the Utes that were in present northern Hinsdale County the most, and the Weminuche Utes were in the south part of Hinsdale County in the summer and fall.

Because of the harsh climate and high terrain, the Utes never lived permanently in the Hinsdale area—they were usually just passing through the heart of the San Juan Mountains in the late spring, summer, and early fall, while hunting game and gathering seeds and berries. But they considered the San Juan Mountains their sacred territory and never allowed other tribes to stay in the San Juans for long. After they started trading with the Spanish and obtained horses, guns, and metal implements like knives and kettles, making life immeasurably easier for them, the Utes led a somewhat idealistic life for the time. Spiritually, the Utes had a supreme God, but they also had many minor gods and could definitely be described as nature lovers.[16]

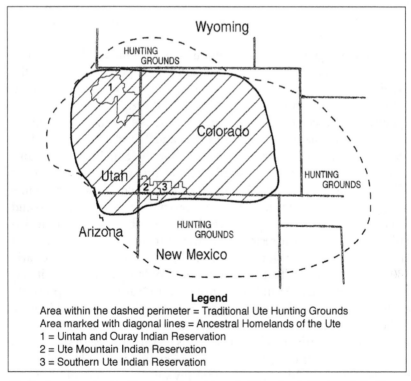

Legend
Area within the dashed perimeter = Traditional Ute Hunting Grounds
Area marked with diagonal lines = Ancestral Homelands of the Ute
1 = Uintah and Ouray Indian Reservation
2 = Ute Mountain Indian Reservation
3 = Southern Ute Indian Reservation

Ute Territory Showing Hunting Grounds and Ancestral Homeland. (Western Reflections Publishing Map)

After 1600, the Spanish occupied New Mexico Territory and were therefore the Utes' southern neighbors. The Utes lived in a very uneasy relationship with the Spanish, sometimes living in peace and at other times waging bitter war. Until about 1760, the Spanish would only occasionally go into Ute territory; but, after 1600, the Utes would often go to New Mexico to trade with the Spanish. About 1800, Spanish settlers began to move up the Rio Grande River from New Mexico; and when they started building communities in what is today's extreme northern New Mexico and southern Colorado, the Utes would often attack them. As author Duane Vandenbusche put it, "The Spanish and Utes, uneasy neighbors, had trouble adjusting to one another."[17] It was not until the coming of the Americans during the Pikes Peak Gold Rush of 1859-60 that the Utes lost any of their mountain territory. Before that time they had been constantly and successfully defending their beautiful and bountiful land from other tribes invading from the east and from the Spaniards who came into their territory from the south.[18]

The Spanish traveled into the eastern San Juan Mountains as early as Juan Oñate about 1600[19] looking for gold, silver, and other precious metals. They found a little free gold and silver; but they, like the later, initial American prospectors, did not recognize that most of the valuable metals were mixed with other elements in ores; or, if they did know the ores contained gold, silver, and other metals, they did not know how to efficiently extract them. The Spanish tried to appease the Utes in the Province of New Mexico by making gifts to them and even pledging to help defend them from their enemies; but, the gifts were few and the Spanish always seemed to disappear when the Ute enemies attacked.

Many place names in the San Juans and Hinsdale County reflect the area's Spanish heritage.[20] The name for the San Juan Mountains themselves came from the Spanish, who at first called the mountains "Sierra de las Grullas" or "Mountains of the Cranes." That early name was given because of the hundreds of thousands of cranes that lived and migrated (and still do, but in much smaller numbers) through the San Luis Valley, and which rested along the numerous streams and small lakes along the eastern slopes of the San Juans. It was not until the early 1800s that the name "San Juan" was commonly used, and then it was always in the singular. "San Juan" translates into "Saint John" — probably a reference to St. John the Baptist, who traveled in the wilderness. Although we know the Spanish were in the San Juans, we have few records of their early travel, because it was illegal for most of them to be in these mountains except by order of the crown. Some physical proof has been found that the Spanish came anyway—a few very old Spanish coins, a few pieces of armor, old arrastras (large grinding mills for ore made out of solid rock), a few early mines and discovery cuts, and some copper mining tools, to name a few. Perhaps the best proof is that there were a few early San Juan Spanish mining claims and mining records filed in Mexico City.[21]

By the mid-1700s French trappers were also in or near the San Juan Mountains, although specific information is limited. They usually traveled in small groups of two to four men, made honest friendships with the Native Americans, and helped them fight their Native American enemies. As a result, they were generally accepted by the Utes; but there were never many of the French present in the San Juans, probably only several dozen or less. They were joined after 1803 by a few American trappers (certainly less than 100 before Mexican Independence in 1821), who felt that the San Juans were now American territory because of the Louisiana Purchase, at least on the east side of the Continental Divide.

The isolationist policies of New Spain changed for a short time after the Mexican War of Independence from Spain ended in 1821 and Mexico became a country. At first the Mexicans not only welcomed foreigners, but actually encouraged them to come to their new country and settle. Some Americans were even offered free land. One reason for the change in policy was the Mexicans in New Mexico were starved for inexpensive trade items at the time and were somewhat backward in their way of living, as Mexico City businesses charged such high prices for goods and transportation that most of its citizens living in New Mexico Province could not afford the Spanish or Mexican merchandise.

Some of the best American trappers and mountain men, like Kit Carson, came early to the San Juans and eventually regarded the area as their favorite hunting grounds, as they contained a large number of "Santa Fe" beaver that brought a very good price. Because many of the Americans were frontiersmen from the East, most had no idea how to survive in the wild and harsh wilderness of the San Juan Mountains; so, learning from the French, many not only became friends with the Utes, but some married Ute women and became honored members of some of the Ute bands. "Old Bill Williams," who trapped in the future Hinsdale area often, had several Ute wives. Many of these French and American fur trappers had homes close to the San Juans in Taos, Abiqui, or Santa Fe that they used when they were not out trapping. They were at least tolerated by the Mexicans, if not fully accepted.

Antoine Robideaux, a Frenchman who became an American by the Louisiana Purchase and later a Mexican citizen, built a trading post in 1828 near today's Delta, Colorado. Although there is no written proof, Robideaux and his men were probably in today's Hinsdale County area, and they most likely used the Lake Fork and the Cebolla/Los Piños shortcuts on some of their trips back to Taos and Santa Fe for more supplies. The Utes traded beaver pelts and buffalo robes with Robideaux for manufactured goods, like knives, tea kettles, and jewelry. The peak of the fur trade in Colorado was in the 1820s and 1830s. Kit Carson, Old Bill Williams, Peg-leg Smith, Jedidiah Smith, Jim Baker, Antoine Leroux, Charles Autobees, Tom Tobin, "Uncle" Dick Wooten, and many other famous mountain men are known to have visited the San Juans often, usually trapping even if they were just passing through, and many of them must have been in Hinsdale County at one time or another. As late as 1846, Thomas "Peg Leg" Smith and six other men were documented as trapping up the Lake Fork and the Uncompahgre Rivers.[22]

During this time, a little known mountain man in the San Juan area named Phil Gardner preceded Alferd Packer, the infamous "Colorado Cannibal," and also resorted to murder and cannibalism. Little is known about Gardner, but Grant Houston, present owner and editor of the Lake City *Silver World*, reports that Gardner, commonly known as "Gardner the Cannibal," was supposed to have eaten at least two Indians and a Frenchman.[23] It soon became obvious to Mexico that most Americans were not immigrants, but rather wanted to occupy their land for the United States or to look for and take Mexican resources like silver and furs. The initial warm welcome by the Mexicans cooled back toward the Spanish level by 1825, but the Americans trapped anyway.

In 1848, during the Mexican-American War, the United States took possession of today's Colorado and New Mexico without a fight, as well as fighting for and taking the rest of the American Southwest. When the war ended in 1849 with the Treaty of Guadalupe-Hidalgo, the United States immediately made a treaty with the Utes (the Calhoun Treaty of December 1849), agreeing that all the historic land the Utes occupied was Ute territory. In return the Utes agreed to be peaceful towards U.S. citizens and allow them to safely pass through their land. The Utes consented to the sovereignty of the United States, but this meant little to them, and their way of life continued on as always. The Utes further agreed to not leave their "normal territory," but no definite boundaries were set in the treaty.

After the Mexican-American War, the United States felt that it would be wise to try to map and explore their newly gained territory before too many American settlers began to flow into the area, so several government expeditions traveled to California while exploring the extreme northern and southern San Juans. John Fremont on his Fourth Expedition tried to go through the heart of the San Juan Mountains in the middle of the winter of 1848-1849 to prove that a transcontinental railroad would be feasible along the 38th Parallel, which passes very close to present-day Lake City. Fremont's guide was experienced mountain man William "Old Bill" Williams, who had pioneered a trail over Spring Creek Pass (also called Rio del Norte Pass by the Spanish, and some mountain men called it "Old Bill Williams Pass.") Williams had initially suggested Cochetopa Pass to the north or Cumbres Pass to the south, but Fremont insisted on passing through the central San Juans to prove it would be a good route for a later railroad. Somehow the group got lost in the La Garita subrange of the San Juans and ten of Fremont's men starved to death.[24] The party was forced to eat all of their horses and mules and were said to have resorted to cannibalism. Afterwards, the humiliated Fremont exaggerated when he said that the San Juan Mountains were "inaccessible to trappers and hunters even in the summertime." However, memories of this disaster may have come back later to haunt Lake City's quest for a railroad.

Precious metals were probably found by Americans for the first time in Hinsdale County by members of the Fremont Fourth Expedition in 1849. A man by the name of Stewart, who evidently joined Fremont after his party retreated and recuperated in Taos (there was no one in Fremont's original group named Stewart) was said to have found gold north of today's Pagosa Springs, in what later would possibly become southern Hinsdale County. This find was made when the remainder of Freemont's group, after problems with Native Americans, skirted to the north of the Old Spanish Trail on their way to California. Stewart, and possibly others in the group, returned but could not find the spot where the initial discovery of gold had been made. Some historians believe Stewart kept the location of the discovery a secret from his companions.[25] Several lost gold mine legends still exist in this area of Hinsdale County.

By the 1850s, the Utes had become rightfully upset that so many American settlers were coming north onto their land in the San Luis Valley. Their unrest surfaced in what was called "The Ute War of 1854-56." The United States responded to Ute aggression by sending troops into the San Luis Valley and building Ft. Massachusetts (the fort was later moved to present-day Ft. Garland).

The "solemn promise" of the United States to the Utes in the 1849 Calhoun Treaty did not last long after the Pikes Peak Gold Rush started in 1858. The Pikes Peak boom brought close to 100,000 Americans to the future state of Colorado in 1859, but almost all of them initially prospected around present-day Denver and Boulder. Many of the hopefuls turned back before even reaching the mountains of Colorado, or returned to the East soon after they arrived; but even so, there were still way too many prospectors compared to the possible mining claims to be found in the northern Colorado Rockies. Agencies had to be built for the Utes to supply them food, as the once plentiful game in the future Colorado was being decimated by the American prospectors.

During the Pike's Peak Gold Rush, William Gilpin, later Territorial Governor of Colorado, actually pushed for someone with money to rise to the occasion and mine the precious metals he had observed in the San Juans during the years after the Mexican-American War. He even gave talks in Kansas City in 1858 about the gold he had seen in the San Juans, and his talk was reprinted as a popular guide book during the Pikes Peak Gold Rush.[26] In early 1860 the *Santa Fe Gazette* also printed an article about precious metals being in the San Juan Mountains. Their article contained a journal of fur trappers and prospectors, Albert Pfieffer and Henry Mercure, describing the gold they had observed in the San Juan Mountains[27] over the previous years. Kit Carson and Albert Pfieffer had both been in the Baker's Park area in the 1830s and 1840s, and Pfieffer reported finding gold there. Pfieffer was the Ute and Navajo Indian agent at the time, and therefore had access to what they could tell him about precious minerals and metals in various spots in the mountains, although the Utes had not yet fully realized the value of silver or gold. It is probable the reports of Pfieffer, Carson, and Gilpin, as well as the *Santa Fe Gazette* article, were major reasons for northern Colorado prospectors to head for the San Juans in the early summer of 1860.

Yet another reason for Colorado prospectors to head south was the realization that a "mineral belt" ran through Colorado. Its north end was near Boulder, then it ran southwest through Clear Creek, California Gulch (the future Leadville area), and evidently kept going southwest toward the San Juans. The Colorado Mineral Belt was eventually found to run all the way to the Mancos and Dolores Rivers in the extreme southwestern San Juans.

By the summer of 1860, many prospectors had worked their way southwest down the Mineral Belt from Denver and Boulder to the Continental Divide, then south down to California Gulch, and then further south along the Arkansas River. California Gulch was swarming with somewhat successful placer miners in 1860. F. R. Rice and S. B. Kellogg were two of those doing well, and Charles Baker convinced them to grubstake him for prospecting in the San Juans. He set out in July, 1860, with six other men, including three named Cunningham, Bloomfield, and Mason. Baker's roundabout route to the San Juans was down the Arkansas River, over Poncha Pass into the extreme northern San Luis Valley, over Cochetopa Pass into the Gunnison River Valley, west to the mouth of the Lake Fork of the Gunnison, south up the Lake Fork to Cinnamon Pass, and then down the Animas River to the park that now bears his name and the present-day town of Silverton.[28] Colonel William Loring and 300 men with fifty wagons had recently gone over Cochetopa from Utah to get supplies from Ft. Union during the "Mormon War" in the summer of 1858; and they had made a pretty good trail over Cochetopa Pass and along the Gunnison River in the process. The trail Baker traveled up the Lake Fork of the Gunnison had been used by Native Americans for centuries when going to the San Luis Valley.

After prospecting in what became Baker's Park, Baker went down the Animas River a short distance, then circled back and went out of the San Juans near the future town of Ouray.[29] Reports of rich discoveries were soon being sent to Denver by Baker and others; although Baker's judgement was surely clouded by the terms of his grubstake that required he not only find gold, but also play up the mining area he discovered, establish a town site, and build a toll road to the new discoveries. Baker spent the winter of 1860-61 in New Mexico and, in November of 1860, wrote a letter to the *Santa Fe Gazette* in which he made the highly exaggerated claim that he had made rich discoveries in Baker's Park and that "there will be not less than 25,000 Americans engaged in mining and agricultural pursuits (in the San Juans) ... within a year, perhaps

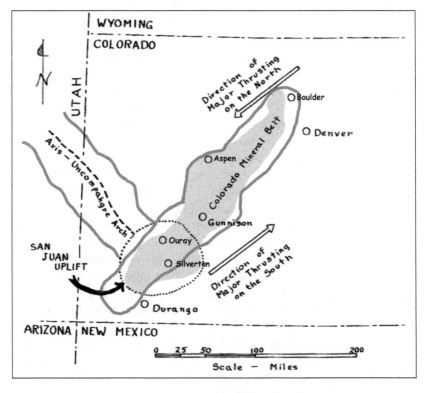

It only took a few years for the Colorado '59ers to figure out that a mineral belt ran through Colorado. Precious minerals, like gold and silver, seemed to be in a line running from Boulder southwest down to (and they hoped through) the San Juans. (Adapted from a U.S.G.S. Professional Paper 166 map)

double that number." As if to validate his bias, in the same letter Baker wrote "I learn with regret that a movement is already on foot to divert the travel and commerce to a more northerly channel...." *The Rocky Mountain News*[30] also printed Baker's letter.

Richard Sopris and newspaper correspondent D.C. Collier were also in the San Juans in 1860, as was another unnamed group. Collier, like Baker, sent exaggerated reports back to his paper in Denver that he had discovered gold. He even claimed to have found diamonds (probably quartz).[31] Later in 1860, other prospectors from California Gulch had used the same route that Baker had followed, but continued on Loring's trail down the Gunnison to the Uncompahgre River and then went south to the area around the future site of Ouray. Some prospectors also went north of the Gunnison River and found gold in the Crested Butte and Tin Cup areas.

On December 14, 1860, based on Baker's and others' positive reports, Kellogg and Rice left California Gulch for the San Juans. They were followed by other men who suspected that rich mineral discoveries had been made. This group is generally called "The Baker Party," although Baker was not in the group. Baker did give specific instruction to come to his newly founded town site from the south over his new toll road from Abiqui, New Mexico. Rice, Kellogg, and most of the hundreds of hopeful prospectors who were following them used this route. Also in the party was Henry Henson, who later would be one of the locators of the famous Ute-Ulay (Ute-Ule) Mine and for whom Henson Creek is named.[32] At times, these followers were estimated at 100 to 300 men, but it was a fluid group with those traveling faster often leaving the slower members behind. After great hardships, the main part of the group made it to Conejos in the southern San Luis Valley on March 4, 1861, and then went to Abiqui, up the Chama River, explored in and near the springs at Pagosa (there was no town of Pagosa Springs yet), and then went west and north up the Animas River to near the present-day Durango Mountain Resort (Purgatory), where most of the party made camp because of deep snows at higher elevations. Kellogg and a few other men soon went on to Baker's Park and camped near the future mining camp of Eureka.

On arrival, they found that Baker had already cut trees and whip-sawn lumber to make sluices to pan for gold, but he was having very little luck. Baker's best days of placer mining for gold were only yielding about fifty cents a day per man. This was at a time when $3 to $4 a day was an average wage-earners' pay.[33] Gold was easy to recognize when placer mining, and most hopefuls felt it would take little work to find a fortune in gold nuggets. Unfortunately, they found only a few small gold flakes. Gold and silver were present in Baker's Park in large quantities, but were locked in ore veins. It would take hard work, a large amount of capital, and a good transportation system to get the precious minerals to the smelters. These early prospectors, in their quest for gold nuggets, totally overlooked very obvious silver veins. The same thing was happening back in California Gulch at the time. California Gulch prospectors did find a fair amount of gold, but it quickly played out, and they did not recognize the silver in their pans that eventually made Leadville famous.

Baker had a motive other than financial profit for wanting prospectors to come into the San Juans from the south. He was a Southerner and evidently wanted the future San Juan Mountain mines to be tied to New Mexico, which he hoped would join the Confederacy when the impending Civil War started. He and others in his group therefore pushed for prospectors from northern Colorado to enter the San Juans from the south by going through the entire San Luis Valley, then west on the Old Spanish Trail along the southern San Juan Mountains, and then using the Animas River Route to go north. It was a very rough and roundabout way to get to Baker's Park, but it made Taos, Abiqui, or Santa Fe their home base. It was much quicker and closer from the Denver/ Boulder area (where most of the prospectors were at the time) to go up the Rio Grande and over Stony or nearby Cunningham passes, or to go up the Lake Fork or the Uncompahgre Rivers from the Gunnison River. A Captain McKee and thirty-six men from California Gulch explored much of the Rio Grande and its upper tributaries in July and August 1860 and passed on information on this "shortcut." In 1861 some men headed to the San Juans by following the Rio Grande River to near its source, which put them in today's Hinsdale County. These groups, which probably totaled no more than a hundred prospectors, panned most of the creeks along the way with only a little success.

Besides being shorter, the Rio Grande route had the advantage of being closer to the American Ft. Massachusetts in the San Luis Valley, later moved to Fort Garland. The fort, which was the only American military presence in the area, had been built during the ""Ute War of 1854-56"and was used to protect Mexican-American settlers and ranchers in the San Luis Valley from marauding Utes. Later the presence of American farmers and ranchers in the San Luis Valley meant nearby food supplies for the Hinsdale prospectors. In fact, in the early 1860s, much of the food for prospectors as far away as Denver and Boulder came from the San Luis Valley.

Although Baker is famous for his promotion of Baker's Park, where Silverton was later founded, in a letter printed in the *Rocky Mountain News* in 1861 he also exaggerated claims for the future Hinsdale County area. He wrote that he had followed the Colorado Gold Belt south:

Ft. Garland, formerly Ft. Massachusetts, was the only military presence within hundreds of miles of the San Luis Valley and the San Juans. (Author's Collection)

The quartz veins reappeared from the Lake Fork of the Grand (Gunnison River), near where it flows out of the mountains… and near its source will be found remunerative gold mines. After spending some time upon the stream, I ascended the Lake Fork to its head and crossed the range to the headwaters of the Rio de los Animas.[34]

The prospectors arriving in 1861 were even more upset at Baker than the men of 1860, as they were still only able to pan about fifty cents in gold flakes per man per day, falling way short of covering their expenses and expectations. The white prospectors were now being joined by a good number of Mexican-Americans who were trying their luck, but no one was having any success. Most of the Mexican-Americans were coming from the San Luis Valley, up the Rio Grande River, and over Spring Creek and Slumgullion passes and prospecting in the future Hinsdale County area on their way to Baker's Park.

Baker had gone back to the park named for him in March, 1861; and within a few weeks, the large number of men, and even some women, from the "Baker Party" were in the area. When Baker heard in 1861 that men were coming in via the Rio Grande and Stony Pass, he was upset and continued his campaign to have prospectors come to Baker's Park from the south. By mid-summer it was estimated that as many as 1,000 gold seekers were in or around Baker's Park. It was almost as crowded in that part of the San Juans as it had been back in California Gulch. Most prospectors were disappointed, but some spread out to examine nearby areas including the Hinsdale area where some discoveries were made on the upper Henson and Lake Fork. The Utes watched all this with interest, but generally allowed prospectors to be on their land, if they came only in the summer and did not build and permanent buildings.

By late summer of 1861, it was generally agreed that the "San Juan Excitement" was instead pure "humbug." By early fall of 1861, the large majority of the prospectors had left due to the remoteness of the area, the outbreak of the Civil War, the "encouragement" of the Utes, and the poor "diggings." Only Baker and a few others stayed until late fall when they too left to join the Confederacy. Union sympathizers prevailed in Colorado at this time, but there were also many men who left to join the Confederacy. There was surprisingly little trouble between the two groups in Colorado itself. Other men who were not taking sides or who were running from the war went west to Arizona or California. Colorado's first wave of prospecting and mining totally died out in the San Juans by the beginning of 1862. The minerals in the northeastern part of Colorado's mountains had mainly been discovered, and those in the south were abandoned. Colorado's entire precious metals industry basically dried up from 1862 until 1869.

The facts of Baker's efforts have dissolved from confusion at the time of his explorations into a muddy mess of fact and fiction at present. Some historians have claimed the whole Baker expedition was a hoax, but it was not. Others feel that he did find gold and silver, but that most prospectors in Baker's Park were too lazy to work the hard rock to make a living. However that also was not true. Many novice prospectors did expect to merely pick up gold nuggets off the ground and get rich; but there were many men present who would have staked the gold and silver veins, even though in Ute territory, if the veins had been noticed. Some historians tell obvious tall tales about Baker, including well-respected Hubert Bancroft:

> *Baker was a mountaineer of note. He had heard from the Navajo and other Indians that the royal metal existed in the mysterious upper region of the Sierra Madre, proof of which was exhibited in ornaments and bullets of gold.*[35]

Due to the Civil War and the hardships endured by most Americans for years afterwards, no written history of any prospecting activity in the San Juans has been found until Baker returned for a short while in 1867, only to be killed shortly thereafter by Native Americans in

Arizona. Then, little, if any, prospecting happened from 1867 until a few prospectors returned to the San Juans in 1869.

However the United States government had been working to gain more Ute territory. In the fall of 1863, Chief Ouray and six other Capote and Tabeguache Ute chiefs were taken to Washington, D. C. by Alexander Hunt and Kit Carson. The United States knew that it would be hard to fight the Civil War and the Utes at the same time. In the "Carson Treaty" of October 7, 1863, the Utes agreed to be peaceful and leave the whites on the Front Range of Colorado alone. Most of the Ute chiefs were reluctant to agree to this treaty and were not bound by such; but it was later ratified by most Utes in the Treaty of 1868, which the United States started negotiating shortly after the Civil War ended. This treaty was made by six of the seven Ute bands (the Yampah tribe in far northwestern Colorado was missing). The Treaty of 1868 was signed in Washington, D. C., on March 2, 1868.

The 1868 treaty, known as the "Hunt Treaty," mainly affected the Capote Utes, who were giving up the San Luis Valley; but it opened a gateway to the San Juans. The "Hunt Treaty" created a Ute reservation in western Colorado described by latitude and longitude, but which was basically that land west of the Continental Divide, called "the Western Slope" of Colorado Territory. The Utes were to receive supplies and annuities, and the U.S. agreed to protect the Utes "forever" from white trespassers. An agency was established west of the summit of Cochetopa

The location of the Ute agency on Cochetopa Pass was not quite this rugged but the drawing does a good job of showing how high it was in elevation. (Harper's Weekly Illustration, Author's Collection)

Pass for the Tabeguache, Mouache, Weminuche, and Capote, after the Utes refused to be moved further west. They were supposed to have been moved to the Los Piños River near present-day Durango, but the Americans solved the problem by renaming a nearby stream the Los Piños River to satisfy the terms of the treaty. The official description in the treaty read that the Ute Reservation would:

> Commence at that point on the southern boundary line of the Territory of Colorado where the meridian of longitude 107 degrees west of Greenwich crosses the same, running thence north of with the same meridian fifteen miles of where said meridian intersects the 40th parallel of north latitude; thence due west to the western boundary line of said Territory; thence east with said boundary line to the place of beginning, shall be and the same is hereby, set apart for the absolute and undisturbed use and occupation of the Indians herein named (the Utes).... The United States now solemnly agrees that no persons, except such officers, agents, and employees of the Government as may be authorized to enter upon Indian reservations in discharge of duties enjoined by law, shall ever be permitted to pass over, settle upon, or reside in the Territory....[36]

The Utes did not understand the surveyors' boundaries and basically accepted that the boundary would be the Continental Divide. Another agency was established at White River for the Grand River, Yampa, and Uintah Utes. The 1868 treaty also provided that no further treaty would be valid against the Utes unless "executed and signed by at least three-fourths of all the adult male Indians occupying or interested in the same," and that no further treaty should "deprive, without his consent, any individual member of the (Ute) tribe to his right in any tract of land selected by him for ranch or agricultural use."[37] The 1868 treaty lasted only four years before the United States would be again trying to get the Utes back to the bargaining table.[38]

In the meantime, a mass of people were starting to return or coming for the first time to Colorado's gold and silver fields because of the total destruction caused by the Civil War and the bad economy afterwards.[39] The Americans were getting closer and closer to the San Juans. By 1872 the Denver & Rio Grande Railroad had finished laying track from Denver to Pueblo, so in 1872 and 1873 most San Juan prospectors were traveling to Pueblo by train, then either to Walsenburg or Cañon City by stage. Those coming from Cañon City went up the Arkansas River and over Poncha Pass to Saguache, while other potential prospectors went further south along the Front Range to Walsenburg and over LaVeta Pass by stage to Ft. Garland and then Del Norte. As the railroad kept building south, the stage agencies moved with them, running their routes from the "new end of the railroad."

Another problem besides the initial gold fever was arising. As Robert Brown put it:

> In the early days, not many people who settled actually thought seriously of making their home in the San Juans. They came for immediate gain and expected to go away as soon as their objective (gold) had been met.... Those who came were not legitimate miners by any means, nor were they always motivated by legitimate intentions. It has been estimated that 30 to 50 percent of the incoming Argonauts were misfits, the first to be unemployed in the great nationwide panic that followed the Civil War.[40]

Three of the legitimate class of prospectors, James Harrison, Joel K. Mullin (also spelled Mullen), and George Boughton, had been in the future Hinsdale County area in the summer of 1869, and they established their main camp in the vicinity of present-day Lake City.[41] It

Even though the Ute Indians, who had lived on their land in western Colorado for at least 500 years, were "legally" given their land by the United States in 1863 and 1868, American prospectors ignored the legalities in their search for gold and silver. The results were many ominous meetings like this one. (Harper's Weekly, October 25, 1879, Author's Collection).

was very dangerous for them, as the Utes not only had possession of the area but also had been given legal title to the land by the United States. By 1870 there were about fifty prospectors in Baker's Park and a much smaller number in the future Hinsdale area. By the end of the summer season, the prospectors were finding some promising claims, as most had finally come to realize that the silver and gold they were looking for were locked in hard rock veins that were easily visible in the mountains, but not easily mined.

It has been estimated by one source that in the summer of 1871 a total of perhaps twenty-five to forty prospectors were in the San Juans, and that they located 100 to 200 claims before going to lower elevations for the winter. However another source claims that in 1871 prospectors started returning to the San Juans in much greater numbers, but they filed only a few claims with the authorities, as they realized they were documenting their trespassing on Ute land; or, perhaps, they wished to keep their discoveries to themselves until they could legally file a claim.

The Mexican-American settlement of La Loma, which was located on the Rio Grande River near where the river exits the San Juan Mountains, and the town of Saguache, at the far northwest end of the San Luis Valley, were the San Juan prospectors' supply points. Both towns, however, were very remote. La Loma was thirty-five miles northwest of Ft. Garland, but the nearest true town was Pueblo, which was 140 miles away. Saguache was only slightly closer to true civilization at 110 miles from Cañon City, but it had no mercantile store until 1873, although Otto Mears and a partner were evidently running a small trading post there. Most prospectors could get a wagon load of supplies to La Loma or Saguache; but usually burros and pack mules were needed to carry the loads into the San Juans from those points.[42]

La Loma was a Hispanic settlement at the junction of San Francisco Creek and the Rio Grande River near where the Del Norte high school now stands. La Loma was already established when Anglo Americans arrived and established their own settlement of Del Norte, just across the Rio Grande from La Loma. Once gold and silver were discovered at Baker's Park, Summitville, and along the Lake Fork of the Gunnison, Del Norte became the first true supply town for the San Juans, but it soon found competition from Saguache to the north and Abiqui became the supply town for the southern San Juan mining communities.

Considerable gold was discovered in the San Juans in June of 1870 at the head of Wrightman Creek at what would come to be Summitville, located only twenty-six miles from La Loma. Since it was just barely on the east side of the Continental Divide, Summitville was not in Ute territory after 1868. The first to find gold in Summitville was a rancher, John Esmond, who found fifty pounds of rich gold ore lying there on the ground in 1870 and filed four claims. However Esmond did no assessment work at all and lost his rights.[43] When he came back, Esmond found that others had relocated his discovery with The Little Annie, Del Norte, and Margaretta Lodes. All three claims were later among the very best producers in the district. In the spring of 1871, hundreds came to Summitville, but most prospectors had left Summitville by mid-September of that year except James L. Wightman and J. Carey French. French sold twenty-five pounds of ore and six ounces of gold dust from Summitville to the Denver Mint in August, 1871, which started another small rush in 1872.[44] The big news came in October, 1873, when three Summitville claims were sold to investors for $410,000, and by 1874 there were hundreds of men and almost 2,500 claims in the district.[45] Summitville was probably the first true mining camp in the San Juans.

In 1871 Summitville prospectors got their supplies from La Loma, while lumber for the sluices at the San Juan prospects came from Otto Mears' and Lafayette Head's lumberyard at Conejos.[46] The unpublished Howard manuscript[47] states that La Loma had only a few residents in 1871, several dozen in 1872, and perhaps fifty in 1873. Del Norte was founded in 1872, and by 1874 supposedly had a population of 1,500.[48]

In the summer of 1871 Henry Henson, Charles Godwin (also spelled Godman), Albert Meade (also spelled Mead), and Joel K. Mullin located a rich claim that became the famous Ute-Ulay Mine on what was then called "Godwin Creek," (later called Henson Creek) about three or four miles upstream from where Lake City would eventually be founded.[49] Henson, Meade, and possibly Godwin, had been part of the large Charles Baker party of 1861 and came to Godwin (Henson) Creek in 1871 through Baker's Park. The Ute-Ulay was the first great discovery in the San Juans. (Silverton's Little Giant vein, which was big news at the time of its discovery, did not last long.) The Utes still legally owned the San Juans, so the Ute-Ulay claim was not legally recognized at the time. Henson became the first senator from the San Juans in 1876. The initial discoverers formally and legally located the Ure (Ulay) vein three years later on July 11, 1874, and filed their claim on September 10, 1874.[50] The same men staked the Ute claim on July 31, 1874, but instead of a recording date the county records show that the original location date was August 27, 1871. The Capitol Lode was located on June 8, 1874, and filed September 31, 1874, and was probably the second officially located mine in Hinsdale County after the Big Casino, which was the first.[51]

Exciting new discoveries were being made not just at Summitville, but all over the San Juans in 1872, and many of the prospectors that became pioneer San Juan settlers arrived that year when the western San Juans were still Ute territory. It has been estimated by many historians that 300 to 400 prospectors were in the San Juan Mountains that summer (although some estimates are as low as 100) and that they located between 2,000 and 3,000 prospects.[52] Although they still could not legally file their claims on the west side of the Divide, the 1872-1873 prospectors knew that the United States was interested in having the Utes cede the San Juans. It is estimated that only 150 or so claims were actually worked, and the others were merely staked or the location was simply recorded on a piece of paper, so as to give the locator some claim over later prospectors if the veins proved to be profitable. Prospectors on the Lake Fork in 1872 included Peter Robinson, O. A. Mester, and B. A. Taft. They filed several claims, which were once again invalid. Albert W. Burrows, for whom Burrows Park is named, came up the Lake Fork in 1872 and prospected in and around Burrows Park, but ended up at Mineral Point on the other side of Cinnamon Pass.[53] A party led by a Colonel Nugent and his son, a Captain Nugent, was reported to have found ore in the present-day Lake City area, but the exact vein location is unknown.[54]

In 1872 Major M. V. B. Wasson (also spelled Wason) left his ranch in Antelope Park (today split by the Hinsdale and Mineral County line) for Santa Fe to seek stallions for his horse herd. While there, he discovered that a heavy load of milling machinery had been brought over the Santa Fe Trail and needed to be transported to Arrastra Gulch near present-day Silverton. Wasson decided to take the job and used ten wagons, each drawn by four yokes (eight oxen) to pull each load. It was the end of August and mine owner, E.M. Hamilton, was desperate to get the machinery to the Little Giant Mine in Baker's Park before the winter snows, so he was willing to pay an exorbitant price. Wasson later told a historian[55] that he made the trip from Santa Fe up the Rio Grande to Antelope Park, but at that point there is a discrepancy in his reported route from what later historians record.

It is generally accepted that Hamilton took the machinery over Stony Pass, claiming he made the first road into the heart of the San Juans at that time. He really just made a mess of the countryside while pulling the huge load. However Wasson later told his biographer that his party left the main trail at Antelope Park and went past Lake Santa Maria, then up Spring Creek Pass and down Slumgullion, which he said had to be done by snubbing the wagons to trees. There was no road, just a rough trail to this point. Wasson often said he had to make his own trail, cutting trees down to go part way up Cottonwood Creek, then over to Burrows Park, and over Cinnamon Pass. There he said he went down the Animas and delivered the machinery to Major Hamilton at the Little Giant Mine. Hamilton and Wasson were in the same party, at least until Antelope Park, but which man gave the correct route? It is possible the two men split the machinery at Antelope Park with each taking some of the load. Neither route could really be called a "road." This author would nominate the Mears toll road from Saguache to Burrows Park for the honor, as neither Hamilton nor Wasson actually spent time building a road, although they did travel across the area.

When Wasson got back to his homestead in Antelope Park, he killed the oxen he had used and said he sold the meat to a few prospectors, who he said had stayed in the future Lake City area during the winter of 1872-73. Wasson said there was no town, but that prospectors had camped on the spot since 1869. In the same interview Wasson claimed "Bear" Jim Harbinson, J. K. Mullin, and George Boughton were among the first to build cabins there.[56] Mullin and Boughton had been prospecting on the Lake Fork of the Gunnison as early as the summer of 1869.

Eighteen-seventy-two was a pivotal year for San Juan prospectors. They were finding gold and silver, but the land still belonged to the Utes under the 1868 Treaty. Since early 1872, the U. S. had been attempting to get the Utes to sell the San Juans, but Chief Ouray asked many times why the United States was not strong enough to keep its promise under the 1868 Treaty, which had basically pledged the land west of the Continental Divide would belong to the Utes "forever," and that the Americans would be kept off the Ute land. The Utes were not particularly attached to the high mountains, but they were beginning to see a trend — the Americans were taking their land bit by bit. As soon as the Utes sold one piece of land, the American prospectors and settlers pushed to have another piece made public.

By the end of the 1872 season, the flood of prospectors into the San Juans had been great enough that U. S. troops were sent to try to keep peace between the whites and the Utes and to move the Americans peaceably out of the area; but, in just a few more months, the focus of the United States would be to get the Utes out of the San Juans.

In late August, 1872, a council was held at the Los Piños Agency to again try to get the Utes to sell. Felix Brunot boldly announced that the Utes did not need the land, and they would be paid a fair price for it ($25,000 a year, which came to about one cent an acre.) Ouray and the 2,000 other Utes present refused to sell.[57] The Americans left the council on September 1, 1872, with nothing being accomplished.

Included among the pioneers in the early spring of 1873 was Harry Youmans, who was trapping while headed towards the new diggings near the future Lake City. He said that there was evidence that many trappers had been in the Cebolla and Lake Fork areas earlier. When he saw moccasin tracks, he became worried about Utes and almost shot V. C. Loutzenhizer, who was trapping while wearing moccasins. The two men joined forces and trapped together for several months along the Cebolla, presumably waiting for the snow to melt in the high country in late spring.[58] Youmans eventually became a famous rancher and lumber man in the Hinsdale area, and Loutzenheizer later lived and had commercial orchards in the Montrose area.[59]

However gold fever ran rampant in Colorado. Even though soldiers were sent to keep the whites off the Ute land, the prospectors still came; and even with Ouray's pressure, the Utes still balked at giving up more land. They pointed out that the United States, under its own law (the Utes had no concept of private ownership of land before the Americans arrived) had recognized this land as belonging to the Utes "forever." Why should they give any of it up if they didn't want to do so? So when over 500 prospectors were heading into the San Juans in the spring of 1873, bad trouble was brewing.

Meanwhile, Felix Brunot, one of the commissioners appointed by the United States to negotiate with the Utes, came up with an idea that

The Ute delegation in Washington, D. C. in February 1868, took time to pose for a photograph. This is just part of a much bigger group photograph but shows (left to right), Lafayette Head (Indian Agent), Waro, Daniel C. Oakes (Indian Agent), Chief Ouray at about age thirty-four, Edward C. Kellogg (brother-in-law of Colorado Governor Hunt), Capote, and William C. Godfrey (translator). (Matthew Brady Photographer, Author's Collection)

he presented to Chief Ouray in early 1873. Ouray then indicated that the Utes might sell the San Juans, although he was not ready to sign a treaty yet. Ouray had been tempted by a promise from the U. S. government that they would find his only son, who had been stolen by the Sioux years earlier, if Ouray in return would get his people to sell the San Juan Mountains. On June 20, 1873, Brunot and Ute Agent Charles Adams reported that they had learned Ouray's son had been captured by the Sioux, then traded to the Arapaho, both enemies of the Utes. Brunot somehow convinced a small group of Arapahoe that evidently included Ouray's son, to meet with Ouray and a few Utes in Washington, D. C. There was little doubt about the teenager's identity because of a scar on his shoulder, the boy being left-handed, and the boy looking very much like Ouray. However the young man refused to admit he could be Ute, a tribe hated by the Arapaho, little less the son of a mighty Ute leader.

A tentative date in August, 1873, was set for another conference with as many of the Utes as possible attending. When the date came, one of Brunot's commissioners was not present, but the other officials went to the Los Piños agency anyway, getting there two weeks late on September 5, 1873. The Utes began by pointing out that a Lt. E. H. Ruffner was putting in stakes for the boundary of the old treaty and was putting them in the wrong places. Brunot stated that the Continental Divide was considered the present boundary by the United States, and that it did not matter where the stakes were put. The Utes were again offered $25,000 a year forever for selling 3.5 million acres of the San Juans. Although it was also part of the treaty that the Utes could always hunt freely in the San Juans, it was something that they were only allowed to do in recent times, without complying with the regulations and fees that non-Utes had to follow. On September 12, the Utes agreed in principal to the terms of the treaty with the understanding that they would go with the surveyors and make sure the new boundaries were where they thought they should be.

Ouray very eloquently stated his reasons:

We shall fall as the leaves from the trees when the frosts of winter come, and the lands which we have roamed over for countless generations will be given up to the miner and the plowshare.... This is the destiny of my people. My part is to protect them and yours, as far as I can, from violence and bloodshed while I live, and to bring both into friendly relations, so that they may be at peace with one another.[60]

After the Brunot agreement was made, but before it was finalized by the U. S. Senate, Ouray asked that a message be taken to the Territorial Governor Elbert:

We want you should tell Governor Elbert and the people in the Territory that we are well pleased and perfectly satisfied with everything that has been done. Perhaps some of the people will not like it because we do not wish to sell our valley and farming lands, but we think we have good reasons for not doing so. We expect to occupy them ourselves before long for farming and stock raising. About eighty of our tribe are now raising corn and wheat, and we know not how soon we shall have to depend on ourselves for our bread. We do not want to sell our valley and farming lands for another reason. We know if we should, the whites would go on them, build their cabins and drive in their stock, which would of course stray on to our land, then the whites themselves would crowd upon us until there would be trouble.... We are perfectly willing to sell our mountain land, and hope the miners will find heaps of gold and silver. We have no wish to molest or make them any trouble. We don't want that they should go down into our valleys, however, and kill or scare our game.[61]

With the signing of the Brunot Treaty the Utes had ceded an area of about sixty by seventy-five miles. Was Ouray a traitor to his people or was he a farsighted leader who realized the Utes were vastly outnumbered and would die if they fought the Americans? The answer

This photo shows the typical terrain at the top of Cochetopa Pass, where some of the Utes camped near the Los Piños Agency for "issue day" in 1873. This was a time when the Utes would "hunt" cattle for their meat, like they had the buffalo in the past. The Utes were also there for the 1873 Brunot Treaty meeting to determine if they would give up the San Juans. (W. H. Jackson Photo, Author's Collection)

probably falls in between these two views. To his credit, or perhaps his dishonor, Ouray kept his part of the bargain even though his son would not recognize him as his father.

The boundaries of the land to be ceded were again done in a way the Utes could not possibly understand:

> *Beginning at a point on the eastern boundary of said (Ute) reservation, fifteen miles due north of the southern boundary of the Territory of Colorado, and running thence west on a line parallel to the said southern boundary to a point on said line twenty miles due east of the western boundary of Colorado territory; thence north by a line parallel with the western boundary to a point ten miles north of the point where said line intersects the 38th parallel of north latitude; thence east to the eastern boundary of the Ute reservation, and thence south along said boundary to the place of beginning...* [62]

It had been decided earlier in 1873 to send an army exploration and surveying party to examine the San Juans and determine how many U.S. citizens were actually there, how many had permanent homes there, and how much they were finding in the way of precious metals. All of these would be factors in the final U. S. decision to make the Brunot Treaty, but an estimate of how much gold and silver was present in the San Juan Mountains was obviously the main concern.

Lt. Ernest Howard Ruffner's report of his 1873 expedition is well worth repeating in some detail, as it is the earliest detailed description of Hinsdale County and a wonderful description of the geography, flora, and geology of the area. Lt. Ruffner's report first detailed the reasons for his exploration:

> *The origin of the recognizance was the disturbed relationship between the Ute Indians and the miners of the so-called San Juan District. This district was reported as embracing claims located on the Animas River and on the Lake Fork of the Gunnison River (then called the Lake Fork of the Grand River) and their tributaries. These districts, formerly opened (in 1860) and abandoned, had become again the center of wild speculation, and prospectors were reported as rushing there from all quarters. To the Ute Indians, occupying a consolidated reservation indefinitely large and embracing certainly one portion of the field and possibly all, the prospects of a wild flood of white men occupying their land without regard to their guaranteed rights was anything but pleasant, and they early protested against the invasion. An attempt was made, in the summer of 1872, to secure a cession from them of the disputed territory. It*

was a failure, however, and when the rush of the miners in the spring of 1873 promised to be greater than usual, the remonstrance of the Ute grew to threats during the winter, and they firmly said the miners must leave or war would follow.

The consequence of war with the powerful and intelligent tribe occupying the entire mountain region of Colorado could not fail to be dire. Of undoubted courage, possessed of all modern improvements in firearms, and with the secure vastness of the mountains to fall back on, the tribe could well put a bold front in the making over their demands — demands undoubtedly just, as being the only fulfilment of a solemn treaty. The Indian Bureau with justice, requested that the miners be kept out of the limits of the reservation, and the request was granted. Orders were issued to the military authorities to send such force as would be necessary and clear the district by a certain time. To do this it became necessary to know where the reservation extended. The eastern boundary was 107 degrees Meridian from Greenwich, probably as difficult a line to establish as could have been chosen; orders were then given to me to prepare a party to determine points on this line, to accompany the expedition while engaged in its unpleasant duty, and to furnish a full descriptive report of the district in question.[63]

It became evident that the Brunot Treaty would be agreed to by the Utes just as Ruffner's soldiers were getting ready to remove the American prospectors, so further surveying of the old reservation boundary and removing the prospectors became unnecessary. Ruffner was instead ordered to give the first official description of the country and its mines. He also was to determine what was truth and what was fiction in the reports coming from prospectors about the mineral wealth of the San Juans and was to analyze the potential travel routes in and out of the country. He left Pueblo on May 5, 1873, and reached Ft. Garland on May 13, where he stayed until May 20, while completing the gathering of provisions and animals needed for the trip. It is interesting to note that he reported Ft. Garland was already "somewhat out of repair." He then went west across the San Luis Valley to the Rio Grande River, "Camp Loma," and Del Norte. Rufner reported that the settlement of Del Norte had fifty buildings and La Loma twenty. He predicted a great future for both settlements as supply towns; but he did not recognize the prejudices the Mexican-Americans would face at La Loma, which was deserted within a few years. At the time of his arrival, the two towns were located at the terminus of wagon roads from Pueblo and Cañon City to the San Juans.[64]

Ruffner went up the Rio Grande, passed Wagon Wheel Gap and Bristol Head, and then noted that nearly opposite "Rainy Cañon" was a dry canyon that held the trail to the Lake Fork. However Ruffner took the route that continued up the Rio Grande River and went to Baker's Park, passing through future southern Hinsdale County along much of the way. He noted that "Lost Trail" was a very rough road that had been made in 1872 by Major Wasson to bring a small mill to the Little Giant Mine. He also noted the great difficulty of going over Stony Pass to Baker's Park.

H. G. Prout, the group's surveyor, and a few other men separated from the rest of the group and explored the headwaters of the Lake Fork and its tributaries. His group called Burrows Park "Delusion Park" because of its thick mass of willows, which from above made the park look like it would be easy to cross. It wasn't. Prout was also the person who named Lake San Cristobal, called simply Lake Cristobal or Cristoval by some at the time.[65]

After checking out the Little Giant Mine, Baker's Park, and the surrounding areas, Ruffner received a message sent by his superiors that he should cut his trip short and return to Ft. Garland because of a possible Ute uprising to the east of the fort. Ruffner decided to take two of his men and go back by way of the Lake Fork and Cochetopa Pass, so as to at least get an overview of the second half of his mission. The rest of the party was to retrace the route back over Stony Pass and travel down the Rio Grande, where Ruffner would meet them in Antelope Park. Even though in a hurry, Ruffner stopped to admire the view of the Lake Fork drainage from the top of Cinnamon Pass:

> *The view is supremely grand. On either hand rise close above the stream gigantic peaks far above any vegetation — bare crags with immense bodies of snow in the deep gulches.*[66]

Then Ruffner descended into "Delusion Park," later to be called "Burrows Park," and on down to "Lake San Cristoval," later spelled as San Cristobal, with which he was greatly enamored:

> *This lake is a beauty. Its waters are perfectly clear, and reflected the mountains which slope into the lake on all sides. It has numerous coves and reaches, and two or three little islands dot its surface. Ducks, teal, mallards, and mud-hens were seen in all the coves with their broods of young, while a flock of ambitious mallards were sailing down the middle of the lake. There are no fish.*[67]

The lake was formed by the Slumgullion Earthflow about 1250 A.D. The earthflow broke loose from Mesa Seco and slid for four and a half miles to block the Lake Fork and form the 342 acre lake. Then another slide repeated the process about 400 years ago, but the second slide has still not reached the lake. A "homesick Englishman," probably H. G. Prout, who was part of the Ruffner Reconnaissance of 1873, is believed to have named the lake for a fictional lake in a poem by Alfred Lord Tennyson (the later Rhoda expedition used Proutt's map which gave the lake's name. The problem is no one has ever been able to find one of Tennyson's poems with a Lake San Cristobal or San Crisoval mentioned in it.[68] The name of the lake was Spanish for Saint Cristopher, the Catholic saint of travelers. Thomas J. Hines, official photographer of the same expedition, took the first known photographs of the two and a half by three-quarters of a mile lake and of many other spots in the San Juan Country. Unfortunately Hines had many problems with his glass negatives — a few were not properly developed and many were broken.

After exploring "the upper falls" (later named "Argenta Falls" but also called Argentine Falls by some) located about a mile below the lake, Ruffner went a few more miles down the Lake Fork. He then returned to the lake and continued south over the Continental Divide to Antelope Park, where he met the rest of the party. There he learned the supposed "Ute Uprising" had fizzled out and he could continue his trip. He returned to Lake San Cristobal by way of Bristol Head and "Lake Mary" (evidently Santa Maria Lake), which he called "a lovely sheet of water." Then he followed Clear Creek and came to North Clear Creek Falls. A mile and a half above the falls on Clear Creek, near today's Continental Reservoir, he crossed the "great Ute trail from Cochetopa towards the country of the Sierra La Plata."[69] He noted that the area he was passing through "is a magnificent cattle-range," which is still its principal use today. He turned to the north, passed over the Continental Divide at the large, high park now called "Jarosa Mesa" (today a favorite snowmobiling spot) and wrote that from the eastern side, it was probably "the easiest grade over the (Continental) Divide in Southern Colorado."[70] He was evidently describing the Cebolla drainage.

From this point he got his first view of "Mount Chauvenet" and noted it was probably the tallest in the region and was "the "grandest I have seen. The miners have sometimes called it the 'Leaning Tower,' and sometimes 'Capitol Mountain.'"[71] Mount Chauvenet was later named "Uncompahgre Peak." He also noted correctly that, because the San Juan rivers ran in all four directions that the San Juan Mountains must have been a giant dome at one time.

Ruffner then began the trip down the Slumgullion Slide (which had no name at this time), which he noted had formed Lake San Cristobal and was composed of bright yellow clay. Somewhere in the vicinity of Slumgullion, he passed the Scotland Mine, which he was told had been sold earlier in Denver for $30,000 but was now abandoned. He also saw burros on the slide, which meant prospectors were probably in the area, although he did not see any. After reaching the lake, he again went downstream on the Lake Fork and mentioned large amounts of roses, cardinal flowers, larkspur, daisies, gentians, Solomon's Seal, and many other varieties of flowers. It impressed him enough that he wrote that the "wild flowers are much more abundant and beautiful than on the eastern slope," and then he commented:

The Lake Fork, especially above the Lower Falls (Granite or Crooke Falls), is a beautiful stream with abrupt, rocky banks, flowing in dalles and cascades with a fringe of timber along most of its course; some fine photographs up and down the Lake Fork and lake were here made.[72]

Ruffner camped at "the Lower Falls" and felt it very picturesque.

From the crest of the first leap to 50 feet down the gorge under the first leap, the water is lashed to a snow-white foam of most lovely shapes, much like the Upper Fork of the Yellowstone. From the foot of the sheet, foam and spray rise high above the walls of the cañon so as to wet my book as I sat above writing. Bright rainbows played about and over the cañon.[73]

Then Ruffner rode up "Godman" (Henson) Creek for about three miles. He mentioned that the north face of the gulch was 2,000 to 2,500 feet high, sloping steeply toward the stream but ending in 200 to 300-foot cliffs immediately above the creek. "The south face is much the same but holds a thin soil with scant timber and vegetation, thus making a trail possible." Ruffner was looking for prospectors to talk with, but found only the tracks of a single prospector, a dog, and several burros. After three miles he turned back.

The party then explored down the Lake Fork from the site of today's Lake City. Ruffner found the Ute trail along the river to be very good except when he had to cross the river, at which points the trail was often very steep. He mentioned that the east side of the nine mile valley was much wider from the river and:

... the hills run down to the river in gentle undulations, here and there opening out into a small level park, are well grassed, watered by small streams, and thinly covered with yellow pine. Here and there an old tree has escaped Indian knives and grown to a good size, and the peeled trees show the valley has been frequented by Indians, but none of them had been peeled within a year or two.[74]

When on the lower Lake Fork of the Gunnison, Ruffner noted what was already called "The Gateway" (now simply called "The Gate" or the "Gates"), the large park below the Gate, and many Native American trails coming into this park. He wrote that the main Indian trail to the Uncompahgre River, which he described as being as wide as a "double wagon road," crossed the Lake Fork just before the "lower" Lake Fork Canyon, and that it was much worn. This crossing later became part of the Mears toll road and the present "Blue Mesa Cutoff" Road. When Ruffner was on Blue Mesa, he found many Utes camped there, but followed the edge of the lower Lake Fork Canyon on the Blue Mesa side down to the Gunnison River. It is only fitting that the Ute tribe now owns a large ranch in this area. Ruffner noted that the Utes were:

Mostly well-armed, well-mounted, and well-dressed, uncommonly clean, smiling, and civil; short men, with broad muscular shoulders; good looking for Indians, bland, courteous, and great beggars.[75]

Ruffner's group then continued by going up "Soda Creek" (the Cebolla), over Los Piños Pass, and up Los Piños Creek to the Ute Agency, where he met Charles Adams, the agent, as well as Chief Ouray and several other Ute chiefs. He mentioned that these Utes went to the Uncompahgre (in the area of the present town of Delta) for the winter, but the agency employees stayed at this high altitude. "Snow is said to be three feet on the level."[76] He noted the San Luis Valley was an "old stronghold of the Utes against the Plains Indians, Kiowa, Comanche, etc." Just as many people often do today, he crossed the summit of Cochetopa Pass without realizing it until he noted the creeks were running to the east instead of north or west. Then he and his men went down the Saguache River; and, near the San Luis Valley, he described fine crops of spring-wheat, potatoes, and numerous small cattle ranches. Ruffner mentioned that the small settlement of Saguache had two blacksmiths, one store, and one saloon. From Saguache his group then returned to La Loma, and their equipment and supplies were packed in wagons for the trip to Ft. Garland, where they arrived on July 21. Unfortunately soldiers from the fort had loaded Hine's glass photographic plates improperly at La Loma and thirty-eight of them were broken. Hines did return with 140 usable but much smaller and less detailed stereoscopic views. Later that summer, Ruffner's group explored the future Gunnison area and the Elk Mountains. By the time Ruffner returned to Del Norte that fall, a wagon toll road was being planned from the town to Baker's Park over Stony Pass. It would also be the first section of a road that would eventually branch off at Antelope Park and go to the Lake City area.

Until the winter of 1873-74, prospecting in the San Juans was believed to be seasonal, in the summer and fall, with the Americans leaving for the long winter. However in the winter of 1873-74 a few men stayed in the area, since the Brunot Treaty had been signed with the Utes and was only awaiting ratification by the United States Senate. Before the winter of 1873-74, Colorado newspaper accounts of the mineral richness of the San Juans were contradictory — at times claiming the San Juans were the richest district in Colorado, and at other times claiming the supposedly rich San Juan discoveries were a total scam. By late 1873, all the Colorado papers had been convinced of the potential riches of the area and promoters were securing some capital for future investment.

However, it was now the United States Senate that was keeping the San Juans from being legally opened to American prospectors. In 1874, the Brunot agreement with the Utes was still considered a treaty with a foreign nation and therefore had to be ratified by the U. S. Senate.[77] However many prospectors did not wait for ratification in the spring of 1874 before they started prospecting, exploring, and occupying the San Juans; although with the deep snow there was not much they could do in the high country until the late spring or summer snow melt.

While the federal government was procrastinating, the Territorial government of Colorado moved forward. When Colorado became a territory in 1861, there were seventeen counties established. The San Juans were originally covered by three counties — Lake, Costilla, and Conejos. On February 10, 1874, before the Brunot Treaty was even ratified, La Plata, Rio Grande, and Hinsdale Counties were added to cover the newly acquired San Juans. Originally Hinsdale was much larger than it is today and covered much of the eastern part of the San Juans. (About one-half of the original Hinsdale became part of Mineral County in 1893 after the rich silver areas around Creede were discovered in 1889.) The Brunot Treaty was not ratified until April 29, 1874. Hinsdale was originally going to be called "San Juan County," but was named "Hinsdale" at the last minute to honor former Colorado Lt. Governor and attorney George A. Hinsdale who died only a month before the county was formed.[78] In 1876 San Juan County was formed with Silverton as the county seat, followed the next year by Ouray County.

Lake City was not the original county seat of Hinsdale. When Hinsdale County was formed on February 10, 1874, a group of men from Denver located a site for a town about twenty miles up the Rio Grande River from the future site of Creede. "San Juan City" was located at the head of Antelope Park and near the present-day Hinsdale and Mineral County line. The settlement was referred to as both "San Juan" and "San Juan City," and was probably located on the present-day San Juan Ranch. Soon, inflated reports were being circulated that the town had a dozen cabins, but it was more like two cabins and a tent. There was also a very small log cabin that was the courthouse. A corral for the horses was also built, as well as a fenced area for a few cows. A post office and a far-sighted road house called "The Texas Club" were established in the cabins in 1874. San Juan City received the first post office in the San Juans on June 24, 1874, although Howardsville near Silverton also received one the same day.[79] A couple by the name of Taft was the original owners, but they sold out to Clarence W. Brooks in 1875. San Juan City was considered a good location because it was near the junction of the roads over Stony or Cunningham passes to Silverton and the road over Spring Creek and Slumgullion passes to Lake City.[80]

Hinsdale County was formed without much thought for geography, as it sits astride both sides of the great east to west bulge of the Continental Divide that occurred because of the formation of the San Juan Dome. The Continental Divide therefore crosses the eastern Hinsdale County line twice. Ray Newburn, in his postal history, points out that this effectively divided the county into three fairly equal parts. The northern part of the county is centered around the Lake Fork of the Gunnison, Henson Creek and the Cebolla; and it is this part that contains most of the ore found in the county and therefore most of its people. The middle part is composed of the upper drainage of the Rio Grande River and was the early route over Stony Pass to the Silverton area. This portion of the county contained many small settlements along the trail (road) to Silverton, mostly stage or rest stops. The southern portion of Hinsdale County contains the Los Piños and upper Piedra Rivers, which drain into the far southern San Juan Mountains and the San Juan River. This portion of Hinsdale County is mostly in the Weeminuche Wilderness but also contains a little ranch land and is usually accessed from Pagosa Springs. Only one small town, Debs, was ever established in this remote area. Nevertheless Debs was an incorporated town.[81]

As mentioned, Hinsdale County was created two and a half months before the ratification by the U. S. Senate of the Brunot Treaty on April 29, 1874, yet there was no great rush at that time, as the San Juans were still an uncharted wilderness. Perhaps the greatest fear was that the Ute Indians might not have left the area. Actually there were only a few Utes left in the entire San Juan Mountains, so it was not nearly as dangerous as before the Brunot Treaty. Most Utes stayed in the lower valleys of western Colorado, land which they had kept under the terms of the Brunot Treaty. Government surveyors were soon in the area, but most of their maps and discoveries were not yet published. Transportation routes were needed into the San Juans, and road building was not the responsibility of the U.S., states or territories, or county governments. The public needed to know the geology of different areas, the drainage of rivers and creeks, information on roads and trails, and at least some official information about the climate. However, the resulting government expeditions were instructed by the politicians to inspect for the virtues of the new territory and not to "dwell" on the negative factors as barriers to progress.[82]

Besides Ruffner, another survey unit in Hinsdale at this time was the Wheeler Survey, which consisted of a small Army unit under the command of Lt. William Marshall. In the summer and early fall of 1873, Wheeler's party worked west of the 100th Meridian. Marshall's group had descended into Bakers Park in November, 1873, when he came down with a terrible toothache. He decided that he must see a Denver dentist. He went back by way of the Lake Fork, then the upper Grand River (later called the Tomichi), and discovered Marshall Pass. A year later he recommended in a letter to a friend that the junction of the Lake Fork and Henson Creek as a perfect town site, saying it was "nearer the San Juan mines by a better route than the Rio Grande and better suited for a mill site than Baker's Park."[83] Marshall returned to work in the San Juans in 1874. His newly discovered route became another Otto Mears' toll road, and cut 125 miles off the trip from Denver to the San Juans. In a few years it became one of the routes of the Denver & Rio Grande Railroad to the San Juans.

The main government survey was the U. S. Geological Survey, which had been established in 1867, and Dr. F. V. Hayden was made its first director. In the spring of 1873, Wyoming and Colorado were being investigated by the Hayden Survey. The San Juans were of particular interest because of the potential for valuable minerals, but it would be the summer of 1874 before the Hayden Survey followed Otto Mears' trail for his new toll road into the San Juans. They reported the Cebolla Valley already partially settled. The Hayden Survey never operated in Colorado as a single unit because of the difficulty of the terrain and the need to quickly finish the operation. Sometimes there were as many as six or seven subgroups working in different locations in Colorado. A.D. Wilson and Franklin Rhoda worked together under the Hayden Survey in the San Juans in 1874. The purpose of this sub-group was to document the geological and mineral resources of those parts of the San Juan Mountains opened up by the Brunot Treaty.[84] In making their survey, they scaled 125 of the highest peaks in the San Juans, including Uncompahgre, Sunshine, and Handies in Hinsdale County near the future Lake City. Wilson published *The Atlas of Colorado* in 1877, and his maps were so accurate that they have proved useful right up to present.

Wilson and Rhoda started on July 24, 1874 from Saguache, then went to the Ute Agency on Cochetopa, where they switched to what Ruffner had called "The Great Ute Trail" (the Colorado Trail now follows much of this ancient Ute route), which ran from Los Piños Creek close to the Continental Divide south to the headwaters of the Rio Grande River. However, at the upper Cebolla, they went over part of Cannibal Plateau and down the Cebolla where they hit the Mears' toll road trail to Burrows (also spelled Burroughs at the time) Park. They went over to the Lake Fork and then upstream where they climbed Crystal Peak and then went down to "Godwin" (Henson) Creek. On August 7, they climbed Uncompahgre (thought at the time to be the highest mountain in Colorado). They surprised a grizzly bear with two cubs on Uncompahgre and noted the bears had been all over the summit. They also mentioned the great view of almost all of the San Juan peaks.[85] Rhoda's and Wilson's first, but minor, Colorado electrical storm experience was on Henson, then they moved upstream to the top of Engineer Pass and American Flats.[86] They went back down Henson and up the Lake Fork, and by August 12, were near the Packer Massacre site near Lake San Cristobal and the present location of "The Dawn of Hope" Bridge, named after a nearby mine.[87]

Rhoda and Wilson were going to climb and make stations on both Red Cloud and Sunshine, but the weather turned bad and they decided to only climb Sunshine. The storm continued to progress until the two men were totally absorbed by it. Rhoda ended up writing seven pages in his journal pertaining to his climb of Sunshine — an extraordinary detailed account compared to his other entries. In part it reads:

On arriving at the summit (of Sunshine) Mr. Wilson hastily made a rough sketch of the surrounding drainage, and then set up the instruments, while I proceeded to make profile sketches of the mountains south and west of us. We had scarcely got started to work when we both began to feel a peculiar tickling sensation along the roots of our hair, just at the edge of our hats, caused by the electricity in the air.... By holding our hands above our heads a ticking sound was produced, which was still louder if we held a hammer or other instrument in our hand. The ticking sensation above mentioned increased quite regularly at first, and presently was accompanied by a peculiar sound almost exactly that produced by the frying of bacon....

As the force of the electricity increased, and the rate of increase became greater and greater, the instrument on the tripod began to click like a telegraph machine.... The effect on the hair became more and more marked.... The cause became apparent, as a peal of thunder reached our ears. The lightning had struck a neighboring peak and the electricity had been discharged. Almost before the sound reached us the tickling and frying in our hair began again....

The (clouds) moved about in a chaotic manner, producing a curious effect. When you consider that the tops of the clouds were not less than 2,000 feet below us, you can get some idea of the strange scene that presented to our eyes in those exciting times....[88]

At this point Rhoda adds a little humor to his report:

We were electrified, and our notes were taken and recorded with lightning speed, in keeping with the terrible tension of the storm's electricity.... The lightning strikes were now coming thicker and faster, but separated by not more than two or three minutes at the time.... The fast-increasing electricity was suddenly discharged, as we had anticipated, by another stroke of lightning, which luckily

Lake San Cristobal looks pretty small in this 1874 photo because of the lower level of the lake. Several small dams over the years have made the lake rise 3 to 5 feet. (William H. Jackson Photo, Author's Collection)

for us, struck at a point some distance away. The instant he felt the relief, Wilson made a sudden dash for the instrument, on his hands and knees, seized the leg of the tripod, and flinging the instrument over his shoulder dashed back. We started as fast as we could over the loose rock, down the southwest side of the peak, but had scarcely got more than 30 feet from the top when it was struck.[89]

They continued up the Lake Fork and said they could easily discern large silver-bearing veins in Burrows Park. Then they went up Grizzly Creek and found prospect holes, stakes, and several location certificates on a good vein.[90] Rhoda and Wilson climbed Handies on August 15, then crossed Cinnamon Pass to Animas Forks the next day. By the nineteenth they had gone down the Animas River and out over Stony Pass. They then went down to the Rio Grande and up to the Rio Grande Pyramid.[91]

Yet another survey party was led at almost the same time by Hayden himself. He went with famed pioneer photographer William Henry Jackson and others along the Continental Divide to Stony Pass, Silverton, and Mesa Verde. Wilson-Rhoda and Hayden-Jackson were to meet on the Animas River and go to Mesa Verde. Travel writer Earnest Ingersol was also with this group and wrote later of the Lake City/Hinsdale area.

Hayden and his various groups were in the San Juans in 1874 and 1875. Hayden remained in Colorado until 1876, doing the research that would be needed by Americans who wished to invest or settle in this land. Hayden's groups ultimately produced a wonderful, large atlas of most of western Colorado. The Hayden maps are considered to be superbly accurate for the time.

Because of several years delay in publication, the findings of these various survey groups would not be of much help to most of the early prospectors in the San Juans; but, their maps and scientific information would be of great use to the thousands of people who would be in the San Juans within a few years.

One of the earliest photographs of Alferd Packer, which was taken about the time of his first trial in 1883. Packer was in his early 40s at the time. (Author's Collection)

CHAPTER 2

ALFERD PACKER —
THE "COLORADO CANNIBAL"

···❦···

he Colorado Historical Society stated that Hinsdale County "has
the dubious distinction of being the site of Colorado's most
sensational crime."[92] There is no doubt that the infamous crime
has become "a fixture in the lore of the Old West."[93] Littleton, Colorado,
which is Packer's burial place, declares in its blog that the perpetrator is
the only person in the United States to be convicted of cannibalism.[94] The
crime has inspired a half-dozen books, dozens of articles, songs, poems,
and even a film and Broadway musical. To top it off, several restaurants
and school cafeterias now carry the killer's name — Alferd Packer.

The event for which Lake City is perhaps best known happened
before there was a town and only a very short time after Hinsdale became
a county on February 10, 1874. Exactly what did happen is confusing,
as for the most part, we have to rely on several different confessions
given by Packer of the events that led to the killings. Parts of his story
were contradicted by physical evidence that was later found. Then the
tale became a legend, with many authors adding a little extra action to
make the story more interesting. Even the spelling of Packer's first name
is contradicted, as he spelled it both "Alfred" and "Alferd." Because he
had his name tattooed on his arm as "Alferd," we will use that spelling,
although Packer later said the tattoo artist misspelled his name, but he
liked it spelled that way. Author Paul H. Gannt writes that Packer signed
his name both ways at various times, but Packer usually referred to
himself only as "Al" or "Packer."[95]

There is no way to present all the details or different stories concerning
Packer's misadventures in this short space, so we will concentrate on
the most likely events, along with a few humorous, but obviously false,
additions that have enhanced Packer lore over the years. If the reader
wants to review all the variations of the details of the story, then Ervan
F. Kushner's book, which can be found in the bibliography, is probably
the best on the subject and the one to review.

Packer was born November 21, 1842, in Allegany, Pennsylvania.[96] That made him about thirty-one at the time this story begins, although he told many people that he was much younger.[97] Packer reportedly suffered from epilepsy since childbirth, which was displayed in rigidity, flaying of the limbs, frothing at the mouth, unintelligible speech, and amnesia. This would drain his strength so badly that he would sometimes need days of food and rest to recover.[98] In 1857 doctors discovered that bromide helped epileptic seizures, and Packer evidently started taking the medicine. It helped slow the frequency of his seizures, but did not totally stop the attacks. According to Packer, the affliction did not slow him down as a young adult. Packer later told others that he was a hunter, rancher, guide, and a scout before the Civil War (when he would have been age twenty); but all of these occupations are unverified. It is known that at least one of Alferd's actual occupations was a shoemaker's apprentice in 1870. During the Civil War, Alferd served eight months[99] in the Union Army before he was discharged as being disabled. His disability, as recorded by the Army, shows how little was known about epilepsy at the time, as his Army record reflects that he caught typhoid while serving and then began experiencing epileptic seizures.[100] Packer had obviously failed to inform the enlistment team in Iowa of his epilepsy, and his discharge therefore gave him a monthly pension of twenty-five dollars for the rest of his life. Packer enlisted in the Union Army a second time in Iowa on June 10, 1863, but was soon discharged, again because of his epilepsy.

Like many other men, Packer came to Colorado as a prospector after the Civil War. He worked as a miner in Georgetown, Colorado, in 1872 and early 1873. Probably while "doublejacking," a sledge hammer hit his fingers and the tips of two fingers had to be removed.[101] Then he moved on to Utah Territory in 1873.[102]

In early November 1873, a group of eighteen Utah miners and prospectors, most or all of them strangers to each other, had decided to travel from Bingham, Utah,[103] to the new gold and silver strikes in the San Juans or the new discoveries in Breckenridge, Colorado.[104] They had decided to band together, as they would be crossing the Ute Indian reservation in western Colorado in the winter.[105] The members of the group were from all over the United States, as well as Scotland, Ireland, Canada, and France; and they had a variety of different occupations. The guide that the group's leader tried to pick could have only been chosen out of the delirium brought on by gold fever. Packer said he knew the San Juans and the area around Breckenridge well and also knew of a shortcut (probably the Cebolla Creek/Los Piños Creek route) to the Ute agency on Cochetopa Pass.[106] Packer had been sentenced to a Bingham chain gang for passing counterfeit money and was working as a convict laborer on the streets of Bingham to pay his fine. He kept telling anyone who would listen to him that he was very familiar with Colorado and would make a good guide. He is said to have told the group of eighteen that if they paid his fine he would be released and would guide them, but his offer was evidently not accepted. Yet another version of Packer's trying to hire on as a guide (this one told by Packer himself) was that immediately before the trip he had been working in the Bingham Copper mines, but he came down with lead poisoning and decided to go back to prospecting. Packer said he was hired by the group's leader Robert McGrue, but McGrue later denied this statement.

Alferd Packer did not look like he could be trusted, but he was the only one the group could find that supposedly knew the route, so he became an "advisory guide." Famous author Gene Fowler, in his book *Timberline*, wrote this haunting description of Packer:

> *He was twenty-four years old,[107] tall, gaunt, illiterate, taciturn. He was dark and wore a frowsy black beard. He was not well-known to many of the adventurers, to some he was an unwelcome addition. He had applied for a position as guide, but a majority of the party demurred.*

The group left in late November or very early December, 1873, but one of the worst winters in Colorado and Utah history had already set in and the men's progress was slow because of extremely cold temperatures and very deep snow. They supposedly had two four-horse teams and wagons, a four-mule team and wagon, and two or three two-horse teams. There were also a few saddle and pack horses. Each man, except Packer, had been charged $50 for food and transportation to Breckenridge by the wagons owner Robert McGrue. Packer paid $25 and agreed to take care of McGrue's teams to cover the rest of the fee.[108] Preston Nutter joined the group at Provo, Utah, and O. D. Loutzenheizer (called "Lout," but sometimes spelled "Lot") joined in Salina, Utah, making a total of twenty-one men including Packer.[109] Packer soon had an epileptic fit and fell into the group's campfire.[110] Most in the party had disliked Packer from the time they met him, but this incident caused many of them to ask McGrue not to allow Packer to accompany them. McGrue later stated that everyone in the outfit except him hated Packer, and that Packer recognized this and hated them back.[111]

It was 325 miles from Salt Lake to the Colorado border. By late January, 1874, the group was only at the Green River. They camped on the Green and built a raft. Their wagons were taken apart and put on the raft with most of their food. However the raft had very poor workmanship, and after it was launched on January 21, it started spinning in the middle of the river and threw most of the supplies and many of the wagon parts into the water. One writer claims that most of the food was lost in this accident, but another historian states the group was already desperately low on supplies.[112] Whatever the case, the lure of gold and silver was too strong for this misfortune to stop them, and they continued on in the belief that they would be able to kill game for food along the way. Soon the men had only an occasional rabbit and the oats they had brought for the horses to sustain them.[113]

The group of very hungry men passed what is now the Colorado-Utah border about January 25, and camped on the south side of the

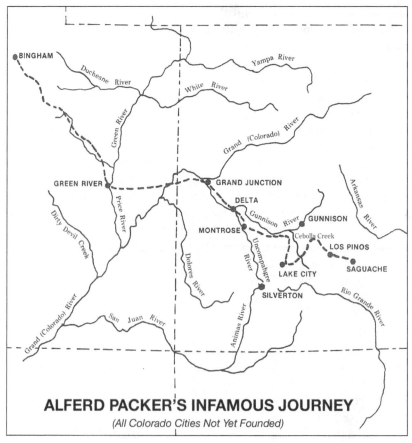

ALFERD PACKER'S INFAMOUS JOURNEY
(All Colorado Cities Not Yet Founded)

The group of prospectors left Bingham, Utah, in late November or early December, 1873. Because of deep snow and harsh weather, it was mid-January, 1874, before they made it to the Green River, where their raft overturned. They crossed the Colorado River a few days later, and then took three more days to get to Ouray's camp near the future Delta. Packer's party left Ouray for the Los Piños Agency February 9, and Packer arrived at the Ute Agency April 10, 1874. (Author's map)

Colorado River (then called the Grand River). They were discovered near the present site of Grand Junction, Colorado by three Utes, who suspected they might be settlers coming to find a new life on the reduced Ute Indian Reservation. Since homesteading by whites was not allowed under the 1868 or the pending 1873 Ute treaties, they were "invited" to join Chief Ouray at his winter quarters at the present-day site of Delta-Olathe, which was about a three day trip. They arrived there half-starved, but physically okay, although they had been on the trail for about two months. When on the move, they had averaged about ten miles a day, but many days they had traveled much less or they could not travel at all.

Chief Ouray treated the men well, after he was assured they were merely passing through Ute territory and were not settlers. He fed them, visited with them almost every day, and warned them to not proceed into the high mountains at this time of year. The snow was much too deep this particular year, and it was way too cold to travel. Ten of the men took Ouray's advice, and the Utes even helped the Americans build permanent shelters to live in until spring. Lout and Packer had an argument, probably on the route to travel; and those who were going to travel on split into two groups. Oliver (O. D.)Loutzenheizer and four other men soon left despite Ouray's warning, and they followed the Gunnison River route that Ouray suggested. Lout's group, and later Packer's men, did not own what was left of the wagons or the horses the group was using, so they were free to travel, but were all on foot. They believed they could make it to their destination — the Ute Indian Agency at Los Piños or the small settlement of Saguache within a week or two.[114] The group chose not to mention the San Juans destination to Chief Ouray, as the 1873 Brunot Treaty had not yet been ratified by the U.S. Senate.

Lout's group was soon in trouble. They were caught in a blizzard, starving, and lost. The group had been in the wilderness for three weeks in the middle of winter when providence intervened. They had gone up the Lake Fork, thinking it was the Gunnison River, the same route that Packer's group would later take. However, about the site of the later settlement of Barnum (near Indian Creek in Dutch Gulch and the Lake Fork and near the later Carr Ranch), Lout's group realized their mistake and went back downstream to the Gunnison River. They had been seeing some game, but only had a single pistol, which is a hard weapon to hunt game with.[115] They staved off starvation by killing a coyote that had a sheep's shank in its mouth.[116] The meat of both animals gave their group about five day's rations.[117] Lout and Mike Burke decided to go for help, while the others stayed behind. It was only by eating a half-dead cow from the Ute agency herd and drinking its warm blood that the two men made it to the Ute cow camp near present-day Gunnison, where they were taken in by Jim Kelly, Sidney Jocknick, and several of the other American cowboys that kept watch on the 800 head Ute cow herd.[118] Kelly and another man went to get the men that had been left behind. The other men in Lout's group wanted to stay where they were for a day or two to regain their strength, so the cowboys pitched a tent for them and left food and firewood.[119]

The rest of the travelers soon made it to the cow camp, where all five of the men of Lout's group rested for nine weeks[120] to regain enough strength to try to make it to the Ute Agency on Cochetopa Pass and then go to Saguache. Once again they encountered deep snows plus gale force winds that are typical in the spring in Colorado, and they again almost died.[121] The men stated later that they had considered casting lots for who would be killed for food for the others.[122] When they left the cow camp, Lout and Burke had snow shoes to use for breaking trail for the whole party through the deep snow,[123] but their group was soon again lost and this time they split up—every man for himself.

In the meantime six other prospectors had decided to leave Chief Ouray's camp — Shannon Bell, Israel Swan, George Noon (a sixteen year-old boy), Frank Miller, and James (Jim) Humphrey decided they would follow the lead of Alferd Packer, who claimed he knew a shortcut to the agency.[124] It is likely that they were going to stay at the Ute agency or Saguache, so as to be nearby and ready to prospect in the San Juans after the spring thaw; but once again, due to the area still being technically the property of the Utes, they mentioned only Breckenridge to Chief Ouray and others. As evidence that they really intended to go to Saguache and then in the spring to prospect in the San Juans, it is noted that almost all of the survivors of the group of twenty-one stayed in the San Juans after the winter was over. Ouray again warned Packer's group about traveling in the San Juans in the winter, but when he saw they would ignore his advice, he gave them directions on the best route to travel in the deep snow, supplied them with a little food, and even drew a crude map that would take them along the Gunnison River to the Ute agency cow camp near today's Gunnison, then on to the Ute agency proper on the top of Cochetopa Pass, and finally down the other side of the pass to Saguache. The men were told to follow the Gunnison River as closely as possible, and Ouray warned that the extremely deep Black Canyon made it hard to keep the Gunnison (called the Eagle Tail by the Utes) in sight. The six men left in a snow storm anywhere between February 7 to 15, but it is generally agreed it was February 9. All the rest of the group stayed with Chief Ouray and enjoyed his hospitality until spring.

Packer and his group estimated the trip would take seven to ten days, and they thought they had enough food with them to make it in that time frame, but only by using short rations. They hoped to kill game along the way to supplement what food they had. Swan and Noon carried rifles, Bell had a hatchet, and Miller (a butcher) had a skinning knife. At least one and possibly two of the men carried pistols, but Packer was evidently unarmed. They were fairly well-equipped for the winter's cold weather with blankets and heavy garments.

Within five days, Packer and his group were in trouble. Like Lout's group, they were lost, freezing, and starving. Whether on purpose or by accident, they too had ended up on the Lake Fork of the Gunnison, and the temperature was going well below zero at night when they reached a site near Lake San Cristobal. At this point, Packer's descriptions of what happened vary, but we will consider them in a few pages.

Let us now skip about six weeks ahead. Mrs. Alva Adams, wife of the Ute Agent at the Los Piños Agency, General Charles Adams, had a strange dream in March of 1874. It happened one day when the clouds came in low and gradually covered the countryside like fog. She was resting and had a vision that someone was lost in this "fog" and pleading for help. She requested that someone at the agency hang a light from a high point. The agency men laughed at her, but she persisted, and the lantern was hung every night. Sure enough, eventually Lout saw the light. He had separated from the other men and lost his way from the cow camp to the Ute agency. He was in bad shape, and the light undoubtedly saved his life. He fainted before the agency men could get him inside the agency building. Men were sent out to guide the rest of Loutzenheizer's party to the agency, but they could not find any of his companions, so they built a big fire and hung provisions on the limb of a tree. The rest of Lout's men, who had become separated from each other, miraculously saw the fire, and the provisions saved their lives. One by one, the men came in to the Agency and all lived.

But there were to be more strange occurrences. Three employees had just sat down for breakfast at the Ute Agency. One of the cowboys, Alonzo Hartman, told in later testimony what he saw in the early morning of April 16, 1874:

> There was no one in the section (around the Ute Agency) nearer than fifty miles, so it seemed strange that a man should drop down from nowhere so suddenly. I was wondering what it all meant when he came up.
> "Hello," I said, are you lost?"
> Packer, for that is who it was, rubbed his eyes.
> "Is this the agency?" he said.
> I told him it was. He didn't seem different from any other man who had been exposed to winter weather. His hair and beard were long and matted; but he showed little sign of having suffered from

severe winter weather, lost in a wild uninhabited country with the thermometer showing between thirty and fifty degrees below zero many mornings. Naturally one would expect that no man could stand the exposure this man had been through and live; but here was the man alive and seemingly none the worse for his experience.[125]

It was about sixty-six days (somewhere between April 6 and April 16) after the second group of prospectors had left Chief Ouray's camp, when Packer arrived at the Los Piños Agency and was met by Alonzo Hartman.[126] Packer carried a Winchester rifle and a coffee can full of live coals for starting fires. His jet black hair was matted; he was about six feet tall and weighed about 165 to 175 pounds. He walked with a limp caused by frostbite to his toes, as his feet were wrapped only in pieces of torn blankets. Although he limped, he was in remarkably good shape for a man who had spent a good part of the winter outdoors in the San Juan Mountains. When he spoke, it was with a very high-pitched, unusual, almost whiney, voice.[127]

Packer told Stephen A. Dole (who was in charge of the agency in the absence of Agent Charles Adams), James Downer (Justice of the Peace for the area), and Herman Lueders (government clerk and agency constable) that early in his group's trip he had become snow-blind and hurt his leg. He said he could not walk without great difficulty and was

Indian Agent Charles Adams, agency employees, and Utes pose at the first Los Piños Ute Agency. Adams is at the center of the front row. Ouray may be the second chief to his left. Tentative identification of the white men in the back row (left to right) are Justice of the Peace James P. Downer, Herman Lauter, Stephen A. Dole, and Herman Lueders. Within this building Packer made his alleged first confession. (Author's Collection)

left behind by the rest of his party. He said he had wandered for several months in the wilderness with no food but berries and an occasional rabbit or squirrel. He stated that he thought the other men had gone to Baker's Park (the future site of Silverton). In most accounts, Packer's first request was not for food, but rather for whiskey. Other accounts say he ate ravenously or that he gagged when he saw meat. The three agency men accepted Packer's story at face value and expressed their sympathy. Dole even offered Packer a job at the agency, but Packer instead sold the Winchester rifle to Downer for $10.

On April 16, two of the men who had stayed behind at Chief Ouray's camp, Preston Nutter and a Dr. Cooper (we do not know his first name), also arrived — having made the trip in two weeks without incident in early April. The two men and Packer decided to go to Saguache, but because of his frost-bitten feet, Packer had to travel in the agency wagon. Saguache was still a small Mexican-American town with only about a dozen white merchants and settlers. It had been founded in 1866, but it was on the verge of expanding rapidly. It was located forty-five or fifty miles southeast of the agency at the northwest edge of the San Luis Valley.

In Saguache, Packer visited the store of Otto Mears and Isaac Gottieb (also spelled Gotthelf as well as many other ways),[128] who had already heard from other members of the party that Packer had been jailed for passing counterfeit money in Salt Lake City. Mears refused to take a bill which he thought looked "funny." Packer then pulled out another wallet and gave Mears a bill that Mears accepted, although he thought it strange that Packer had two wallets.[129] Packer spent $100 at Mears' store — $70 on a horse and $30 on clothes.

Packer stayed for eight or nine days in Saguache with Larry Dolan, a saloon keeper, who became a friend of Packer and noticed that Packer occasionally displayed large sums of money while drinking and playing poker at Dolan's saloon.[130] Packer also spent large sums of money buying drinks for his friends, and he lost often at gambling (one day alone he lost $37). Dolan later testified in court that Packer spent "about a hundred dollars in the saloon" and was "a frequent customer." Dolan also testified that in addition to what Packer spent, he saw two fifty-dollar gold notes and lots of smaller bills in Packer's possession. At one point, Packer offered to loan Dolan $300, but Dolan never took him up on the offer.[131] The other members of the Utah group all wondered where the money had come from, since Packer had told them he had only $20 after paying his half fare of $25 to McGrue for transportation.

While Packer was having a good time, the other members of the Utah party who had stayed with the Utes near present-day Delta-Olathe, as well as their winter host Chief Ouray, reached Saguache in late April or very early May. All had an easy trip after the snow melted or hardened. Ouray supposedly made the comment that Packer was in "extremely good shape" for the hardships he said he had endured, and everyone was suspicious of Packer's story.

The members of the original Salt Lake party told others that Packer had much more money now than he said he had in Bingham. Preston Nutter sought out Packer to ask about the other men who had been with him.[132] Once, when drinking heavily in Saguache, Packer displayed items that members of the original party knew belonged to the other men who had gone with Packer. Among these items, they were sure he had sold Israel Swan's Winchester rifle and still had Frank Miller's prized skinning knife. Packer was also discovered to have a pipe, pocket knife, and a few other items that belonged to the men who were missing.[133]

On May 1, General Adams arrived in Saguache on his way to the Ute agency. Mears, Nutter, and several members of the original party mentioned their suspicions about Packer to General Adams, who talked with Packer and was told the same story that had been given the agency employees, but this time Packer added that he had been given the Winchester rifle that he sold when the other five men in his party left him alone in the wilderness. The others in his group had supposedly left him a few days' provisions, and he said he had shot a rabbit with the rifle and had eaten rosebuds to help his hunger.

Adams was suspicious and decided to try to get Packer to come to the Ute agency with him, as Adams thought he had police jurisdiction over Packer there, since the crime, if any, had occurred on the then Ute Reservation.[134] When Adams first talked to Packer at the agency, there were many inconsistencies in Packer's story about being left alone by the group. Foremost, it was the "law of the wilderness" that a hurt comrade was never left behind. No one really believed Packer's version of the events. When General Adams later questioned Packer about where he got his money, Packer said the Saguache blacksmith, Jim Kincaid, was a friend of his family and had loaned him the money. However, Adams sent an employee to check with Kincaid, who said Packer had never even asked him for a loan.

Adams asked Packer to guide a search party to be sent from the Ute agency to look for the missing men. At first Packer gave many excuses why he could not go, but eventually he consented and went back to the agency with Adams and several members of the original party. Adams then became much more aggressive with his questions and interrogated Packer for hours.

According to several sources,[135] on the way to the agency Packer was caught throwing items into Cochetopa Creek. When asked what he was doing, Packer said it was just trash he was throwing away. Later it was assumed that the "trash" included two of the dead men's wallets.[136] Along the way, Nutter noticed that Packer had Miller's hunting knife; and when questioned, Packer said Miller had stuck it in a tree and evidently forgot it when he and the other four men had left him alone. By this time it had been learned from other travelers that none of the men with Packer had reached Baker's Park, where Packer had said they might have gone, since they had not shown up at the agency or Saguache. There were a dozen or so other men present when Adams again asked where Packer got the large sums of money he was spending in Saguache. This time Packer said he had borrowed the money from a friend, but he could not remember the friend's name.

Adams continued to confront Packer well into the night with the group's suspicions that he had killed the other members of his party. In the late evening of May 4, Packer changed his story.[137] Afterwards Adams wrote down the substance of the oral confession, awoke Justice of the Peace Downer, had Packer sign the document, and Downer notarized it. It read:

> *Old Man Swan died first and was eaten by the other five persons about ten days out of (Ouray's) camp. Four or five days afterwards Humpreys (sic) died and was also eaten; he had about one hundred thirty three dollars ($133). I found the pocketbook and took the money. Sometime afterwards, while I was carrying wood, the butcher was killed — as the other two told me, accidently — and he was also eaten. Bell shot "California" with Swan's gun and I killed Bell. Shot him, I covered up the remains and took a large piece along. Then traveled fourteen days into the agency. Bell wanted to kill me with his rifle—struck a tree and broke his gun.*
>
> *I, A. G Packer, do solemnly swear that the above statement is true and nothing but the truth, so help me God,*
> *Signed, A. G. Packer*
>
> *Sworn and subscribed to before me the 4th day of May, 1874*
> *James P. Downer, J.P.[138]*

Packer said his companions had died of hunger, exposure, or been shot by others in the party at various points along their journey, and since burial was impossible because of the frozen ground, their bodies were left where they died, and they had taken each dead person's belongings to return to their loved ones. The only person that he admitted killing was Bell.

At the time of Packer signing his first written version, Adams in his monthly report to the Commissioner of Indian Affairs, wrote:

...Soon after the first party left Ouray's camp, another party consisting of six persons left in the same manner against the advice of Ouray with the intention of reaching this Agency. They left camp about the first of February and on the 16th of April one of the party, A. G. Packer, after being out two and a half months arrived at this Agency, evidently in good health and condition.

Upon being first questioned what had become of his companions he said that shortly after leaving Ouray's camp he had frozen his feet, that his companions had left him with some provisions and a rifle, and that after getting well he had managed to get through here by himself and that his companions had probably died from hunger and cold since they left him to his fate.

The story at first I believed, and made arrangements to send out and find the bodies, but Mr. Packer finally confessed under oath that one after another of these five persons had been killed, the last remaining man within only about 20 miles of the Agency. He excepts only that the two first men victims of whom he speaks as having died from starvation, and that they had eaten the dead bodies first, before commencing to kill each other.[139]

Adams brought up a new discovery to Packer — the Utes had found strips of human flesh along Packer's trail to the agency. At that time, Packer said he had thrown away the rest of Bell's dried flesh. It was decided that a search party would be sent out to get Bell's body. Packer said that Bell was killed near a large lake, and the Utes all said they knew where the lake (San Cristobal) was and that it was about fifty miles away. Adams and Mears agreed that if the search party found Bell's body and the broken rifle that perhaps Packer was telling the truth and Adams would try to help him.[140]

The search party consisted of some of the men who had been in the original Utah party, two agency employees, and three or four Utes. Paul Gantt writes the party consisted of Nutter, Dr. Cooper, and James McIntosh from the original Utah party of twenty-one men, as well as Indian Billy and two other Utes.[141] Herman Leuders, the agency constable, went with the search party to keep a close watch on the manacled Packer during the hunt for Bell's body. Packer seemed to know where he was going until they reached the Lake Fork of the Gunnison, where he said he was lost and had never seen that part of the country before. He said he did not know where to go next.[142]

Some authors write that the party was out searching for two weeks and found one of the party's campsites, but nothing was found there, so they returned to the agency. Other sources, including Kushner, write that they found two camps — one of which contained a pill container with Dr. Cooper's and Packer's names on it. These were supposedly the pills that Packer took for his epilepsy.[143] Robert McGrue, the leader of the Utah group of twenty-one, later stated that Dr. Cooper never gave Packer any medication because he especially hated Packer, and Packer hated him back and would never have asked for medicine.[144]

The search party even drained a beaver pond near the first camp, hoping to find the murdered men's bodies, but they found nothing. A few of the men in the search party went all the way downstream and found another of the party's camps near the future site of Sapinero. On the trip to look for bodies, Preston Nutter confronted Packer and told him he knew Packer had killed the other men and that he should be hanged. Supposedly on the way back to the agency, Packer made an attempt to kill Herman Leuders, the agency clerk and constable and the leader of the search party. Packer was ultimately jailed at the Ute Agency.

The more Packer talked about his ordeal, the more contradictions appeared in his story; but Packer was not the only one getting his story mixed up. At the time, there were three versions of who found the bodies of the murdered men. The most likely version of the discovery was carried in the Del Norte *San Juan Prospector* on August 22, which published an article that stated that prospectors, Captain C. H. Graham George Nicholas, and F. P. Wells (who was also the coroner), had found the bodies. The *Rocky Mountain News* of August 28, 1874 carried the same article. The Packer party appeared to have been camped at the spot where the bodies were found for only a short time, perhaps just a day. Another camp, which was the one found by the search party from the Ute Agency, looked as if it had been occupied for some time — at least several weeks but probably by only one man. The prospectors who found the bodies went to Saguache to report the grisly discovery.

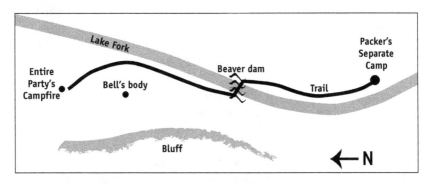

This sketch, with a few additions, was made at the Packer trial at the direction of O.D. Loutsenheiser. Lout testified that Bell's body was 2 rods (about 33 feet) from the main camp, and that Packer's wickiup was further away and across the river. (Base map from Kushner, Alferd Packer)

The second version was that John A. Randolph, an artist and photographer for *Harper's Weekly*, found the bodies about August 20, 1874,[145] two and a half miles south of present-day Lake City and about a mile north of Lake San Cristobal. It is very possible that Graham took Randolph to the spot and Randolph came back later after the prospectors left for the Ute agency and claimed the discovery for himself. The party sent out from the agency to identify the bodies found four of the men close together, laying practically shoulder to shoulder, their skulls crushed with a hatchet. Preston Nutter, from the identification party, testified to this in court, as well as Bell's body being some distance away. Randolph's drawing does not look like this and even shows Bell's body in the drawing when everyone who saw the site agreed the body was some distance away. Since Randolph and Graham's party were in a wilderness with no nearby settlements, it is possible that both found the bodies at different times and thought they were the first. Either Randolph moved the bodies after discovery or took an "artist's license" to draw the bodies in a different configuration from the way they were found. Regardless of how the bodies were found, their being together was absolutely contrary to Packer's first written confession that the men had died along the trail. The bodies had been decomposing since the first spring thaws (about three or four months) and the smell was supposedly terrible.[146] Within a few years, the spot where Packer killed the men was (and still is) known as "Deadman's Gulch," and the area above it is still called "Cannibal Plateau."

Randolph's *Harper's Weekly* article stated:

> They were living in a gloomy, secluded spot, densely shaded by tall trees, at the foot of a steep hill near the bank of the (Lake Fork of) the Gunnison River.... Marks of violence on each body indicated that the most terrible crime had been committed there. The bodies lay within a few feet of each other, in their blankets and clothes. There had been no attempt to conceal the remains.[147]

Yet another version of the discovery at the time was that Enos Hotchkiss, or one of his men, who were working on the Mears' toll road at the time, found the bodies of the dead men under a high, steep bluff in a very thick forest of spruce trees with thick branches that went almost all the way to the ground. This version simply didn't happen, although it was reported in the *Silver World*. However the confusion is understandable, as it was later disclosed that the Hotchkiss party did find Packer's later camp that was a short distance away from where the bodies were found. James Fullerton, who was working on the road with Hotchkiss, stated that the road crew camped near Lake San Cristobal

John Randolph's drawing for Harper's Weekly *has many discrepancies' from the testimony at trial. The bodies are scattered around, Bell is in the middle of the other four bodies, two heads are missing (not one), and the flesh is gone from the waist down on all the bodies. Why he did this is unknown, but it was a grizzly scene either way. (Harpers Weekly, October 17, 1984, Author's Collection)*

for several days on their way back to Saguache. They were probably prospecting on Hotchkiss Mountain and at the time were no more than a few hundred yards from Packer's camp, but they did not initially see anything because of thick brush. Fullerton eventually noticed Packer's camp, investigated, and later noted Packer made a very good winter camp, protected from the wind, and with a stone wall to project heat into his shelter. The camp looked well used.[148] Hotchkiss later said he and his crew never searched in the area of the other camp where the bodies were found.

After the bodies were discovered and reported, a group was sent from Los Piños to identify and bury the men. Preston Nutter was a member of the recovery party, which found a butcher knife (as opposed to the skinning knife carried into the agency by Packer) and another rifle at the site, but no mention was made of whether the stock of the rifle was broken.[149] The Lake City *Silver World* of April 3, 1883, the time of Packer's first trial, reported that two hunters later found a "pepperbox pistol" at the murder site. The pistol had six barrels and three were loaded. The *Silver World* also gave its version of the tale, but it was unfortunately full of bad information.[150]

When Nutter testified later at Packer's trial, he said it looked like no flesh had been cut from Swan's body, but it did look like someone had badly torn Swan's clothes as if searching his body for something.[151] Four of Packer's victims lay some distance from Bell's body. The skulls of all the men were cracked open with a sharp object like a hatchet, and it looked like Bell had also been shot in the back while running away.

Miller's head was missing. There was no sign of a struggle. Since Packer had lived for almost sixty days in the wilderness, it seemed obvious he had killed them all early on during their stay there, and then lived in the other camp for quite some time. However, there was later court testimony that only two of the men had flesh cut off their bodies and that those were small pieces. A year later, Miller's skull was found some distance away from where his body was found. It was speculated that perhaps animals had pulled it away at some time during the six months before the bodies were found. Miller's skull seemed to indicate he had been hit many times before a blow was fatal. The others looked as if they died instantly. It was estimated at that time that Packer had stolen from $1,400 to over $2,000 from his five victims.

After the bodies were found, Packer was officially arrested and taken from the agency to Saguache. The little town had no real jail, so Packer was kept at Mears' home the first night and afterwards in a small stone or adobe building at the Saguache Sheriff's ranch. On June 11, 1874, Adams was removed as agent at the Los Piños Agency for political reasons. Different Christian groups were now being appointed as Indian agents, and Adams was the wrong denomination.

Packer escaped from jail on or about August 8, 1874. Someone (many claimed that it was the Saguache sheriff, Amos Walls, who had become friends with Packer) had given Packer a handmade key to his cell.[152] Packer claimed later that Otto Mears told him, "You fool, you ought to skip." Packer later said other men had told him to escape. At the time of the escape, the sheriff had been called away to testify in District Court in Del Norte[153] and had left Packer guarded by an eighteen year-old boy.[154] John Lawrence, the Saguache County attorney at the time, later made an affidavit in which he stated that he and Mears had agreed to turn Packer loose because they thought a trial would bring bad publicity to Saguache, which was just beginning to boom. Lawrence said:

> *Packer was given provisions, etc. and turned loose.... When the bodies were found, of course, it created a nine day wonder among the few who were in the country. But Packer was gone and no one*

had any idea of where he was or that he would ever be caught and all soon died out and all went on in even tenor.[155]

Yet another version of the escape is that Packer bribed the young guard.[156] There is no question that someone gave Packer a key made from a knife blade and a file, but he either did not know the identity of the man who gave him the key or Packer was never to reveal it,[157] and no one was ever able to prove who gave it to him. Members of the original Utah party looked for Packer in the Saguache area for months after his disappearance but did not find him.

It was almost ten years later that "Frenchy" Cabazon, also spelled "Caberazon" by some writers, one of the members of the original Utah party, recognized Packer's unusually high-pitched voice in a hotel in Ft. Fetterman, Wyoming, and the "Colorado Cannibal" was recaptured. He was using the name John Schwartze. Newspapers of the day had a field day calling Packer different names and using cannibal slurs and puns in their articles.[158] Packer was seemingly anxious to make a second confession to General Adams, who was asked to come to Ft. Fetterman to identify whether the prisoner was indeed Packer. Packer had been arrested March 11, 1883, and on March 16, gave a second confession to Adams that was very different from his first.[159] This time the confession was taken down in writing by General Adams at the Arapaho County jail near Denver, where Packer spent the night while being taken to Lake City from Wyoming. Packer's confession was released in full to the Denver press the next morning. In the same newspaper articles that carried the confession, Packer was accused of many other unsolved crimes in various Western states.

This example from the Denver Republican *newspaper shows some of the extremely bad publicity given Packer when he was kept overnight in the Arapaho jail on the trip back to Lake City from Wyoming to stand trial. (Author's Collection)*

HUMAN JERKED BEEF.

The Man Who Lived on Meat Cut From His Murdered Victims.

The Fiend Who Became Very Corpulent Upon a Diet of Human Steaks.

A Cannibal Who Gnaws on the Choice Cuts of His Fellow-Man.

Packer Arrives in Denver and Meets and Recognizes General Adams.

He Makes a Confession, But Studiously Ignores the Five-Fold Murder.

He Says He Subsisted For Sixty Days Upon Human Flesh.

Particulars of the Tragedy From Denverites Conversant With the Facts.

His confession reads in part:

> *...When we left Ouray's camp we had only about seven days food for one man, we traveled for two or three days and it came a storm... We came to a mountain, crossed a gulch, and came on to another mountain, found the snow so deep we had to follow the mountain on the top, and on the fourth day we had only a pint of flour left.*
>
> *We followed the mountain until we came to the main range (presumably the Continental Divide), do not remember how many days we traveled — living on rosebuds and pine gum and some of the men were crying and praying.*
>
> *Then we came to the main range. We camped twice on a stream that runs into a big lake, the second time just above the lake. The next morning we crossed the lake, cut holes into the ice to catch fish, there were no fish[160] so we tried to catch snails. The ice was thin, some broke through.*
>
> *We crossed the lake and went into a grove of timber, all the men were crying and one of them was crazy. Swan (the oldest man in the group) asked me to go up and find out whether I could see something from the mountains.[161] I took my gun, went up the hill, found a big rose bush with buds sticking up from the snow, but I could see nothing but snow all around.*
>
> *I was kind of a guide for them but I did not know the mountains from that side. When I came back to the camp after being gone nearly all day I found the red-headed man (Bell) who acted crazy in the morning near the fire roasting a piece of meat which he had cut out of the leg of the German butcher (Miller).*
>
> *The latter's body was lying the furthest from the fire, down the stream, his skull was crushed in with the hatchet. The other three men were lying near the fire, they were cut in the forehead with the hatchet, some had two, some had three, cuts.*
>
> *I came within a rod of the fire, when the man (Bell) saw me. He got up with his hatchet towards me when I shot him sideways through the belly. He fell on his face, the hatchet fell forward, I grabbed it and hit him on top of the head. I camped that night at the fire, sat up all night.*
>
> *The next morning I followed my tracks up the mountain, but I couldn't make it, the snow was way too deep, and I came back. I went sideways (presumably alongside the river) into a piece of pine timber, set up two sticks, and covered it with pine boughs and made a shelter about three feet high; this was my camp until I came out.*
>
> *I went back to the fire, covered the men up, and fetched to the camp the piece of meat that was near the fire. I made a new fire*

near my camp and cooked the piece of meat and ate it. I tried to get away every day but I could not, so I lived off the flesh of these men, the biggest part of the 60 days I was out.

Then the snow began to have a crust and I started out up the creek to a place where I saw a big slide of yellowish clay seemed to come down the mountain, then I started up but got my feet wet and having only a piece of blanket around them I froze my feet under the toes, and I camped before I reached the top, making a fire and stayed all night.

The next day I made the top of the hill and a little over. I built a fire on the top of a log, and on two logs close together. I camped. I cooked some of the flesh and carried it with me for food. I carried only one blanket. There was $70 among the men. I fetched it out with me and one gun.

The red head had a $50 bill in his pocket. All the others together had only $20. I had $20 myself. If there was any more money in the outfit I didn't know about it and it remained there.

At the last camp, just before I reached the agency I ate my last piece of human meat....[162]

After arriving in Lake City, Packer was transferred to the Gunnison County jail from the Hinsdale County jail by Sheriff Claire Smith in the dead of night and with a large party of guards, as mob violence was deemed likely in Lake City. However there was time for Henry Olney, editor of the *Silver World*, while Packer was in the Lake City jail, to ask Packer why this second version of what happened was so different from his first confession. Packer said he was "crazed" at the time of the first written confession, because he was sure he was going to be hanged and hoped the bodies would not be found until he was out of the area. When asked if he was guilty of any of the many other crimes the Denver papers had blamed on him, Packer said:

They are all false.... Since my arrest, it seems that every crime committed in the mountains by unknown men has been charged to me.[163]

Justice was swift in those days. Packer was brought back to Lake City and indicted April 6,[164]and the latest signed, sworn confession was entered into evidence when Packer stood trial between April 9 and April 13, 1883, in Lake City. Preliminary matters had been heard by Judge Melvin B. Gerry by March 28. It was almost exactly ten years after the crime was committed, and the trial was less than three miles from where the crime had occurred. Packer was only tried for Swan's death at this trial, as he obviously had taken Swan's money. John C. Bell was the District Attorney and prosecutor, assisted by J. Warner Mills, another Lake City attorney. Packer was defended by Aaron Heims and A. J. Miller. Packer's attorneys first tried to get a change of venue because of the bad publicity, but this was summarily denied. Then his lawyers pointed out that he was on the Ute reservation at the time of the killing. As the Brunot Treaty had not yet been ratified by the U. S. Senate, it was thus a federal offense for which he was being tried, and the trial should have been in the federal courts. This motion was also denied, although both motions were probably valid points.

Then, before the start of the trial, Packer's attorneys moved to quash his indictment, as the crimes were not committed in the State of Colorado or County of Hinsdale, as there were no such places at the time of the commission of the crime.[165] The judge indicated that the indictment should be amended to show the "Territory of Colorado," instead of "State of Colorado," and no decision was made on the "Hinsdale County" point. The next day, a new indictment was presented and Packer's attorney brought up that the Colorado Territorial statute in force at the time of the commission of the crime had been repealed without a savings clause to keep it in force for crimes committed during that time but discovered or tried after the repeal, and that District Attorney John Bell had not signed the indictment. These were both valid objections, but Judge Melvin B. Gerry merely overruled them. Seating a jury was difficult, as feelings ran high against Packer, but eventually twelve men were picked after fifty-six potential jurors had been questioned.

Both of Packer's signed written confessions were entered into evidence. Preston Nutter, who had stayed in the San Juans after Packer's escape and was now very respected (even having been elected a state legislator from 1881 to 1883), was the first witness for the prosecution and was basically able to lay out the prosecution's case, because he had been present at most of the discoveries or confessions that had been made. Otto Mears testified that there was usually plenty of game along the route Packer and his group followed in southwest Colorado, but that if there was a lack of game he thought Packer was justified in eating human flesh. When General Adams testified, he said Packer had told him that he had to eat the bodies of the men in order for him to live, and he was ready to die for doing so, if he had to.[166] Evidence was also produced from others in Packer's trial that there had not been as much snow as normal in the winter of 1873-74, that game was fairly plentiful that winter, and that there was nothing to justify the eating of human flesh.[167] However, this testimony did not reconcile with Ouray's warning, the ordeal of the Lout party, or the statements of several other witnesses.

Packer took the stand in his own defense and spent six hours describing the details of his party's ordeal in a barely audible voice, after being allowed by the judge to talk without interruption instead of answering questions presented to him by his attorneys. Mostly, he stuck with the story as detailed in his second written confession. He said the party was short on supplies because each man was supposed to have brought his own food, and they soon discovered that several of the men had brought nothing to eat and others only had a few days of food. He said that several days after leaving Ouray's camp, they stewed George Noon's moccasins for one meal. An amusing confrontation occurred at the trial over this point. Prosecutor Bell asked Packer when the group ate Noon's moccasins, and then asked, in a very sarcastic voice, "Did the eating of the moccasins gratify you?" Packer answered curtly, "It was something near what we relished — Salt."

Packer continued by saying four or five days later they ate Shannon Bell's moccasins and started eating buds and roots. Packer also recounted they camped by a huge pine root that had already been part of a fire someone else had built. The next day the group came to a lake, or at least he thought it was a lake, because it was large, flat, and had no vegetation.[168] It was at this point that the men, for the most part, gave up and decided they could not go any further. When they ran out of matches, they carried embers in a coffee pot to start the next fire. Packer stuck with this story the rest of his life. He said he left camp to search for food or help; and when he came back, Bell attacked him and he had to kill Bell in self-defense. Packer consistently said he only killed Bell, but other details of the crime varied in his story over the years.[169]

Several witnesses testified for Packer, but they all just said that he should be pitied for what he went through, rather than prosecuted. The case went to the jury about 5 p.m., but after just two hours of deliberation they adjourned until the next day. The next day, after only one more hour of deliberation, the jury returned with a verdict of guilty of murder in the first degree.[170] The first jury ballot had produced an eleven to one vote in favor of conviction. The one juror who had voted not guilty on the first ballot had, however, quickly yielded to the others.

Some of the facts that probably contributed to Packer being found guilty included his lying in his first two (one oral, one written) confessions, his trying to keep the search party from finding the scene of the crime, and that Miller had obviously been in a life and death fight before he was killed. The question was whether the fight with Miller was instigated by Bell or Packer. Packer at one time had said the party cast lots to see who should die. Also, the trail he described the party as following would have put them upstream from Lake San Cristobal crossing Engineer and Cinnamon in mid-winter and then coming downstream to Lake San Cristobal — this was a virtually impossible task during the winter months and especially during the severe weather of the time of year of the killings. Further the money the dead men had on them did not add up. Packer's sworn statement said they only had a total of $80, and he had only $20 at the start of his journey. Later he had spent over $200 at Saguache alone, he still was seen afterwards with a large sum of cash, and he had offered to loan Dolan $300. Obviously he was trying to minimize his motive for robbery and the murders. The real sum of the money the members of the party had with them was finally determined to be at least $2,000, which in those days was the equivalent to $50,000 or more today.[171]

There was also the testimony that Bell was shot from behind, apparently retreating and not coming at Packer. A member of the jury said they all believed Packer killed the other men with the hatchet while they were sleeping, except for Bell, who woke up and was running away from the scene when Packer shot him in the back and then finished him off with the hatchet. One major point brought up by the prosecution at the trial, and which prompted much discussion, was that at the time, before the arrival of the white man in any numbers, there was *always*

This painting of Packer's trial was made by Herndon Davis, whose most famous painting was "The Face on the Floor" at a Central City saloon. The courtroom still looks almost exactly like this today, even after being remodeled on several occasions. (Author's Collection)

game in the area in winter — mountain sheep, rabbits, deer, and elk. If there was plenty of game, many historians questioned why Lout's group had so much trouble? At the trial the answer was given that Lout's group only had one working pistol as opposed to two rifles and at least one pistol in Packer's group. A pistol is not a very accurate weapon with which to shoot game at any distance.

Another factor against Packer was his demeanor and physical appearance. Charles F. Huntsman, who was a school boy in Lake City at the time of the trial, later said:

> *(Packer) was a very peculiar man, having a large head and almost no forehead, the cranium sloping back from the eyes. The man was broad shouldered and had a wax-like complexion, a small goatee, and a very peculiar voice.*[172]

Judge Gerry later said he thought Packer deliberately led his group to where they died to steal their money. As in all jury trials, it must be remembered that both the judge and the jury heard all the testimony and were able to see the demeanor of the witnesses. There seemed to be little doubt in the jury's minds, as shown in their short deliberation, that Packer was guilty of murder.[173] Eighteen years after the trial, three of the jurors summarized the jury's beliefs in their deliberations.

> *To cross two mountain ranges, as Packer had asserted in his confession and in open court, the party would have had to cross either Engineer Mountain of the range at the head of the Cimarron River, near Uncompahgre Peak, and then the range between Burrows Park and Henson Creek. It was considered an utter impossibility to make such a trip without snowshoes in the middle of winter.....*
>
> *The jury believed that the party followed the Gunnison River until it reached the Lake Fork and that Packer misled the party to the scheduled spot where the crime was committed.*
>
> *The jury deduced ... with respect to the location of the bullet hole that the bullet was fired at Bell from behind. This indicated the belief of the jury that Bell was retreating instead of advancing when he was shot. It was the belief of the jury that all of the victims had been struck in the head while asleep and that Bell upon being hit, jumped up and started to run, when Packer shot him, and then finished him with a hatchet blow.*
>
> *It was established beyond any reasonable doubt that Packer was broke when he left Utah and that he possessed considerable money when he caroused in Saguache. The jury believed that the sole motive in committing the crime was robbery.*

The fact that weighed heavily in the mind of the jury composed of miners, prospectors, trappers, and hunters, was Packer's claim that the men could not find anything worthwhile to eat. Loutzenheizer had testified that his party had encountered "plenty of game." The doom of that party was predicated on the scarcity of game, but on the fact that the men were insufficiently armed... Packer himself admitted that he was an experienced trapper.... The jury assumed he could have easily caught beaver in Lake San Cristobal.[174] Lastly, some of the jury knew from their own experience that despite the heavy winter in 1874, game was not scarce in the region.[175]

There were six possible verdicts that the jury could have come back with. Murder in the first degree (premediated murder), murder in the second degree (no premeditation), voluntary manslaughter (the act was not planned), not guilty, self-defense, or temporary insanity. (Packer did have epileptic fits that could have been brought on by the stress of the ordeal.) The jury nevertheless found him guilty of murder in the first degree.

Judge Gerry made a very eloquent summation of findings and sentence — perhaps some of the most eloquent words ever used by a trial judge in a murder case. In fact, his masterpiece was widely quoted in schools of law at the time.[176] With great emotion he pronounced the sentence:

It becomes my duty as the judge of this court to enforce the verdict of the jury rendered in your case, and to impose on you the judgment of which the law fixes as the punishment of the crime you have committed. It is a solemn, painful duty to perform. I would to God that the cup might pass from me! You have had a fair and impartial trial. You have been faithfully and earnestly defended by able counsel. The presiding judge of this court, upon his oath and his conscience, has labored to be honest and impartial in the trial of your case and in all doubtful questions presented you have had the benefit of the doubt.

A jury of twelve honest citizens of the county have sat in judgment on your case and upon their oaths they find you guilty of willful and premeditated murder—a murder revolting in all its details

In 1874 you, in company with five companions, passed through this beautiful mountain valley where now stands the Town of Lake City.

At that time the hand of man had not marred the beauty of nature. The picture was fresh from the hand of the Great Artist who created it. You and your companions camped at the base of a grand old mountain, in sight of the place you now stand, on the banks of a stream as pure and beautiful as was ever traced by the finger of God upon the bosom of the earth. Your every surrounding was calculated to impress your heart with the omnipotence of the Deity and the helplessness of your own feeble life.

You and your victims had had a weary march and when the shadows of the mountains fell upon your little party and night drew her sable around you, your unsuspecting victims lay down on the ground and were soon lost in the deep sleep of the weary, and when thus sweetly unconscious of the danger from any quarter and particularly from you, their trusted companion, you cruelly and brutally slew them all. Whether your murderous hands were guided by the misty light of the moon, or the flickering blaze of the campfire, you only can tell. No eye saw the bloody deed performed, nor ear save your own caught the groans of your dying victims. You then and there robbed the living of life and then robbed the dead of the reward of honest toil which they had accumulated, at least so say the jury.

To the other sickening details of your crime I will not refer. Silence is kindness. I do not say these things to you to harrow up your soul, for I know you have drunk the cup of bitterness to its very dregs, and wherever you have gone the stings of your conscience and the goadings of remorse have been an avenging Nemisis which has followed you at every turn in life and painted afresh for your contemplation the picture of the past.

I say these things to impress upon your mind the awful solemnity of your situation and the impending doom which you cannot avert. Be not deceived. God is not mocked, for whatever a man soweth, that he shall also reap. You, Alferd Packer, sowed the wind; you must now reap the whirlwind.

Society cannot forgive you for the crime you have committed. It enforces the old Mosaic law of a life for a life, and your life must be taken as the penalty of your crime. I am but the instrument of society to impose the punishment for which the law provides. While society cannot forgive, it will forget. As the days come and go and the days of our pilgrimage roll by, the memory of you and your crime will fade from the minds of men.

With God it is different. He will not forget, but will forgive. He pardoned the dying thief on the cross. He is the same God today as then—a God of love and of mercy, of long suffering and kind forbearance; a God who tempers the wind to the shorn lamb and promises rest to all the weary and heartbroken children of men; and it is to this God I commend you.

SENTENCE OF DEATH.

Judge Gerry Pronounces the Words which Number Packer's Days.

All Efforts to Arrest Judgment and for a New Trial Overruled.

The Cannibal Sobs like a Child when his Aged Father and Mother are Referred to.

If the Supreme Court Does not Interfere the Prisoner will be Hanged on May 19th.

Guilty Packer.

Special to Daily Review-Press.

LAKE CITY, Colo., April 14.—The terrible strain and agony of the Packer trial is over and the case was given to the jury at half-past six on Thursday evening. The jury agreed at eleven, but court having adjourned till this forenoon the fact was not known to the public. At 9 a. m., on reassembling, the jury rendered a verdict of guilty as charged and killing premeditated.

The headline from the April 14, 1883 Gunnison Daily Review noted that Packer was to be hung May 19, 1883, if the Colorado Supreme Court did not stay the execution pending appeal; but this did happen and Packer had to wait for almost three years to learn if his conviction would be overturned. (Author's Collection)

Close your ears to the blandishments of hope. Listen not to the flattering promises of life, but prepare for the dread certainty of death. Prepare to meet thy God; prepare to meet the spirits of thy murdered victims; prepare to meet that aged father and mother of whom you have spoken and who still love you as their dear boy.

For nine long years you have been a wanderer upon the face of the earth, bowed and broken in spirit; no home, no loves, no time to bind you to the earth. You have been, indeed, a poor pitiful waif of humanity. I hope and pray that in the spirit land whither you are so fast and so surely drifting, you will find that peace and rest for your weary spirit which this world cannot give.

Alfred Packer, the judgment of this court is that you be removed from hence to the jail of Hinsdale County and there be confined until the 19th day of May, 1883 and that on the said 19th day of May, 1883, you be taken thence by the sheriff of Hinsdale County, to a place of execution prepared for this purpose at some point within the corporate limits of the Town of Lake City, in the said Hinsdale County, and between the hours of 10 A.M. and 3 P.M. of said day, you then and there, by said sheriff, be hung by the neck until you are dead, dead, dead, and may God have mercy upon your soul.[177]

Despite Judge Gerry's eloquent judgment, Larry Dolan, the Saguache saloonkeeper who had spent so much time with Packer when he came to that town after his ordeal, ran to his nearby Lake City saloon on Bluff Street (Dolan had moved his saloon operation from Saguache to Lake City in 1875) and gave his famous version of Judge Gerry's sentence:

Stand up you man-eating son-of-a-bitch; stand up. Then pointing his finger at him, so raging mad he was, he says — There was seven Democrats in Hinsdale County and you ate five of them. God damn you. I sentence you to be hanged by the neck until you are dead, dead, dead, as a warning against reducing the Democrat population of this state.[178]

Dolan was by the time of trial a well-respected saloon owner in Lake City and was called "one of the striking characters of the San Juans for the stories and tales that he told."[179] Even though Packer's attorneys announced in court shortly after the verdict that they would appeal, immediate preparations were made to hang Packer. There had been fifteen men killed in Hinsdale County in the seven years before Packer's first trial, but Packer was the only one to be convicted of murder and sentenced to hang.[180] Sheriff Smith therefore had no experience with conducting a hanging. Smith placed an order for a noose and received plans for building a gallows. He also printed "tasteful" invitations to the hanging.[181] The gallows for hanging Packer was said to be erected close to the spot where he killed the men, but more than likely it was at Ball Flats inside the city limits of Lake City.[182]

On May 11, 1883, less than a month after the verdict, Packer's appeal was accepted and his execution stayed. That same day the Colorado

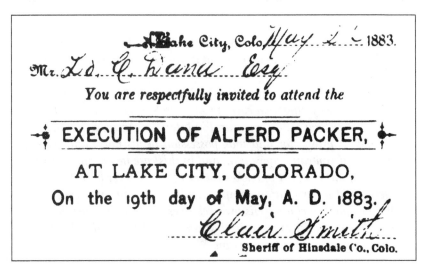

The "tasteful" invitation that Sheriff Clair Smith had printed for Alferd Packer's hanging was even signed and dated by the sheriff himself. Note that Packer's name is spelled "Alferd." The execution was supposed to take place in Ball Flats, but of course was cancelled after the execution was stayed. (Author's Collection)

Supreme Court decided another case declaring all murders during Territorial times were to be held on hold because of the lack of a savings clause. This ruling actually saved the lives of six men, but Packer was by far the most famous.[183] So, Alferd Packer did not get to meet that loving God that Judge Gerry talked of, at least not then. Packer had been turned over to Gunnison Sheriff Doc Shores for protection while awaiting his hanging, because it was felt that in Lake City a mob would try to hang him. Gunnison continued to house Packer during his appeal in Gunnison's new $8,000 brick jail, which was part of the courthouse complex and had steel cells. Shores did not have anything good to say about Packer, and wrote that, like most bullies, Packer was a coward at heart.

In his autobiography Shores wrote:

Of all the prisoners that I held in custody during my eight years as sheriff, Packer was the only one that I failed to find at least some good qualities. He was slow-witted, cowardly, vicious, and a natural bully.[184]

During the three years Packer was in Shore's jail, Packer told Shores he had committed other murders and serious crimes for which he was never arrested. Whether any of these claims were the same as the *Rocky Mountain News* had previously mentioned is unknown. Shores continued:

It was a diabolical crime, but after becoming closely acquainted with the killer, I came to realize that it was entirely in keeping with his character....[185]

Shortly after his escape from the Saguache jail, for example, he murdered two young men east of Colorado Springs and stole their team and wagon. Later on near Tombstone in Arizona Territory, he killed a prospector and took possession of his horse and pack mule. So if you can believe him, and in this case he has no motive for lying, this is a part of Packer's story that has never been told.... Packer had a persecution complex and took it out on everybody that he could, including his own relatives.... Among other things he accused (his sister) of neglecting him, and threatened to kill her when he was released from prison.[186]

Evidently Packer was eligible for a $5,000 bond that would have freed him from jail between the time of the first and second trials, but his sister and other relatives in the East, who did have some money, would not loan him the cash for the bond. Packer consistently said he was going to kill them for not coming to his aid.

This is the "official" photo of Packer, which he was allowed to sell for fifty cents each while he was in the Gunnison jail. He was in jail for a little more than three years while awaiting a decision on his appeal from the first trial. (Author's Collection)

While Packer was waiting for his retrial, Shores got to know Packer's version of the cannibal story pretty well. Packer said his group actually was going to prospect in the San Juans and was not trying to get to Breckenridge. Shores also wrote that General Adams told him that when Packer told him so many contradictory stories that he became convinced of Packer's guilt.[187] Doc Shores' wife also got to know Packer and said he behaved well and kept his cage clean (he had a steel bar "cage" that was his cell at night). He liked to talk with the Shores' little boy Frank. Tourists would come to the Gunnison jail to stare at Packer or to pray with him. Packer was even allowed to sell photographs of himself for fifty cents each to visitors. Mrs. Shores, who felt Packer was definitely guilty, went to Packer's second trial and said he told:

a cunningly conceived defense, and had he told the same story at Los Piños in 1874 and always adhered to it, at the same time telling the whole truth about the attendant circumstances, he probably would never have been accused.[188]

The Colorado Supreme Court overturned Packer's murder conviction on appeal on July 6, 1886, as well as the convictions of the five other Colorado murderers who had committed their crimes before Colorado became a state in July of 1876. They had all been convicted under the laws of the State of Colorado, when Colorado was a territory and there was no "savings clause" of the territorial crime of murder. Also Gantt[189] writes that the 1868 territorial legislature established the penalty for premeditated murder as death, but in 1870 the law was changed so that the jury had to specifically find the murder to be premeditated in their deliberations for the death penalty to be imposed. This was not done at Packer's first trial. Then in 1881, the penalty for murder was modified again and the old law was repealed without a savings clause. This argument had been made before Packer's first trial, but it was rejected by Judge Gerry.[190]

The defense attorneys in the second trial asked for and received a change of venue to Gunnison because of the bad publicity in Hinsdale County. The defense attorneys also asked for and received a recusal of Judge Gerry from the second trial of the case.[191] Because of the Colorado Supreme Court ruling, in the retrial Packer had to be charged with manslaughter; but instead of being tried for just Swan's death, he was tried for the death of all five victims. Unfortunately this was done without Packer's permission, which led to a possible appeal from his second trial.[192]

Packer's retrial was held in Gunnison between August 2 and August 5, 1886. William Harrison was the judge.[193] The witnesses and testimony were basically the same as at the first trial, except this time evidence was introduced from several more witnesses, including Enos Hotchkiss, who had been on the Lake Fork most of the winter of 1873-1874, that there was an abundance of game in the area when the group passed through. Several witnesses testified that there was little doubt Packer's group could have shot rabbits, beaver, and deer. Preston Nutter, who admittedly was not fond of Packer and thought him guilty beyond a shadow of a doubt, testified about the whole event. This time he added to his testimony that Bell had a blanket over his face, the fibers of the blanket were pushed into his skull (as if the blanket had been over his head when he was hit with the hatchet), and that he was shot while running away. Nutter also testified to the then well-known fact that the camp in which the bodies were found looked like the whole party had not been there more than one or two days, while the other camp looked like one man had been there many weeks, with a well-worn trail between the camps.

Kushner gives a good synopsis in his book of the long rambling testimony of Packer at his second trial, a summary of which follows:

Packer began his testimony by explaining the circumstances of a condition that caused him to suffer fits. He describes how he met his company on the prospecting trip, his duties, and the group's preparation for departure. As provisions grew short, the men began to quarrel. The party reached Ouray's camp and subsequently divided, heading in different directions. In his group, provisions again grew short, conditions worsened, tempers flared, and they became lost. He described his scouting attempts, his return to camp, and his encounter with Bell. Packer then related his state of mind when he found himself alone and described his preparations to leave camp, and his attempt to reach the agency. Then he describes his trip to Saguache and his financial condition at the time. He returned to the agency, told his story to Preston Nutter and others, and attempts to retrace his route for the men. They became lost and returned to the agency. Packer then questioned the testimony of the former witnesses, described his eventual return to Saguache and imprisonment. At that point, Packer said Otto Mears advised him to escape.[194]

During his testimony at the second trial, Packer cursed Judge Gerry and most of the witnesses from the first trial, and he answered all of the questions asked of him in a very gruff and sour way. Packer also made many disparaging remarks about the District Attorney, and swore at the first jury whenever the first trial was mentioned. He would not answer questions on cross examination from the District Attorney unless made to do so by the judge or requested to do so by his attorney. These actions certainly would not have helped his case. Testimony in the case lasted two days, and the jury found him guilty of voluntary manslaughter in two and one-half hours. The jury sentenced Packer to forty years of hard labor at the Colorado State Penitentiary—eight years for each victim, with the sentences to run consecutively.

The second jury was said to have been sympathetic toward Packer at the beginning of the trial, but changed their minds as the trial went on.[195] During sentencing Packer still claimed he was not guilty. When sentenced, the judge asked Packer his name and to spell it. True to form, Packer reportedly told Judge Harrison he had a tattoo on his arm that showed he was "Alfred" Packer, but later the tattoo was shown to read "Alferd."

Instead of a long statement from the judge at the time of sentencing, Packer gave a very long statement saying he had a fair trial and, with the evidence presented against him, "I think I would have convicted myself." Yet he also said he had been convicted unjustly, and that he hoped the whole mystery would be cleared up someday. Packer also asked Judge Harrison to give him the maximum penalty only for killing Bell. The Judge, however, gave him eight years for each man. The case was again appealed, but this time the appeal was denied.

This prison photograph of Packer, was made while he was serving time at Cañon City, Colorado's maximum security prison. He is beginning to show his age, so this photo was probably taken shortly before he was released. (Author's Collection)

At the state penitentiary, Packer was a model prisoner. Excused from hard labor because of his epilepsy, he worked in a flower garden that he established. In addition to his military pension, he also made considerable money by selling very attractive horsehair watch fobs, beautifully fashioned canes, and a variety of other objects. Today, a doll house made by Packer is on loan to the Hinsdale County Museum from the Colorado Springs Pioneer Museum. The general public snapped up his works, apparently because they were anxious to have something made by "The Colorado Cannibal."

A friend of the author, Lake City resident Henry Woods, tells the story of a good friend of his father being the warden of the Cañon City prison when Packer was housed there. The son later told the story that when the warden wanted to leave on an extended vacation, he evidently chose Packer to babysit his son in his family's absence. When his case came up for parole, Warden C. P. Hoyt wrote the parole board that Packer, who was then sixty years old, should be let out, as he suffered from Bright's Disease as well as epilepsy. The parole board did not agree.

Although the *Rocky Mountain News* had written an editorial upon sentencing that Packer's sentence was much too light for the crimes he had committed, around the turn of the century a reporter from the *Denver Post* named Polly Pry took an interest in Packer's case. She soon declared she was convinced he was innocent and aroused public sentiment in his favor. She blamed Otto Mears, who she claimed was afraid Packer would kill him if he ever got out of prison because Packer believed Mears had used his political power to keep him in the penitentiary. She also blamed the judge at the second trial for sentencing Packer to forty years (eight for each victim), when she felt the sentences should have run concurrently and thus would have only been eight years. This point had been appealed at the end of Packer's second trial, and then again at the end of his first eight years in prison; but the Colorado Supreme Court denied the appeals. Packer did repeatedly threaten to kill several of the witnesses who had testified against him at one or the other of his trials, as well as Judge Gerry and some of the witnesses' families. Packer had in fact received the longest sentence for manslaughter ever given in Colorado. Polly Pry felt Packer was guilty only of cannibalism, and stated he was justified in eating the men under the circumstances. She also viciously attacked those who felt that Packer was at least partially insane because of his epilepsy.

John Lawrence, independent of the *Denver Post*, was also working on a parole or pardon at the same time for Packer. Lawrence was with the Baker party in the San Juans in 1861, and was living at Saguache when Packer came there after the murders. As mentioned, Lawrence admitted in an affidavit that he and Otto Mears helped Packer escape from the

Saguache jail. Lawrence did a pretty good job of proving by affidavits that Packer's companions all disliked him, and they were scared of his epilepsy, to the point that Packer felt his companions might kill him.

Lawrence further talked with George Tracy, who told him that when Packer was captured and brought back to Lake City, that Tracy thought Packer was going to be immediately hanged, but that the Sheriff talked the vigilantes out of it. Lawrence further pointed out that none of the members of the second jury had lived in Colorado for over a year and a half, and none of them were mountain men who would realize what it was like to be lost in the San Juan Mountains in the middle of winter.[196] Lawrence's plea for a pardon was delivered to the Governor's office the day Packer was paroled.[197]

After Packer spent seventeen years in the Colorado penitentiary at Cañon City, the last official act of Governor Charles S. Thomas on January 8, 1901 was to parole Alferd (spelled Alfred by the Governor) Packer. The original document shows it was a parole, although the Governor later referred to it several times as a pardon. Parole means that the prisoner is released early from his sentence. Pardon means that the record is wiped clean as if the crime never happened. There is some evidence that a condition of the parole was that Packer not exhibit himself as "The Colorado Cannibal," since Packer had recently mentioned the idea to several people as a good way to make money. He also said he had an offer from the Sells-Floto circus to appear in their sideshow. Colorado officials were worried about the bad publicity. Another condition of Packer's parole was he could not go near any of his relatives,[198] since he had repeatedly said he was going to kill them when he got out of prison. The written parole agreement does not contain any of these restrictions, but ex-Governor Thomas later wrote a letter to the *Silver World* stating:

> *The* Denver Post *bedeviled the life out of me during my whole term as Governor to pardon (Packer), and its proprietors were bitterly vindictive because I would not do so. It so happened that I was in possession, through former Sheriff (Doc) Shores of Gunnison County, of somewhat extended one-sided correspondence consisting of letters from Packer to relations. They were the foulest compositions that I ever read with all sorts of threats against them in the event he regained his liberty. I was under pledge not to make them public, but they were sufficient to justify a refusal of pardon even if he had any claim for consideration. I saw him several times during this period and talked to him at considerable length, but saw nothing in his attitude to change my opinion. Finally, however, and in view of reports concerning his health, and also in view of the outstanding*

fact that his cannibalism was due to the pressure of starvation, I consented to pardon him), conditioned in the most positive way, however, against him leaving the state or attempting to further communicate with his relations. I do not know what became of him ... but I am sure that he was of no use to the community and probably a burden to himself.[199]

The *Silverton Standard* saw the *Denver Post's* efforts from a different angle:

Alferd Packer, the "Man Eater," a term formerly applied by the newspapers throughout the state is at present being lionized by the ladies of Denver, and we can soon look forward to the papers of that city to dub him the "Lady Killer."[200]

Packer walked away from the Cañon City penitentiary a free man, attired in a new suit, and carrying a railroad ticket to Denver that the State of Colorado bought for him. He had $400 in cash in his possession, which he had saved over the years from his pension and items he had made and sold while he was in prison.[201]

At this time the *Lake City Quarterly*, in its first issue, speculated they had found the reason for Packer murdering the other men. Their theory was Packer and his companions had found what was later called the Golden Fleece Mine, and Packer killed his companions not only for their money but also to get sole title to the mine. The Golden Fleece is located almost directly across the Lake Fork from the site of the murders,[202] but there is no record that Packer ever tried to claim any mine, much less the Golden Fleece.

Perhaps the wildest version of what happened in the Packer ordeal of 1873-74 appeared shortly before Packer was released from the penitentiary in an article in a Utah paper. The article claimed Packer and his group had found a fabulously rich, but now "lost" gold mine in the Uncompahgre drainage, and that Packer drew the location on a map shortly before his release. Packer and Bell supposedly murdered their companions over the mine, then Packer murdered Bell. The Utah paper announced rumors that unknown men had convinced Packer to take them to the mine after he was released and would reward him well. Nothing ever came of this tale.[203]

Packer only stayed a few months in Denver after being released, and then lived in a shack in Littleton, Colorado (a southern suburb of Denver). After that, he moved to the town of Sheridan, Colorado, not far from Ft. Logan, where he built a small house. He ate his meals at the Sheridan Hotel and was said to have loved discussing politics. In 1905 he moved to a friend's ranch in Deer Creek Canyon. In all these places he was loved by the local children, for whom he bought candy and told tales of the pioneer days. The *Englewood Enterprise* newspaper described him as a "Pied Piper to the youngsters who followed him in droves every Saturday afternoon to thrill to his stories and much candy...."

Even Packer's death is surrounded in controversy and misinformation. One authority states Packer died in Littleton, Colorado in January, 1911. The Colorado Historical Society writes that he died April 5, 1907, at the age of sixty-five. One author writes that he had walked to a neighbor's house in July, 1906, and collapsed. Most likely, Packer had an epileptic fit in July of 1906, while caretaking at his friend's ranch. He was found unconscious on the ground by Charles Cash, a game warden, who took him to Cash's mother's house. He languished there for nine months, sometimes ranting and raving that

Packer's grave in the Littleton Cemetery lies in an isolated, rarely visited corner of the cemetery. His victim's lie near the "Dawn of Hope" Bridge over the Lake Fork of the Gunnison, under "Deadman's Gulch" and "Cannibal Plateau," near Lake City. (Author's Collection)

he was innocent of "the crimes." Packer's tombstone in the Littleton cemetery states he died April 23, 1907, while Gantt states he died April 24, 1907 at 7 p.m.[204]

Packer was buried with Grand Army of the Republic (G.A.R) rites in the Civil War Veterans section of the Littleton cemetery. His death certificate supposedly reads that he died of "troubles and worries."[205] Most present-day Lake Citians are somewhat embarrassed that the Packer crime is the best known event that occurred in or near Lake City — even though there was no town at the time. However over the years, in other parts of Colorado, Packer's name has been sarcastically given to a number of government and school cafeterias. In recent years, Packer even had a cook book named after him. It is also said by some that Packer died a vegetarian.[206] A bust of Packer, which was made for the University of Colorado's cafeteria, was temporarily installed in the Colorado State Capitol building in 1982. In accepting the bust, Governor Richard Lamm gave a short speech, almost entirely composed of cannibal jokes. Phil Oches wrote the ballad of Alferd Packer in honor of the event.[207]

One strange after note to Packer's life was a ceremony absolving his sins, which was presided over by Bishop Frank Rice of the Liberal Church at the Littleton cemetery in September, 1940. Six of the Bishop's followers also participated — five dressed as the ghosts of Packer's victims and one dressed as the spirit of Packer. The six were chained together and wore black robes over white robes. The sins of Packer and his victims were transferred to a nanny goat (a scape goat). The chains and black robes were then symbolically laid over the goat's back. The goat was said to take this burden "meekly."

In 1989 George Washington University law professor James Starrs decided to exhume Packer's victims to see if forensic science could shed any light on the case. Starrs was evidently known for digging up the bodies of famous frontier villains and victims. His group concluded that all victims had both blunt and sharp force trauma, and that almost all the meat had been removed from every one of the bodies.[208] Starr's group also reported that Bell put up a heroic fight with dozens of hatchet cuts on his arms and head. Starr decided Packer was the killer because an old wound on Bell's skeleton supposedly showed he would have not been able to use a hatchet very well.[209]

In 1994 David P. Bailey, Curator of the Museum of Western Colorado in Grand Junction, realized a pistol in the museum's collection, an 1862 Colt Police Model with three bullets still in the chamber, had an accession card that read: "This gun was found at the site where Alfred Packer killed and ate five of his traveling companions." The pistol was badly rusted, the grips were rotten, and it had a rusted cylinder that contained three live bullets. The pistol had been found at the massacre site in 1950 by a young Western State student named Richard Ronzio.[210] Bailey researched the Alferd Packer case and decided that Alferd was not guilty of murder. He decided that he would try to get permission to dig up the victims' bodies and see if he could find forensic proof to help Packer's case. He was further allowed to examine soil samples taken by Starrs from under the bodies. He was able to prove that the gun in his museum was the gun that shot Bell, but Packer always admitted he shot Bell, claiming it was in self-defense. Bailey felt he had "vindicated" Packer, but in this author's opinion as an attorney and judge, it seems that he did no more than prove the gun in his museum was used by someone in some way to shoot Bell. Starrs then disclosed that he felt the hole in Bell's hipbone was made by an animal and not a bullet, and the most likely scenario was that Packer killed all five victims with an axe. Bailey countered with testimony from the trial by the local coroner, who was one of the first to respond to the scene, that one of the victims had a bullet hole in the hip and that an empty wallet at the scene also had a bullet hole in it.

In 1993 Trey Parker and Matt Stone, students at the University of Colorado produced *Cannibal! The Musical,* based on Packer's tale. The men went on to produce the hit series South Park, but Alferd's tale was a failure.

So the question of how many of the victims were killed by Packer still remains unresolved. A heavy steel plate was placed above the victims' burial site after the last reburial to prevent vandalism, but it will probably crush the victim's bones and make another inspection impossible. It is an admitted fact by Packer that he killed Bell (in self-defense) and ate the flesh of at least two of the men, but it still remains up to each individual to decide who killed the four victims found in a row and to decide how it happened.

Doc Shores wrote in his biography in the late 1920s, that:

After identification, the bodies were buried where they were found.[211] *The burial ground was surrounded by an iron enclosure (now gone) and a bronze tablet on a nearby rock (still there) reads:*

This tablet is erected in memory of Israel Swan, George Noon, Frank Miller, James Humphreys, and Shannon Bell who were murdered on this spot early in the year 1874 while pioneering the mineral resources of the San Juan country.

Today the graves are surrounded by a wooden fence just below Deadman's Gulch with Cannibal Plateau in the background to the east and 50 to 100 feet above the spot on the river where the men were killed. The memorial does not mention why or who killed the men, who had not yet started "pioneering the mineral resources of the San Juans."[212] A nearby information sign does give more of the actual story, but makes no statement of Packer's guilt or innocence, except that a jury convicted him. Hopefully this chapter will give you an opportunity to make up your own mind.

For now, the tale seems to be a classic story to tell kids around a campfire when they are camping out in the woods on a dark night–especially if they are near Lake San Cristobal, with the wind blowing, and a full moon hiding behind the clouds.

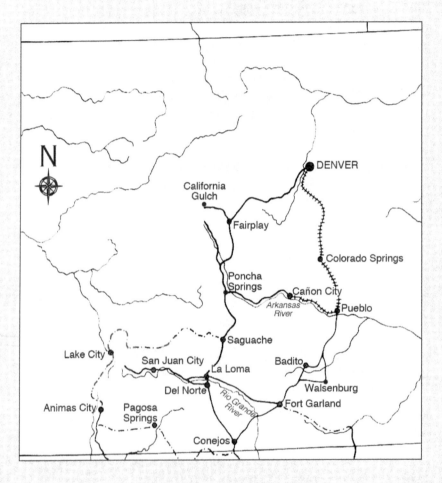

Map of Routes into the San Juan Mines in 1874. (Western Reflections Map – Modified from Cathy Kindquist, *Stony Pass.*)

CHAPTER 3

A Very Good Start

L et us now back up to the spring of 1874, shortly after Alferd Packer had eaten at least some of his companions and left for the Los Piños Ute Agency on Cochetopa Pass. By this time the San Juans had already been divided informally into a few large mining districts — the Animas District (Baker's Park), the Lake District (Lake City), and the Summit District (Summitville). Lake City, Ouray, and Silverton soon formed what was called the San Juan Triangle. It was within this triangle that the greatest riches were discovered in the San Juans. Hurricane Peak, near Animas Forks, is close to the center of this mineral rich region.

A logical way into the newly acquired San Juan Mountains was from the west, but the Utes still owned and controlled this area after the Brunot Treaty. Although the land to the south of the San Juans had been explored and partially settled by the Spanish as early as the 1760s, the terrain became rougher by the mile as one headed north. Two practical trails into the new San Juan mining areas being used at the time were from the east from Del Norte over the very steep Stony Pass or from the north over a much easier but longer route over Cochetopa Pass, down the Cebolla, then west to the Lake Fork and south (upstream) through the area that soon held Lake City. Both of these routes were rough trails, and passable only by men on horseback or on foot. Supplies were carried by mules or burros. A wagon road was badly needed.

Perhaps no other man can be given more credit for the opening and development of the San Juan Mountains than Otto Mears. Mears was one of the founders of Saguache, which competed with La Loma and then Del Norte for the business going to Baker's Park, later Lake City, and finally all over the San Juans. Mears knew Del Norte was planning toll roads to the new mining camps that everyone realized would be built in the San Juans Mountains after the Utes were removed. Del Norte built the first road to Silverton over Stony Pass, but the route was virtually impossible for wagons. Meanwhile, in 1874-75, Mears built a trail to

Lake City from Saguache, and in 1875 he upgraded it into the first true wagon road into the San Juan mines. Mears' wagon road beat Del Norte to Lake City, if only by about six months. Both Saguache and Del Norte came to be known as "The Gateway to the San Juans."

In 1874 Otto Mears was still early in his career, but he had already built a toll road over Poncha Pass in 1867 to transport wheat to California Gulch (later the site of Leadville); and, in 1870, he and other Saguache merchants and farmers built a road from Saguache to the Los Piños Indian Agency, which was located slightly north of the summit of Cochetopa Pass. Mears and other Saguache business men transported food items, like flour, corn, and other vegetables, as well as other merchandise to the Agency to sell to the Utes and agency employees.

Otto Mears was a true Horatio Alger story. He was born in Kurkland, Russia, on May 3, 1840, was orphaned at an early age, and was raised by an uncle for a short time, until he was sent to live with another uncle in England. He was then sent to the United States to live with a relative in New York, but soon was sent by boat to the West Coast to live with yet another relative. This man, however, had left the country by the time Mears arrived, so Mears grew to be a young man while taking care of himself. He worked at a store in California and eventually saved a little money, which he invested in California mining stocks. After an initial success, he lost all his money in another mining investment. He joined the Union Army during the Civil War and was stationed in New Mexico for three years under the command of Kit Carson. He moved to Santa Fe after the war, where he worked as a clerk in a store. In 1865 he moved to the southern San Luis Valley, where he operated a general store in Guadalupe on the Conejos River, and then

Otto Mears was a self-made man, who eventually earned the nickname of "Pathfinder of the San Juans," since he built so many trails, roads, and railroads. He was responsible, in great part, for the founding and rapid growth of Lake City, into the "Queen of the San Juans." (Author's Collection)

he operated a local grist mill in partnership with Lafayette Head, agent for the Mouache and Capote Utes in the southern San Luis Valley. Mears and Head mainly furnished their flour to the Ft. Garland army post in the east-central San Luis Valley, but they also ran a lumber mill. In 1866 Mears bought land near present-day Saguache to help grow more wheat for the grist mill in Conejos. Unfortunately, the price of wheat soon fell radically at Ft. Garland (from $10 per hundred pounds to $5), and Mears needed a new market. Before Mears built his own mill in Saguache, he would haul the grain from Conejos to Charles Nachtrieb's mill in Nathrop, Colorado, (located in the Arkansas River Valley) to be ground into flour.[213]

Mears later told the story of his meeting Territorial Governor William Gilpin after Mears' wagon had tipped over on Poncha Pass and spilled a good part of the grain being carried in it (grain was carried loose in those days and not in sacks). Mears related:

> In 1867 (Gilpin) owned the Baca Grant, one hundred thousand acres of land in the San Luis Valley. He was a very able man but rather crazy. He asked me why I didn't take out a charter and build a toll road; that it would only cost me $5 and I could make a lot of money out of it. He said that someday there would be thousands of people in the San Luis Valley, and we could raise lots of things there.... So he told me to make a road out of that, and I started in. I did not have any regular tools for it, but I had axes and shovels, and built a road to get my wheat down (over Poncha Pass), and finally got it to Charles Nachtrieb's mill in the Arkansas Valley.... I went to Denver and got a charter and made a good road in 1867.[214]

The charter allowed Mears to operate a toll road for twenty years. Nothing more was required to get a toll road charter in those days, other than the payment of $5 and the filing of a simple statement of the beginning and ending points of the road, with perhaps a general statement as to where the rest of the route would be located. The Poncha Pass Toll Road was officially incorporated on November 8, 1870, with Charles Nachtrieb and Otto Mears being the major shareholders.[215]

Gilpin not only explained the toll road system used in Colorado to Mears but also convinced him to build a good enough wagon road over Poncha Pass to support heavy freight wagons, stage coaches, and later be used for a railroad grade into the San Luis Valley. Gilpin also gave Mears the idea to obtain investors to help raise the money to build his roads, usually local merchants. Gilpin's advice was a financial plan that Mears used to his advantage for the rest of his life. Mears usually walked his toll routes prior to construction, then worked directly with the surveyors to pick the best way for the road, and then often oversaw the actual construction of his roads. Most importantly, Mears had a special way of convincing investors to put up capital, and he was good at gaining the cooperation of towns along his routes. Some authorities write that Mears built the Poncha Pass Toll Road with his own hands, but Michael Kaplan writes that Mears paid $14,000 to have the construction done.[216] Mears soon found out, however, that maintaining a toll road was more difficult than building it. Weather and heavy traffic "took a toll" on the roads, and Mears sometimes sold out and moved on to another project fairly soon after initial construction was finished.[217]

The lush area along the Saguache River above the present-day town of Saguache was east of the Continental Divide and had been homesteaded for ranches and farms since 1866. Mears settled in Saguache after completion of the Poncha Pass Toll Road, married, and fathered three daughters, one of whom died in infancy. He also started a small trading post, which served the Utes, in partnership with Isaac Gottieb (also spelled many other ways including Gotshelf). When Saguache was made a county in 1867, Mears was elected the first Treasurer. Most of the local residents were poor, and Mears often took items in kind and then sold them to pay the taxes owed. In 1873 Mears and his partner expanded the trading post to a general store. In 1874 he started the *Saguache Chronicle* newspaper to publicize the northern San Luis Valley. A Mears' newspaper became a trademark in many of the towns his toll roads connected, including the future Lake City. The town of Saguache was officially founded the same year as the newspaper. Saguache was in a good location to become a major supply town for the northern San Luis Valley, the Ute Indian Agency, and the men that soon arrived to prospect in the San Juan Mountains. It was also quite evident that Cochetopa Pass might be used if a railroad was constructed to the Western Slope of Colorado.

Otto Mears, along with David Heinberg, Isaac Gottieb, and John Lawrence, were the men who pushed the farming community of Saguache to prominence; and they formed a close knit business group in the late 1860s and early 1870s. Mears' and Gottieb's store in Saguache was popular with both the local whites and the Utes.[218] Mears had the vision to not only see how good transportation systems would be very helpful to new San Juan mining areas but also how related businesses, such as newspapers, merchandise at wholesale and retail, freight companies, mail contracts, stages, and later railroads could tie in and bring good profits during the inevitable booms that followed. Mears was eventually known as "The Pathfinder of the San Juans."[219]

Martha and Henry Ripley wrote:

Roads there must be, burro transportation being too slow, and Otto Mears and Enos Hotchkiss undertook to build a toll road to Lake City. The need was urgent and no pretense was made of building a finished road. After locating the route, the immediate object was to build the trail, and finish it up as soon as possible. This being done, quite naturally the first to pass over it were not especially outspoken in the praise of it, in fact the tenor of their remarks were in the other direction.[220]

Even though a very smart and good businessman, Mears was evidently very insecure and was constantly proving or testing himself.

His life-long friend Judge John Bell (prosecutor in the Packer case)... remarked that being rich meant little to him (Mears), because what he really desired... was to do anything other people could not do.[221]

Mears had started furnishing cattle to the Ute Agency on Cochetopa Pass in 1869, and made all kinds of supplies available to the agency in 1870. He soon had many other Saguache merchants voluntarily working on the construction of the road to the Ute agency, as well as helping him with repair and upgrading costs. The road to the agency was incorporated as a finished toll road in 1871.[222] However, later in life, Mears did not claim the agency road from Saguache as "his" toll road, writing in his memoirs that the Lake City Toll Road was his second after Poncha Pass. It was reported that the agency road was fifty-five miles long and very rough, sometimes no more than a trail. It took an ox wagon eleven days, instead of the usual five on flat ground, to get from Saguache to the agency.[223] Freight wagons were pulled by ten or twelve oxen or six large draft horses, usually Percheron or Belgian (or a cross of the two breeds). Mears soon invested in a freight company to haul supplies to the agency.

Sidney Jocknick, in his autobiography *Early Days on the Western Slope*, wrote that Mears by 1872 supplied 100 head of cattle per month to the Ute agency, as well as oats, beans, hay, potatoes, and flour.[224] The people around Saguache also supplied turnips, cabbage, corn, beets, parsnips, and carrots.[225] Mears eventually became friends with Chief Ouray and the other Utes at the agency and came to speak the difficult Ute language himself. He therefore helped with the Brunot Treaty in 1873, and he served as an interpreter on several occasions when the Utes were taken to Washington, D. C.

It was also well-known from the experiences on the eastern slope of Colorado that a mining town was important to an area. As mentioned by Duane Smith:

The mining frontier was different from (ranching, farming, or fur trapping frontiers) in a significant manner, for here not one man or a small group of men participated, but hundreds, even thousands, joined the initial rush. Gone was the self-sufficiency of earlier pioneers. The miner and the mining camp resident were after one thing, quick wealth. He did not have time to plant crops, make clothes, or manufacture needed tools; these services were provided by others. The mining camp grew overnight in response, and consequently, it, and not the individual, became the cutting edge of the frontier. This, then, was an urban frontier in every sense of the word, with urban life developed before rural—a unique development in its sweep and impact on the course of American history.[226]

As historian and geographer Mel Griffith noted, there was a radiating network of mining camps that supplied the San Juan mines. All larger mines had mining camps nearby to meet the miners' and prospectors' needs. A few of these camps grew to a population of more than 300 people; however, most never had more than a dozen or two dozen residents. The mining camps had a system of trails and roads that might be called the "primary" system. Outside of the primary ring there was a secondary ring of bigger towns that were much easier to get to from the outside world and which supplied the mining camps and larger mines. In the San Juans these towns included Lake City, Del Norte, Ouray, Silverton, Telluride, Rico, Durango (originally Animas City), and later Creede. All of the towns in the outside or secondary ring were soon connected by good wagon roads and eventually by railroads to the outside world.[227] Lake City, Del Norte, and later Creede supplied most of the mines on the eastern side of the San Juans and many of the mines in the central San Juans.

Mears had recognized as early as 1871 that the San Juans would be taken from the Utes and filled with mining towns and camps that would need good roads, and he and other Saguache merchants organized a company in that year to build a toll road into the future San Juan mining districts. Of course, the road from the agency could not actually be built until the Utes ceded the San Juans, but Mears was ready to move quickly. The first part of the route for the "Saguache and San Juan Toll Road" was to be along the already existing road from Saguache to the Ute Indian Agency. The rest would pass up Los Piños Creek (now a jeep road) and down Deldarado Creek into the Cebolla drainage, following the east bank of the Cebolla nearly as far as today's Powderhorn.[228] Mears' road crossed the Cebolla about three miles upstream from Powderhorn, then went over the divide to the Lake Fork of the Gunnison, connecting at the future site of Barnum, and finally proceeded south up the Lake Fork to the future site of Lake City.[229] Mears planned that The Saguache and San Juan Toll Road would be used by wagons at least as far as the future Lake City area, as wagons could economically carry much bigger loads than burros or mules. On the way back to Saguache from the mines, Mears hoped the wagons would carry ore to the smelters at Cañon City and Pueblo.

When the toll road was first conceived in 1871, the principal men of Saguache backed Mears in this endeavor, with Enos Hotchkiss and Isaac Gottieb being the main investors. However, both men ran into financial difficulties, and Mears bought them out before the toll road construction was actually started in 1874.[230] Mears' new road company was incorporated on March 11, 1874. Evidently Enos Hotchkiss received a contract to survey and build the toll road for $16,000.[231]

Mears already realized the great potential of Hinsdale County when it was formed in February, 1874.[232] Construction of the toll road began shortly before the Brunot Treaty was ratified by the Senate on April 29, 1874, but Mears first had Hotchkiss construct a good trail to be later upgraded into a wagon road. The trail would allow a chance for small modifications to be made after Mears himself carefully checked the road. Duane Vandenbusche writes that Mears personally oversaw the final construction of the road until it reached Indian Creek near the Lake Fork and that Hotchkiss took over at that time.[233]

The toll road eventually covered 130 miles, of which approximately the first 100 miles were to the future site of Lake City and were usable as a trail by early August of 1874.[234] Hotchkiss was joined during the trail construction by John Lawrence, Byron Bartholf (also spelled Bartlof), and James Fullerton. John Lawrence, who was a lawyer, later wrote about making the trail in an affidavit he made in favor of Alferd Packer's pardon.

We got ready, at once to start. We took two horses each. One to ride and one packed. On account of the snows and ice we would encounter we got all the horses "rough shod." We were well prepared for a long stay if necessary....

We were stopped by three "of the hands" of the Agency, who asked our business. We told them. They said, "All, right." They thought we were prospectors and that the Agent (Adams) did not want any prospectors on the "reserve" as it might cause trouble with the Indians, and also that the Agency thought if we went a few miles farther south that we might be off the Reservation and that no fault could be found to the road and no one would stop us.[235]

James Fullerton also later made an affidavit, which included a few more details on the construction of the trail:

> *In the months of February and March, 1874, a company was formed here in Saguache, Saguache County, Colorado, to be known as the "Saguache and San Juan Toll Road Company." The object being to build a toll road from Saguache past where Lake City now is to the San Juan, presumably to where Silverton in San Juan County now is.*
>
> *On March 30, 1874, the said company called a meeting to appoint three "viewers" to view and lay out said road. Enos Hotchkiss, Byron Bartlof and myself were appointed…. We started on or about April 1, 1874 to "view out" said road. When we went farther south from the agency, we viewed out different places till we got to the headwaters of the Cebolla creek or river. Viewed out different places from there went down said creek over to and across the "Powder Horn" up to and down Indian Creek to the Lake Fork of the Gunnison, crossing and re-crossing it on to Burroughs (Burrows) Park about 15 or 20 miles above where Lake City is now.*

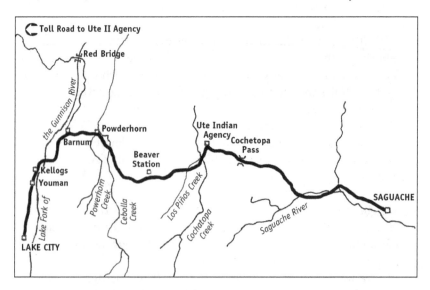

Map of the Saguache and San Juan Toll Road, which was the first road to Lake City and the San Juans. (Western Reflections Map)

All this time we were blazing trees with an ax, cutting back brush in places when we thought it might be the best place for a road... so that by the tracks of our roughshod horses in the ground and mud in places and in the snow in places and with our blazing of trees and cutting of brush and our camps and beds, we left a big and open trail that anyone could follow.[236]

...When I returned to camp (on the way back at Lake San Cristobal and then Saguache) I told my companions about the camp I had found. The next day when we started on our return trip we all went in and examined the camp again.... Packer came to see me (in Saguache) and said he was told that I had found the camp where he was supposed to have stayed for some time while he was lost in the mountains. I told him I had.[237]

As mentioned, it was 1875 before the toll road was truly usable by wagons to Lake City, but Mears still beat the Del Norte Road by almost six months.

It took several more years after 1875 before Mears' "wagon road" made it to Animas Forks; and even then, it was very hard to travel by wagon from Lake City to Animas Forks. Later Mears built a good toll road from Animas Forks to Silverton. Mears said in his biography that Burrows Park was the real goal for the original termination of his toll road and that it was only later that he decided to try to get the road to Animas Forks and Silverton.[238] The change of the destination was probably due to Mears' receiving the mail contract from Saguache to Baker's Park and Silverton for 1875 through the winter of 1877. Everyone agreed that the portion of the road from Lake City to Animas Forks was a disgrace, especially in the early days, and many said it could never be truly called a wagon road. The portion of the road along Lake San Cristobal was often under a foot of water, so the toll booth was located about a mile above the lake.[239]

After the winter of 1876-1877 the mail contract to Silverton was switched to Stony Pass, the Henson Creek Toll Road was built, and the railroad came to Silverton in July, 1882. Because of minimal use and lack of maintenance, the upper Cinnamon Pass part of the Mears' road was soon totally unusable by wagons.[240] The part of the road from Sherman to Burrows Park also fell into disuse in the early twentieth century.

While Lawrence was collecting his affidavits to help pardon Alferd Packer, he also got one from John R. Pond, which included information about the early Lake City area:

About the first of May, 1874 I went with others up to where Lake City now is. There were quite a number of prospectors in there. We

knew Enos Hotchkiss was about to build a toll road in there for the
"Saguache and San Juan Toll Road Company." We also knew (of)...
the Ute and Ouray (Ulay) mines near there, some years before but
(they) were only holding and working their assessments.... We were
generally camped along Henson Creek, but one log cabin was being
built.[241]

Mears himself said:

Lake City had a boom that started bringing people there, and this
(my) road gave them a chance to get in....[242]

In June 1875, Mears almost had his wagon road completed to Lake
City, but Del Norte had concentrated on getting its toll road to Silverton
over Stony Pass (but it was still unusable by a stagecoach), and only a
trail existed from Antelope Park to Lake City. Jarod Sanderson, one of
the owners of the Barlow and Sanderson stage line, went to Del Norte
at that time and told the town fathers that if a true wagon road to
Lake City or Silverton was not built that year that the stage company
would start pulling back its service to Del Norte. This threat spurred
the merchants into building a toll road to Lake City from Antelope
Park[243], but Del Norte had to scramble to catch up with Mears.[244]
The Del Norte-Lake City road started near San Juan City. The road
was built by J. T. Phillips and not Otto Mears. After it was finished in
November 1875, the Del Norte-Lake City toll road had an advantage

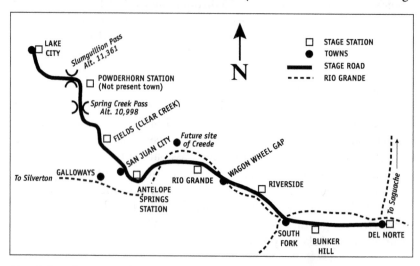

Map of the Del Norte-Antelope Park-Lake City Toll Road. (Western Reflections Map)

over the Mears Toll Road, as it was a little shorter for most people traveling to Lake City. After both Saguache and Del Norte had toll roads to Lake City, people coming from South Park and the Arkansas River Valley would usually use the Saguache Road, and those coming down the Front Range to LaVeta Pass, or coming up the Rio Grande from New Mexico, would travel the Antelope Park Toll Road. Mears was originally against the Del Norte Toll Road, but eventually bought a ten percent interest in the project and opened a store in Del Norte, as well as Lake City and Saguache, evidently feeling there would be plenty of business for both towns.[245] Until the arrival of the railroad in Lake City in 1889, Del Norte and Saguache were very profitable spots for freighters and wholesaler merchandisers that were shipping into the entire San Juans.

Most of the first part of the Del Norte-Lake City Toll Road was an easy grade, but the Slumgullion part of the road was always a frightening adventure. Not only was it steep, but the clay-like soil was slippery; so much of the road was "corduroy," made by placing logs across the road for better traction. This made the ride very rough, a fact mentioned by almost everyone who wrote of traveling over Slumgullion. Even the Lake City *Silver World* wrote:

...no person who ever traveled over these yellow billows of tenacious mud or was seated on a coach when it ran over the old road, saw the horses floundering on it, cannot forget the name.[246]

Crofutt said it gave the effect of:

walking backwards up the stairs, and then sliding down with the feet slightly elevated. The dirt when wet seemed to have no bottom and will stick as close to anything as some hackmen to a tenderfoot.

By late 1875 and spring of 1876, the toll roads from Del Norte and Saguache were booming with people and Lake City was to soon became a true town. In Lake City's first year, it was estimated that up to thirty-five wagons, horseback riders, or pedestrians used each of the toll roads per day. The Lake City *Silver World* of May 22, 1880, reported that in the summer of 1876, six to twelve vehicles, some totally filled with people, were paying a $3 toll from Saguache to Lake City.

Mears kept on building toll roads in the northern San Juans well into the 1880s. Mears also built a road from Barnum on the lower Lake Fork to the Los Piños II Ute Agency near today's Colona and then continued on to Ouray in 1877. However, because Mears' road over Cinnamon was so bad, in 1877 Lake City merchants also built a toll road over Engineer

Pass to Mineral Point, Silverton, and Ouray, but this road was only open to wagons over its full length for three or four months of the year.

There had been enough of a rush of prospectors by 1875 that it was obvious the San Juans needed a mail route. The Ute Agency initially agreed they would take the mail meant for early prospectors, but the agency soon moved and someone else needed to take it from Saguache to the new towns of Lake City and Silverton. As mentioned previously, Otto Mears, probably using his political connections, got the mail contract; and, when necessary, supposedly used sled dogs to bring in the mail that winter.[247]

In 1874, when Enos Hotchkiss first surveyed the Saguache Toll Road, built a trail, and prospected near Lake San Cristobal, he spent time at the large flat area where Lake City now stands. By that summer, just months after Alferd Packer had eaten at least some of his companions; it was already obvious that the land at the junction of Henson (Godwin) Creek and the Lake Fork of the Gunnison River would be a good town site. Although somewhat marshy, there was plenty of level ground, good well water, and many good mines were being located near the spot. After arriving at Lake San Cristobal in August of 1874, Hotchkiss came back down river four miles to the intersection of Godwin (Henson) Creek and the Lake Fork of the Gunnison. Common agreement is that he and John D. Bartlof (also spelled Bartholf) each built a log cabin, so they could later file a homestead or town site claim;[248] and then they traveled back up the Lake Fork to catch up with the rest of the road building crew.[249] Some historians report that Hotchkiss built two cabins at Lake City on or about August 11, 1874.[250]

However, in a letter written by one of John D. Bartholf's sons to *Silver World* editor W. C. Blair in 1931, Eugene Bartholf states that after hearing about the Lake Fork area's potential from sons Byron and Will Bartholf in 1873, John Bartholf, Otto Mears, and Enos Hotchkiss got a charter for a toll road to the area and completed it in late September of that year. The son stated:

> *That summer my father took up a ranch where the town of Lake City now is. We built a cabin just back of the Elephant Corral, which he built later. The cabin faces the cliffs, just west from the San Juan Dance Hall, which was built later. It was the first cabin built in Lake City. Twenty-seven of us wintered there — the winter of 1874 — including myself, father, and brother; a few at the Hotchkiss Mine; Charlie Bunch (sic) and Will Hunter at the Falls, Pike Snowden and partner up Henson Creek a ways. My father and my brother-in-law, Henry Finley, and Enos Hotchkiss formed the Town Company and a Mr. Newman surveyed it (fall of 1874). Enos*

Hotchkiss built the first cabin after the townsite was surveyed. Neise and Chanute Lee, I believe, built the second one.

By the summer of 1874 the future Gunnison County also had a fledgling camp called "Richardson's Colony." Sylvester Richardson started the colony in that year near the future site of today's town of Gunnison. He brought twenty men from Denver to settle there, but some of the group went back almost immediately. The colony was just a few miles from the land retained by the Utes after the Brunot Treaty and was often visited by them. Twenty log cabins were started during the summer of 1874, with Richardson's being the first to be finished. By mid-summer Richardson had lost another third of his original party to the future Lake City area, and those that stayed with Richardson left in 1875 to join the excitement in the San Juans. Richardson's sawmill was taken with them, as there was no demand for lumber in their colony. Richardson's Colony was basically abandoned by the spring of 1876.[251]

Although unofficial mining claims had been filed in what became Hinsdale County as early as 1870, the first mining claim to be officially recorded in Hinsdale County was the Big Casino Lode, which was located by William Moss and Jas. J. Holbrook on Henson Creek, on June 15, 1874, four months after Hinsdale became a county and less than two months after the Brunot Treaty was ratified.[252] The Centennial Lode with five other connecting lodes (including the Yellow Jacket Lode) were the second claims located and were staked by John Hancock on June 23, 1874, and filed in San Juan City on August 19, 1874. There was also a millsite filed at the site.[253] Prospectors had made some good mineral discoveries in the San Juan Mountains in 1874, but there obviously was no major rush, because the San Juan Mountains were too remote and rugged as well as still considered to be dangerous Indian country. The Saguache and Del Norte Toll Roads quickly changed that situation.

Before we get further into San Juan mining, let us discuss the important difference between a prospector and a miner. Many people think the terms are synonymous, but nothing is further from the truth. A miner worked for another man for wages (from which room and board was often taken), while helping develop a mine. Usually someone with money owned the mine, because mine equipment and the wages paid miners were expensive. A miner's life was very hum-drum but was often punctuated by extreme danger like a premature explosion or nearly falling down a 300 foot shaft. Miners did a lot of drilling; and, therefore, often had lung problems (miners' consumption) later in life, which often killed them at an early age.

A prospector worked for himself. Usually he had put together a little money to buy staples, but basically he lived off the land in the great outdoors. The prospector did what and went where he pleased, which most of the time was to the newest mining boom. Prospectors were a very special breed. They usually lived and worked by themselves but might well have a partner or at least a burro or a dog along to keep them company and to use as an early warning system of predators and other humans. A self-reliant, independent man could very easily be drawn to the life of a prospector. It was an especially good life in the new territory of beautiful Colorado. Dan O'Connell, who spent nearly fifty years prospecting in the Colorado mountains, described why a man stayed a prospector, even if he never struck it rich. It was very near the feeling of why a man keeps fishing, even if he does not catch a fish.

> *There is a lure in the great out-of-doors, in the broad vision which the hills afford, in the quest for something that is ever evasive, but which may turn up at the next strike of the pick, and above all being able to come and go when you please — in being your own man in surroundings of your own selection.*[254]

But back to the beginning of the Lake City boom. Not only did the Mears toll road open up transportation to the future Lake City, but it also led to the discovery of one of Hinsdale County's most famous mines. When Enos Hotchkiss and his men were first working on the trail for the toll road from Saguache to Burrows Park, they noticed very promising ore near Lake San Cristobal, near the spot where the Hotchkiss (later called the Golden Fleece) Mine would soon be located.[255] The history of how this rich mine was found, lost, or abandoned, like many of the famous Colorado mines, is somewhat foggy. There is little doubt that Enos Hotchkiss was focused on the toll road and evidently did not realize just how rich the ore was, or possibly he did not see the rich outcrop at all, so he continued his work on the toll road that summer.

It seems most likely that two brothers named Hall, who were working for Hotchkiss on the road, succumbed to their prospecting instincts and took time off from road building to explore. They evidently found "float" (exposed rock that had crumbled from the vein and over the ages by gravity had rolled downhill) that was very rich.[256] The two men picked up the rich ore, sacked it, and put it in two wagons. They later sold the rich gold and silver ore in Denver for $1,000 per bag with a total of eighteen bags. At today's value the ore would have been worth over a quarter of a million dollars.[257]

However, finding loose rock did not qualify for the formal location of a mine, which had to be done on a vein. Nineteen year old Monet (also spelled Monette and Monett) Hotchkiss was also helping his father build the toll road and was left behind to find the vein and later became a partner in the Golden Fleece. Enos Hotchkiss is said to not have been much of a prospector, while Monet was very interested in mining. When Enos finished his work on the toll road in late August, he came back to Lake San Cristobal to help work the claim.

Evidently one of Hotchkiss' workers convinced Enos to file on the vein and call it "The Hotchkiss Mine." William M. Simmons wrote that his father told Hotchkiss:

> *Enos, there is a mine up there. Someday go up there and locate it; and if you don't mind, locate me in.*[258]

The sons of Simmons both later said their father wasn't made a partner because so many people wanted in on the mine that he was overlooked.[259] Simmons had tried to send supplies to Enos with his two sons, age seventeen and eighteen, but Hotchkiss was surveying in Burrows Park, and the kids could not get their wagon and supplies to his location, as much of the work that had been done by Enos had been washed out by recent heavy rains.[260] The boys ended up going to work for Enos and said he made it to Animas Forks that year. They claimed that the portion of the "road" that realistically was only a trail down to Animas Forks was "one of the most wonderful roads of the day," but remember these were adventurous teenage boys.[261]

As news of the discovery of the Hotchkiss Mine spread and the Mears wagon toll road neared completion in 1875, a number of prospectors started heading towards Lake City. John Lawrence wrote that after the Utes were moved, he and Hotchkiss quickly changed the beginning point of the toll road back to the agency to better accommodate prospectors, and Lawrence also wrote that he took out a charter on the part of the road from Saguache to Los Piños Agency, upgraded it, and called it "The Lawrence Toll Road."[262] He further stated that Mears took an assayer to Lake City who assayed the Hotchkiss Mine's ore and made an offer of $250,000 on the spot. This quite possibly was a great publicity stunt, as the news quickly made the San Juan excitement grow even more. For example, the *Rocky Mountain News* of February 9, 1875, carried an article that the owners of the Hotchkiss Mine were approached by an assayer in Denver to whom Otto Mears had shown the ore:

> *It is said that the owners of the Hotchkiss Mine, located in the new mining district of Lake, had $250,000 in greenbacks shaken in their faces.... They figured out a million or two in sight and two or three million more that can't be seen.....*[263]

Evidently it took Hotchkiss a little while to locate the vein from which the loose rock came, probably the very rich but pocketed "comb" that is still very visible today. When Hotchkiss located the Hotchkiss Lode "in what is known as Monument Gulch" on November 2, 1874 (filed February 22, 1875), he did so in several names — a one-fifth interest to himself, his son Monette, James Sparling, Ben Hall, and B. A. Bartlof.[264] The original owners were evidently not able to finish the legally required assessment work by November, 1874; so the claim was relocated on February 22, 1875 with Henry Finley (a good friend of Hotchkiss), W. C. Lawrence, Byron Bartholf, Monette, and Enos as owners.[265] During late 1874 and early 1875, the men sold or traded their shares or bought each other out.

Clarence Foster, head farmer at the Ute Agency (he taught the Utes how to farm) and an early Hinsdale pioneer, verified that it was the Hall brothers who first noted the outcrop of the Golden Fleece and took the rock to the Grant Smelter in Denver.[266] He also said that

A man named Finley, traded a Sharps carbine rifle for a fourth interest in the Golden Fleece, which, by the way, was on the location where the Halls had taken out their fortune. It was thought that they had only found a pocket and that it had played out. The mine broke Hotchkiss and it was sold on default of assessment work. A man named Davis secured a lease on the mine, and at this time C. P. Foster, who was operating a market in Lake City, furnished him with supplies. Foster was afraid that Davis would not be able to pay him, and told him so. Davis then said if he did not strike good pay ore the next time he tried, he would quit. He went up to work again, but finally gave up in disgust, and when there was only one stick of powder left, he quit and started out. The man who was with him decided to use the stick, and so shot off a pot shot in a bulge in one wall. The shot opened up a pocket and they took out a thousand dollars' worth of gold. Proceeding on that vein they took out more gold, and Davis, fearing the pocket would play out, sold out for $75,000 to Stearns, Stewart, and Bartheldes of Denver.

The new owners worked out the pockets they found and were losing money on the mine, but, figuring that they had invested too much to stop, they kept on with the work and opened up a chimney of fabulously rich gold.[267]

The ownership of the mine was confusing during this time. Monette traded his one-fifth share to his father for shares in Saguache and San Juan Toll Road.[268] On June 19, 1875 the *Silver World* reported that Hotchkiss sold a one-fifth interest to John Crooke.[269] The deed to Crooke states that Henry Finley got $2,000 and that $1,000 each went to Enos Hotchkiss, his son Monette, and W. C. Lewman, so they were evidently the owners at the time.

In November, 1876, Hotchkiss apparently still owned part of the Hotchkiss Mine and is reported to have had a bad accident when for some reason he went into the mine at night without a good light and fell down a thirty-foot shaft. Hotchkiss was saved from death when he was slowed down by striking a board on the way down and then hit four feet of water in the bottom of the shaft, which cushioned his fall. Still, he was seriously injured and was taken to a nearby cabin. Supposedly he remained unconscious for ninety days. Hotchkiss not only survived but went on to lead a very full life, although he was blind in one eye.[270]

Frank Hall, in his four volume *History of Colorado* reports that the name "Lake City" came to be used for the area because of the many lakes in its vicinity,[271] but it is almost certain the town was named by Hotchkiss for nearby Lake San Cristobal.

The Lake City town site survey was finished by Henry Finley on November 2, 1874, and covered 260 acres; but with winter coming, it was necessary to wait until the spring of 1875 to make sales. The town was divided into 72 blocks with 32 lots in each block; however, the lots were only 25 feet wide, so many people used two lots to build on. Bartholf, the Lee brothers, B. A. Sherman, Henry Finley, and James Sparling soon built cabins in Lake City near that of Hotchkiss. By the end of 1874 Lake

This woodcut is identified as the first cabin built in Lake City, probably the one built by Enos Hotchkiss. Unfortunately, it burned down just a few years after it was built. However Bartlof probably built the first cabin on a ranch homestead within the present-day city limits but we don't have a good photo of it. (From Tiny Hinsdale of the Silvery San Juan)

City had thirteen log cabins plus a few tents. As spring of 1875 arrived, the town would grow quickly.

As mentioned, Hinsdale County was created on February 10, 1874, and San Juan City was made the first county seat. The first meeting of appointed county commissioners was held June 5 of that year at San Juan City, although it was probably only an organizational meeting with little, if any, actual business done. Because the number of actual residents grew very slowly in 1874, the first election of county commissioners was not held until September, 1875, at which time Lake City was the county seat. Lake City was not very big, but it did have a much better site than San Juan City and was much closer to the new mines that were being discovered; so on February 23, 1875, a little more than a year after Hinsdale County was formed, a vote was taken by residents of the county, and the county seat was moved from San Juan City to Lake City. It is very possible that Otto Mears, through his political connections, made this vote possible.

Enos Hotchkiss was one of the first newly elected commissioners, indicating that he was or claimed to be a resident at the time. However Hotchkiss evidently did not consider Lake City his home at the time. It was not until April 11, 1876, that John Lawrence of Saguache reported that Enos got his horses together and moved from Saguache to Lake City. His brother Preston joined him.[272] However it is possible that Lawrence was actually writing of Enos moving to his ranch at Powderhorn at this time. Enos operated a tollgate for the Mears toll road on his Powderhorn ranch for several years near the junction of Powderhorn and Cebolla Creeks. In 1882 he sold his homesteading rights on the ranch to Elijah McGregor and moved, but his ranch remained a stage stop for several more years.[273]

By late May, 1875, the town's population was estimated at 300. The growth of the town in 1875 was phenomenal.[274] By October 1875, when the town was incorporated, there were sixty-seven finished frame buildings and a population estimated at between 500 and 800. The Lake City town company had been organized to oversee lot sales; and Hotchkiss, Finley, and Otto Mears were among the directors. Henry Finley, F. Newton Bogue, and William T. Ring evidently formed the Lake City Town Company and elected officers on April 3, 1875, but it was largely financed and encouraged by Otto Mears and a few of his associates.[275] Henry Finley was elected president. As was typical for the time, all of the founding fathers received a number of free lots from the town site company. Bartholf and possibly Hotchkiss "homesteaded" 160 acres that were covered in the town site, but they both took a good number of city lots instead. One of the first actions of the townsite company was to remove squatters from the land covered by the new town. Hotchkiss and D. P. Finley had filed a placer claim at Granite Falls on May 28, 1875 to secure the use of the falls to power their saw mill.[276] By the end of 1875 Hotchkiss' and Finley's saw mill at Argenta Falls was being operated twenty-four/seven and still could not keep up with the demand for sawn lumber. The Bartholfs, B. A. Sherman, the Lee brothers, Henry Finley, and James Sparling were among its first residents. The rich discoveries at the Ute-Ulay and the Hotchkiss Mine were causing Lake City to become the center of the southwest Colorado mining excitement, a status it would hold until 1879.[277]

It has been claimed that in 1874 and 1875 alone, more than 1,000 claims were located in the Lake District; but a later report counted only about 100 claims, so many of the early claims probably had no assessment work done on them.[278] The first boom in Lake City lasted from 1875 thru 1878 with the peak in 1877. Almost all the area's principal mines were discovered during this time.[279] The most active mines were the Ute-Ulay, Hotchkiss, Dolly Varden and the Ocean Wave. The Galena District was formed and included many of the Henson Creek mines.

Williams Tourist Guide wrote:

Before the snow had left the valley and while the mud on the range was ankle deep (the miners) came pouring in like clans at the summons of their chief. A store opened in Lake City almost every day.

Lake City's new newspaper, *The Silver World*, published its first issue on June 18, 1875. It was the first paper on the Western Slope of Colorado. Mears continued to be very active in encouraging the development of the Lake City area, and he financially backed the *Silver World* to bring publicity to the area. Harry M. Woods and Clark L. Peyton were the first editors. Woods was a young man from California, who was very self-confident. Peyton was a small man, who was described as having "dash" and "versatility."[280]

One of the first actions of the *Silver World* was to complain about the lack of efficient mail delivery, which was a problem throughout the San Juans at the time. Woods wrote:

Our mails come in on bull teams and go out by chance, and yet there are between 500 and 600 persons who receive their mail at this point.[281]

The feeling of the community and the publicity about the bad service evidently did some good for as previously mentioned the primary mail route into the San Juans was soon established from

Saguache through Lake City to Silverton over the Mears toll road. After July, 1875, the Barlow and Sanderson stage was used to carry the mail to Lake City. From Lake City the mail route went up to the Tellurium post office in Burrows Park and over to Animas Forks, a very difficult and undependable route in the winter.[282] Mears was required by government regulations to keep the mail regular with a predetermined number of deliveries per week. As a result, the mailmen from Burrows Park to Animas Forks and in other areas of deep snow, strapped the mail on their back, and used long, homemade wooden skis (called snowshoes in those days) to deliver the mail, with what was called "superhuman feats of endurance and perseverance."[283]

The first Barlow and Sanderson stage from Saguache arrived in Lake City July 11, 1875, before the wagon road had even been finished to Lake San Cristobal. However it was reported that Hotchkiss and a twenty man crew were quickly converting the trail into a good road and in the process had shortened its original length by eight or ten miles and eliminated the "delectable" places such as Devil's Canyon and Hell's Delight.[284] It was the first of what originally was three times a week stage service, soon to be made daily.

By April 1877, the Barlow and Sanderson stage ran daily until the heavy winter snows in the mountains slowed or stopped their progress. In the fall and spring, when the roads were partially blocked and muddy, horses were sometimes used by passengers. Travelers could buy tickets and wait for the stage at any of the stations. Large concord stages were used, pulled by four horses on the level and six horses on the steep slopes.[285]

John Bell was particularly impressed with the equipment and quality and care of the stage company's animals:

> *Every horse had to stand as critical an examination by an expert judge, as is required of an applicant to Annapolis or West Point.... The coaches were run on as close time and with as much system as are the cars on the Pennsylvania Railroad, and they had no more accidents or breakdowns, and passengers were treated with as much consideration by the employees. Many of the horses lived from thirty to thirty-five years. A trained veterinary was always looking after their feet, teeth, and general health.*[286]

Stage riders were offered plenty of excitement in the mountains. Besides the rough roads and steep drop-offs, there were avalanches, storms, and the impossibility of sleep for days at a time. Bell said there were as many as seven passengers inside the coach and nine, including the driver, outside. Many of the people going throughout the San Juans first came to Lake City by stage, but an equal number walked or rode horseback to the town. Lake City was described during this boom period as "a constant stream of humanity pouring into the San Juans through this metropolis."

Freight rates from either Saguache or Del Norte at the time were 2 to 2 ½ cents a pound from either city and in the winter were 3 to 4 cents a pound.[287] Because of the relative ease of access offered by the stages running over the toll roads, women and children arrived early at Lake City.

Barlow and Sanderson Stage Company was small compared to Butterfield or Wells Fargo, but it did very well and was very important to Lake City and the entire San Juans from the mid-1870s through the 1880s. Early stage coaches had some amazing suspension systems. Concord stages used thick, long, layered leather straps that were usually 3 or 4 inches wide and stretched from the front to the rear of the chassis. The ride was a difficult one, as the coach swung from side to side, as well as up and down, causing many passengers to report "seasickness." It did however allow the coach to find its own center of gravity on steep, sloping roads. The horses that pulled the stages were changed every ten miles or so in the mountains and the changeovers were done quickly — usually taking three minutes or less, unless the station was a rest stop.

There were only a few small settlements along any of the roads coming into Lake City in 1875 or 1876, so it was the custom that the men passengers slept with the teamsters in the stage company's barns and women and children would sleep in the main station building.[288] The roads were harsh, even when new, and storms and floods really messed them up. Of course being private, toll road owners tried to do only a minimum of maintenance. Expert drivers, who seemed to have no fear, drove the coaches and actually had very few serious accidents. Unfortunately, not many passengers had the nerve and pluck of the drivers and diaries of the time are full of fearful rides along the San Juan Mountain roads.[289] Many shady characters rode the stages at the time, trying to pickpocket a passenger, steal a gun or luggage, or work some kind of a scam while on the stage. Then there were holdups along the routes. Guards were armed, and robbers were usually hung within days of being caught. Robbers along the Lake City route included the LeRoy brothers and the Allison gang.

The Barlow and Sanderson Stage Company thrived by taking passengers off the end of the line of the railroads and transporting them into the Colorado mountains. To some extent the stage drivers acted as tour guides, stopping, for example, to let passengers look at the "Gate" or Clear Creek Falls. A driver for Barlow and Sanderson, who stuttered, had a full coach on the Saguache to Lake City run when he stopped

An ad for the Barlow and Sanderson Stage Line shows it took five days from Denver to Lake City or four days from Cañon City to Lake City. The trip from Cañon City to Del Norte was two days. Not only was the trip long, but it was also very rough. (Author's Collection)

at Gateview to let the passengers admire the sight. Two women were on board; one, the wife of the *Silver World* editor, was lavish with her praise, but the other woman, who had recently moved to Colorado from Iowa, acted unimpressed and said "I would rather see an Iowa cornfield." The driver quickly stuttered back at her — "S-S-S- So would a h-h-h- hog."[290]

The mountain freight wagons of the time were very large (some loaded rigs were said to weigh 5,000 pounds or more) and were built to take heavy loads over rough and rutted roads. Oxen were used if the load was extremely heavy (like a boiler), or while traveling very steep stretched in the mountains, with as many as ten teams (twenty oxen) pulling the load. At many places the loads had to be transferred to mules or burros for the last part of the trip to the mines.

In 1875 a railroad was already being considered across Colorado's Continental Divide. Even at this early date, Lake City wanted and anticipated the coming of the railroad to the town. As the railroads continued building towards the San Juans, the stage agencies kept transporting from the end of the railroad line. The route over Cochetopa seemed the easiest and least expensive for a railroad. One of the Wheeler Survey's jobs in 1873 was to check out the Antelope Park to Lake City route for a possible railroad. From Lake City, it was even considered that the railroad might go up Henson Creek to American Flats and then down to the Uncompahgre, and this route was found to be possible! Wheeler liked the Rio Grande route even better than Cochetopa, going over Spring Creek and down the Cebolla to the Gunnison.[291] The Hayden Survey also liked the Rio Grande route. Both surveys felt that even Stony Pass might be a possibility for a railroad route.[292] Of course, it would have been very expensive and dangerous to construct; and, perhaps it would have been shut down in the winter.

Although Otto Mears was the driving force and made the town financially viable, Enos Hotchkiss, not Mears, is credited as being the "Father of Lake City." Hotchkiss picked a good site for a town, built at least one of the first two cabins on the town site in 1874, served on the original town board and board of county commissioners, and spent a lot more time in Hinsdale County than Mears. Hotchkiss' original cabin was destroyed in 1879 or 1880, probably by children, but the present-day building used as a garage at 121 Gunnison Avenue is near the spot of the Hotchkiss cabin and was probably built only weeks or months after Hotchkiss built his cabin. It is of very similar construction, except Hotchkiss used a dirt roof.[293] The garage is probably the oldest surviving cabin in Lake City.

Even though the town company had surveyed hundreds of Lake City's lots, there were so many people in Lake City in 1875 that many camped or even built cabins in the streets and alleys.

Cabins and rough shacks were thrown up without regard to alleys and streets. Streets and sidewalks, if allowed for at all, were cramped, winding trails through the mass of cabins and tents. During the spring (of 1875) streets became muddy thoroughfares, wagons and residents alike plowing through the muck to reach their destination.... The Board of Trustees for Lake City passed certain ordinances designed to make the town of Lake City into an organized settlement.... The rough shacks were moved, the streets widened and the town of Lake City began to take on the aspects of a city.[294]

Lake City was no different as far as its need for urbanization and was without a doubt the early forerunner of the San Juan boom towns, at least during the first five years of the San Juan rush. City services like lawmen and fire protection were needed by all the early Colorado mining towns, and Lake City was no exception. The condition of early streets was a problem, with stumps often left where trees were cut for lumber mills or early cabins; and there were usually no plans for drainage. Strict sanitation was also badly needed in the close quarters of a town. Lake City was to meet all these challenges admirably and quickly.

To help finance these functions, Lake City turned to licensing merchants early on in its existence. The town licensed saloons, auctioneers, hotels and boarding houses, lumber dealers, stables, restaurants, bowling alleys, grocery stores, and many other types of mercantile. Some of the less respectable businesses paid the highest fees. For example a saloon license was $300 per year and a small hotel $25.[295] A single prostitute might pay a $25 per year fee. Lake City, by the end of 1875, already had these businesses and more — meat markets, general stores, an assay office, a shoe shop, a newspaper, and the inevitable attorneys. Merchants were the pillars of the community and often grubstaked local prospectors for a percentage of their discovery. Costs were high, but Lake City's wagon roads made the costs lower than other San Juan towns of the time, where pack trains or burros were required for transport of supplies and ore.[296]

Mining towns like Lake City also lured miners and prospectors with recreational activities. Saloons were probably the most popular attraction for men all over the country, not just in mining camps. A saloon was usually one of the very first businesses to open in any mining camp, regardless of the size of the place. Prostitutes also arrived early. The south end of Lake City's Bluff Street had its red light district, but it was not nearly as big or as rowdy as the other large San Juan towns. South Bluff Street was known by most of the local men as "Hell's Acre." Gambling halls were popular throughout the town and fit the personalities of the prospectors. Other recreation, like bowling and billiards, appeared in Lake City within a year or two after its founding.[297]

Lake City was growing fast. As the *Silver World* put it:

Last fall the traveler through the valley of the Lake Fork of the Gunnison might pass from its mouth to the source without encountering a single human habitation, save it might be a wigwam of a roving Ute. What would be his surprise now to view the bustling and thriving village at the junction of that stream and Henson Creek, a place of already some thirty-five or forty buildings and many more in the process of erection?[298]

The year 1875 was a year of many firsts for the new town — the first wedding, stage arrival, and the first child's birth to name a few. There was also the first reported crime (not counting Packer). A newcomer slashed a man in the back with a knife. There was talk of hanging him, but he was instead taken to the Del Norte jail.

Quite a few "respectable" women came to Lake City in 1875. When the first child was born on July 8, 1875, many of the nearby residents came to hold and see the new baby. Married women put their own unique stamp on early mining communities. They insisted on picket or board fences around their homes to keep out wandering livestock, especially the voracious burros that freely wandered the streets. Even if living in a log cabin, a woman would usually have flowers planted outside her home. They planted shrubbery and whatever vegetables would grow in the high, thin air, and short summers of the San Juans.[299] Many of the huge cottonwood trees in present-day Lake City were planted by these pioneer women.

Soon, only a few lots were left for sale in the original town site, so the additions of Foote and Richardson, Samuel Wade, the Casco Placer on the west side of south Bluff Street, and West Lake, on the west side of north Bluff, were added. The *Silver World* joyfully and humorously proclaimed:

The cry is lots! Lots! Lots! Everybody wants to build on a lot, and lots of them want to build on two lots. When we cast our lot in Lake City there was lots of room for lots of people but now lots of houses have been built and the first inquiry that a newcomer makes of the oldest inhabitant is, can we get a lot?[300]

The first business in general merchandise had arrived in Lake City in May 1875. George C. Merritt opened the first restaurant "before the town even had a name." It was a 10 by 12 foot log cabin with no windows and only one table that could seat four people. The "kitchen" was a log fire out front of his establishment on what later became Silver Street. It was said that he always had beans on the stove.[301]

Lake City had its first "official" celebration of the Fourth of July in 1875. It was also the first such celebration on the Western Slope of Colorado. There was no American flag to be found, but one was made out of red flannel long underwear, a blue flannel shirt, and several white handkerchiefs. "Perfect except there were no stars."[302] The festivities included a parade, contests, fireworks, and a public dance that lasted all night. There were reportedly about a dozen ladies in town at the time, "all arrayed in good taste." The Fourth of July tradition still stands today, except the dance ends a little earlier. It is the really big Lake City celebration of the year (and that of most other San Juan towns). At the first Fourth of July celebration, the holes in anvils were packed with powder and fired thirteen times.

The July 3 issue of the *Silver World* claimed Lake City had twelve American and two Mexican women and that 122 lode claims had been located already in the Lake Mining District, as well as nine mill sites.[303] The many mill sites were a sign of times to come. Other early businesses in the town included the general store of Foote and Kellogg and the Miner's Supply Store of Major J. W. Brockett, which included Brockett's Hall on the second story. Early entertainment in Lake City included musical concerts, plays, lectures, and dances; but, of course, the saloons, dance halls, and gambling establishments were also very popular with the men.

Even with its known treasure chest of minerals, San Juan mining, as opposed to prospecting, continued to open up slowly. Mining required not just the discovery of rich minerals, but also capital for equipment and a good transportation system to ship the ore to the smelters. Besides the prospectors being generally much too poor to build milling or concentrating facilities, they did not want a regular job; they wanted to move on to look for the next big discovery. If a prospector did anything with his ore, other than have it assayed for value, it meant the ore had to be shipped from his mine. A burro could only carry 150 pounds and a mule 250 pounds of ore. It could cost fifteen or twenty dollars or more per animal to get the ore to the eastern slope Colorado mills, and the trip could take two weeks.

As Frank Fossett put it:

Promising as were the numerous discoveries of the San Juan country in 1873-74-75, they were generally of no immediate benefit to their owners, on account of the distance from an ore market, wagon roads, and railroads. The region labored under a peculiar disadvantage. It was made up of almost inaccessible mountain ranges, and at the time, was so remote that capitalists and mill men were not inclined to investigate its mining wealth. The pioneers who had been making discoveries of rich veins were too poor to build works for extraction of the precious metals, and it cost too much to get ore to market to admit of attempting it, unless it was wonderfully rich, and money was at hand to defray shipping expenses.[304]

Hinsdale County and Lake City were an early answer for both of these needs in the San Juans. Fortunately for Lake City, W. H. Van Giesen had moved from New York to be part of the San Juan rush. He originally had a concentrating mill at Del Norte and had consigned the smelting of some of the ore from Bakers Park to the Crooke Smelter in New York City. All assays ran from $1,000 to $5,000 per ton, which greatly interested the Crooke family. Van Geison soon thereafter purchased the North Star Mine near Silverton for the Crooke brothers for $30,000, but smelters did not work well in Baker's Park. Within a few years both Van Geison and the Crookes had smelters in Lake City, thereby supplying capital and mills for the local mines.[305]

The two wagon and stage roads to Lake City from the outside world, and the type of people they brought to Lake City tended to mean more money to invest in Hinsdale County mines and mills. The Crookes original reduction mill was finished in late 1875. The mill used the water power of Granite Falls, but their later smelter imported Crested Butte coal. Later, fifteen charcoal kilns were built at Crookes to make coke for the smelter (coke burns hotter than coal). The Van Gieson's Lixiviation Works was built in Wade's Addition near the mouth of Henson Creek, and it opened in 1876. Lixiviation was a process that used a large quantity of water (in this case from Henson Creek) to leach the ores. The mill and its machinery cost $35,000, and it had a sixty foot smokestack. Unfortunately, it was not very efficient with local ores. It operated for only a short time, and then was torn down for salvage in the 1890s, although the smoke stack stood until 1902.[306] The Ocean Wave Mine would also soon have a smelter in Lake City in 1876. The first boom in Lake City reached its peak in 1876, with the opening of the Ocean Wave and the constantly growing Hotchkiss and Ute-Ulay Mines. Still, shipments of San Juan ore increased slowly — there was no ore shipped in 1874, $90,517 in 1875, $244,663 in 1876, $377,472 in 1877, and $434,089 in 1878. A great deal of ore was being produced at the local mines, but little of it was being shipped because of the high cost of transportation, and the fact that the mills and smelters were having to experiment on the best ways to process the unfamiliar local ores.

However, ore was shipped to Lake City's mills from mines all over the San Juans and could be there in a few days, be concentrated, and then be on its way to the smelters in a wagon that could hold 1,000 to 2,000 pounds of concentrates. Therefore much of the early ore that was shipped from the San Juans came through Lake City.

Otto Mears' newspaper made sure that the rest of the United States knew about Lake City and its nearby mines. As mentioned, the *Silver World* newspaper printed its first issue in Lake City on June 19, 1875 with Harry Woods and Clark Peyton as editors. Legend has it that the first issue of the *Silver World* was printed in a tent. However editor Woods described the *Silver World's* earliest place of business:

> *Our office is a log cabin built on a sand bed, and is, in places, four or five inches deep with fine dust.... We lack all the conveniences and many of the things usually considered necessary in a printing office. But we still are happy and present this issue with some satisfaction.*[307]

From the start, the paper pushed Mears' toll roads, including an ad for the Saguache to Los Piños route "with connections for Gunnison," which must have meant the Gunnison country, as there was no town at the time. The paper's stated objective was to let the people of the outside world learn about the new silver and gold discoveries in the San Juans.[308] From its start, the *Silver World* pointed out the beauty of the San Juans and the restorative powers of several hot springs in the area.[309] The editors hoped that outside papers might pick up positive articles on the Lake City area and prospectors might respond. It was a time when all local papers were expected to publicize the benefits of their area to the point of grossly over-exaggerating. This was especially important when printing mining news. Editorially, Woods and Peyton stressed the potential riches of the new mining areas, emphasized the desirability of Lake City as a home, and promoted the civic improvements which they felt to be necessary.[310] The local paper was so important that Helen Searcy claimed it was the reason for the first great Lake City boom of 1875 to 1879.[311] Editor Woods was so anxious to promote Lake City that he carried the first newspaper to Del Norte, about eighty-five miles away, to the post office. From their first issue and throughout the early history of Lake City, Woods and Peyton strove to provide "...full and complete reports from this and adjacent mining districts." [312]

The *Silver World* stated:

We dip out colors to the public to supply the need of the San Juan country for a paper. The Silver World *has now been inaugurated and now makes its bow. We don't believe our mission is to make or unmake nations, hence we shall not dabble in politic; believing that all our miners and prospectors are full supplied with religious reading, we will preach no sermons. Thus we will have nothing pressing on our time to prevent us giving full and complete reports from this and adjacent mining districts....*

The scenery adjacent to Lake City is well entitled to rank with the grandest on the continent. Mt. Uncompahgre is the highest peak in the Rocky Mountain range,[313] distant a few miles from Lake City, but shut out from view by intervening range. Born of the snows of these rocky heights, the Lake Fork of the Gunnison flows down thru many a scene of wild beauty for a few miles, then spreads out into Lake San Cristobal, a body of water some three miles in length and one in width, of most marvelous clearness and immeasurable depth. Its waters pass on thru a rocky canon, where are the upper falls now called Argenta, over which the waters leap in a series of precipices for 150 fifty feet. No more wildly beautiful spot in nature exists than these falls, whose thunderings may be heard from afar, and make the eternal requiem of the five victims of Packer's hellish atrocity, whose lonely grave lies about a mile below.[314]

Henry Olney bought *The Silver World* paper on September 7, 1876. The second Lake City newspaper was the *San Juan Crescent*, started on July 19, 1877, by the former *Silver World* editor Harry Woods, but it did not last long. The Lake City *Mining Register* and the Lake City *Phonograph* were later papers.

The *Silver World* soon moved to more permanent quarters on Third Street between Gunnison Avenue and Silver Street.[315] The *Silver World* reported there were three stores, a restaurant, and a saloon when it arrived in early 1875 and that all the houses were log cabins with dirt floors and sod roofs, and only two had glass in their windows. As was expected, the *Silver World* used a great deal of its space to promote the richness of the local mines and the great scenery and weather in the area. Only occasionally were there gunfights, burglaries, or horse thefts reported in the paper, which printed that there were no physicians in town, but that the city felt no need for a doctor, since Lake City was such a healthy and safe place to live.

Prospectors on their way to the San Juans usually used burros, which they would need while prospecting. (From Fossett, Colorado)

By the end of 1875 Lake City was "beginning to take on proportions and capital was coming in."[316] Lumbermen, ranchers, mining engineers, professional men and business men saw a real future in Lake City and moved there with the idea of making it their permanent home....[317]

The first post office in Lake City was opened on July 1, 1875. The Wrights in Tiny Hinsdale of the Silvery San Juan label this building as the first, but it is unlikely it looked like this at that time, as this type of construction didn't start for another year or two. The first post office was probably log, although it could have been later sided with sawn lumber. (From Tiny Hinsdale of the Silvery San Juan.)

The first post office opened in Lake City on July 1, 1875, and once again there was a major celebration, as yet more proof of civilization was in the area. Mail was delivered from Saguache three times a week and included such items as eastern newspapers and weekly magazines. In the winter, the mail was carried to Lake City and on to Silverton and Ouray on sleds or snowshoes when the roads were impassable for wagons or the stage.[318] Another stage passenger expressed his fears, this time from the winter conditions on the stage road:

The road was icy and steep; far below was the bottom of the canyon; the stage driver swished around the curved at a perilous rate. The horses slipped and sometimes fell on the icy spots and the stage coach careened from side to side.[319]

Later the mail was switched to come from Del Norte and then after 1880 from Gunnison, where it was sent by stage from the D&RG Railroad at Sapinero until the Lake City branch of the D&RG arrived in Lake City in 1889. The railroad mail stopped in 1933 with the demise of the Lake City branch and then a Star Route was established from Gunnison.[320]

In 1875 Lake City was the largest, safest, and easiest to get to of all the San Juan towns. Silverton would catch up by 1880, but some of the other San Juan towns of today like Ouray, Telluride, and Rico had not even been founded in 1875. Although the next few years were to be boom years, life in Lake City was actually pretty quiet compared to most western mining towns. Only one man died violently in 1874 or 1875, but there were plenty of accidents and more than a few men were wounded in fights.[321] Most crimes were minor, like petty theft; yet Lake City was plagued by horse thieves (a capital crime at the time) in its early days. The *Silver World* reported:

> *Some horses and mules have been stolen from this vicinity either by an organized band of thieves, or by parties who want a cheap yet expeditious way of leaving the county. Anyone found with a stolen horse wouldn't be bothered by questions, but would be allowed a few moments' meditation and prayer before ascending upward —* on a rope. [322]

This article was followed the next month by another warning:

> *We are not particularly fond of scenes of violence, but we don't know anything that would afford our citizens more pleasure than the hanging of a horse thief.*"[323]

This warning was followed by the sheriff and a posse traveling to Del Norte, where they caught two horse thieves and brought them back to Lake City. That night the sheriff went to check on the prisoners without giving any warning of his presence. His deputy mortally wounded him, thinking he was someone either coming to free or to hang the two men. The horse thieves got away in the ensuing confusion.[324]

Saguache suffered in 1875 when the first Los Piños agency was moved to the Uncompahgre River near present-day Colona. After that time Saguache was supplying only Lake City and was having major competition from the much bigger Del Norte. When the Ute agency was moved, Alonzo Hartman kept the first agency's cow camp cabin near the future Gunnison, and he and Jim Kelley had a store and a ranch at the spot. There was no town of Gunnison until 1879,[325] and Lake City had made Richardson's Colony a ghost town. The Crookes' road for obtaining coal at Crested Butte allowed Lake City merchants to use Hartman's Gunnison ranch as a place to buy hay and produce for Lake City merchants.[326]

People continued to flock to Lake City and the San Juans, in great part because of the *Silver World*. On October 9, 1875 it declared:

> *The influx of strangers is astonishing, not an hour passes but our streets are thronged with new faces; and every day sees some new families who have pitched their tents in our midst.*

By November 1875 Lake City had sixty-seven completed buildings, although most were log cabins, and about 400 inhabitants,[327] but there were also forty-five structures in the process of being erected and seventy-nine foundations had been laid,[328] so that construction could continue during the winter.

The first Christmas Eve celebrated in Lake City was in 1875 at Finley Hall with 311 people attending a free community supper. Many gifts, most of which were handmade for friends and family members, were brought to the hall during the day. Kris Kringle made an appearance, delivered the presents, and kept the audience in continuous merriment.

The number of people present exceeded what was supposed to be the population of the town. Thirty-five married ladies, seventeen babes in arms, and innumerable children between the ages of three and fifteen were among the celebrants.[329]

After the dinner there was dancing and music. Christmas breakfast was served the next morning, and then those that were still left retired to their homes. Christmas is still a very important part of Lake City life.

The Ute-Ulay, Hotchkiss Mine and other mines were all being worked hard in the Lake City area. The Crooke mill was now busy concentrating ore. There were several mines in the local area that looked promising, and mines as far away as Silverton were shipping their ore to be concentrated in Lake City. Almost overnight Lake City had changed from a stop on the way into the San Juans to a good-sized town in its own right that could truthfully proclaim that it was the "Gateway to the San Juans."

The *Silver World* reported:

A large number of families are arriving in Lake City, some from the East and a great many from the Animas country (Baker's Park), all intending to remain here and build. Homes are going up so rapidly that a citizen leaving town for a day's excursion has to inquire his way to his own domicile in the evening. And if he goes across lots to see his girl in the evening he is likely on returning home to run his proboscis (nose) against a house where none existed when he started. For a distance of six blocks, extending from 2nd to 8th and Bluff to Water Streets, a width of four blocks is almost entirely covered with buildings and houses in the course of erection and the area is rapidly enlarging. So the "Gateway of the San Juan," combined with delightful climate and other natural advantages, is rapidly reaping its rewards and the result is growth unrivaled by any other town or city in southern Colorado.[330]

By the end of 1875, the effects of the Brunot Treaty, the several Government surveys, the completion of the two new toll roads and a concentrating mill, and the effect of a newspaper with wide distribution had started a drastic increase in the number of prospectors and merchants coming into Lake City and the San Juans. The draw was bolstered by discoveries of even better ore at the Ute-Ulay and Hotchkiss Mines, and Lake City was officially a booming mining town. By the end of 1875, the *Silver World* estimated that five million pounds of freight had been brought into the town—all brought in from Saguache or Del Norte over the rough toll roads.

Drawings like this grossly over exaggerated the ease of discovery of the local silver veins in the San Juans (represented by the white streaks in the drawing). As a result many people came to prospect that were not qualified, and who left empty handed and broke within a few weeks after arriving. (Author's Collection)

One of the first actions any "legitimate town took was to elect a town council. Politicking in the San Juans was often a rough and humorous affair. Elections were sometimes won by the best joke-teller or the person who could buy the most drinks. Most campaigns were won or lost in the saloon. (Harper's Weekly, September 29, 1888, Author's Collection)

CHAPTER 4

LAKE CITY BECOMES A TOWN

⬤

The first great Lake City boom (1875 to late 1878) was caused by the opening of the San Juans to Americans and the discovery and operation of the Ocean Wave, Hotchkiss (later called the Golden Fleece), the Ute-Ulay, and other large mines in the area, but was also due to the initial surge of people coming into the San Juan Mountains along the Saguache and Del Norte Toll Roads. Many of the incoming prospectors bought their supplies in Lake City; and there were others who had initially planned to pass through Lake City that saw opportunities in the town and stayed. By the end of the first boom, the great mines in Hinsdale County had mostly been discovered; and the true prospectors were generally gone from the area after hearing of rich discoveries in Leadville and the Gunnison Country.

In 1876 Lake City was able to add to its list of businesses that of mining supplies and wholesale groceries for the many small mining camps that were opening in the mountains around it. Lakeshore, Sherman, Whitecross, Burrows Park, Tellurium, and Carson eventually spread out along the upper Lake Fork; and Capitol City, Henson, and Rose's Cabin were soon on Henson Creek.[331] Another reason for the boom was that in early 1876 the Crooke brothers announced they would buy ore from anywhere in the San Juans during the coming summer. Lake City was at that time one of the few places in the San Juans where it was economical to ship ore to be milled. In addition, the good production of the Hotchkiss and the Ute-Ulay Mines and the opening of the Ocean Wave Mine and Mill, made 1876 a very promising year.[332] The Crooke brothers bought the Ute-Ulay in 1876, and news of the $135,000 purchase price solidified Hinsdale County's reputation for being rich in minerals. Little but assessment work had been done on the Ute-Ulay up until that time, but the Crookes started doing serious development and production at the mine. The Ocean Wave also sold for $80,000 in early 1876 for a three-quarter[333] interest, then was resold a few months later for $140,000. The three Lake City mills processing ore by the end of 1876 were almost constantly running.

English and East Coast capital started arriving in Lake City in late 1875 and early 1876. Among the most prominent men were the Crooke brothers, William Van Geison, John Hough, and John J. Lewis. The Crookes (Robert, Charles, Lewis, and John) bought the Granite Falls sawmill site from Enos Hotchkiss and D. P. Church, and built a concentrating mill during late 1875 and early 1876 and in 1876 added a smelter, which unfortunately did not originally work very well. The Van Geisen Lixiviation Works was being built at the junction of Henson Creek and the Saguache and San Juan Toll Road. W. H. Van Geison was a Wisconsin capitalist and his operation covered almost four acres. The Ocean Wave Mill was built at the north end of town just a little later.

Hundreds of people flocked to Lake City and Hinsdale County in the spring and summer of 1876. Miners were still scarce; but prospectors were numerous.[334] Unfortunately, many of the new arrivals were neither miners nor prospectors, and had no special skills to earn a wage. Most of these men left the San Juans when they realized it took hard work, mining knowledge, and capital to get the ore out of the ground, and then transported to a mill or a smelter to get the precious minerals out of the ore. The flood of prospectors continued to flow in and through Lake City but:

A large part of these wanderers were disappointed. They came, as many do when traveling place to place, looking for the pot of gold at the end of the rainbow. Most of this type of people were unprepared for any trade and knew nothing about mining, so they came and went. But capitalists, business men and trade men came (to Lake City) in great numbers in the first few years and stayed; many for years.[335]

Even many of the skilled prospectors left when they realized they did not have the money to work their hardrock claims, although most tried to sell their "mine" if possible. Many did so for only $10 or $20.

As Frank Fossett put it:

(Lake City) has grown from a mere cluster of cabins in 1875 (to) a thriving business center of from 1,500 to 2,000 population, its mills and reduction works comprising the most extensive system of mining machinery in all the San Juan Country....[336]

Merchants flooded into the town bringing with them all kinds of merchandise, as well as supplies for the prospectors. Almost all of

Lake City's visitors in 1876 noted that the town was very refined for a new mining camp that was less than two years old. There were fine restaurants, jewelry and clothing stores for the many women in town, and two cigar factories as well as two breweries for the men. There were four sawmills, a planing mill, and a shingle mill trying to keep up with the construction going on in Lake City. The town had two assayers, two banks, five blacksmiths, three bakeries, two brickyards, two drug stores, four Chinese laundries, fifteen lawyers, and seven saloons among many other businesses.[337]

Mining claims were continually being bought and sold during Lake City's first boom, as speculators felt that good discoveries were being made in the area; however, very few mines were doing any real development or exploratory work. Some mines changed hands many times and never had any work done on them other than the minimum assessment work required for an unpatented claim. Values were generally inflated at this time, even when working mines were sold.[338]

Lake City became a true town in the summer of 1876. One of the families that came with both capital and milling experience was that of the Crooke brothers. Through the efforts of John J., they opened their ore concentrator on July 4, 1876,[339] and in December 1876, the Van Geisen Lixiviation Works opened. By the spring of 1876, all the original town lots were sold and the editor of the *Silver World* could write:

Buildings of every description; the crude cabin and the enormous warehouse; the Sanctuary and the gilded saloon; log, frame, brick and adobe rose on every hand. The hammer and saw never ceased. So rapid was the growth that no one pretended to keep pace with it even for a block each way on his own street. The oldest resident would scarcely recognize the town after a week's absence; long trains of six mule teams rumbled through the streets bringing stores for mine and kitchen. The flannel shirt and buckskin pants gave place to the wonders of broadcloth and cassimere. Ladies appeared upon the streets and in their parlors wearing the elegant costumes of a gay city. Nearly every luxury that gratifies the palate in New York or Chicago could be bought of our merchants at very reasonable prices. Two banks furnished their much needed facilities. Jewelry glistened in the show room windows. The daily newspapers of New York, Chicago and San Francisco were on sale at the news stands. The almond-eyed celestial brought his pigtail and his chopsticks and erected a cabalistic sign over his cabin door. Lawyers and assayers swarmed into town like the locusts in Egypt. All was bustle and activity.[340]

Several of the early Lake City business buildings were made of adobe, such as the O.K. Clothing Store built in July, 1876, by Louis Kafka. His store continued in Lake City until the turn of the century. The number of people in town was swollen by men who were only in the area in the months without snow, but the correspondent for the *Rocky Mountain News* in June, 1876, estimated a population of 1,000 in town and 2,000 more in the nearby areas.[341] The *Silver World* represented the population of Lake City at the end of 1876 to be 1,500. It was truly amazing growth, seen only in places like California Gulch and along Clear Creek near Denver. Unfortunately, there were signs the town was possibly being overbuilt, but no one seemed to recognize it at the time.

Banks came early to Lake City. The town's Hinsdale Bank was the first bank on the Western Slope. Then S. C. Foote and John Hough helped procure a branch of the Colorado Springs National Bank that opened in Lake City under that name on June 17, 1876. The frame bank building was located on the east side of Silver Street between 2nd and 3rd Streets in what is now the town park. Its first President was H. A. McIntire.[342] The *Silver World* acknowledged the important move by writing that the bank building was "neat and complete in all its appointments, well-furnished and an ornament to Silver Street."[343] The bank did very well;

The "Stone Bank Block" was not a full block, but it was the pride of Lake City. It was originally occupied by The First National Bank of Lake City for a few years, but then for decades Miners and Merchants Bank operated from the location. The O.K. Clothing Store can be seen at the left in this photo. It was an early establishment that lasted into the 1900s before it closed. (Author's Collection)

and, by February, 1877, it had its own charter, additional capital, and was renamed "The First National Bank of Lake City." The legal change occurred on May 14, 1877.[344] John Hough agreed to build a new building for the bank to be called "The Stone Bank Block," as it was to be made of cut stone, quarried in Slaughter House Gulch at the northwest end of town. The stone building was shared with his dry goods establishment. The Hough-First National Bank building was constructed in 1876 and 1877 at the southwest corner of Third and Silver Streets at a cost of $15,000. It was very substantial and still stands today.

The cost of the building's furnishings was another $7,000, by August the bank's new safe had arrived, and by late August, 1877, the building was occupied. H. A. McIntire was an extremely well-liked man in Lake City, both socially and in business; but he suddenly resigned as President of the bank on March 16, 1878. It was soon learned that he had embezzled over $40,000. By mid-June, 1878, the bank was in liquidation. McIntire was convicted of embezzlement in January, 1880, and was sentenced to prison; but U. S. President Rutherford Hayes pardoned him. Banks were not generally trusted, so many people kept their cash hidden at home. A Lake City blacksmith was said to have built a secret compartment inside his big leather bellows to store his excess money.[345]

The Bank of Lake City was formed in December, 1876, and operated in a brick building at the northeast corner of Third and Silver Streets. By the summer of 1878 it was out of business, at which time it was bought and incorporated into the Miners and Merchants Bank, which was a branch bank of the famous Thatcher Brothers of Pueblo. John A. and Mahlon D. Thatcher were highly successful financiers in Colorado in the late 1800s. They started with a small mercantile business in Pueblo, but later opened a series of banks throughout Colorado. Later their holdings included railroads, irrigation canals, factories, and miscellaneous heavy industries. Mining interests were also part of their portfolio, but loans for mining slowed down after 1900 and were non-existent in Lake City after 1910. John Thatcher died in 1914 and M.D. Thatcher in June 1916. Their estates were valued at over $9 million, the richest in Colorado history at the time.[346] Their bank had purchased and moved into the Stone Bank Block building in 1881. After this time there was only one bank in Lake City for many years. Miners and Merchants was one of the Thatcher Brothers most profitable banks until 1914, when it was closed after the death of John Thatcher. Its closing left Lake City without a bank until 1983. In the interim, the building was a hotel, liquor store, cocktail lounge, and then the Elkhorn Hotel.[347]

By 1877 *The Silver World* reported that "homes are going up so rapidly that a citizen leaving town for a day's exercise has to inquire of his own domicile in the evening." Besides mining, there were many families in town that made a living supplying the miners and prospector's needs (called at the time "mining the miner"). As the mercantile business became more important, the cost of lots in town rose to an average of $100. Farmers, ranchers, and lumbermen were also succeeding in the Hinsdale area.

Although several of Lake City's "halls" rented cots and some homes were open to boarders, Lake City's first real hotel was the American House, built in 1876. It was located on Gunnison Ave, between Third and Fourth streets and was a frame structure, two and a half stories high, with a kitchen and dining room downstairs and rooms upstairs. It had large woodstoves for heat and separate outhouses for men and women. Although somewhat crude, it was known throughout the early San Juan mining towns. It was later destroyed by fire.[348] Lake City's first big hotel was the Hinsdale House, which was also built in the summer of 1876 on Gunnison Avenue. The financial backer of the hotel was Otto Mears.[349]

The Pueblo House was first operated in 1885. It was on the east side of Silver Street between Third and Fourth Streets. The south part of the dining room was made from hewn logs, probably incorporating an early miner's cabin. Later the logs were covered over, and it was made into a two-story building. The building survived or was rebuilt after three different fires until it finally closed. Adjoining the dining room was a bar; and some, but not all, rooms had a woodstove for heat. The kitchen had a huge wood cooking stove about seven feet in length. The second floor was later removed by owner Max Hersinger.[350] Unfortunately what remained of the hotel burned in 2012.

Another American House was opened in 1897. The first American House had by this time burned. The Occidental, at various times, was located in two different locations and three different buildings. It opened in 1885 on Silver Street and was a large two-story frame building. It had fourteen rooms, each heated by a wood stove. The original building burned but was immediately rebuilt. Then a second fire destroyed the hotel; but rather than rebuild, the owner bought the American House hotel and changed the name to the Occidental. A fire also destroyed much of this hotel in 1937. The LaVeta Hotel was located at the corner of Third and Gunnison. It also was two stories with a kitchen, dining room, and offices on the first floor. Eventually all of Lake City's hotels were unfortunately destroyed by fires.

The Wrights, in their book, *Tiny Hinsdale of the Silvery San Juan*, report thirty saloons in Lake City by July 1877. Some were respectable and some were "honky-tonks." The main difference in these establishments was the class of people who frequented them. Ladies did not drink in public in those days, but some of the nicer saloons had a special back or side door, so a respectable woman could accompany a man, if they so desired.

It was generally agreed that the unusually large number (proportionate to other mining towns) of women in Lake City brought a civilizing influence, and that they worked hard to make sure the children of the town were educated, that good morals prevailed, and that law and order generally ruled.[351] However, it was not just women who brought class to Lake City. One man wrote that Lake City men "are intelligent, even aristocratic, many of them quote Shakespeare."[352] The Reverend George Darley wrote that the men who came to Lake City included many who "had been trained in fine eastern homes."[353] Lake City's residents organized a dramatic association as early as January, 1876. It was reported that many of the members had previous stage experience in their schools, community, and even professionally.[354] Their first play was presented in early February and the second on February 19, 1876. By 1877 Lake City also had a Shakespeare Club. Both clubs' productions were always well-received in town. Several bands and vocalists gave performances in 1877 and for years afterwards. There were also traveling shows, lectures, and dramas.

The earliest settlers of Lake City combined talent, friendliness, community spirit, and native surroundings with a desire to utilize leisure times in a wholesome manner and evolved a program of varied interests in the field of recreation and public entertainment. The rough and bawdy type entertainment and recreation, which is still commonly associated with mining camps, was present, but it was segregated, for the most part, in the area known as "Hell's Acre."[355]

Early recreation for the locals included mountain climbing, roller skating, fishing, raffles, military drilling, firemen contests, ice skating, skiing, sledding, football, baseball, tennis, and boxing.[356] Billiards was popular in town and several establishments had only billiard tables and liquor for entertainment. A situation involving gunplay occurred at the Star Billiard Hall on the night of July 3, 1876. Johnny Roche and Dan Emmit settled their argument with guns. Roche was killed and an innocent bystander wounded. Emmit was arrested and was allowed to make bond, but he was re-arrested for assault with intent to commit rape and was then held without bond in jail. It wasn't until June, 1876 that Lake City had its first real jail—just a log cabin, used mainly to house drunks until they sobered up. The day shift of the police department was paid $5 for each arrest and conviction. Those on the night shift were paid a flat $50 a month. In February, 1876, $150 had been allocated to make the jail more escape-proof, yet a few weeks after being jailed Emmit dug under a wall and escaped. No attempt was made to recapture Emmit, but the police force was increased at the time.[3577] The jail really was not used much, but not because of a lack of violence. When the first court was held in the new courthouse in June, 1877, two of the nine defendants were found not guilty, and the seven other defendants had left town and forfeited bail.[358] Murder was actually the exception in Lake City in 1875-77. There was crime in town, but it was generally minor.[359]

Many mines were prospering near Lake City in 1876. These still included the Hotchkiss Mine, the Ute-Ulay, and the Ocean Wave; but also the Golden Wonder and the Black Crooke. Besides the Crooke Brothers' new smelter, the Ocean Wave and the Van Geison Lixiviation Works were now concentrating ore to be shipped to the smelters. All were only relatively successful compared to the Silverton smelters, which evidently had problems with the high altitude among other things. Many San Juan mine owners in 1876 felt smelters should be built near their San Juan mines to keep transportation costs low, but there were two problems. First, San Juan ores were very complicated and needed experimentation and very experienced men to make the smelters produce a good percentage of the metals contained in the ores. Secondly, smelters of any type did not tend to reach high enough temperatures in the rare atmosphere of the high mountains. These were hard and expensive lessons to be learned in the future. When the Crookes bought the North Star Mine on King Solomon Mountain near Silverton, they also filed on mill sites near Mineral Point and Silverton, but they never built a mill in either place.[360]

From the start, Lake City citizens had strived to create a strong religious and moral atmosphere in their town. The churches served the intellectual, social, and religious needs of Lake City. The churches were, and are still, an important part of community life; so much so in the early days that one longtime, but unnamed, resident supposedly noted that in the 1890s the gambling halls and saloons donated part of their profits to a church selected by them each week. One longtime resident observed that "the decent element in town took charge and ran things, though the other element was present."[361] Within a few years after its founding, Lake City had six church denominations — Presbyterian, Episcopal, Methodist, Baptist, Christian (nondenominational), and Catholic. Only the Methodists are missing today. Presbyterian minister Alexander Darley and, at the time, his lay brother, George, were the second ministers to arrive in town on June 17, 1876. George Darley, early on, solicited books and began a drive for a building to house a library and reading room. By 1876 Darley, his wife Emma, and his two sons were living in Lake City.

Three church buildings were built in Lake City in 1876 and 1877, including the first church building on the Western Slope of Colorado. The Presbyterian and the Episcopal churches were started across the street from each other by famous Colorado pioneer ministers. The Presbyterian building was dedicated on November 19, 1876, and the Episcopal Church was dedicated in February or March, 1877. The Catholics followed suit in September 1877. In addition, these Lake City clergymen also started churches in Ouray and Silverton and gave services in many smaller mining camps and even at some of the larger mines.[362]

George Darley came to Del Norte in 1876 and then went to Lake City with his brother. Although he never finished high school, he became a college president, pastor of Denver's largest Presbyterian Church, and received a Doctor of Divinity Degree. (From Darley's book, Pioneering in the San Juan)

The Darley's first service in Lake City was on June 18, 1876 and 115 people attended. There was even a substantial choir present. At first, George came for services once a month from his location in Del Norte, but soon he was ordained and became a resident Lake City minister. George had neither college nor seminary training, but went to Del Norte early in 1876 to join his brother. George sensed his calling to the ministry while he was living in Galveston, Texas, where he preached to dock workers and jail inmates. His brother Alexander went back from Lake City to be the minister in Del Norte.[363] George Darley later wrote:

Lake City was a 'live mining camp', largely made up of young men of that class who were willing to prospect and take all kinds of chances to make money; but they had no desire to work underneath the ground. Miners were scarce; while prospectors were numerous. No class of men knew better how to treat a minister they liked in a royal manner than the men that were in southwestern Colorado during the great San Juan "excitement" of '75, '76 and '77.[364]

Darley traveled to the smaller mining communities constantly.[365] As Colorado historian Duane Smith put it:

To go beyond Lake City meant to go where there were no bridges across streams and in some districts no wagon roads. The trails were often rough and the distance between cabins so great that the traveler was forced to sleep on the ground. To give the first sermon in Ouray (Darley) walked 125 miles, more than half through snow, and waded all the streams.[366]

Before he was even ordained, George was sent to Silverton in the winter to check out the possibilities of a church there. He made it on horseback to Burrows Park ahead of a snowstorm, but then went over Cinnamon Pass with legendary mailman, Gus Talbot, in a blizzard. The two became lost, but finally made it to Animas Forks. Talbot told the people of Silverton that:

They could tie to George M. Darley, for, out of more than 100 men he had piloted across the range, the Presbyterian preacher was the only one that had the grit to keep up with me all the way.[367]

According to Darley, he would usually go to a saloon when he first entered a mining camp. The men would stop gambling, cover the liquor with sheets, sing hymns, pray, and listen to sermons with tears in their eyes.[368] Darley found respect there, as well as a well-filled offering plate.

Not all of Darley's experiences were good. One night he returned home in Lake City after Sunday services and discovered his house had been broken into and a number of his personal effects had been stolen. Darley went to seek help at Larry Dolan's saloon, found a police officer there, and asked him to help locate his stolen goods. They first checked the other gambling halls and then went to Hell's Acre. At the first dance hall they went to, they were told a carpetbagger had just left with a coat over his arm and a valise in his hand. They stepped outside to look for the man and Darley casually noted in his memoirs that inside the dancehall the bartender had just shot a man in the neck. Darley's belongings were found the next day, but the thief had disappeared by that time.[369]

Darley had a great knack for relating to the miners. In one of his sermons he said:

Sinner, whether you are a mining sinner or a prospector sinner, do you wish to be "staked" in on this lode, and have your name recorded in the Book that our Creator keeps in which are written the names of all who are interested in it? If so, go to Christ, tell him you have thus far sought the gold and silver that perisheth with the using — the "vein" of silver and gold — but now you desire an interest in imperishable riches... [370]

One of the very important and unfortunately necessary functions of early preachers was to perform funerals, both for members of their congregations and for those who had never seen the inside of a church. Darley answered both calls without hesitation. He kept a log of funerals that he performed, which in part reads:

> *George Elwood — saloon keeper killed*
> *Luther Ray — murdered in a gambling hall*
> *John Ferguson — killed by a landslide*
> *Alfred Shepard — died from exposure in storm*
> *Harry Pierce — killed by a premature blast in the Ute-Ulay*
> *Charles C. Curtis — killed in a snowslide* [371]

Avalanches were a problem on anyone's trip into the backcountry in late winter. There were a dozen or so slides just between Lake City and Capitol City, and many more avalanches higher up the trail. Darley

The Sunday School posed at the Presbyterian Church, which was built in large part by its first minister George M. Darley. The church did not yet have its steeple or bell, but it was a proud addition to Lake City. (From Pioneering in the San Juan)

141

related holding services for two men killed in an avalanche on Engineer Mountain and buried at the IOOF Cemetery.[372] The service was held in one of the men's (Jackson Gregory's) home. He left a wife and eight "stair-stepped children, the youngest still at its mother's breast." The second man was a bachelor. Darley told how "the men present provided for the needs of the unfortunate family in the months that followed."[373]

As Grant Houston put it:

> *Whether in a simple wooden marker or a rounded river rock, polished Italian marble or cool cast iron, the headstones in the Lake City cemetery are more a tribute to the strength and determination of the early settlers than any one individual.... Their attempt at taming an otherwise untamable area has put them in a small category of those that were willing to sacrifice everything for an ideal.*[374]

Darley also showed compassion to those who led a seedier side of life in Lake City. His first convert to Christianity after coming to town was said to be an orphaned twenty-year old local prostitute.[375] The story of Magg Hartman that occurred years after Darley had left Lake City also shows this side of Darley:

> *A man named Crowley was sick with pneumonia in a cabin above Sherman. The doctor who went there on snowshoes to attend him said that he must have a nurse. There was none available in Sherman or Lake City. A girl (Magg Hartman) from one of the dance halls in Lake City volunteered to go and nurse Crowley. She was up there a week before they brought him to Lake City, but owing to the exposure she had suffered, the girl came down with the same disease. The men were taking her (to town) on a toboggan during a snowstorm and were forced to stop at Boyd's cabin, two miles above the mill.*
>
> *One of the men stopped on his way to Lake City and Mary Franklin heard the girl's story.*
>
> *"Bring her in at once," Mary ordered.*
>
> *"But—," the man started to explain the girl's reputation.*
>
> *"Never mind telling me about that," Mary ordered, "Bring that child here. I will take care of her and do all I can for her."*
>
> *During the next week Mary hardly left the bedside of this sick girl. Nothing else counted until the patient had recovered enough so that the doctor said she must be taken to Lake City. This however should not have been done, because the girl lived only a few days after being taken away from Mary's loving care....*

In spite of the heroism the girl had displayed, a preacher in Lake City refused to permit her body to be buried from the church. Mary was furious. She succeeded in getting the beloved George M. Darley to come to Lake City and preach the sermon.[376]

As the service was held in a house, Darley shook hands with all the girls who came and spoke a kind thought or two to each. He also went to the burial ground after the service.

Darley was a strong supporter of the Temperance movement and preached constantly against the dangers of liquor. Most of these talks were packed with people. Over 600 Lake Citians signed a pledge that Darley had prepared, agreeing not to drink. Darley wrote:

To do this work in a "live" mining town, where so many were engaged in the devil's own business, needed wisdom as well as courage, that the work might be pushed vigorously without creating a feeling of hatred toward those who favored temperance.

When first mentioned I met opposition where I least expected it — from Christian men, officers in the church....

I said to the church officers: "If I cannot deliver my lectures in the church I will deliver them some other place." No objections were made to my using the church building.

The first lecture was given December 18, 1877—subject: "Come, Take a Drink...." The posters were placed everywhere, not forgetting to put a liberal supply in the saloons.... Every night while the meetings were held, our church was packed.... Over six hundred signed the pledge.[377]

Church buildings were important to a town and a source of real pride. Darley basically built the Presbyterian Church building himself (he and his brother were carpenters). Then he built most of the pews and furnishings for the church.[378] Later the manse for the church's minister was also built by Darley, and was the first for such use on Colorado's Western Slope. Darley finished it in just over four months in May, 1879. A Christmas Eve service was held at the church that same year, a tradition still held up to the present.

Winter was when church attendance increased dramatically. Most of the higher mines closed because of deep snow, and unemployed miners flocked into the bigger towns. Church services provided not only spiritual uplift, but a welcome diversion that provided a chance to spend time with some of the local families.[379]

All of the Lake City churches held benefits and programs, but the Presbyterians were especially active and added greatly to the social life of the town. George Darley served as minister of the church until 1880, as well as organizing and serving a church in Ouray. He describes his life in Ouray and Lake City in his book *Pioneering in the San Juan.*

In 1876 the Episcopal Reverend C. Montgomery Hogue, who had been working as a missionary on the Front Range and in the Wet Mountains, conceived the idea of "The Associated Mission of the San Juans." He held services in Lake City, Ouray, and on the San Miguel River. Like the Darleys, Parson Hogue was a carpenter and built many of the first churches in the San Juan mining camps with his own hands; but he was also comfortable wearing a six-shooter and holding services in a saloon, when there was no church building. It was said that after services at a saloon he sometimes gambled the plate to "increase the Lord's share."

The Episcopal Church organized in December, 1876,[380] and bought an existing carpentry building across the street from the Presbyterians. The church building was dedicated in February or March, 1877, with regular services held within a few months, but soon the members worshipped without a priest until May, 1880, when the first rector arrived. Then, in 1882 he was transferred to Gunnison. Services continued for years with only an occasional priest or bishop presiding. The Episcopalians sponsored dances in the armory to the chagrin of several other denominations in town.[381]

The Catholic Church arrived in Lake City in September, 1877. Reverend Father Hayes from Del Norte solicited funds to construct a building. The first services in the new church were held on January 6, 1878, although the building was not yet finished. The 22 by 55 foot building was finished in March, 1878, and Father J. H. Brinker was the first full-time local priest; however, by February, 1881, Father Quinn from Gunnison was coming weekly to Lake City to hold services. The Catholic ladies put on many social events, including a Christmas Eve Ball that was a tradition for many years.[382]

The Christian Church, which was formed in 1882, turned its efforts to the youth of Lake City. It held Sunday School classes at the school house and received its first minister in July, 1883. The group then rented a building it called "Christian Hall." Lectures and exhibits were also held there. In 1891 services were switched to the American House Hotel, until the church disbanded in 1898.

The first Baptist service was held on July 9, 1876, with James Finch from Denver presiding; however there is no record of further Baptist services until September, 1883. At that time it was reported that eighteen local Baptists were considering a church, and that regular meetings

The Catholic Church of St. Rose of Lima was built on a bluff south of Henson Creek by George Boggs. The Foote-Vickers house is on the left in the photo. The Foote house was built by Smith C. Foote in 1880 but later the house was owned by John and Vera Vickers and it was added to several times over the years. (Colorado Historical Society Photo)

and bible studies were being held. A church building that included the beautiful stained glass windows that are still present today was built and occupied in September, 1891, but there still was no regular pastor for quite some time.

A Methodist minister, Rev. J. Moffat actually held the first church service in Lake City, but he never had a church building in the town. Later services were held at the Presbyterian Church, and then in the courthouse. However the Methodists disbanded in 1881 without ever building a church.[383]

Lake City's churches and their Sunday Schools were a major factor in the high moral values and intellect of the town's earliest settlers, and the persistence of that moral influence is still recognizable and lauded today. A community-wide Christmas Eve celebration was held in 1875 and every year right on up to present. In 1877 the non-denominational Christmas service was held at the new courthouse. Two large spruce trees were decorated upstairs and ladies were on hand all day to accept presents to put under the tree. Families brought presents for each other as well as presents for friends. There was singing, recitals, and instrumental music. Other social functions, not necessarily celebrating a religious holiday, were held throughout the year at various churches. The children would often give plays, usually charging a small admission to raise funds for various projects. As mentioned, the Christian Church had the most active children's program. Every Sunday evening its young people held a "song service." The church socials and church activities declined a little after 1884, but only because of school activities, the opera house (armory), and the fraternal organizations that were blooming in town.

Unlike some mining communities, where "respectable" townsmen had little to do with laborers at the mines, Lake City churches discovered and utilized the unusual talent of various mine workers in their programs and socials. At the February 21, 1882, Presbyterian Church program, a black quartette of miners from Roses' Cabin made their first public appearance in Lake City. At the same program George Harris and Richard Cruse from the Ute-Ulay Mine presented a flute duet.[384]

Not all social activities were at the churches. As Perry Eberhart put it:

Lake City was not lacking in cultural and social life. There was much drama and music to pass the time. Dances were held at the drop of a hat. Some of the top personalities of the day passed through the

The Baptist Church's Sunday School class, teachers, and possibly some of the parents posed for the camera in 1898, shortly after the church was built. (Denver Public Library Photo)

© Colorado Historical Society

city.[385] *The first Thanksgiving was celebrated in Lake City in 1876. Besides the food that was everywhere and for everyone, there was a masked ball and a community supper that included oysters, ham, sirloin, chicken, lobster, relishes, potato salad, pies, cakes, puddings, fresh fruits, candies, and nuts.*[386]

Harry Woods left the *Silver World* in 1877; and he and Thomas Reynolds started another paper, the *San Juan Crescent*. His move was made mainly to operate a Democrat paper to compete with the Republican *Silver World*.[387] However, the town was not big enough for two newspapers, and Woods' paper failed within eighteen months. Henry C. Olney had bought Woods' one-half interest in the *Silver World* when Woods left, but did not start working at the paper until October, 1876. By March 1877, Olney owned the whole paper. Olney had a lot of experience in the "Wild West" and knew a considerable number of famous Native Americans, as well as Buffalo Bill Cody, Wild Bill Hickok, and Bat Masterson. He was a correspondent for a time with *The Chicago Tribune, The New York Tribune,* and *The Rocky Mountain News*.[388] Olney was appointed Registrar of the U. S. Land Office when it came to Lake City in February, 1877, and served as registrar for about six years.

Although Lake City had town marshals, it was not until 1877 that Hinsdale County had its first sheriff — James M. Swiney, and then Swiney was followed by Enos Hotchkiss' friend Henry Finley. Just to show how great the optimism in Lake City was, *William's Tourist Guide and Map of the San Juan Mines of Colorado* in 1876 reported that:

Lake City, the principal town in the (Lake) District, is also the largest town in the San Juan, and from its accessibility and central location, it being also the depot for supplies for the largest portion of the San Juan country, it will undoubtedly become large and important, and always remain the leading city of the southwest.... Its population is not less than 1,500, principally gained during the year 1876.... Its growth has been magical, and has few counterparts in the history of Western progress.[389]

That Lake City has already become the great entry spot of the San Juan country, is no longer disputed. Prices of goods and provisions here are generally as low as in Saguache or Del Norte. The large wholesale houses here propose to keep the heaviest stocks of goods to be found outside of Denver. Nature has made this the supply point, and no circumstances can thwart its design.[390]

William's guidebook also reported in 1877 that Del Norte had 2,500 citizens, but:

Del Norte itself lost considerable trade and population by the building up of towns within the heart of the mining region, but more particular through the rapid growth of Lake City.[391]

As to Saguache, Williams reported:

Its population has fallen off during the past two years, owing to the building up of the towns in the San Juan country, which now take the trade that heretofore supported it.... The town derives its main support from its being the nearest market to Lake City and other points in the San Juan, which it supplies with grain, vegetables, butter, eggs, hay, beef and mutton, the products of the county.[392]

January 10, 1876 was when Lake City's first school opened. Even the earliest residents had recognized the need for a school in Lake City, because most of the town's people were educated and wanted their children to get a good education. They also realized a school was needed if the town was to prosper.[393] The first school was paid for by subscription. The school included adult education in English, bookkeeping, and mining law. Mr. W. A. McGinnis was the first teacher and twenty-eight students attended.[394] McGinnis worked for a salary of $55 a month. The Wrights write that the first school was held in a six room house on Gunnison Avenue.

In September of 1876 the first public school had 103 prospective students ranging in age from six to twenty-one; but the school's tax levy was not being paid by many, and there were financial problems that held up the start of classes. By late 1876 Lake City had 317 perspective students, as well as 178 children under the age of six. Money came in slowly and the school's rented building was not working out well, so a bond issue was passed to build a new school house in 1880. The plans showed a stone building with four class rooms on the second floor, as well as a full basement to be completed later. However the completed building was of brick with two large rooms and a small room between them on the second floor. The cornerstone was laid for the school on October 9, 1880.[395] The first school building was occupied only on the lower floor in October, 1881, with 107 students enrolled.[396] Attendance would continue at that level for a decade.

By this time there were also small Hinsdale County schools at Capitol City, Lake Shore, Henson, Cathedral, Hermit, and Debs. Most were one room schoolhouses, but the school at Capitol City was a very large frame building. It was torn down for its lumber about 1960. The school at Henson (the Ute-Ulay Mine) was a log cabin, while Hermit, Sawmill Park, and Debs held school in private residences. Schools in these last three towns were held in the summer.

Half to two-thirds of the students ended their formal education with the eighth grade, but for those who wished to continue on, most of the San Juans provided a high school.[397]

The Lake City School had only a few pupils in the 1940s and 1950s but started rebounding in the 1960s, although high school students still had to commute to school in Montrose or Gunnison until more recently.[398] At the time of this writing, Lake City again has over a hundred students in its K-12 school.

Some 1,500 people lived in Lake City during the winter of 1876-77, even though a thousand more had left until the next spring. By this time, some were calling Lake City the "Queen of the Mountains."[399] Lake City took on a permanent look in 1877. Many of the new buildings in town were expensive and well built. The increase in population was "not rapid but substantial." Lake City had not only a lot of people, but the town itself started to look like one. Until that time, most of the buildings were log with a few small and quickly built frame residences and commercial buildings. By 1877 there were several hotels that were usually full, some nicely constructed brick and stone buildings, many large homes and commercial buildings, as well as church buildings, two schools, and a new courthouse.

The Hinsdale County Courthouse was built in 1877 and looks substantially the same today. This photograph was taken in the early 1950s. It is most famous for being the scene of the first Alferd Packer trial. (Author's Collection)

Until 1877 county officials were using rented facilities on Gunnison or Silver Streets. By the end of June of that year a new 30 by 60 foot wooden, two-story facility was ready for use. The entire second floor was set aside for judicial use, while other county offices occupied the first floor. Since it was the largest building in Lake City at the time, it would often be used for dances, social affairs, church gatherings, and lectures.

Well-known freighter Dave Wood had a livery and freight business in Lake City by 1877, and his company was critical to the town from 1876 until the late 1880s, when the railroad arrived. He used to tell people who asked if he could handle their job that "Sure I Can! I Hauled These Mountains In Here!" Wood hauled much of the machinery and supplies for the Crooke's Mill to Lake City, and was one of the best known and most liked businessmen in the San Juans. In 1876 he had started a livery stable in Pueblo that quickly became a freight business. His very first connections in the San Juans were at Lake City, where by 1876 his father, mother, and sister lived. Most of the time, when moving freight to Lake City, Wood went south down the Front Range to La Veta and over the pass to Alamosa and then into Lake City via Slumgullion. In the spring of 1877, he started a "fast line" in a light wagon for passengers going to Lake City and Ouray. His route was quicker than taking the train to La Veta or Alamosa and then switching to stage coaches for the rest of the trip.[400] He thrived by quickly moving freight from the end of the railroad tracks to its final destination, mostly in the San Juans. In one day in 1881, his company hauled out 400,000 pounds of ore and moved in 100,000 pounds of supplies and equipment — a real feat when even the huge freight wagons usually carried less than two tons.

When Dave Wood moved his operations to Ft. Garland (Garland City), the *Silver World* reported that Garland City was now the terminus of the Denver and Rio Grande Railroad (D&RG) and that Wood had erected a large livery stable and feed stables there.

> *He will also carry passengers to and from that place to Lake City. From personal knowledge of him, we can recommend him to the public as a man worthy of their confidence and patronage.*[401]

Wood traveled over rough routes. After he followed the D&RG tracks to Alamosa he wrote:

> *From Alamosa we freighted to Silverton, Lake City, Ouray and other San Juan camps.... Without a road we had to cross rivers and small creeks where there seemed no bottom at all. Several times we had twenty yoke of oxen — forty head — on one wagon.*[402]

Duane Vandenbusche wrote:

Wood's name became a household word in Western Colorado in the 1880s. He had ample capital, large warehouses, the best wagons and drivers, the best stock, and was thoroughly dependable.[403]

Wood sold his Alamosa to Lake City oxen in 1878, but his mule-powered freight wagons continued on the route. Wood helped build the D&RG railroad over Marshall Pass in 1881, and then followed the railroad west. He still had plenty of Lake City business, hauling from Sapinero to Lake City, as well as from Montrose to Ouray and Telluride. *The Gunnison Daily Review* of January 1, 1883 wrote:

His trade has now become so extensive he is constantly filling orders for every mining camp in the great southwest.... [404]

Wood then changed much of his operation to hauling from Cañon City to Leadville. Wood continued to run freight and passengers from Gunnison to Lake City after this time, but wrote:

The trade to Lake City was not heavy. We handled mail and people by buckboard from Gunnison and freight by teams from Sapinero. Six sixes in two outfits (three teams) did most of the work. [405]

The Silver Panic of 1893 pretty well put Dave Wood out of business, as he held some major mining interests by that time.

By late 1877 the population of Lake City expanded to over 2,000, including the prospectors that were in and out of town.[406] The *Rocky*

Dave Wood's freight wagons carried plenty of advertising over what he called "The Magnolia Route." This eight horse team is hauling two of his freight wagons on level ground (probably in the San Luis Valley). (Denver Public Library Photo)

Mountain News reported that 1,000 houses were completed or under construction,[407] although this was probably a major exaggeration. To help entertain all these people, Kelly's Hall was built in April, 1877. It was very well furnished for a building in a new mining town, although it was basically one room with fine woodwork, a beautiful bar, and ornate mirrors. It even included a shooting gallery. Brockett's Hall was also dedicated in April 1877, with a ball and concert given to raise funds for the town's new band. It had dances and concerts, as well as many other uses. In June, 1878, the Lake City Beer Garden was opened about a half mile up Henson Creek. Its clients were reported to all be "high-class."[408] Besides tables and chairs, its outside furnishings included arbors, rustic walks, swings, and a bridge to an island in the creek behind the hall.[409] It served beer and provided music for dancing. Unfortunately, most of the premises were washed away by a flood of Henson Creek in the late 1880s.

William F. E. Gurley, who later became a prominent University of Chicago professor, was impressed with the quality of Lake City's merchants and prospectors as this time:

> *They were real men of sterling quality, belonging to that class which future generations will delight to honor as pathfinders, trailblazers, and empire builders. Oft indeed do I feel grateful that it was my good fortune to associate with such men during the formative years of my career.*[410]

People continued to pour into Lake City in the fall of 1877. As the *Silver World* confirmed in their year-end review of 1877:

> *In 1877 property advanced rapidly in value; lots for which on the first of December (1876) or January (1877) could not find purchasers at $250 or $300, on the 1st of March readily commanded $500 and $600. Buildings went up like magic, and arose on every hand. So great was the demand for lumber that the mills could not supply the demand, and the planing mill, although running night and day a large portion of the time, could not turn out dressed lumber as fast as it was required, while dry and seasoned lumber could scarcely be had at all. Active building continued until midsummer, and up to late fall was continued in but slightly diminished number.*
>
> *From actual count the number of buildings erected during the year was 136, costing $212,680. Many of these were costly structures, and nearly all were far more substantial in character than are generally erected in a new town.*
>
> *... The class of newcomers (was) far more superior to those who usually rush into frontier mining town, and especially a mining camp....*

During April, May, and June the roads leading into town were perfectly lined with newcomers, pedestrians with packs on their backs, or on burros and jacks, men on horseback and in wagons—a constant stream pouring into the San Juans through this metropolis. Of course the largest share of these newcomers were disappointed. They come with no adequate idea of the country, totally ignorant of the character of the mines or mining; in fact, comparably few were practical men, and the largest proportions were either adventurers or men who were masters of no trade, perhaps ready to do anything, but unable to or how to or in what channel to direct their energies. The exodus of this class of men was about as rapid and great as was their incoming. Meanwhile, businessmen, merchants, men of capital or worth, came in great numbers and stayed, and today Lake City can boast of the best class of citizens to be found in any town east or west. The legitimate population is fully 2,000; many good judges place it at 2,500. The number of buildings in town is over 500.

In just two years, Lake City had passed from a mining camp to a true town. More stone and brick commercial buildings were being built. The Ocean Wave Smelter was at the north end of town, where the

This photo was taken about 1877 or 1878, only about two years after the first cabin was built, and shows the large amount of growth in the town. (Photo from Tiny Hinsdale of the Silvery San Juan)

153

Country Store Grocery is today, and had eight connected buildings that contained the mill, offices, storage for coal and lime, assay offices, and a blacksmith's shop. It started operations October 12, 1877.[411] The stone Henry Finley building at the corner of 2nd and Silver was also built in 1877, and still stands — being used today as the Hinsdale County Museum.

The Lake City *Silver World* reported that immigration to the San Juans was beyond calculation or the expectations of those who had tried to get the original interest of the public. By 1877 guide books were being printed about how to get to and what to bring to the San Juans. *The San Juan Guide,* published for the Atchison, Topeka, and Santa Fe Railroad, and *William's Guide to the San Juans*, published for several railroads, are examples. Newspapers in Lake City, Pueblo, and Colorado Springs also published guides.[412] Telephone service even tried to come to Lake City in 1878 under the auspices of the San Juan Telephone Company. The company tried to sell stock in Lake City, but was laughed at, as even Denver did not get phone service until the fall of 1878. The system had to wait until 1881 and the Colorado Telephone Company.[413]

From the town's founding, most Lake City residents had a high appreciation for the arts. The local events included holiday celebrations, sports events, lectures, debates, theatrical presentations, and balls. Although there was always a conflict between the cultured and the rougher elements in town that preferred the saloons and brothels, the more refined citizens seemed to have always been a strong majority.[414]

John J. Crooke came to Lake City in 1876 and was among the leaders of early Lake City business and social society, as he was young, had money, and provided employment for many of the townspeople.[415] The Crooke family had twenty-five years' experience as metallurgists, except that smelting the San Juan ores would prove to be very different than those back East. They opened their concentrator in 1876, and it soon included a smelter, as most big mines soon had their own concentrators. Lake City became the early smelter center of San Juans. A lead based smelter came first at Crookes in the fall. The Crooke Smelter was about a mile south of Lake City, and its cloud of smoke usually hung above the city in the early photographs of the town.[416]

The Crooke brothers came from New York and had a smelter there. Early on, they entered into a very aggressive ore-buying program, which ate into the business of mills in other parts of the San Juans. One of their main acquisitions was in 1876, when they bought a good size interest in the North Star Mine on King Solomon Mountain near Silverton. Its ore was so rich in silver that it paid to bring it to Lake City for concentration and smelting. At first the ore had been sent to the Greene smelter in Silverton, as well as to the Crooke in Lake City; but it was only a year before all the North Star ore was going to Lake City. The Crooke Smelter runs of North Star ore assayed at 27,000 ounces of silver, 110 ounces of gold and 130 tons of lead in 1877 and 1878 alone. In 1879, the ore was reported at 150 to 240 ounces of silver per ton, as well as 50 to 60 percent lead. In 1877, it was learned that the Crookes had filed for mill sites on the upper Uncompahgre River at Mineral Point and at Boulder Gulch, just outside Silverton. The Crookes kept saying they were going to build a mill near Silverton, as well as one in Mineral Point, but they never did.[417]

John J. Crooke married Nellie Mendenhall, the daughter of another early Lake City pioneer.[418] John J. also represented a London firm for financial support of his many projects in the San Juans, and the Crookes eventually had a better concentrating mill and two smelters in Lake City, in which they processed the majority of the Lake City ores before 1884.[419] As an indication of just how important the Crookes were to Lake City's economy, production figures for Hinsdale County almost tripled in the first year after their mill was working.

The Crookes were one of the main forces behind Lake City's early prosperity and were major factors in the growth of the San Juans. They brought perhaps the most important single factor to hardrock mining — capital. They started their Colorado investments in Summitville in 1875. There the Crookes purchased the Little Annie and Golden Queen, which were very successful gold mines. This gave them the money needed to buy and develop Lake City mines and to build mills and smelters; but they soon chose to move to Lake City (although they kept their Summitville interests) because of its relatively easy access by wagons and the rich initial strikes in the area. In August, 1876, the Crookes purchased the Ute-Ulay, which proved to have plenty of ore, even though none of it was of bonanza quality; but it was close to their mill and smelter. In 1876 the Crookes had not yet finished their smelter, so the ore was being concentrated by them and sent to their smelter in New York for smelting. Still the Crookes managed a net profit of $12 per ton on their ore.[420]

On August 24, 1877, Enos Hotchkiss, Henry Finley, John Shaw, William Van Gieson, and William Lewman supposedly lost the Hotchkiss Mine in a foreclosure, with Robert Crooke taking full title to the mine; but a mechanics lien was filed for the same amount in September, 1877. Evidently the Crookes had advanced development money that was not paid back because of poor ore at the mine at the time, and the Crookes foreclosed on the other owners through a mechanics lien. This type of scenario happened several times at the mine. Owners would hit rich pockets, gear up for major development, and then the ore would play out, as it was not on a substantial vein. John J. Crooke supposedly offered a $50,000 reward to any miner who found the "mother lode" in the Hotchkiss Mine, but no one did until well after the Crookes were gone.[421] The Crookes became disenchanted with the mine and sold their interest.

The Crookes began getting quite a few customers from Mineral Point and Silverton, although it only paid to send the most high grade ore to their operation in Lake City. Josef Reef, who the Crookes knew from Summitville, even served as a resident agent for the Crookes in Silverton.[422] In 1877 Preston Nutter, later a U. S. Senator from Utah,[423] claimed he built a new trail from the Animas River that was meant to allow San Juan County ore to be brought to Lake City to be processed by the Crookes. The trail was up Maggie Gulch from the Animas, and then down Cottonwood Creek to Sherman.[424]

However Durango was to take over the San Juan smelter business in 1883 when the D&RG came to that town and more efficient smelters were constructed there at a lower altitude and with railroad transportation to the site from Silverton. The first copper smelter in the San Juans was "blown in" in Durango in November 1884. This was probably why the Crookes closed their operations and moved out of Lake City that same year.[425] When the Crookes closed their interests in the area in late 1884, production for Hinsdale County fell from $208,703 to $11,362 within a year.[426]

A small community called Crookesville soon grew around the Crooke's mill. In a few years the Crookes added a second smelter and chlorination works. Granite Falls provided cheap power, but the Crookes also built a road and imported coal from Crested Butte for their smelters. The Ute-Ulay gave the Crookes their steadiest supply of ore for their mill.[427] The Crooke Smelter and Mill complex burned to the ground in 1924.

The Van Gieson Lixiviation Works was on the south side of Henson Creek near the entry into town. It used a chemical leaching method, then roasted the ore, and used salt to wash out the precious metals. Their process did not work very well on the San Juan ores. The Van Gieson mill was abandoned in the late 1870s and burned in 1900.

John C. Bell was another pioneer of Lake City who came in 1876. He later wrote the book, *The Pilgrim and the Pioneer*, describing his adventures as a prospector and a prominent attorney in the San Juans (he prosecuted Alferd Packer in the "cannibal's" first trial). He later became a district judge in Montrose, Colorado, and a Colorado legislator.[428] Bell had gone to live and work in Saguache in 1874, after he heard the Utes were being moved out of most of the San Juans, and that Saguache was likely to boom. He knew that area had "native grass in great abundance, and had attracted many wealthy cattle and sheep men." He thought it might be a good place to set up his brand new law practice.

There were also many old and reliable Mexican families with large herds of sheep, and some attractive senoritas and senoras here, besides, a liberal number of pretty and bright American women in the valley. Many new buildings were being erected, and many business men were waiting for rooms in which to embark in some unrepresented lines of business. They were received with open arms by the old settlers who showed them the things of public interest, and gave their ideas of this place as the real gateway to the great San Juans.[429]

Bell and a friend found Otto Mears and three other men trying to draft a partnership agreement, with which they were having a lot of trouble. Bell drew up an agreement for them from his book of legal forms and quickly impressed the group. Mears immediately took Bell to the Saguache county commissioners, who appointed him the County attorney at a salary of $50 a month, which allowed Bell to stay in Saguache. About a year later, Bell reported the boom was over in Saguache and the excitement was in Lake City. When he traveled to the new boom town, he happened to meet Otto Mears, who at the time was doing wholesale business in Lake City, and Mears took him to the Hinsdale County commissioners, who gave Bell the Hinsdale County attorney's job for $1,000 a year.[430]

Besides the beautiful natural surroundings and several of the local rich mines, Bell was extremely impressed by Lake City's streets, "so level

The building that housed John Bell's law office is still standing across from the main Armory entrance. Bell himself poses before the house/law office. (Author's Collection)

and smooth that they would have made ideal race tracks."[431] Someone evidently had recently done a good job of fixing the streets. Bell also wrote:

Tents, cabins, and camps were on every side, and the streets were alive with all kinds of people—Americans, German, Hebrew, Irish, Cornish, Swede, Canadian, French, Italian, English, Negro, Chinese, Japanese, etc., and all tongues were spoken there.[432]

Bell left Lake City for Montrose in 1885, but he continued to own his Lake City cabin for many years afterwards. Bell's house and law office still stand across from the armory, occupied by Hinsdale Public Health and Community Services at the time of this writing.

John Hough came to Lake City in the 1870s and built the Hough Block on the northeast corner of Silver Street in 1880. His building is at the time of this writing owned and used by the Lake City Arts Council. Hough was a first cousin of Ulysses S. Grant; and he ran for governor of Colorado on the Democratic ticket, but was defeated by Frederick Pitkin. Hough was also a member of the Colorado Territorial legislature and was the Hinsdale County Judge for many years. He was a close friend of Kit Carson, and even shared a house in Boggsville with Carson and his family in Kit's later life. Hough inherited one or more of Kit Carson's beautiful buckskin shirts.[433] Lake City's Hough Fire Company was financed by him and he served as a mayor of Lake City. He did as much as anyone ever has for Lake City until his death in 1919.[434]

Lake City had few deaths until 1876, so it was not until that time that a cemetery was considered. The "City" or "Lower" Cemetery was started that year, next to present-day Highway 149 at the north end of town. Unfortunately graves were dug somewhat at random and many of them were only marked by crude wooden markers, if anything at all. Furthermore, no formal records of burials were kept and many paupers were buried in the lower cemetery. A large number of those buried were miners working in the area or members of their families. There are, however, sections of the cemetery designated for paupers, blacks, Catholics, Italians, and other ethnic groups. The first burial was in October, 1876, and the cemetery filled up very quickly. Grant Houston has estimated that at least 475 of the more than 700 people buried there are unknown. Today there is an effort underway to at least determine where all the graves are.

The "Upper" or "IOOF" Cemetery was started in 1877. The local lodge of the International Order of Odd Fellows started their cemetery with the first burial in April of 1877. Most of the "important" people of Lake City are buried there, many with elaborate headstones and iron fences surrounding family plots. The IOOF Cemetery was originally a private cemetery for the members of the lodge. It sits in a secluded spot on a hillside northwest of town. By 1900 members of other lodges could also be buried there; and, eventually, it became a public cemetery operated by Hinsdale County, which appointed a board in 1968 to take care of the cemetery.[435]

There were also many small cemeteries located outside Lake City in Hinsdale County. Before World War II, it was estimated that there were twenty-one graveyards in the county.[436] Some of the bodies in these cemeteries have been moved to other sites, some still lie in graves with only three or four others buried around them, and some are in cemeteries that cannot now be found. We will therefore never know the names of most of the deceased.

A decorative fence surrounds a family plot in the old Lake City Cemetery. Wrought iron stands up much better than the more usual wooden fence and wooden grave markers that were used. (Denver Public Library Photo X-54)

Besides the dangers of working in the mines, Lake City miners faced avalanche dangers that plagued the San Juans because of the steepness of the mountains and the considerable amount of snow. The first avalanche death was believed to have been at the Dolly Varden Mine in 1880. Henry C. Repath died trying to save two of his friends, whose names are not known. The next fatal slide was in January, 1916. Fred Davidson, Harry Youmans, and Otto Bowers were coming down the Nellie Creek road from a sawmill Youmans operated, when the group was swept to the bottom of the gulch by the slide. Bowers was only partially covered and managed to free himself and locate Youmans, whom he rescued. Davidson was ten feet under the snow and was dead when reached.

Perhaps the worst avalanche was at the Empire Chief Mine and Mill on a night in March, 1929. Everyone was sleeping when the slide roared down and almost covered the two-story bunkhouse. A one-story addition was completely covered. The night watchman was thrown out of the building, but was uninjured. The woman cook also escaped without injuries. Two men were dug out from ten feet of snow but survived after being buried for almost twelve hours. However, F. Wickersham, J. Color, Elmer Johnson, and Keith Cutting were killed. The Empire Chief was again hit by an avalanche eighty years later, shortly after being partially restored by the Bureau of Land Management and local contractor Native Son. It was badly damage, but no one was at the mine at the time. In February, 1932, the Independence slide "ran" at the mine of the same name, hitting and killing F. A. Walburg. The weather was so bad, the danger of more snow slides so high, and the snow so deep that Walburg's body was not found until May.

There were also plenty of fatal accidents that sent people to the cemetery. Many of Lake City's new arrivals were newcomers to mining or prospecting and did not realize the dangers of the occupation. One of the most hazardous problems was that drill bits left minute particles of hard rock in the air that stuck in the miners' lungs when they breathed, causing respiratory problems and possibly death within a few decades. The high altitude also caused bronchial problems. Pneumonia in the high altitude without today's antibiotics was almost always fatal, especially among the young and the old. Living conditions of the time spread diseases we do not hear about today, such as cholera, typhoid, and diphtheria; but these were dreaded, deadly diseases in the 1800s. Scurvy was also common due to a lack of Vitamin C in the winter when there were little or no vegetables and fruits available.

We know the cause of death of many Lake City's residents, many of them at a young age. Besides the diseases mentioned, there were events like childbirth that took a terrible toll. Many of the graves with stone markers show a young mother who died shortly before or after childbirth. Often their newborn child is buried beside them. Women worked hard during these times, sometimes literally working themselves to death or dying because they were forced to have too many children. Child mortality rates ran as high as fifty percent before children reached age ten. A close examination of Lake City's cemeteries will reveal all kinds of people, causes of death, and ages:

From 1874 ... to 1899, statistics provide an interesting look at causes of death. Pneumonia held the lead, followed closely by accidents—with almost two fatal mining accidents for every fatal non-mining accident. Children's diseases and tuberculosis shared third place. Fatalities from avalanches were next, although many of these deaths occurred on or near mine sites. Homicides, influenza, and drug overdoses were close together for fifth, sixth and seventh places. Old age related causes of death ranked quite low, but it must be remembered that frontier populations contained very few individuals more than fifty years old.[437]

Perhaps one of the most unusual and touching tombstones in the Lake City cemeteries is mentioned by Ken Reyher in his book *Through the Valley of the Shadow of Death*. The tombstone is located a short distance into the IOOF Cemetery. It was dedicated to all the children buried there and includes the entire poem, *Come Little Leaves*, written by George Cooper, who was a collaborator of Stephen Foster.

Come little leaves, said the wind one day
Come o'er the meadow with me to play
Put on your dresses of red and gold
For summer is gone and the days grow cold.

Soon the leaves heard the wind's loud call
Down they came fluttering, one and all
Over the brown fields they danced and flew
Singing the glad little songs they knew.

Cricket, good-bye, we've been friends so long
Little brook, sing us your farewell song
Say you are sorry to see us go
Ah, you will miss us, right well you know.

Dear little lambs in your fleecy fold
Mother will keep you from harm and cold
Fondly we watch you in vale and glade
Say, will you dream of our loving shade?

Dancing and whirling, the little leaves went
Winter had called them, and they were content
Soon, fast asleep in their earthy beds
The snow laid a covering over their heads.

Although they are not buried in Lake City, lore has it that Billy the Kid visited Lake City,[438] as well as Jesse James, Poker Alice, Bat Masterson, and Soapy Smith, although no authentication of such has been discovered except for Poker Alice. It is known that all of these people were in the San Juans and very possibly could have been in Lake City. Wyatt Earp was hired by a saloon in Silverton for a year and also was a faro dealer in Gunnison for the winter of 1882-83, so he very possibly could have visited Lake City.[439] It was rumored that Doc Holiday was with Wyatt during some of the time he was in Gunnison. Bat Masterson and Soapy Smith were in Creede during its boom in 1891, and at times were deputy marshals there. Generally such characters were not welcome, but all could have easily visited Lake City.[440]

This photograph is classic Poker Alice. As an older woman she traveled all over the West gambling, especially at poker. She smoked a cigar and carried at least one pistol at all times, but as a beautiful young woman she lived in Lake City, where she learned how to gamble. (Wikipedia Photo)

Poker Alice (Alice Ivers) did come to Lake City as a young woman, but she later spent more time in Creede. She was famous as an older woman for being a cigar smoking, pistol toting gambler, who killed at least one man. It was said she never sat at a gambling table without at least one gun on her person. She usually had a pistol in the pocket of her dress and another in her purse. Alice was an English girl raised in the American West. Frank Duffie won the attractive woman's hand in marriage and brought her to Lake City to live. Alice, bored of being "just a housewife," learned to play poker from her husband and some of his friends and started attending the local gambling halls. Soon she was dealing cards as a faro and blackjack dealer every night. Her husband was killed in a mining accident, and Alice became a traveling professional gambler and did well. People came to see her play because of her reputation as a winner.[441]

By July 1877 there were twenty-nine establishments that served liquor in Lake City and Crookesville. Some of these were very respectable and offered a high level of entertainment and socialization. Most of the owners of these establishments were highly respected citizens. At the other end of the spectrum were the bawdy houses.

Lake City did have a red light district that, of course, served liquor and was sometimes called "Hell's Acre." It was located at the far south end of Bluff Street. One sad incident that occurred there was the shooting of young Louis Estep, who hoped to marry one of the girls living in Hell's Acre. His girlfriend was in a fight with a man, drew a gun, and shot Estep by mistake. He died, and she was convicted of murder. While at the penitentiary, she caught pneumonia and came back to Lake

City to die. She requested a Christian burial from one of the town's ministers, but her friends were denied use of the church by one of the congregation's trustees. The service was still performed by the minister in another building. The trustee was later given a severe beating by two women who had previously lived in Hell's Acres.[442]

In an attempt to make sure the town remained quiet and peaceful, the town trustees hired four more marshals and built a new jail in 1877. One of Lake City's somewhat rare gunfights occurred on April 9, 1877, between Tom King and William Brock, who King had publically threatened to kill. The two met at the Third and Silver Street intersection and fired at each other from a distance of about eight feet. King's gun got stuck in his holster; and although he was hit first in the stomach, he soon returned fire and hit Brock in the groin and then in the arm and shoulder. Brock's gun jammed, and he ran from the scene. King died a week after the gunfight, and Brock was later acquitted of murder.[443] The winner of a gunfight like this was often acquitted by juries, and most of the time there was no trial at all. Even if a man was found guilty of murder, the sentence was usually light — six or eight years being about average and usually there was parole after just a year or two. Several other shootings occurred in the next few years, all arising from disagreements over election results. Most of the winners of these disputes were found not guilty.

Daily wagon service was coming to Lake City from Pueblo in 1877, bringing travelers and supplies.[444] Otto Mears' toll road over Cinnamon Pass was now so difficult, if not impassable, that Lake City merchants hired F.C. Garbutt and J.J. Abbott to direct the construction of The Henson Creek and Uncompahgre Toll Road. Unless travelers wished to pass through the Ute Indian Reservation to the west, and most did not, this wagon road was to be the only viable access to the outside world for Galena City and supposedly Ouray, but only in the summer. However the part of the new road from Mineral Point to Ouray was so difficult that the builders abandoned its construction in favor of travelers going to Silverton. On August 1, the road was finished to Mineral Point and a road already existed from there to Silverton. On August 10, 1877, nine businessmen from Lake City went across the narrow wagon road to celebrate its opening. They were well-received by a welcoming party in a local Silverton saloon. The establishment of this toll road was part of the reason for a boom in Galena City, soon after called Capitol City.[445] Since the Henson Creek Toll Road was passable by wagons, it meant that virtually all the ore along the Henson Creek route could come to Lake City.

William's Guide to the San Juan Mountains, a short book that was used by people wanting to come to the San Juans from the East, pointed out in 1877 that there were now several routes into the San Juans:

There is a connection with the Denver and Rio Grande Railroad (narrow gauge), which will land (the traveler) at Colorado Springs, Cañon City, or La Veta, at either of which points an outfit can be procured for the trip to the San Juan, or Barlow and Sanderson's great line of six-horse coaches will take him whirling through Del Norte, and thence to Lake City; time from La Veta to Del Norte, in the summer, fifteen hours, from Cañon City to Del Norte, twenty-five hours; from Del Norte to Lake City, stopping overnight, thirty-six hours. The route via Cañon City is practically discontinued by reason of the extension of the D&RG beyond La Veta to Wagon Creek (nine miles east of Ft. Garland).... If desired, outfits can be acquired in either Del Norte or Lake City.

For prospecting, a very simple outfit is needed: pick and hammer, provisions and blankets, packed up to patient burro or upon the back of the owner. Don't invest in rifles, carbines, or revolvers, for they are so seldom needed.[446]

Lake City for a few years was now the main mail route to Gunnison and its mines, and in June 1880, Otto Mears added a road from Powderhorn to the new town and the mines in and around Crested Butte. Mears' employees were taking three days in the year 1877 to get the mail from

An early view shows how the Henson Creek Toll Road was narrow and rough — so narrow that two wagons could not pass each other in most places. (Author's Collection)

Lake City to Silverton,[447] but that was in the winter through deep snows and over Cinnamon Pass. Still the people in Baker's Park complained that their mail should come over Stony Pass, which was a much rougher route. In 1877 Mears decided to open a store in Ouray, besides the stores he had in Saguache, Del Norte, and Lake City. *The Saguache Chronicle* wrote:

> *Mears is now in Lake City, and we wouldn't be surprised to hear he had bought the town and moved it to Ouray.*[448]

By July 4, 1877, the local lodges had expanded Lake City's Fourth of July celebration into dances, parades, games, races, and community picnics. There was also a concert by the town band and a reading of

A woodcut from Tiny Hinsdale of the Silvery San Juan shows the toll gate to the Henson Creek Toll Road after it was opened in 1877. The toll gate was almost in the city limits and right next to Hell's Acres, which probably bothered more than a few women of the day who rode the stage or went on horseback up the road. (From Tiny Hinsdale of the Silvery San Juan)

the Declaration of Independence (which could not be done in 1875, as no one could find a copy). A big dance was held at the armory and lasted until the next morning. Most of the early celebrations would have mining and packing contests. There were also celebrations at Lake San Cristobal, with boating, singing, croquet, and, of course, alcohol and food. For years afterwards, the day was usually started with a keg of black powder, a case of dynamite or a string of dynamite sticks being set off at day break.[449] No one seemed to object that some of the windows in town were broken by the blasts. There were also some citizens who brought fireworks. Later Fourth of July celebrations included torchlight parades, shooting matches, firing of cannons at dawn, and a parade by the Pitkin Guards in 1884.

Drilling contests on the Fourth were usually held in the years when mining was important to Lake City. A huge boulder of granite was set up and men raced to see who got their drill to a certain depth using both single-jacking and double jacking. One of these boulders still resides in Lake City's Town Park, although this particular boulder was drilled by an air drill in a later contest. In the early celebrations:

Any miner who cared to compete brought his big hammer and drills into town, and in the main square was set up a big rock, usually granite, for the harder the rock the better. There was a time limit for drilling; there were judges, and a crowd. Big muscles worked hard and fast for the cash....[450]

An actual library building and reading room was opened in Lake City in April, 1877. Besides books, all the major Colorado papers and many Eastern papers were received. Stationery and desks for writing were also available for the miners. The *Silver World* felt it was "a great moral and intellectual aid to this area." Denver's *Rocky Mountain News* wrote that "the miners' free reading room and library at Lake City is a great success."[451] A miners' library in a San Juan mining town was quite unique and gives insight into the type of culture of the town. Many miners were laid off in the winter because ore could not be

In this photo a hard rock drilling contest was being held on Silver Street in 1897. The object was for teams to get the furthest into the rock (usually granite) in a certain amount of time. Such a rock is still in the City Park by the restrooms. These contests usually had big money prizes for the winner — a month's pay or more. (From Tiny Hinsdale of the Silvery San Juan)

shipped from their mine. A great number of them left the mountains for the winter, but many stayed, doing odd jobs in Lake City to make a living.

The library was not just meant for the miners:

The people who were responsible for the stable life of (Lake City) were adamant in their desire to establish a cultural and intellectual atmosphere for the young people. Their efforts resulted in a social pattern which has endured. The early residents of Lake City were interested in improvement through education. They appreciated art, music, and literature. The children of the families who settled there were not denied an educational foundation. Today, descendants from those pioneers, and some who have known no other home, engage in the same cultural pastimes of reading, studying, writing, and listening to music.[452]

Several large frame residences and new commercial buildings were included in the 136 new buildings built in the town in 1877. The new courthouse (which still stands) was completed in June 1877 at a cost of $4,450. The courthouse looked basically the same as it does today, with five offices on the first floor, and two offices for the judge and court clerk and a large courtroom on the second floor.

Almost any type of food could be found in Lake City by 1877. Lake City stores offered fresh eggs, butter, and garden vegetables obtained from locals or shipped in from Saguache. White flour came from Denver. Exotic foods like canned oysters and caviar were also available. However the altitude played havoc with some of the newcomers' recipes.[453]

On September 20, 1877, Susan B. Anthony came to town on horseback to speak at Lake City's Hinsdale Courthouse, but so many people turned out for the woman suffragette that the meeting had to be moved outdoors. Her speech on woman suffrage went well, but afterwards a vote was taken of those present and only 322 out of 893 thought it a good idea to let a woman vote. In spite of the vote, her talk was so well received that she was invited back the following day after she had to cancel a trip to Ouray. The *Rocky Mountain News* reported that:

Miss Anthony was here (in Lake City) last Thursday and Friday evenings (September 20 and 21). The first evening she addressed the largest audience that ever assembled in the San Juan country. The Court House would not hold half the people so the meeting was adjourned to the outside. There is a strong feeling here in favor of the movement, and it would not be much surprised if Hinsdale County should give a majority in favor of Women's Suffrage.[454]

John Bell was extremely impressed by Anthony and wrote many pages in his book, *The Pilgrim and the Pioneer* about "a remarkable speech in behalf of democracy and in behalf of the equal and natural rights of the sexes."[455]

When she had finished, an acre of bronzed-face miners sent up a shout of applause and said, "You are quite right, my good lady; we shall stand behind you until full justice is done to your sex in Colorado." And they kept their word.[456]

Susan B. Anthony spoke in front of the Hinsdale County Courthouse in 1879 to hundreds of interested miners. She had to come outside as there was not room for even half the crowd inside. (Drawing from John Bell's, *The Pilgrim and the Pioneer*.)

"The Duel" from Bell's book shows the duel at Henson Creek Canyon, so that is evidently where the duel took place. It was right at the edge of town near the Henson Creek toll road booth, where Doc Kaye was supposed to have run and hid right after the duel. (From The Pilgrim and the Pioneer)

In 1877 the U.S. Land Office was established at Lake City. This brought even more people to town to file their location certificates or to apply for their mine's patent, which gave them full title to the land. The next closest office at that time was at the far southern end of the San Juans at Animas City (later a part of Durango). The Lake City land office was moved to Montrose in 1883.[457] David A. Hoffman, the first doctor, came to Lake City in 1877.

Lake City continued to have crime, although not nearly as much as most early Colorado mining towns. In September of 1877,[458] Lake City was the site of a very unusual and amusing duel that was actually a hoax, but there are several versions of what happened. "Doc" Kaye supposedly insulted a man known as the "Tailor." William Harbottle wrote that a man by the name of Taylor (not the same as the Tailor) provoked the fight between the two.[459] They decided to settle their differences with shotguns. Doc, a small man, fortified himself with whiskey, while the Tailor seemed much calmer. The duel was reported to have been held a short distance up Henson Creek, or in Deadman's Gulch, or at "Charlie Allaire's cabin." Taylor evidently controlled the duel. The two men stepped off their agreed distance and fired on each other at almost point blank range. Doc's shot struck the Tailor, while the Tailor's shot went into the air, and he fell to the ground with a red stain spreading in the snow. Kaye was so upset that he ran to the nearby tollgate at Henson Creek and jumped into a pool of water. Or, according to another account, he got on a horse and escaped into the woods. But later, to Doc's amazement, the Tailor appeared unhurt. Everybody but Doc knew that the shotguns were loaded with blanks and the red stain was ink. The two men apologized to each other and became friends.[460] John Bell writes, although perhaps his account is fictionalized, that he was the other party in the duel against Doc, that Bell did not know the shotguns were loaded with blanks, and that the undersheriff of Hinsdale County provoked the fight by telling Doc that Bell as county attorney was going to disallow some of Doc's bills for treating indigents.[461]

Some very real violence occurred at this time in and around Lake City. For example, "Oregon Bill" Speck settled on a farm near Lake City. When he had an accident and had to go to Lake City to the doctor, he was kept in bed for some time. While he was gone, a Frenchman named Derocia jumped his homestead. Oregon Bill killed Derocia, fled Lake City, and eventually went to Saguache; but the Lake City Justice of the Peace had issued an arrest warrant for Oregon Bill, and it was soon discovered where he was. A deputy brought him back. Bill was afraid he might be lynched, but the charges against him were dropped, since it was said that Lake City had no use for claim jumpers.

Some very dubious claims of self-defense or being intoxicated were often accepted at face value in the Lake City courtroom. There seemed to be no rationale to the punishment given in those days throughout the West. As Betsy Wallace put it in her book, *History with the Hide Off*:

> *One of the most striking things about pioneer lawlessness was the infrequency of punishment.*[462]

On one occasion, a young man killed a man named Davis in a cabin not far from Lake City. The young man had a small .32 caliber revolver, and Davis was teasing him to not pull the gun unless he intended to shoot. On the day of the shooting, Davis had been teasing the boy unmercifully, and the two men got into a fight. Then Davis hit the boy in the head with an axe handle and the boy shot Davis through the eye, killing him instantly.[463] As in most cases in early mining areas, the boy was acquitted of murder or any other of the lesser included crimes.

In October 1877 the Ocean Wave Smelter turned out its first bullion — about 5 tons worth. The Crookes Smelter was operating at this time and shipped 300 tons of concentrates worth $48,000 during 1877, yet its slag dump was later twice reworked at a profit, meaning its recovery of precious metals from the ore in the early days of the Hinsdale mills was not very good. The generally low value of Hinsdale ore made concentrating plants necessary at the bigger mines; and unless this was done, many of the mines could not make a profit because of high transportation costs. However if the concentrating mill was not efficient enough to capture at least 60 or 70 percent of the precious minerals, then the process was usually not used because of the loss of so much precious metals.

The Van Geison Lixiviation Works was reported to have sent out $35,000 in silver in just the fall of 1877. Their silver product ranged from .850 to .952 purity.[464] Lake City's population continued to grow throughout 1877 and reached its historical peak about November, 1877, when there were supposedly 3,000 people living in the town, and it was reported that there were over 500 houses. It was during the winter of 1877-1878 that Lake City's first big boom started to wane. Those who had come expecting quick riches were beginning to leave. The *Silver World* pointed out that:

> They had come with no knowledge of the country, mines or mining, and most had no special skills. The exodus was as great as their coming, and as rapid.[465]

Also, new routes were opening into the San Juans, and Lake City's role as a supply town for the prospectors was slipping. Even though its population dropped a little in 1878, the town was still taking on a more permanent nature. Rev. Darley noted that:

> Among the men who came to the camp were many who had been taught in fine eastern homes, or by pious parents, that man's chief and highest end is to glorify God and fully enjoy him forever.[466]

The downturn in the Lake City economy was unfortunately a cycle that would repeat itself several times during the next few decades. This cyclical nature was brought on in great part by the discovery of rich pockets of ore in the local mines that later proved to be limited in quantity. The area contained large deposits of low grade ore, but most of the ore was simply not worth shipping. The population of the town began to dwindle, and a few of the marginal businesses closed. Helped along by the embezzlement of some of its deposits, the First National Bank of Lake City closed. This closure hindered further investments of capital in the city and the county's mines. It did help, however, the other two banks located in the town, Lake City Bank and Miners and Merchant's Bank, with Lake City Bank absorbed into the Miners and Merchants Bank in order to continue operation.

The 1878 State Business Directory confirmed Lake City's 1878 population at 3,000. One of the reasons Lake City had initially grown so fast was it contained many specialty businesses that could not make a go of it in a small camp. This included banks, smelters, assayers, sawmills, etc. The larger towns could also tax their residents and support schools, law enforcement, roads, and, later on, water and sewer systems.[467] In 1880 Del Norte had the largest population in the San Juans and Lake City was next, followed by Silverton.[468]

In 1878 Hinsdale County still held the distinction of being the top producing county in the San Juans. This was due in part to the statistics being for silver, gold, and other metals shipped out of the area, and many San Juan mines outside Hinsdale County were shipping much of their ore to Lake City to first to be concentrated, milled, or smelted by the Crookes and others before shipment. Transportation costs ate up the potential profit of all but the very richest mines, and even those had no desire to give most of the value of their ore to freighters. Most of the San Juan mines seemed to be stockpiling their ore until their area had better mills and smelters or a railroad for cheap transportation. The end of the first boom came when it was realized that the area was a long way from almost everywhere and could only be reached over steep and dangerous trails and roads. However, there was talk of a railroad coming to the San Juans, and Lake City's citizens assumed any railroad coming to the San Juans would first build into Hinsdale County.

Inefficient recovery and high transportation costs eventually closed all the Lake City mills and smelters — Van Geison in 1879, Crooke in 1883, and Ocean Wave in 1891. The first boom also became a bust because newer and bigger booms were occurring in the Gunnison, Leadville, and Summit Districts.[469] In 1878 it was already clear that many Lake City businesses were not making it and, at the same time, the population was not only *not* growing, but was starting to decline. Some businesses closed, others were absorbed by competitors.

However there were some positive developments. The Hotchkiss Mine discovered several new gold veins that seemed to be valuable; and the Golden Fleece Lode was located November 3, 1879 (although the mine continued to be called the Hotchkiss for a few more years). The mine took that name in the 1880s when it was realized just how valuable the new vein was. The Golden Wonder was also producing some good gold.

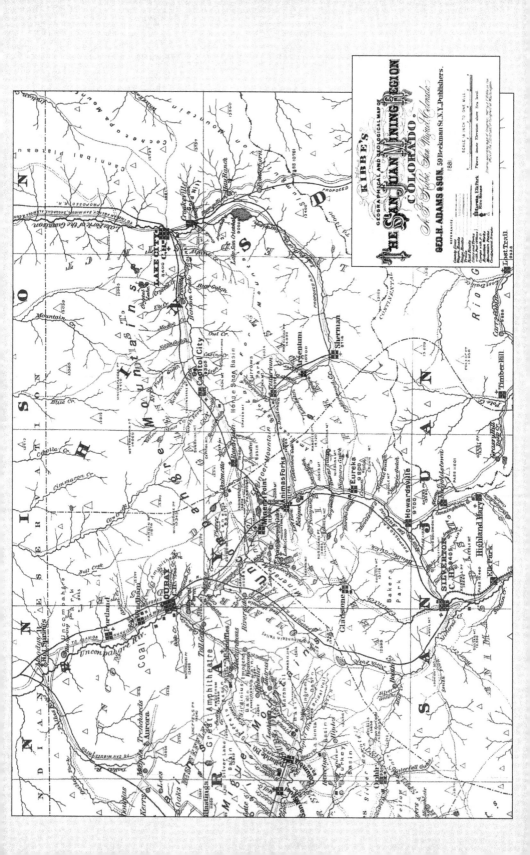

CHAPTER 5

The Boom and Bust Cycles

Eventually there were three major boom and bust cycles in Lake City's history, as well as several smaller ones. The first boom, described in Chapter 4, was from 1875 to 1878, the second boom from 1880 to 1882, and the third from 1889 to 1903. In between these dates were the bust cycles. After 19035, Lake City slowly slipped into almost three-quarters of a century of depression, not starting to rebound until the 1970s.

Hall blamed the bust at the end of 1878 and beginning of 1879 on:

a lack of market for ores, inexperience of the miners, the great cost of supplies, the distance from the great centers, and general inaccessibility began to undermine the courage and endurance of the people…. To crown the disaster on the 8th of November, 1879, a destructive fire occurred which swept away the better part of the business center of Lake City.[470]

Fossett put it a little more gingerly:

For some time (Lake City) has been the most populous place in the San Juan country, although Silverton is gaining somewhat at present (1879). This place grew rapidly in 1876-7 following the development of many silver veins…. The situation is wild and romantic, beside the Lake Fork of the Gunnison and Henson Creek and surrounded by lofty mountains.[471]

(Preceding page) This segment from Kibbe's Geographical and Geological Map of the San Juan Mining Region Colorado—1881 does a good job of showing the many small towns and roads in the San Juan Triangle Region of the San Juans. It is extraordinarily detailed considering it covered land that was Ute Indian land just a few years earlier. (Author's Collection)

The Rocky Mountain News of June 22, 1879, blamed the slump in Lake City in 1879 on "too little money available, weak faith, and apathy."

The year 1880 would mark the beginning of the second big, but short, boom for Lake City, as mines expanded into places like Palmetto Gulch and Capitol City. The Golden Wonder Mine, near Deadman's Gulch, was the most talked about mine during this time. It further seemed very likely that a railroad would soon be in Lake City to help transport the lower grade ores to the Front Range smelters, but the second boom ended abruptly near the beginning of 1882, when the D&RG announced it would not complete the branch line it had already started from Sapinero to Lake City. Instead the D&RG was building into Crested Butte, Gunnison, and west through the Black Canyon.

It also was soon learned that the D&RG would turn south in the San Luis Valley rather than continuing west to Lake City. The D&RG Railroad made plans for a great loop to the south, then west to a new town that would be called Durango, then north to the San Juan mining town of Silverton. This decision may have been made since Silverton is approximately in the center of the San Juans. However this meant that the low grade ores predominant in the Lake City area could not be economically shipped and the amount of ores shipped to Lake City's smelters from other parts of the San Juans greatly decreased. Silverton was now the "Gateway to the San Juans."

Almost as a harbinger of things to come, the oldest cabin in Lake City, which was only five years old, fell into disrepair and was destroyed by vandals in the fall of 1879. This was followed by a series of disastrous fires.[472]

Fire was a constant danger in all the new Colorado mining towns, as most buildings were made of wood and only primitive efforts were available to fight a fire. In addition to the Lake City mining bust, Lake City had a number of large, disastrous fires in its business district, which resulted in the town being in "more or less in constant turmoil from being rebuilt."[473] Fire after fire swept the business district. The first city jail, located at the corner of Third and Henson Streets, had burned in 1876, but there was no fire department at the time. Evidently the fire in the jail was started by an incarcerated and very drunk prisoner, Kit Carter, who was smoking. His charred body was found later in the ruins.

The first Lake City volunteer fire department was organized in 1877 and soon contained seventy-five members. When the volunteers fought their first Lake City fire at the Bon Ton Saloon on October 18, 1877, it was obvious they were disorganized and poorly trained. To deal with fires, Lake City's inhabitants had bought a hook and ladder truck. This was a wagon frame that was light and long and had ladders, rows of buckets, and long poles with hooks on one end for pulling down burning lumber. A hook and ladder wagon was purchased for $975. Firemen pulled the wagon and a hose cart by hand to the fires, because there was no time to harness a team of horses.[474]

When the volunteer fire department was formed in 1877, a system of ditches was proposed to supply water, and the Presbyterian Church bell was used for a fire alarm. The Lake City fire company had been supplied with fancy uniforms, helmets, and belts, but unfortunately received little training. As a result of the Bon Ton Saloon's total loss, a night watchman, whose job was simply to look for fires and sound the alarm, was hired by Lake City merchants.

On November 14, 1879, the first really disastrous fire swept through the heart of the town's commercial area. Many of the best businesses in Lake City (a good portion of one block of Silver and Third Streets) were reduced to ashes. Over a million dollars in damage was supposedly done to buildings and merchandise by the fire that had spread quickly through the night. The firemen who fought the fire badly mishandled the affair, and the event brought about the formation of a formal fire department. One great problem with the big 1879 fire was that the fire bell (reportedly a large triangle at that time) had broken during a celebration the previous spring and no one had it fixed. Still, Lake City

The June 15, 1901 fire burned a good part of the west side of Silver Street, even though the efficient Hough Fire Company responded. (Colorado Historical Society Photo)

rebuilt quickly after its fires and in many instances rebuilt with brick, stone, or firewalls between buildings.

Yet another fire destroyed buildings on Silver Street, including the Occidental Hotel located between Third and Fourth Streets. In addition, the buildings on Third Street, between Silver and Gunnison, were all totally gone. Many of Lake City's finest stores and quite a few saloons were destroyed. Yet another fire burned the Crystal Palace on Bluff Street. The county (as opposed to the city) jail was also completely burned to the ground in 1950. Like most jails in the San Juans at the time, the second story of the building contained the sheriff's apartment. He escaped by jumping from a second story window. Fortunately there were no prisoners in the jail at the time. The last big fire was when the Occidental Hotel burned yet again between 3rd and 4th Streets on Silver Street. Because of all the early fires, these blocks now only hold the Stone Bank Block, the Hough Block, and five or six original wood structures. Several of the pioneer log homes still stand in Lake City, but most are covered with siding and incorporated into a house or are now used as garages or out buildings.

Almost as disastrous as the physical damage done to the buildings, was that many of the commercial buildings held supplies that burned that had been shipped in before the winter snows and were being kept in storage for use at the surrounding mines and mining camps. It was very hard to get freight into Lake City for three to four months during the winter. Although the people of the town and the surrounding areas made it through the winter after the fires, there were some pretty tough times for many people before new supplies could be brought in.

Then to make matters even worse, although the Utes had ceded the San Juans in 1874, many Utes either did not approve of the action or did not really understand the terms of the agreement. More than anything else they realized that the United States was trying to change their nomadic way of life and make them settle in one place and become farmers and ranchers. In late September of 1879, this tension broke into outright hostility with the Meeker Massacre, in which northern Utes massacred agent Nathan Meeker and all eight male employees at the Ute agency. Three women at the agency were taken hostage. The final straw for the Utes had been when Meeker plowed up their horseracing track (the Utes' favorite pastime was horseracing) to plant vegetables. Then on September 29, 1879, the Utes attacked a U. S. cavalry rescue party led by Major Thomas Thornburg and killed thirteen soldiers, including Thornburg, with forty-three more being wounded. Thirty-seven Utes were killed in the confrontation that was called by Colorado newspapers "The Milk Creek Massacre." To its credit the U. S. government did consider Milk Creek to be a military engagement that it lost. [475]

The Utes massacred the white employees at the Meeker Agency, and then attacked the U. S. Cavalry unit coming to the rescue. No one felt safe in Colorado after that, until they knew that the Utes had been removed to an agency outside of Colorado. (Colorado Historical Society F873)

General panic from fear of a full-scale Ute uprising quickly spread throughout all of western Colorado. Chief Ouray took charge of the situation, and a delegation under Agent Charles Adams[476] was sent to the agency to try to obtain the release of the three white women. He was successful, and the women were taken to the Los Piños II agency near today's Colona. Although there was no longer a threat from the Utes, it did not help matters that at this time Colorado Governor Pitkin sent a telegram message throughout Colorado that read:

Indians off the reservation, seeking to destroy your settlements by fire, are game to be hunted and destroyed like wild beasts.... General Hatch rushing regulars to the San Juans.[477]

Rumors quickly spread around Colorado that the Ute Indians were burning and killing everywhere, and that Ouray was not able to control the Utes, although Ouray in actuality had complete control of his people, including those in the north.

The Americans in Lake City, as everywhere else in Colorado, had always been somewhat concerned about a Ute attack. One of the biggest buildings at Crookes Mill and Smelter was arranged to double as a fort in case of Indian attack.[478] When the news first came about the Meeker Massacre, all of the women and children in Lake City and its vicinity were taken to a mine on Henson Creek (probably the Ute), where they were guarded underground. The men in town armed themselves, retired to Crookes mill and smelter, and sent out scouts to warn them of approaching Utes. The event spread mass hysteria throughout Western Colorado. Marauding Utes were supposedly seen behind every tree and rock. Untrue rumors spread that some San Juan towns had been attacked and burned to the ground.

Lake City was no exception to the overwhelming fear and panic of a Ute attack. A rumor spread that Ute Chief Colorow (a large 300 pound Ute known for his aggressiveness) and his band of northern Utes had Lake City surrounded, and they were going to attack the town at any minute as part of a general Ute uprising throughout Colorado.[479]

The U. S. military tried to help with the crisis and moved many of the troops from Ft. Garland in the San Luis Valley over to the Western Slope; but this seemed to only increase the public feeling that an attack was imminent. About two dozen soldiers camped near Lake San Cristobal for two weeks (Nora Smith relates that they camped in Wock's Gulch) in order to be quickly available in case of an attack on Lake City.

While Lake City's citizens rushed to defend themselves, the Utes had actually taken no other hostile action after the massacre. They themselves were just as afraid that the whites would take the opportunity to kill them all. Since Lake City had been basically defenseless, the town's citizens had formed the Pitkin Guards in 1878; its own State Militia, Company A, Second Regiment, named for the first Governor of Colorado, Frederick W. Pitkin. The town further built a brick armory several months before the uprising for the protection of its citizens and for the Guards to have somewhere to store their equipment.

The Wrights state that the Pitkin Guards was formed at the time of the Ute unrest with a total of thirty-eight men, and was Company C, 1st Regiment of the Colorado National Guard. The Pitkin Guards never fired a shot for any reason other than target practice. The *Silver World* called Chief Ouray "devilishly sly" but also called him "a diplomat, one of the brightest of the age."[480] In May, 1879, the Guards were reorganized with new membership and new arms and ammunition (Springfield black powder rifles with removable bayonets).[481] The Pitkin Guards remained organized for many decades afterwards. They bought beautiful uniforms (received just before Christmas 1881), formed a drum and bugle corps and a brass band, and constructed a rifle range with a club house, so they could practice their shooting. The Guards performed for the citizens of Lake City often, and their best riflemen were sent to Denver each year for a state competition. The Guards members appeared in parades and also marched and played their instruments on the streets for the enjoyment of the town's citizens. The band would sometimes play concerts for the general public. The Wrights recorded that, after their drills, members of the Guards would sometimes go to the armory in their uniforms and have contests with the public at the roller skating rink that had been established there. The Pitkin Guards were a major force in Lake City social life and the armory still stands today.[482]

John C. Bell was a member of the Pitkin Guards and very proud of it. He said that when first formed, the company met nightly for drills. He wrote that when the Meeker Massacre occurred Governor Pitkin sent a telegram to the Guards stating "Bring in, dead or alive, all hostile Indians found off the reservation." Some men questioned how they would tell if an Indian off the reservation was hostile. They were told to consider all Indians off the reservation as hostile.[483]

The cry was now raised throughout Colorado that "The Utes Must Go!" *The Silver World* and many other Colorado newspapers carried this headline, and the *Silver World* added that "An Indian War is Certain." The article read in part:

> *There is no safety in Colorado until the Utes are removed from its borders, until the management of the Utes is in charge of the War Department, and until a cordon of military posts is put around the Indian country.*

Otto Mears was on the U.S. commission that forced a treaty upon the Utes that provided that they would be moved to the Grand Junction area; but the treaty also contained a provision that if sufficient farm and ranch land was not found there, the new Ute reservation could be moved to another place. Unbelievably, the commission found the Grand Junction area non-fertile, even though it later became the fruit capital of Colorado, and the commission moved the Utes onto totally barren land in Utah. This action opened up the rest of the Western Slope of Colorado to American homesteaders. Mears lied and mistreated the Utes so much during this time that they started a plot to kill him, so he

"The Utes Must Go! became the battle cry of every newspaper throughout Colorado. This paper even included a cartoon of a soldier chasing a scared Ute. (Author's Collection)

The Utes Must Go.

But don't forget to patronize the Pioneer Grocery of Colorado.
WOLFE LONDONER.

resigned from the commission and no longer had anything to do with the Utes.[484]

Jack Nichols writes:

Many historians point to the Ute displacement as one of the most abysmal example of lack of good faith extended by the government to Native Americans. Colorado Governor Frederick Pitkin said, "My idea is that unless removed by the government, they must be exterminated."[485]

As a result of the many fires that were occurring in early Lake City and the lack of firefighting organization and skills, the John S. Hough Fire Company was organized by John Hough on March 6, 1882. As mentioned earlier, John S. Hough had constructed a beautiful building in the town, known as the Hough Block; and was the owner of the Frank Hough Mine (Frank was John's son), located slightly below the top of Engineer Pass. The mine brought him considerable money, although he was wealthy before he came to Lake City. Hough's company contained only twenty-three men, but they were very organized, well-trained, and were equipped with the best equipment available — three force pumps, 600 feet of hose, a hook and ladder wagon, and six portable

The John S. Hough Fire Company was organized by Hough in March 1882 to replace the original inefficient Lake City fire company. In 1893 Hough Fire Company #2 was also formed. (Author's Collection)

"Babcock" fire extinguishers. Hough also donated a 300-pound bell and a large hose reel to the town.[486] Like the Pitkin Guards, the Hough Fire Company became a social organization, but they also continued to have a very useful purpose. Socially, the fireman's Masquerade Ball became "the event" of the winter season.[487] The new hook and ladder wagon had leather buckets for carrying water, which wouldn't get hot like a metal bucket. In 1911, a cart with chemical extinguisher tanks was also purchased. The Hough Fire Company disbanded about 1940.

Eben Olcott, a mining engineer whose Lake City's letters to his wife are printed in Duane Smith's book *San Juan Gold*, came to live in Lake City and Silverton at the request of the Crookes from late 1879 to early 1881. The Ute-Ulay Mine was owned by the Crookes at the time, and Eben particularly liked the mine and felt that after further development the Ute-Ulay would pay a twenty percent dividend annually to its shareholders for many years to come. He also liked Lake City the best of the San Juan towns, and he noted that Lake City's American House advertised that "no pain will be spared to make its patrons comfortable," and that the advertisement truly described its first class service. He attended the Presbyterian Church regularly, but if it was not holding a service, then he went to the Episcopal Church and was thankful for its presence. He noted that the Crookes still owned the Little Annie in Summitville at the time, and that it was one of the best developed mines in the San Juans. The Crookes had bought several other good San Juan mines before building their ten-stamp mill in Lake City. Olcott noted that Summitville had become the first mining district in the San Juans to produce over a million dollars in ore.[488]

Mining was good enough in the Lake City area by 1880 that the Lake City *Mining Register* began publication on May 21, 1880. The paper seriously challenged the *Silver World*, and lasted well into the bust cycle in 1885. The purpose of the newspaper was:

> ... the development of the mining interests of the San Juan and the business interests of this city and county.

The Ocean Wave Mill was still running, but the ore from the mine was disappointing. Rich ore was discovered in the Hotchkiss Mine during the winter of 1879-1880, but the discovery was kept a secret from the general population until a sale was made to Louis Weinberg, which gave him more time to file on or buy adjoining claims. Unfortunately, the discovery of rich ore in Hinsdale County had barely gotten started when the huge Leadville rush began. Leadville drew tens of thousands of men like moths to a flame, including most of the prospectors in Hinsdale County.

Numerous photos of Lake City were taken in the years 1880 to 1883 and all show the plume of smoke coming from the Crooke Mill and Smelters and filling the valley in the background. It was a sign of prosperity and a growing community. Lake City was at its peak when this photo was taken in 1882. The Hinsdale Courthouse is left center, the Occidental below and a little right, the Hough and Bank Blocks at the intersection of 3rd Ave. and Silver Street. Note how many commercial buildings were on Gunnison and where the city park is now. Crookesville was under the plume of smoke and Van Geison's Lixiviation Works, at right center on Henson Creek was not working. (Colorado Historical Society, X7673)

A telegraph line was established to Lake City on November 4, 1879. The first message sent out was to the Governor, who responded. By October, 1881, there was also an operational telephone line to Lake City, which was extended to Capitol City.

Even with the amazing Leadville boom occurring, Hinsdale County mining picked up again in 1880, and the town began its second big boom. The Ute-Ulay Mine was at its peak production under the Crookes, and the mining camps of Sherman, Burrows Park, and Capitol City were now established. Lake City was the service center for a very large area. That year the Crookes' smelters and mills were running full blast, and the Crookes were especially looking forward to a railroad coming to Lake City, so they could bring in coal from Crested Butte by rail instead of by wagon. The same was true for the Ocean Wave. The Golden Wonder, near the Packer massacre site, was producing very high grade gold ore, and Lake City's population was back to over 2,000 people.

Frank Fossett, in his book *Colorado, Its Gold and Silver Mines, 1879,* wrote:

Hinsdale County is the most easterly of the important silver districts in the San Juans. Its metropolis is Lake City dating from 1874-75 located at the junction of Henson Creek and Lake Fork of the Gunnison.... There are numerous silver lodes in the lofty mountains that rise almost perpendicularly for a half mile on every side—many of them worked extensively.... The site is decidedly romantic, surrounded as it is by stupendous mountains.... From a mere cluster of cabins in 1875 it has grown into a thriving busy center of from 1,500 to 2,000 population, its mills and reduction works comprising the most extensive system of mining machinery in all the San Juan country. It has churches of almost every denomination, three or four hotels, good schools, several banks, five saw mills, a free reading room and library, two excellent and energetic newspapers, and other evidence too numerous to mention of substantial and lasting prosperity.[489]

As optimistic as Fossett sounded, the official 1880 census reported only 1,487 persons living in the entire county, probably because the census was taken in the winter and many of the summer people had left for lower elevations. Also, as mentioned, the fall and winter of 1879-1880 was full of rumors of a Ute uprising, and quite a few people left the area as a result. But once again, new discoveries were made in Palmetto Gulch near the top of Engineer Pass, as well as around Capitol City. The Crooke Smelter, which was processing Ute-Ulay ore, as well as the

Palmetto Mill, which had been built above Rose's Cabin, were both operating at full capacity. Ernest Ingersoll reported:

Over five million pounds of mining machinery and supplies were taken in by way of wagons during 1880 at a cost of over a million dollars for transportation alone.... At the beginning of 1881 about 2,000 people lived in the town itself (Lake City), not counting the great number of men in the mountains round about.[490]

The *Silver World* in the early summer of 1880 wrote:

Lake City has not grown as rapidly as many hoped, but it is on a sound basis. Mines are being developed and look better all the time. People are investing confidently in the mines, as their worth has been proven.[491]

Although there was a major boom going on at Carson on the Continental Divide in 1881, that district really did not depend much on Lake City in the early 1880s. Heavy snows at Carson and a dangerous and slick when wet road to Lake City that ran down the north side of the Continental Divide, all took their toll. Most supplies came in and ore went out to Del Norte.

Crofutt describes Lake City in the early 1880s:

(It is) pleasantly situated on the west bank of the river, beyond which the mountains rise... The stranger visiting here will be surprised to see the great number of stores, hotels, livery stables, saloons, and shops of all kinds, all of which appear to be doing an unusual amount of business for the size of the place. The explanation can be found in the fact that the city is located in the center of a score of small mining camps, numbering all along up to 300 populations each. These people from the very geographic position of the city, find it the best and most convenient place to purchase their supplies, spend their money, and sojourn for a season of recreation....[492]

Electricity came to Lake City about 1880. It was probably first used by the Ocean Wave, which built a dam at the Ocean Wave bridge and used the Lake Fork to power a Pelton Wheel. Steam had originally been used for power at the Hinsdale County mines and mills, but later water power or electricity produced by water power was used almost everywhere. There was a power plant at Fourth and Henson that furnished electricity for the street lights in town. At this time the electric plants were only run at night, as lighting was originally the only use for electricity. Later, diesel powered generators were used. It was not until 1957 that electric power came to Lake City from outside the county.[493]

Many of the local Lake Fork and Henson Creek mines were being worked in 1880. The Golden Wonder was perhaps the most celebrated mine of the boom, out producing even the Golden Fleece (Hotchkiss) and the Ute-Ulay. James Downey's newspaper, the *Lake City Mining Register*, within a year had a circulation of 600 subscribers. The paper did well for five years, but closed its doors in April, 1885. The mines of the upper Lake Fork, around the town of Sherman and in Burrows Park, were doing well. The U.S. Census of 1880 showed that Lake City had seven lawyers, four doctors, one assayer, eight wagon makers and blacksmiths, three bakers, five druggists, one banker, and two engineers. Among the other businesses in town were three meat markets, two cigar-stationery stores, six saloons, five hotels, two jewelry stores, six clothing and shoe stores, four hardware and miner's supply establishments, and seven grocery stores.[494]

An act of violence occurred on September 6, 1880, when Joseph (Big Joe) Nevis and Andrew MacLauchlan fought after an all-night poker game. Nevis hit MacLauchlan in the forehead with an axe (the axe seemed to be the weapon of choice in many Lake City fights), but MacLauchlan was still able to shoot Nevis in the forehead and instantly killed him.[495]

By the early 1880s, Lake City's leaders knew they needed to take action against the bawdy houses and the rougher saloons and dance halls, but they could not quite figure out what to do. In February, 1881, they passed an ordinance that was very harsh for the time that read:

No bawdy house, house of ill fame, house of assignation, disorderly house of any description whatever and house or place for promiscuous dance after the usual manner of a dance house was allowed. Furthermore no house or place for dance or other amusements injurious to the morals of the town and its inhabitants would be allowed. Violators could be fined $100 to $300 and (violators could be sentenced for 30 to 90 days in jail.[496]

The problem was that although such places were desired and frequented by a large percentage of the male population of the town, no one would admit to this. Even many of the women in town wanted the bordellos to stay, as an alternative to their staying in a constant state of pregnancy. As far as the moral issues were concerned, one resident, who knew the girls of Hell's Acre well, explained that it was actually best for the girls, as "some of the (girls) stayed on the line because that represented the kind of life they wanted to live, while others were forced there by circumstances."[497]

In this later class was one young orphan who had heard about "the good times in Lake City." As Duane Smith writes:

> *Expecting to find work there, she found none and had "fallen prey" to one of the so-called madams. She had never "wanted to be bad." The same observer said, "she is not the only girl there who did not want to be bad."*
>
> *....The census of 1880 disclosed some interesting facts about the local prostitutes. Belle, Mattie, Hattie, Millie, Gertrude, Mollie and their friends were all between twenty and twenty-two, with one exception, a girl who was twenty-four. Most came from the Midwest, except two from New York, and all were white and American-born. One was widowed and the rest were single.*[498]

The result was that the law against prostitution was on the books but was ignored or circumvented, as shown by another ordinance in October, 1884, which stated that none of the places mentioned in the February, 1881, ordinance would be allowed in the city limits of Lake City *except* in one area — "south of town and west of Bluff Street." Then in 1888 that exception to the law was repealed, and in January, 1893, no such place was to be operated within three miles of Lake City (the Lake City ordinance was of questionable legality outside the city limits). The possible fine for the offenses was dropped from $100 to $300 to $5 to $100.

The city fathers also passed ever changing laws to keep up the morality of its young people. In 1876, no person under twelve could go to a billiard parlor or a "ball alley" (probably what we now call a bowling alley). Then, in 1881, no one under twelve could go to a bowling alley, billiards parlor, or shooting gallery. In 1884, this ordinance was broadened to forbid anyone under the age of twelve to assist in a dance hall or remain for any purpose in a bawdy house or dance hall.

Freighting rates for supplies and machinery coming in to Lake City by wagon were exorbitant, and weather often shut down the roads to Lake City from December to March.[499] Everyone realized this situation could not continue.[500] A road to Gunnison was completed in June, 1880, shortening the distance to the D&RG Railroad after it arrived in that town in August, 1881, to about forty-five or fifty miles, but this was still unacceptable. Everyone knew a railroad was the answer to the problem, but getting one to come to Lake City was totally out of the town's control. The first boom had ended, in part, because of the huge costs of transporting freight in and ore out of Lake City by wagon. Now it looked like the lack of the promised railroad might end the second boom. The citizens of Lake City could not believe what was happening!

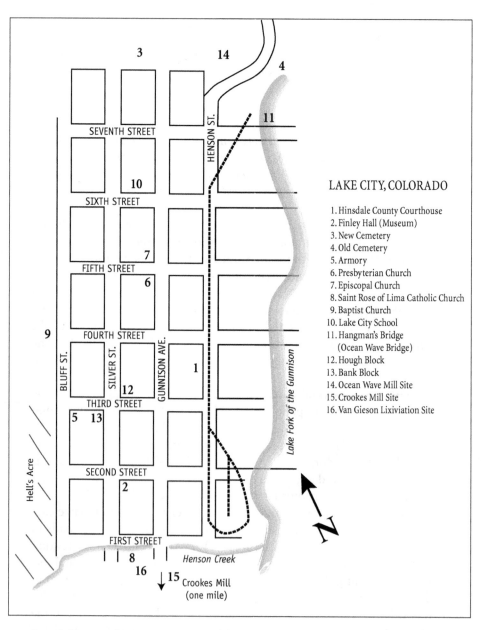

Map of the Town of Lake City. (Western Reflections Map)

As early as 1873, John Evans of the Denver, South Park & Pacific had suggested a railroad to the San Juans. The San Juan Railway Company was even created by Lake City businessmen to bring a railroad to the town, but neither of these dreams ever materialized.[501] In 1875, the Atchison, Topeka and Santa Fe had expressed an interest in building to the new boom town of Lake City, but they also never did anything. Otto Mears started the Marshall Pass Toll Road in April, 1879. About this time, Mears also built the Cebolla to Gunnison Toll Road.[502] This at least cut a large number of miles from freight going to or from Denver, Pueblo, and Cañon City.

When the Denver and Rio Grande decided to move across the Continental Divide into western Colorado in the fall of 1880, the railroad bought Mears' Marshall Pass Toll Road for $13,000 and began laying track to Gunnison. The railroad let it be known that their main line would then go west from that town. They also stated that Lake City would finally get its railroad, but as a branch and not on the main line, which would have meant a lot more growth for the town proper; but at least Hinsdale County's mines would be able to ship lower grade ores.

There was other disturbing news for Lake City's citizens. Eben Olcott sadly noted that in January, 1881, John J. Crooke announced he was retiring from being in active charge of the operations of the Crooke Brothers' mines, mills and smelters in the Lake City and San Juan area.[503] By late February of 1881, more than 1,000 men were working on the new D&RG Railroad route from Poncha Springs (near Salida) to Gunnison. Although they were basically following Otto Mears' toll road grade, it was slow going, and by mid-May the crews were still on the eastern side of the Continental Divide; yet a survey crew was already on its way to survey a branch to Lake City.

In the summer of 1881 telephone service was extended to Silverton and Ouray, whose merchants found it very handy to order supplies by phone from Lake City. By October the telephone was being used for vocal and musical performances by local residents,[504] who played instruments and sang solos, duets, and even held concerts over the phone lines, some of the events lasting for hours. Everyone who owned a telephone was invited to listen in. The concerts, however, only lasted during the winter of 1881-82. A franchise had originally been given for the town's telephone service, but no action was ever taken. The Colorado Telephone Company was given a franchise in 1909, then the Hinsdale Telephone Company was given the franchise in 1950, and finally dial service came to Lake City in 1961. Besides Lake City, there was also early telephone service to many of the nearby mines and small settlements, including Capitol City, Rose's Cabin, and Mineral Point. Despite the lack of a railroad, Lake City did not seem to be quite so isolated from the outside world.

Lake City was also keeping its civilized reputation, as the town's *Mining Register* of January 1, 1881 reported:

> *The social status (of Lake City) is far above the average Western and frontier cities, and no mining camp in the world can boast of more intelligent, cultured, and peaceful citizenship. A street brawl is the rarest of occurrences and for months the log cabin that served for a caboose (jail) is tenantless. The miners, not only of Lake City, but of the entire San Juan area are, as a general thing, intelligent, industrious, and ambitious. There is too much activity here for drones and the "loafer" is not known. Nearly every miner has a prospect or two of his own into which he puts his earnings.*

The same issue also boasted:

> *Our grand mountain canyons echo today with the music of the school and church bells, while the clatter of the busy printing press is heard in every camp and the smoke from the smelters and mills veil the snow-clad summits of our towering mountains....*[505]

Many old timers claimed that the people of Lake City never locked their cabins during these times, and those living outside town would usually leave staples like beans and coffee in their kitchen in case someone else found the cabin empty and needed them. It was customary for the person who ate there to leave a thank you note with his name, but no monetary payment was expected.[506]

However, Hinsdale County did have crime in 1880-1881. The Lake City papers reported that stage robberies were becoming a major problem along the Del Norte to Lake City toll road. The Barlow and Sanderson stage from Alamosa to Lake City was robbed five times between late 1880 and early 1881. The robbers were evidently after currency being sent into the area by mail, but were also robbing the passengers of their money and jewelry. Several of the stage passengers were wounded, all were scared to death, and local businesses were losing money because of the bad publicity.

Billy Le Roy (his real name was Arthur Pond) was an escaped prisoner from the Detroit penitentiary, where he had been sentenced to ten years, and was known to be "desperate and extremely dangerous." Besides Detroit, Le Roy was infamous in the eastern San Juans for his many crimes, and he had been arrested once in Colorado for a stage robbery but had escaped while being taken to prison. He came back to the Del Norte and Lake City areas in May, 1881 and brought with him another criminal. Le Roy and his friend joined up with Le Roy's brother in Del Norte. His brother was also infamous, using the alias of Frank Clark. Both brothers were about as bad as they came.

On May 13, 1881, Le Roy and the two other men tried to stop the Barlow and Sanderson Stage near Antelope Park, but at that time they only managed to spook the stage's two lead horses that ran away with the stage in true cowboy movie fashion. The Le Roy gang never caught up with the stage that day.

On May 18, the Le Roy gang tried again. It was a trademark of the gang to return to the scene of their crimes a few days later and successfully rob the same stage and a new group of passengers, and then give the stage horses a scare to get them running. Often they would fire a volley into the coach as it whirled away. That was exactly the way the robbery went on this occasion, and one passenger was wounded by one of the gang's bullets. The robbery caused a "profound sensation" in Del Norte, where worried citizens raised a $1,400 reward and a posse was formed by Sheriff L. M. Armstrong and Deputy James Galloway of San Juan City. The posse set off in hot pursuit and had little trouble in following the robbers' trail. Billy Le Roy and his brother were captured after three days, and Billy was shot in the leg in the process. The third man evidently had gone to Lake City for supplies, and managed to escape the posse.

After having apprehended the culprits, the posse decided to take them to the jail in Del Norte. Under the cover of darkness Sheriff Armstrong threw the Le Roy gang into the Del Norte jail sometime after midnight. Armstrong was exhausted from having been on the trail for three nights with little sleep, so the Sheriff made his way home and went to bed. In the meantime, a lynch mob was hastily being formed. Some of the citizens of Del Norte were determined to put an end to the lawlessness on their stretch of the road — It was ruining their town's reputation. The mob was evidently composed of the same group that had put up the $1,400 reward. They were especially worried about a jail break, since Le Roy was known to have escaped so many times before after being captured. The vigilantes found Armstrong at his home, made the Sheriff return to the jail, and hog-tied him. They then took the keys to the jail cell and escorted the Le Roys to the nearby Rio Grande River. There, they hung the two brothers in a cluster of cottonwood trees close to the water. Half an hour later the lifeless outlaws were returned to their bunks in the jail and the posse went home.[507]

It was said that the Le Roys died because of "stoppage of breath," occurring while they were guests of honor of the local "Uplifting Society." One concrete result was a decline in such activities along the Del Norte to Lake City route for the next several months.[508]

Eben Olcott, the very well-thought-of twenty-six year old mining engineer from back East, took the time to write home almost every day and he explained to his wife what was going on in this rough and tumble part of the world.

> *We had a serious mail robbery on the road this week. We lost considerable mail and I a package of some value which I needed very much. One of the passengers on the coach was wounded. Two of the three highway men have been arrested....We are getting very indignant and the first man that is brought into Lake City and known to be connected with this high handed robbery will have Judge Lynch after him inside of 12 hours.*[509]

Evidently Olcott had not yet heard about the hanging in Del Norte or did not want to worry his wife about the event. Olcott also spent considerable time writing of the culture of the people of Lake City and the amazing beauty of the scenery in Hinsdale County. He had originally been hired by the Crookes in December, 1879, to help plan and build a smelter that the Crookes wanted to construct at Boulder Gulch near Silverton. Plans for the smelter got delayed, and Eben stayed for months in Lake City helping the Crookes with their Summitville and Lake City smelters, doing some work at the Ute-Ulay, and running errands for the Crookes in Denver and other places. It was not until June 11, 1880, that he was sent to the North Star Mine near Silverton. In August, 1880, he signed a contract with the Crookes to become their superintendent of the North Star Mine. Olcott realized the mine was a very rich one (his first ore sample sent to the Crooke smelter in Lake City ran 563 ounces of silver and one ounce of gold to the ton), but he strongly felt the Crookes needed the Silverton smelter to avoid the high transportation costs to their smelter in Lake City.

Olcott lived and worked for the Crookes in both Silverton and Lake City during 1880 and therefore gives us a good comparison of the two towns and some idea of the Crookes themselves. Silverton at that time was just becoming the largest town in the San Juans, a title it would keep for several decades over all the other San Juan mining towns. However, Olcott made it clear that Lake City was still the most refined town in the San Juans. One example of why Olcott liked living in Lake City much better than Silverton was the poor quality of his hotel in Silverton (one of the best in that town at the time):

> *... For the most part I am in a hotel where they open their eyes at your wanting any better place to wash than the common sink off the office, and think you are stuck up if you ask for a bed alone, not to say a room.*[510]

He further complained:

The mail has not gone out (of Silverton) for two days... When I get to Lake City, I will be within telegraphic communication at any rate, and probably the mail will be regular there....[511]

Olcott mentions the churches of Lake City (Silverton had none at the time), although noting they were occupied mainly by women and children and usually only a dozen or so of them. Duane Smith, editor of the book, wrote that part of the reason for the lack of miners at church was that:

Sunday being a wide-open day in the western mining communities, the only day in fact that many miners did not work, churches had to compete with everything for a miner's attention, from business to the red-light district to sports.[512]

Olcott was paid the very good salary for the time of $500 per month when he worked for the Crookes as the manager of the North Star. Olcott felt strongly that Silverton had better mines in its area,[513] but he liked the connection of Lake City to the outside world and its more civilized nature, including the Lake City restaurants being much better in his opinion. Eben gives us some idea of the food available in Lake City, if you could afford it:

I thoroughly enjoyed the dinner... The old landlady got up a most credible meal — Julian soup, roast veal, Boston-browned potatoes and tomatoes, asparagus, plum pie, coconut cake, and coffee...[514]

Eben also shows throughout his letters that many of the people of the time enjoyed and noted the beautiful scenery:

There are some most beautiful things about this country. The mountains today look superb with a light covering of snow. The majority of the trees here are mountain spruce but there are some aspens, which are now yellow and red with the autumn change and contrast most picturesque with the dark evergreens.[515]

And later:

It... indeed is a magnificent sight to look out upon this sea of mountains. The full moon and Jupiter have just risen to add their brilliancy to the picture and you could almost see to read out of doors... I can give you no idea of the mountains of snow.... I should like you to see the frost effects some morning... every tree, shrub and twig is covered with brilliant frost work, some leaves and crystals in it an inch long.... (The sun) has the effect of loosening many of the thin crystals of ice which are so light that they float in the air, making a perfect cloud of spangles, which reflect and decompose into light until you see every color of the rainbow.[516]

And Olcott hints of Lake City shopping hours — most merchants evidently stayed open until midnight at least on weekends:

It is a most magnificent night. The moon shined almost as bright as day and there were more people on the streets than if it were daylight, which is often the case with mining towns.[517]

Olcott also gave us some insight into John Crooke. J.J. Crooke evidently felt about his mines much like one might feel about their sweetheart. When someone disparaged the Ute-Ulay Mine, Eben wrote that J.J. said:

Those dogs gave only the tribute of a sneer to the best and loveliest property in the San Juans. It was a case, a practical case, of "casting pearls before the swine."

In the same letter Olcott mentioned that one recent ore sample from the Ute-Ulay Mine had carried 563 ½ ounces of silver and one ounce of gold. Then Crooke went on to say "It is a queer mine and you can't tell what surprises may be in store for you."[518] Eben mentioned fairly often in his letters that he felt the Crookes needed to be more careful with the way they spent their money, and that J. J. was a little odd. Evidently this was an opinion held by several others besides Olcott.[519] By 1879 the Crookes had invested over $400,000 in Lake City — in mines, smelters, and other properties. Their mines near Lake City and Silverton included perhaps each areas' best mine at the time–the North Star (Solomon) and the Ute-Ulay.

Olcott was very disturbed about the Crookes' decision not to build their Silverton smelter, which required that the North Star Mine's ore be packed by mules or burros to the Crookes' Lake City smelter. This process was very expensive, but the North Star ore was so rich they still made a good profit; but it entailed giving up a large share of their profit to freighters, which bothered Olcott. Building a smelter near a good paying mine with a lot of ore in sight was a typical engineering plan at the time, but what Olcott did not realize was that none of the smelters built near Silverton ever worked well because of the lack of oxygen at

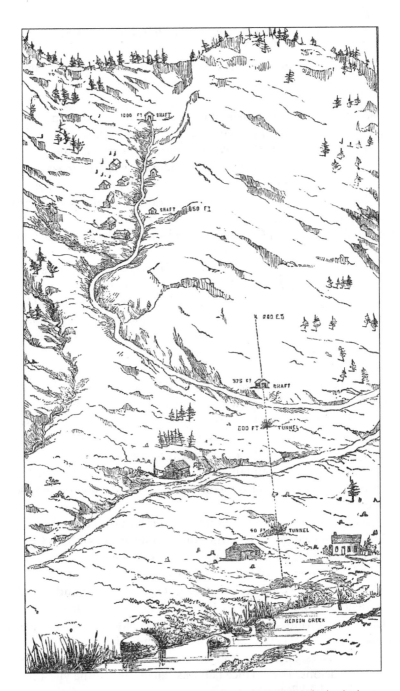

The Ute-Ulay Mine was shown in Fossett's book about 1880. The beginnings of the town of Henson can be seen at the top of the upper road. The engraving shows how far it was to the upper shaft and how many shafts were already on the property. The property was not fully developed until a few years later. (From Fossett's Colorado)

197

high altitudes and the resulting low temperatures. Because of this, the Silverton smelters often recovered less than half of the ore's precious minerals.

Olcott, like many other men of the time, often walked or snowshoed from Lake City to the mine near Silverton in the middle of the winter. If he was walking, he would make each part of his trip at night or early morning, so the snow would hold up under his weight. He stressed in his letters that he tried to carry as few items with him as possible, so as to not break through the hard crust of the snow in the morning. Despite the slump in Lake City's economy, he described his normal trip from Silverton to Lake City and repeated what he had said about Lake City:

> *We expect to accomplish 18 miles (from Silverton) on the journey to Lake City on Monday, stop at Rose's Cabin overnight and make the remaining 14 or 15 miles on Tuesday. It is so much more comfortable at Lake (City) and we have telegraphic lines and very much more of a feeling of civilization pervades the place. Last winter the mail only missed one day.*[520]

The Polar Star Mine also started steady output in January, 1882, with a ten man crew that grew to twenty by April of the same year. By October the Polar Star had a crosscut tunnel that opened on both sides of Engineer Mountain. The mine was owned by the Crookes and Henry ("Hank") A. Wood,[521] so the ore was sent to the Crookes' mills on the Lake City side of the mountain. Part of the big excitement at the Polar Star was when it was revealed the miners had found a 600 pound piece of pure silver.

One of Lake City's worst and most famous crimes occurred on April 26, 1882, when George Betts, owner of the notorious San Juan Central Dance Hall (and local brothel) and James Browning, who is sometimes described as a co-owner of the San Juan Central, shot Sheriff Edward N. Campbell. Browning was only a boy of eighteen at the time, and probably just a friend or employee of Betts. Everyone said that Betts had complete control over Browning, and evidently Betts persuaded Browning to help him rob one of Lake City's nicest homes. Both of the men were known to be lawbreakers, and Betts had been accused of robbery on several previous occasions. Their dance hall was called "one of the vilest in the San Juans" by the *Silver World*.

The house in Ball Flats that they chose to rob was originally built by T. W. M. Draper, superintendent of the Golden Fleece Mine and a prominent mining engineer, although it was unoccupied at the time and was then owned by W.G. Luckett, a local furniture dealer and coffin merchant. When the men robbed the house the first time, they took some valuable articles. This tempted them into trying again. However Luckett had checked at the home and found articles missing. Highly respected Edward N. Campbell had been elected Hinsdale County Sheriff in 1879 and was charged with maintaining Lake City's reputation as a generally peaceful town. He was very well liked by the people of Lake City.[522]

When Luckett reported the robbery to Sheriff Campbell and his deputy (also the City Marshall) Clair Smith, the two law enforcement officials went to Luckett's house to see if the robbers might return.[523] They were given a key and waited inside in the hallway. About one in the morning, the thieves showed up, and one of them struck a match that illuminated his face. When the sheriff ordered them to drop their guns and raise their hands, Betts fired and fatally hit the sheriff. Campbell called for Smith to catch the men and then died. Smith stayed with the sheriff until help arrived, as he had recognized the perpetrators and knew where to find them. Betts was captured in Del Norte by a posse. He carried a .44 revolver with one spent cartridge still in the chamber. The bullet that killed Campbell was a .44 caliber. Browning, evidently didn't realize he had been recognized, and was arrested in Lake City at the San Juan Central Dance Hall, and his gun was found to be a .38 caliber. Therefore everyone knew it was Betts and not Browning who had killed Sheriff Campbell.

Betts was described as a "graceless scamp as ever insulted the ground of Colorado" and "a bawdy house pimp, a thief, and a blackguard."[524] After the men were captured and jailed, irate citizens immediately started talking of a lynching. The enraged citizens of Lake City began to gather at the deceased sheriff's home at 11:00 p.m. the next night. They were all masked and armed, most with rifles. Some carried ropes and others sledge hammers to break into the jail. Three men were reported to have tried to persuade the crowd to at least not hang Browning, because he had not fired a shot and was so young, but they had little success. Soon it looked like every able-bodied man in town and many of the local miners were part of the mob.[525]

City Marshall Smith had asked six armed Pitkin Guards to guard the prisoners, but the reaction of the citizens of Lake City was immediate. The *Silver World* reported that:

All day Wednesday, the people talked of the happenings of that early dawn. They evinced a determined feeling, and many openly advocated immediately inflicting the proper penalty. As the cyclone silently gathered its deadly power, so did the tempers of the people gathered resolution that the murderers should during the night be hurled to hell.[526]

The mob was told to back off but was not persuaded to do so. That night it was dark, so dark that one man evidently gave orders to the mob by using a metal whistle as the crowd slowly moved toward the jail. Shortly before midnight, a large number of armed and masked men appeared in front of the jail. Although law officers and some of the men of the Pitkin Guards tried to reason with the crowd, the men broke off the jail's lock with a sledge hammer. The Pitkin Guards ordered the mob to stop but gave no resistance when the crowd broke into the jail. The guards were told to throw up their hands and no one in the heavily armed crowd would shoot. They were said to have stood in a row with their hands raised.

At the jail, the young Browning begged for someone to help him and kept bowing his head when the vigilantes tried to put a rope around his neck. It took five tries to get the noose in place, because he bobbed his head as he begged for someone to *please* help him. A woman from the San Juan Central Saloon evidently begged for someone to stop the hanging, but no one helped or even talked to her. Betts asked for a chew of tobacco and cursed the crowd. He did not fight the rope when it was put around his neck at the jail. He asked if he had any friends in the crowd. The answer came back a resounding "No." He then asked if his dead body could be taken to his dance hall after his death and was told it would be.

Both men were taken to the Ocean Wave Bridge (the Ocean Wave Smelter was a very short distance away), and the loose end of the ropes, which were already in place around Bett's and Browning's necks were thrown over the beams at the top of the bridge. Browning continued to plead for mercy and made three attempts to seize the rope when he was lifted off the ground. The bodies of the two men were left hanging until the next morning as a warning to any other lawless people in town and to act as a lesson for the school children who were brought to see the bodies still hanging the next morning. The cut rope was left hanging from the beams for years.[527] Betts and Browning were buried the next morning, well before the funeral of the sheriff, which was attended by a very large crowd that gave him a large and honorable funeral.

John Bell, prosecuting attorney at the Alferd Packer trial and later a Colorado District Judge, writes in his book that he was at the hanging and that most of the crowd was miners. He writes that the Pitkin Guards was detailed to guard the two murderers but that the Guards only pretended to put up resistance. Bell claims he was one of the three men who tried to get the vigilante crowd to disburse and that the other two were also members of the Guards; but this may have been pure fiction on his part.[528]

Bell also commented on the fate of Betts' girlfriend, the "scarlet woman," who tried to get someone to stop the hanging. Soon after the event, her daughter evidently died of scarlet fever, which drove her into deep despair and an even greater depression. Bell writes that she came to his law office to have him prepare her will, because she was going to commit suicide. He writes that he discovered her father was a preacher and sent for him. He came to Lake City and she agreed to go back East as soon as she made a marker for Betts's grave. She evidently was able to start a new and moral life when she got back East.[529] However this scenario must be taken with a grain of salt, as Bell writes that his book's purpose was to teach moral lessons.

The Hinsdale County Courthouse flew its flag at half-mast and all the town's public buildings were draped with black crepe in honor of Sheriff Campbell.[530] The sheriff left a wife and six children.[531] Sheriff Edward

The Ocean Wave Bridge was the site of the hanging of Betts and Browning, as shown in John Bell's book. The Ocean Wave Mill is in the background in the area of today's Country Market Grocery Store. Everyone who was there described how Betts' eyes bulged out after the hanging and a later ghost had the same characteristics. (From The Pilgrim and the Pioneer*)*

Campbell is buried beneath a Civil War headstone in Lake City's IOOF Cemetery. His grave marker is located about 100 yards inside the main (east) gate and a little to the right. A coroner's jury officially proclaimed that Betts and Browning had died by unknown hands. Campbell is listed as a peace officer killed in the line of duty on a memorial plaque at the Colorado Law Enforcement Academy at Golden, Colorado.[532] The hangings received publicity throughout the State of Colorado, and most of the out of town papers agreed that the townspeople had done the right thing.[533]

Some citizens of Lake City may have been embarrassed or angry about the hangings, but most were not. Henry Olney of the *Silver World* wrote in his editorial of the event:

> *When in the course of human events it becomes apparent to an order loving people that statutory law is weak or inadequate to suppress or punish crime, or is inefficiently administered, then it becomes necessary to invoke the highest law of the land — the law of dire necessity, the edict of the people.*
>
> *Such was the state of affairs in this community, which sternly demanded action on Wednesday night and Thursday morning. During the past five years several murders and heinous crimes have been committed in this county, and in but few instances have the perpetrators been brought to justice through the procedure of the courts. With crafty lawyers to defend them, who resorted to all types of tricks of the profession, the invoking of the law's delays, the packing of juries, changes of venue to counties where by the side of the unprincipled agents and assistants, packed juries were more easily obtained and by aid of perjured witnesses. Justice has been cheated of her rights and thereby criminals have become emboldened and vice and crime encouraged....*
>
> *We fully and unequivocally endorse the recent action, not that we gloat over it but because it was a dire necessity. We rejoice in the evidence so sternly demonstrated that the people are not dead in spirit, callous in nature nor over awed by the baser element present in the community, but that deep down in their natures be the seeds, the very foundation of justice....*
>
> *This is not a lawless community. Life and property are respected here to the fullest extent and because of this fact was the recent action taken. Instead of a reproach it must and should reflect credit upon our people; for where statutory law does not protect the first law of human nature, the law of self-preservation must and will.*

The recent lynching was the first in the history of the town. Had it been resorted to long ago, precious lives might have been saved. The necessity which called it forth may never occur again. We hope it will not; but should it, we have faith that the people will answer to the call as determined upon the occasion.[534]

There is not space here to delve into Lake City's many ghost stories, but some of the many stories that involve this event deserve repeating.[535] George Betts, the more notorious of the killers, has been reported on many occasions since the hanging as wandering near where his corpse was left hanging. Many of the school children who were let out of school the morning after the hangings to view the bodies, of course, had nightmares; but later many also said they saw a ghost with bulging eyes and a red face, or sometimes they just saw a red face with no body but with bulging eyes. It was evidently Betts, whose ghost was also reported to have appeared many times later at his dance hall with the same bulging eyes and red face.

Although Betts was not a respectable man, many of the citizens who participated in the lynch mob came to regret their action, as Betts had been a local businessman (even if of unsavory character) and Browning was young and did not commit the murder. Some of the citizens who participated were literally haunted by the event. Many of the men in the vigilante committee also began to see Betts' ghost walking near the bridge.[536]

Browning's ghost showed up at the Hinsdale County Courthouse. He did not look ghastly but rather was well dressed in his best clothes, as if wanting to be afforded a trial. His ghost is supposedly seen or heard at times in the courthouse even today.[537]

But let us now get back to history. In 1880, mining reporter Robert Strahorn called Lake City "the Metropolis of the northern San Juans" with 1,100 inhabitants. Strahorn also reported that the Town of Ouray had a population of 900, Silverton 800, Durango (swollen with D&RG workers) 2,000, and Rico 1,100. (Rico was experiencing a major, but very short, boom at the time.)[538] Evidently Durango was to be the "Metropolis of the Southern San Juans." The early 1880s were a time when Lake City continued to mature. The Temperance movement grew, the churches grew, true fire protection was established, and the more wicked saloons and brothels were segregated into Hell's Acre.[539]

In 1881, Lake City's future looked good. The D&RG Railroad had started grading on its Lake City branch and work was being done on the lower Lake Fork canyon out of Sapinero. Robert Strahorn displayed this optimism when he wrote about Lake City's future:

The San Juan country will in two years be penetrated from end to end by at least two lines of railroads. It contains every element desired to build up several of the richest mining communities in the world, and has only lacked this advance of the iron horse. Its climate, though rigorous, cannot prevent underground operators the year round. Its smelting facilities of fuel, lime, water, and all varieties and grades of ore, are unexcelled. To say that some of the largest smelting works in the world will now soon spring up in the San Juan Mountains, and that they will turn out millions of dollars where thousands are found now, is entirely reasonable. That thousands of poor prospectors will be in this great wilderness yet "strike it rich," and that thousands of capitalists will by making judicious investments reap still greater rewards, is in such a country simply inevitable.... It now only remains for us to see who will be the fortunate participants in the work which will attain this gratifying end.[540]

In the summer Lake City had a stagecoach traveling to Silverton over the new Engineer Pass road:

From Lake City the Rocky Mountain Stage and Express runs coaches daily to Capitol City and Rose's Cabin, up Henson Creek Cañon, and over Engineer Mountain to Mineral Point and Animas Forks, where connections are made with coaches for Silverton, Eureka, Howardsville, and other points; and to Sherman, Burrows Park, and up the Lake Fork of the Gunnison.[541]

Lodges became very popular in Lake City at this time and included the IOOF (the International Order of Odd Fellows), OOH (Order of Humility), G.A.R. (Grand Army of the Republic), W.O.W. (Woodsmen of the World), R.A.M (Royal Arch #9), the Good Templar Lodge (a temperance order), the Pitkin Guards, AOUW (Ancient Order of United Workmen, Hough Fire Department, Crystal Lake Lodge # 34 of A.F. & A.M., O.E.S. #35 Rebecca, and the Improved Order of Redmen.

This time there was a "seeing is believing" attitude about the railroad among residents. It was time for Lake City citizens to take comfort in each other, while they waited for the railroad to actually arrive. By the next summer (1881), it was evident that Lake City was in trouble again. The *Silver World* editor tried to make lemonade out of lemons:

Our town has been largely deserted by the bad characters; snide operators have found their level and have been driven out by public sentiment or inability to no longer ply their vocation; our business houses are now in fair proportion to the demand of the surrounding camps.[542]

One reason for the end of Lake City's first boom had been that Gunnison and the mining areas to its north were enjoying their own boom from new discoveries, coupled with the arrival of the D&RG Railroad at Gunnison on August 6, 1881, which opened up the vast coal deposits at Crested Butte.

Dave Wood took advantage of this situation and opened a huge warehouse in Gunnison from which he shipped all over western Colorado, including Lake City. He kept 500 draft horses and mules at his Gunnison operation (his corral covered twelve lots) for use on his teams.[543] By January, 1881, the D&RG was surveying in the Black Canyon, probably the biggest natural obstacle the railroad met in Colorado. The route through the deep and rugged canyon was completed in the summer of 1881 at a cost of $165,000 a mile, a phenomenal sum of money in those days. Even more than the financial cost was the cost of human lives in men killed while building this section of the railroad.[544]

During this time Lake City was in another vicious cycle. As it became apparent that Hinsdale mining was slowing down at the end of 1881 (mainly because of doubts over the railroad coming), the Denver and Rio Grande stopped construction on its branch line to Lake City from Sapinero, evidently because of concerns over how much business Lake City could give them. It was becoming evident that there might be no inexpensive transportation of Lake City's ores. Lake City's prominence in the 1870s suddenly disappeared in the 1880s when the railroad officially announced in 1882 that it was not building the Lake City branch. That announcement and the overwhelming Leadville boom led to yet another bust in Lake City, yet the town kept going. The Polar Star was still shipping ore to Lake City, as was the Mountain Queen at the top of California Gulch near Animas Forks.[545]

In 1882, the armory was being turned into an Opera House, which opened in the fall of 1883.[546] The Pitkin Guards' equipment was still there but was taking up a small space in the big building, which had been built larger than needed so that a great number of soldiers could be housed there, if they were needed. Many of the larger events in town were (and still are) held in the armory. It could hold up to 400 dancers. The partial second floor of the 120 by 50 foot brick building housed several small club rooms. Numerous benefit plays and other events were held at the armory to help repair and upgrade the facility.

Evidently very few tax dollars went into the armory building, although it was being used constantly by the entire community. Before this time, shows were usually comprised of locals and were held in the courthouse, churches, or halls. Traveling companies now performed regularly at the armory (soon called the "Opera House"). Shakespeare, plays, lectures, magicians, and musical concerts now came to Lake City's Opera House. Even dog and pony shows, "hobo" musicians, and local talent shows made appearances.[547]

The main excitement in 1881 was the building and opening of the large brick Lake City schoolhouse. Attendance was about 100 in the 1880s, but would rise to almost 200 by the end of the century.[548] The old brick school house was torn down in 1987 to make room for the new one, which now has an enrollment of about 100 students, kindergarten through high school. Current residents are very proud of the school, which usually ranks as one of the top schools in the state for its size.

The Ute-Ulay Mine closed in 1883 and the Crookes closed their mills and smelters and left town in 1884, probably disgusted that the railroad

The new Lake City School was built in 1880, but this photo was taken in 1897 at the height of the school's enrollment. (From Tiny Hinsdale of the Silvery San Juan.*)*

206

was not coming to haul their concentrates to efficient smelters at lower altitudes. Lake City went from hard times to a full scale depression almost overnight. Later the *Lake City Times* would say this bust period made Lake City "one of the deadest towns in Colorado."[549] Fortunately, by this time there was a core of old timers who stayed on, despite the continuous repetition of boom and bust cycles.

DELMONICO RESTAURANT,

W. W. JONES,   -   PROPRIETOR.

Sleeping Rooms Attached.

Lake City,   -   Colorado.

REFRESHMENTS AT ALL TIMES DURING THE SEASON.

Even though in a bust cycle, Lake City's elegant air was still shown through the Delmonico Restaurant's ad from 1884. The Delmonico was part of the Occidental Hotel and was one of Lake City's nicest restaurants. Note however that almost all the customers were men. (Author's Collection)

CHAPTER 6

STILL A TOUCH OF ELEGANCE

≡O≡

Lake City's second major boom had been brought on by the D&RG's decision in 1880 to build a branch to Lake City; and by late 1882 Lake City's boom ended in a terrific bust after the D&RG announced it was not going to continue construction on Lake City's part of the line. The railroad saw more value in high grade ore being shipped from other areas. Their reasoning was sound, for if the price of silver and gold slipped even a little in value, it might not be worth shipping low grade ore from Lake City. This is exactly what happened to end Lake City's third boom, but by that time the railroad had been tempted to build into Hinsdale County by rich gold deposits that were unfortunately depleted in a few years. It seemed as if every time a Hinsdale mine hit a rich pocket of ore or a new discovery was made in the county, the ever optimistic prospectors, miners, and merchants rushed to the Lake City area in the hopes of getting rich. Then the rich ore would play out, leaving the mines with only low-grade ore. It was a cycle that happened in many places in the San Juans — not just in Lake City—but somehow it happened more often and caused bigger swings in the Hinsdale's economy than in most of the other San Juan mining districts.

After the railroad announcing it was not coming in 1882, even the Crookes put their mines and mills up for sale; but, evidently found no purchaser, and ended up refinancing their debt with a bond issue.[550] Even in their first full year of operation (1878), the Crookes' smelter had produced $85,498 in silver, $23,698 in lead, and $2,925 in gold.[551] Nevertheless the Crooke Mining and Smelter Company closed its mill, smelter and mines in Lake City in 1883, and Lake City's mining economy fell to almost nothing. The value of the production of silver, gold, and other base metals in Hinsdale fell from $208,703 to $11,362 in the year after the Crooke departure. With the D&RG railroad having built into Silverton and mills and smelters opening in Durango, the Crookes had lost much of the business that had previously come their way from the owners of other San Juan mines. However, it was to be only a few years before the Crooke Mill and Smelters would reopen under new ownership.

As author Duane Smith wrote:

Despite being given a "great deal of credit" in the Engineering and Mining Journal *(January 17, 1889) for their pioneering smelting efforts, the article went on to explain they had gone through years of costly experiments to find a treatment process. Still, not all of the problems were resolved, and this led to temporary closure. The* Silver World *told its Lake City readers, April 7, 1883, that the cost of fuel, flux, and labor, plus the expense of hauling ore from the mines, had caused a temporary closure. The editor also blamed unspecified company policy for this situation.*

Nor did some of their mines pan out as anticipated, particularly the Ute-Ulay. The result hampered operations until the closing of activities in November 1883. The Lake City Mining Register *(November 2, 1883) praised "Uncle John" Crooke as the "chief engineer of the city's prosperity." It blasted the "cheerful idiot who did not see a faint idea of what one man's conceptions, executions, ambitions, and grit are worth." Other sources blamed "trouble among themselves" for the company trials.*

High expenses, low grade ore, debt, perhaps some poor leadership or choices, and a local district that did not produce as expected doomed their efforts. The company's assets were sold at public auction in May, 1866 in New York City. Once again hope blossomed. The Engineering and Mining Journal reported, on June 19, 1886, that as "soon as proper arrangements can be perfected," the new owners could then work again. Primarily this meant the Ute and Ulay Mine.[552]

Although in a bust cycle in 1883, Lake City did not close down and become a ghost town. Only somewhat in desperation, Lake City's merchants and residents nurtured the first inklings of a tourist town. The town was visited by a series of Colorado tourist guide authors during the mid-1880s; and hardly any notice was given in their guides to the downturn in mining, or at least they showed Lake City's economy in its most favorable light.

Later in 1885, after the second large bust, Fossett was again drawn to write of the beauty of the town:

The location of the town is grand and beautiful and resembles Georgetown (Colorado). There are numberless silver lodes in the lofty mountains that rise almost perpendicular for a half mile or a mile on every side—many of them worked extensively.[553]

Another well-known travel writer of his day was George Crofutt, who was able to report in 1885 that:

The stranger visiting here will be surprised to see the great number of stores, hotels, livery stables, saloons and shops of all kinds, all of which seem to be doing an unusual amount of business for the size of the place. The explanation can be found in the fact that the city is located in the center of a score or more small mining camps, numbering all along up to 300 in population each. The people from the geographical location of the city, find it the best and most convenient place to purchase their supplies, spend their money, and sojourn for a season of recreation (winter in Lake City)....

The district, of which Lake City is the commercial center, is most prosperous, as well as splendidly developed, owing, principally to the fact that it is the most accessible at all seasons of the year, and its altitude being much lower, mining can be carried on all through the year. A great amount of the work done is called assessment work. The mining law requires a certain amount of work to be done on each mine to perfect and hold the title, otherwise the claim can be "jumped" and relocated by other parties....

At present the city is reached by two wagon roads, one of which is open all seasons of the year, and the other, the "Slumgullion," from Wagon Wheel Gap, with one exception has not been closed on account of snow since it was constructed.

The scenery is most beautiful, and in the near future this will be one of the most charming summer resorts in the state. The Lake is owned by J.M. Gummy, Esq.,[554] who in addition to native trout, has placed in the waters a stock of salmon and Michigan white fish, that are doing well.

From the city there are many objects of interest that should be visited by the tourist, too numerous for us to enumerate, at all of which, the beautiful and the instructive predominate. Come and see for yourself; and if you can secure friend Olney, of the Silver World, as a companion, you will be assured of a pleasant and delightful tour; one never to be forgotten.[555]

Crofutt named the American and Occidental as the two "primary hotels" of Lake City. He also noted that there were now three breweries in town. He either did not know or did not care to relate that the Crookes were gone and their operations shut down at the time, when he wrote:

> The Crooke's Concentrating Works are located a half mile above the city and are the most extensive works of the kind in the state, with one exception, the Argo.... Near the works, quite a little village has grown up, with stores, hotels, saloons, etc., all of the residents being employed by or dependent upon 'the works.'[556]

Travel writer Ernest Ingersoll also reported in 1885 in his travel guide, *Crest of the Continent*, but his opening statement was a backhand slap at the lack of a railroad.

> Lake City is a mining town at the foot of the San Juan Mountains thirty miles south of the railroad station at Sapinero (the latter named after a sub-chief among the Utes who was looked upon by the whites as a man of unusual sagacity). It was at that time reached by buckboard carrying mail and passengers.[557]

Ingersoll proceeds to list many of the natural sites along the stage route to Lake City, more than a few of which he describes incorrectly. Then he resorts to describing even the stage stops and ranches:

> Half way to our destination, the crazy buckboard rattles us painfully down a steep and stony hill, where there is room for several ranches....The best of these is Barnum's, where there is also a store and post office, and where your "humble correspondent," supposing himself to be about to lay his head upon a soft bag of oats, nearly dashed his brains out by hurling it in misplaced confidence against a marble solid bag of salt.[558]

Ingersoll, about this time, for some reason also wrote a very positive article titled "Lively Lake City," which he incorporates into his Lake City chapter in *The Crest of the Continent*. However most of Lake City's accomplishments are given in the past tense:

> (Lake City) is not now so active as formerly. It stands in a little park at the junction of the Lake Fork (of the Gunnison) with Henson creek—both typical mountain streams, each wavelet flecked with foam and sparkling like the back of the trout that it hides. Henson Creek became especially famous among prospectors, who found

that, however large an army of miners might flock there, new veins were always to be had as the reward of diligent searching. Thus a populous and highly enterprising town arose, which became the supply point for a wide mountain region, owing to its accessibility from both north and south; and though it was over one hundred miles–mountain miles at that!—from a railway, more than ten million pounds of merchandise and five million pounds of mining machinery and supplies were taken in wagons in 1880, at a cost of over a million dollars for transportation alone. A very good class of people went to Lake City too, so that a substantial and pretty town arose, school houses and churches were built, and I have never seen a mining camp, where the bookstores and newspapers were so well furnished and patronized. At the beginning of 1881 about two thousand people lived in the town itself, not counting the great numbers of men in the mountains round about and three factories for the treatment of ores were in operation.

Since then, however, Lake City has retreated somewhat; not that the mines have proved false to the confidence placed in them, but because it has been shown that until cheaper methods of transportation and more economic treatment can be devised, the mines cannot be worked to the same profit which a similar investment in some neighboring districts will return. This is due to the fact that the ore, of marvelous value when mass is considered are too low grade, as a rule, to afford a high margin over the expenses of working.

This by no means condemns the district; it only causes its stores of wealth to be held in abeyance for a while before their coinage.... It will not be long before ... the reviving of Lake City's mines will occur, and enable her to catch up with her more fortunate sisters, in the wide circle of the San Juan silver region.

But when that time comes, the Alpine grandeur of the scenery cannot be lost, the splendid shooting and fishing which now makes the village one of the favorite resorts of the West, will have disappeared, and there are some of us, more sentimental than world-wise, who will regret the change.... Deer now throng, and even an occasion elk and antelope are to be seen. In the rocky vastness the bear and panther (mountain lion) find refuge and every little park is enlivened by the flitting forms of timid hares and the whirring escape of the grouse.... One wonders how this railway company is to support itself amid the wilds, this future must be remembered.[559]

Acknowledging that times were bad, but looking to the future, in the spring of 1885 an article in the *Lake City Register* declared:

We talk about the future of Lake City and Hinsdale County as though they had neither a past nor present. Lake City is an established fact. The hand of fate has simply silenced them (mines) for a time. The first of June may find this city the busy, laughing, prosperous metropolis it naturally always was and FOREVER will be, even if its streets are a little quiet.[560]

Yet on April 24, 1885, the *Lake City Register* announced it was closing its doors and the editor was moving to a new job in Montrose. Then, even the *Silver World* closed on March 31, 1888, although other papers were to appear in Lake City over the next few decades.[561]

Both the Ocean Wave smelter and the Van Giessen Lixiviation Works did a fair amount of business after the Crooke's operation shut down, but they were losing a good percentage of the metals from the ores they were processing. To make matters worse for the average local mine owner, the smelters only paid sixty to seventy percent of the value of the metals they did recover. Most smelters said such high fees were necessary because of the high costs of operation and the profit they felt they needed to make because of the risks involved.[562]

In 1887, considerable ore was shipped from the re-opened Ute-Ulay, Vermont, and Yellow Medicine Mines. The shipments fell off drastically in 1888 at the Yellow Medicine, although the other two mines continued to ship ore. The D&RG completed a branch from Montrose into Ouray

The Van Giesen Lixiviation Works was still running, but by the early 1880s it had become evident that the leaching process didn't work very well on Colorado ores, and as a result there was only one other Colorado mill that used the process and it was located in Denver. The mill was dismantled in 1898. (Courtesy of Denver Public Library, X-60845)

in December, 1887, but there was still no news of a Lake City Branch. Although Lake City mining had been in a major slump for six years, by 1888 the Denver and Rio Grande Railroad announced it would finish its branch line up the Lake Fork of the Gunnison from Sapinero in 1889. Once again the boom and bust cycle had been affected by the decision of the railroad.

The third major Lake City boom started about 1887, after the Ute-Ulay Mine was bought at a foreclosure sale, reopened, and began producing a lot of good silver ore. The mine produced $113,000 during the first year it reopened and did even better in 1888. At almost the same times as the D&RG announced that it would finish the Lake City line, very rich gold ore was found at the Golden Fleece Mine. When the railroad arrived in 1889 and low grade ores started to be shipped, the Golden Fleece was mining very rich ore. A single train car of petzite gold ore brought $50,000 (about $2 million dollars in today's values).

Work on the D&RG branch continued through the summer of 1889, with 700 to 800 men working on laying track and building bridges, as most of the right of way and grading had been completed in 1881. Work was completed by August and the first regularly scheduled train arrived in Lake City on August 15, 1889.[563] For the first time, Lake City had cheap transportation to the outside world. Lake City residents could dream big dreams again. A road was started up Cottonwood Creek in 1889, following the trail that went over the divide and down to Minnie Gulch and up the Mears' toll road from Silverton to Animas Forks and Mineral Point, which two settlements had no railroad nearby. Some said it was a better route to Lake City than Cinnamon Pass, but the San Juan County ores that Hinsdale County folks hoped would be shipped to the Lake City branch of the railroad never came and the road soon fell into disuse.[564] Then the Silverton Northern would be built to Animas Forks in the early 1900s, making this totally unnecessary. Still, the Lake City mining districts were greatly revived by 1891, and the mines in the area continued to do very well until about 1902. Renowned geologist Charles Henderson felt that the period of 1891 to 1902 "was the most productive in the history of the county."[565]

The railroad brought back actual prosperity to Lake City. The Ute-Ulay produced $400,000 in one year and had a monthly payroll of $20,000.[566] During this boom Lake City's residents built sidewalks and renovated run-down houses. Many of the old Victorian homes still standing today were built during this period. This time, however, after two previous booms and busts, residents were a little more cautious.

The city completed its first water works in 1890, and an electric power plant was built and a town-wide electric system installed in 1891. In January of 1891, another paper opened in Lake City in competition

Lake City looks ready for a boom in this photograph in October, 1887, but it would still be a year and a half before the railroad arrived. Note the Ocean Wave Mill at the upper right of the photo., the new school in the middle of the photo, and the number of commercial establishments in the area bounded by Silver and Gunnison and Third and Second Streets. (Author's Collection)

with the well-established Lake City *Phonograph*. The Lake City *Times* was backed by local businessmen who wanted to promote the town and its nearby mines. This was done by their newspaper and also by brochures, pamphlets, and even small books that were sent to interested parties.[567] A.R. Arbuckle became the editor of the town's new paper. The first issue appeared January 15, 1891. The paper swore it would not exaggerate the local business and mines as in the past. "The *Lake City Times* only expects to show Lake City to outside interests as a good place to invest capital."[568] The paper lasted until 1917, but the editors changed often. In 1893 the newspaper became the Lake City *Times and Silver World*. All of Lake City's papers were of exceptional quality and publicized not only town news, but all of the San Juan news, especially mining.

By 1890, after the arrival of the railroad, there were twenty mines in the Lake City area shipping ore. By the end of 1891, the population of Lake City had risen from below 1,000 to over 2,000. Culture still persisted in the town, and the Lake City Band was formed. Don and Jean Griswold wrote in their book *Colorado's Century of Cities*:

> *When the Lake Fork branch of the Denver and Rio Grande Railroad reached Lake City in 1889, the camp returned with vigor*

to its mining and allied industries; new people; new businesses; and outside capital came to Lake City; the long vacant houses were occupied again, and the hardy citizens who had, as Hall observed, 'endured the horrors and hardships of business activity for years' again wore 'the smile of gladness and joy.' This was the beginning of the most productive period in the district's mining history. From 1891 until 1902 at least a half million dollars' worth of ores was shipped each year. Then the year 1903 marked the start of more quiet years, which finally culminated in the abandonment of the railroad in Lake City in 1933.

To name all the mines of this region, where the records show the existence of over 5,000, would require a large volume.[569]

In the late fall of 1891, the flu epidemic called "Le Grippe" at the time hit Lake City hard. The flu often progressed into pneumonia with Hinsdale County's cold weather and high altitude. Area miners were especially susceptible as the local mines were almost all damp — some mines even contained a foot or two of water that the miners had to work in. Without antibiotics, pneumonia was a killer, often resulting in death within a few days. Most of the sick men came to Lake City to

Lake City about 1890 does not look like it has grown much since 1887. There are still plenty of log cabins, but the city was on the verge of its third boom, during which many of its Victorian buildings were built. The dump on the center right is from The Red Bird Mine, almost located within the town's limits. The photo is looking west. (Denver Public Library, Author's Collection)

seek medical help, but there was little the doctors could do for them. As the flu and pneumonia spread, Lake City citizens also began to die. The town fathers, in utter desperation, even turned on all the fire hydrants in town and tried to wash the germs away. Soon there was a major epidemic and four or five people were dying each week. Eventually more than 100 residents and local miners died during the winter of 1891-92.[570]

As bad as that outbreak was, it was followed by a more devastating flu outbreak in 1919-20. This was the influenza and pneumonia called the "Spanish Flu" that killed millions around the world; and, with the high altitude, it weakened the lungs of the miners and the large number of small children present in the San Juans. The flu hit so hard in Silverton that there were not enough healthy people to bury the dead that winter, and victims were simply stacked in the cold like firewood to await a later burial. Finally a mass grave was dug and many of the victims were buried together.[571] The flu hit hard in Lake City, but not as bad as Silverton.

By 1892, the Ute-Ulay was owned by the Thatcher Brothers Bank in Lake City. In late 1892 they tried to make a deal with freighter Dave Wood to haul the mine's ore to the railroad in Lake City. He bid $10 a ton, a reasonable price, but the bank tried to get him down to $9.50. When Dave would not budge, the bank hired a much less experienced man to do the work at a slightly lower price.

The man soon came to Dave wanting to buy his local equipment to help keep up with his transfers of ore to the railroad in Lake City. Dave agreed to let him use twelve six-mule teams and wagons for a month, but at the end of that time he had to either buy the wagons and teams or pay a high rental for the use of the equipment. He also required that the bank co-sign the agreement, which they did. At the end of the month, the bank again offered to hire Dave but again tried to haggle him down on his rates; but when Dave pointed out the deal that had been made and that it had been guaranteed by the bank, they had the other freighter buy the teams the next morning. In no time the man who bought the teams failed in his business. Thereafter the bank used Dave and agreed to his terms. Meanwhile the 1893 Silver Panic had hit Colorado hard, and the price of silver fell to a fraction of its former value. Dave Wood realized the man who had gone out of business had failed to move much of the bank's ore, which was now worth only a fraction (about half) of the value it had been a few months earlier when Dave made his original bid to move it. Dave loved to tell this story to show how important it was to use reliable, experienced, and trustworthy freighters.[572]

In the early 1890s Lake City and the San Juans as a whole had been experiencing a boom, but there were dark clouds on the country's economic horizon that would crush the economy of a major part of the American West and especially Colorado. There was a movement for the United States to be only on the gold standard (gold backing its currency) and the elimination of the double monetary standard that included silver. The price of silver was fluctuating wildly.

The Sherman Silver Purchase Act required the federal government to purchase 4 ½ million ounces of silver a month, and this artificially propped up the price of silver. When the act was repealed in 1893, the resulting crash was devastating. Silver fell from over a dollar to 62 cents an ounce within a few days of the repeal of the Sherman Silver Purchase Act; and half the mines in Colorado and much more than half in the Hinsdale area closed.[573] Banks failed, out of work men roamed the streets begging to work for food, and the city coffers were empty and most government projects ground to a stop. When the mines started closing, other local businesses also shut down, and those that did remain often asked their employees to take a cut in salary.

The entire state of Colorado suffered a major depression. Many of Colorado's mining camps became ghost towns overnight, but as in the past, Lake City struggled on. The gold discoveries at the Golden Fleece, the Golden Wonder, and even some at the Ute-Ulay, allowed Hinsdale mining to continue. Wilbur Stone in 1918 wrote about the Silver Panic and the way Lake City was able to respond to it:

The Crooke's operation had been abandoned by 1892 when this photo was taken, as it was set up to mill silver at a time when Hinsdale County would begin to mine gold; but it is a good view of Granite (Crookes) Falls. (Photo by Clark Studio, Courtesy of Denver Public Library, X-61418)

Following the advent of transportation facilities (the railroad in 1889), there was a marked revival in all the mining districts. The general depression of 1893 again retarded advancement for the reason that nearly all the ores developed at that time were lead, silver, and copper. Since 1894 the advance of (Lake City) has been steady, and in common with many other sections, the existence of gold-bearing ore has been demonstrated.[574]

Silver production was at an all-time high in Hinsdale County in 1893 when the bottom fell out of the silver market, but gold production in Hinsdale County tripled in 1895. It had been known since Lake City's founding that there was gold in the Hotchkiss (Golden Fleece) Mine, and, in fact, it had been the reason for the initial rush into the future Lake City area. Owner Charles Davis had struck an extremely rich gold and silver pocket in 1892. Some of the ore assayed as high as 125 ounces of gold and 1,255 ounces of silver. "Some of the ore was so rich, according to reports, that it was hammered into jewelry without smelting or refining."[575]

Very rich silver strikes were found near the future Creede in 1889, and Mineral County was created from part of Hinsdale County in 1893, thereby making further statistics not fully comparable. The late 1890s were, however, still a boom time for Hinsdale County with the Hidden Treasure, Golden Fleece, Contention, and many other mines doing well, mainly in gold production. The rich discovery of gold at the Golden Fleece caught the attention of Denver capitalists, who purchased the mine and formed the Golden Fleece Mining and Milling Company in 1894. The mine continued to produce well — $274,421 in 1895 alone.[576] In 1897, the Hidden Treasure shipped its first rich gold ore. Lead and silver were also being found in larger quantities at some of the local mines, although the silver was almost a byproduct, compared to the gold.

Even with the Silver Panic depressing the Colorado economy, by 1893 more space was needed in the Lake City school building for the elementary children, and a high school was also added. Despite tough times, the second story of the school was finally finished. School attendance increased to 166 in 1897, and 180 in 1898. Until this time there had been private schools off and on that held session in Lake City (including dancing, singing and foreign language schools),[577] but they closed after the Silver Panic.

Because of the local gold discoveries, Hinsdale County mines were actually doing pretty well at a time when most silver mining camps (and Hinsdale had been a silver mining camp until gold was discovered) were becoming ghost towns. During the year 1897, an average of 493 men were employed at the mines and new prospects were being explored. Hinsdale mining, although declining a little, was still doing well.

During these tough times, it would have been easy for many of the town's young people to be drawn into the general (but limited) lawlessness of Hell's Acre, but a real effort was made to provide decent entertainment. In fact the *Lake City Times* noted:

> *In one sense of the word, Lake City is the young people's paradise. The younger class seems to enjoy themselves to the full extent, with parties and social gatherings, and the parents and older ones seem to take pride in helping the young people in their pleasure.*[578]

Life went on in Lake City. The town still had the red-light district of an early mining town located near Henson Creek at the south end of Bluff Street. One of the most famous madams on Bluff Street was Clara Ogden, who had arrived in Lake City in the late 1880s, when business was beginning to pick up with the announcement that the D&RG would continue to build their branch line to Lake City. Ogden had torn down several of the local cribs and built a large ballroom and several entertainment rooms on the first floor of her establishment. A piano player was usually pounding out tunes on the piano downstairs. She built the Crystal Palace dance hall, which was by far the largest and grandest dance hall and bordello in Hell's Acre. On the ground floor of Clara's establishment, the rooms were furnished with crystal, mahogany, mirrors, and fancy carpeting. The second floor included dozens of bedrooms.

Clara, being an acute business woman, believed strongly in the power of advertising, and she was known to often fill her elegant carriage, which she bought along with two matching bay horses in 1895, with some of her girls and drive out to the nearby mines and mining camps to show off their wares. It was a very unusual but successful way of advertising what she had to offer. Clara was forced to shut down near the end of the nineteenth century when there was a shooting in her establishment.[579] It was said that at one time she hoped to open a chain of bordellos in the outlying areas, but she never did.[580]

Shortly before the turn of the century, L. A. Vinton & Co., dealers in real estate and mining properties in Leadville and Lake City, published a small pamphlet, entitled *Resources and Mineral Wealth of Hinsdale County, Colorado*, extolling the virtues of Lake City and its surrounding area. The book stated that "this booklet is issued for the purpose of advancing and perpetuating the mining industry of Hinsdale County.... It is respectfully dedicated to thoughtful and intelligent readers wherever they may be found." In a way, it was a last desperate effort to bring in capital and revive mining, but it also showed that there was still hope in Lake City. The pamphlet stated:

The recent discovery of the yellow metal throughout the San Juan country, which includes our own district, has aroused a new inspiration of hope in the breasts of mining men of this section, and has instilled new life into the mining industry of Hinsdale County.[581]

The authors submitted that the "Silvery San Juans" should be renamed the "Gilded San Juans."

The great progress made in the discovery and development of gold leads throughout the San Juans during the past two years is something phenomenal in the history of mining.[582]

Thus began an extensive review of all the mines still operating in the county. This included the Ute-Ulay, which employed 200 men (down from 300), and was still producing silver and lead in large amounts, but

This photo is from about 1900, taken to the north to probably show the flooding of Henson Creek. It also gives a good view of the railroad yard at the upper right. Note that there were two bridges over Henson at the time — one on Gunnison and one on Silver Streets. (Author's Collection)

only $6 a ton in gold. A review of the Capitol City mines showed they were all still producing mainly low grade silver, but some had gold. The mines in Palmetto Gulch were closed. The Golden Fleece had shipped $288,000 in gold ore in the year ending September 1, 1895, and was "anticipating" $378,000 in the next year. The Black Crooke was not operating. There was "surface prospecting" going on in the Slumgullion District. This evidently meant just picking up rich pieces of ore off the ground, which ultimately were shown to have been brought down by the Slumgullion Slide. The Golden Wonder's past was reviewed, and it would prove to be a good-paying gold operation after more development was done. In short, there were no solid factors to support the optimistic declaration of an era in rich gold mining, although the L. A. Vinton Company did a good job of making prospects look hopeful. Lake City itself was also reviewed:

> The town is handsomely built, with large brick and stone business blocks and residences. Beautiful shaded, paved[583] streets, wide sidewalks, electric lights, water works and irrigation ditches, all combine to make an ideal spot for the transaction of business among pleasurable surroundings.... Every branch of business is well-represented in this city. This publication is not for the purpose of soliciting new business houses.[584]

This last statement was obviously made for the protection of the existing businesses in Lake City. The merchants could not afford to lose any business they had at the time to newcomers.

In 1899, Lake City, like most San Juan towns, was hit by labor violence. Union miners at the Ute-Ulay and Hidden Treasure struck. About 140 men were involved in the union, of which about eighty were Italians who had recently joined the Western Federation of Miners. Most of the Italians were upset over a company order that all single men working at the mine must live in the company's boarding house, which had high rates compared to some of the boarding houses in Lake City. One of the major events of Lake City history occurred on March 14, 1899, when Italian miners at the Ute-Ulay and Hidden Treasure Mines went on strike over the requirement. The miners met the day shift on that day, and would not allow them to enter the mine. Some of the non-union men were attacked. It was soon discovered that fifty Springfield rifles and 1,000 rounds of ammunition were missing from the armory at Lake City. Then it was announced that the Italians had bought every gun and box of ammunition that was available in Lake City. The sheriff arrested twelve Italians and charged the secretary of the local union with the theft of the armory guns and ammunition.

Some indication of the racism that existed at the Ute-Ulay could be found earlier in the Lake City *Phonograph* of March 3, 1894:

J. C. Spargo's ability to work men to an advantage (at the Ute-Ulay) speaks of itself. It has been rumored that in the near future the force on these properties will be composed of white men only.

By March 15, 1899, the sheriff was convinced that the Italians who were not in jail would become violent, and he telegraphed the governor for help. The response was that 326 Colorado militia men were sent to Lake City, accompanied by the Italian consulate from Denver. Wilbur Stone reported in great detail on the strike in his book, *History of Colorado*:

On March 14, 1899, a strike of miners began at Lake City, Hinsdale County, Colorado, or, to be more exact, at the Village of Henson, which is three miles from Lake City (at the Ute-Ulay Mine). Two mines were affected — the Ute-Ulay and the Hidden Treasure. The Aulic Mining Company leased and operated the Ute and Ulay mine and mill in which about 100 men were employed, of which about forty were Italians. The Hidden Treasure Mining and Milling Company employed about the same number of men with about the same proportion of Americans and foreigners. The Italians were members of a local union of the Western Federation of Miners, which had been organized only a few months previously. Some Americans were also members of this organization.

The cause of the strike was a requirement of the company that all single men in their employ should board at the company boarding house. The Italians refused to comply with this order. They sought to induce the Americans to strike, but the latter continued to work. The Americans were unaware of any disturbance until the day shift started to work on March 14, when they were met by the Italians armed with rifles. Not a man was allowed to enter the mines. The Americans having been driven away from the mines, a few returned to go to work, but they were beaten by the Italians, who threatened to shoot them if they returned.

The discovery was made that the state armory at Lake City had been broken open and that the arms and ammunition therein, fifty Springfield rifles and 1,000 rounds of ammunition, had been removed. Investigation also proved that within a few days the Italians had purchased nearly all the Winchester rifles and other firearms on sale in the town.

Governor Charles S. Thomas on March 16 ordered four companies of infantry and two companies of cavalry to the scene of the disturbance, and wholesale arrests followed.

The military officers, civic officers, mine managers, citizens, and the Italian consul reached an agreement on March 20 under which the prisoners should be released under the understanding that the single men should have to leave the county within three days and the married men within sixty days. The agreement further provided that employees of the company might board wherever they pleased. This settlement was received with general approval except by the Italian strikers, but as the managers of the company had already resolved not to employ Italians, the foreigners really had no inducement to remain in Hinsdale County.... On March 20, 1899, the troops were withdrawn from the county.[585]

During this affair, it was rumored that the D&RG Railroad track into Lake City was mined, so the train carrying the National Guard was preceded by a "pilot engine with a box car." At Lake City, the troops were met by a group of locals eager to join in the excitement. Dr. Cuerno, the Italian consul, and Charles Mairo of Lake City met with the Colonel in charge of the militia. A letter was sent to the mine from Cuerno with Mairo carrying the message.

When the State militia headed up Henson Creek toward the Hidden Treasure and the Ute-Ulay, Dr. Cuerno went to the scene and intercepted the troops a few miles out of town. Dr. Cuneo asked to speak with the miners and permission was granted. Then the consul requested that everyone — locals, National Guard, and militia, meet with the miners at Henson to discuss the matter. Cuerno then dressed with a high silk hat, an overcoat with a fur collar, and patent leather shoes, and was driven in a buggy with a white flag attached to the buggy's whip. The troops brought up the rear of this procession.

Half a mile below Henson a company of six men waited for them, and after exchanging salutes and bows the men cheered the consul and kissed his gloved hands. The procession went on to the mine and town, where shawled women and their children were, as well as workmen. Although it was bitterly cold the consul then stopped the buggy, got out, took off his hat and unbuttoned his overcoat so as to display the full evening dress underneath complete with a red, white, and green ribbon (the colors of Italy) across his shirt. The crowd cheered and the consul made a speech to the miners and commanded them to salute the militia officers and surrender to the sheriff. The Italians did as told and started walking down the road to Lake City, accompanied by their women and children.[586]

Perry Eberhart called the drama at the end of the strike one of the most unusual the San Juans had even seen:

> *Dr. Cuerno had promised the miners to do his utmost to secure a fair hearing and just settlement. Under his insistence the miners submitted. But they — and Dr. Cuerneo — were double crossed. Instead of a fair hearing, the unmarried strikers were ordered to leave the area within three days and the married strikers were given sixty days in which to leave town.*[587]

Besides the strike at the Ute-Ulay and Hidden Treasure in 1899, Lake City had a major small pox epidemic, which had spread throughout much of Colorado. Hinsdale County had such an epidemic every five to ten years, but this one was especially deadly. Unfortunately, it was at first diagnosed in Lake City as pneumonia, and it had spread throughout the area by June before any precautions were taken. The situation was bad enough that guards were deployed at roads leading in and out of the city. No one could come in or go out without the permission of the town board. The smallpox epidemic was especially prevalent at the Hidden Treasure, and the men at that mine and mill were not allowed to leave. Four guards were placed at the mine to make sure no one tried. A "pest house" was established in Ball Flats in Lake City for those known to have the disease. As bad as it was, newspaper reports began to be printed in other parts of Colorado that grossly exaggerated the state of affairs in Hinsdale County. By June 30, the *Gunnison News* reported that four people had died and many more were sick, and train service to the town was being discontinued. By July matters were getting better, but the last fatal victim of the plague did not die until July 29.[588]

Capitalists still came to look at the local mines after 1900. Frank Hough wrote in his diary on June 13, 1901:

> *There were 33 Bostonians came to town last night on a special train. They came in at 6:30 p.m. and went right to the Contention Mine. Quite a crowd gathered at the depot to see them come in.*[589] *However, all was not rosy in Lake City during this boom.*

Prosperity began a long, slow decline in Hinsdale about 1902. There were still a few booms to come, but they were all small and short. One of Hinsdale's minor booms occurred when placer gold was discovered in the later 1890s and early 1900s, twenty-five miles north of Lake City in the Lake Fork Canyon. As news of the discovery spread, an area known as the "gold belt" was found to extend to the northeast and was eventually called the "Gunnison Gold Belt," as it was in Gunnison

County, but well on the south side of the Gunnison River. By 1905, there were over 100 acres of placer mines in the Lower Lake Fork Canyon, and this brought a short boom to the area about ten miles north of Hinsdale County. During its time, the Gunnison Gold Belt boom was as big as most Colorado booms and brought about a frenzy of exploration and development. Between August, 1904 and October, 1906, more than twenty-five lode claims were filed in Lake Fork Canyon alone, but the boom was short.

The overall bust in the early 1900s was so gradual that it was not until well into the 1900s that most people in Lake City even realized it was happening, but there were signs. Street brawls became more regular, and racism was to show its angry face. By 1903 gold production was slowing down.

> *Lake City's final boom of the late 1890s did not conclude with any great event. Rather the economy and population simply started a gradual decline.... Ore production decreased, and predictably, the railroad operating the Lake City Branch — by then known as the Denver and Rio Grande Western — began to cut back on its service.*[590]

Although the citizens of Lake City seemed to still be refined and moral, crime was rising as economic decline took its toll. The *Lake City Times* headlines complained in 1898 that there had been:

> *"Three Murders in Four Years," all because of drunkenness. Not one of these crimes would have been committed had the perpetrators of the deeds been sober.... Is it not time to make an effort to discourage drunkenness?*[591]

Yet elegance and taste still existed enough in Lake City that the *San Cristobal Quarterly* was started as a literary magazine in Lake City in March, 1901. The magazine:

> *.... early established itself as a 'literary' undertaking, and did not engage very actively in argumentative matters, although the third edition acknowledged an argument with Col. Meek over the spelling of (the word) 'newsstand.'*[592]

To some extent Lake Citians made their own entertainment. When President Taft came to Montrose for the opening of the Gunnison Tunnel in September, 1909, W.C. Blair, ex-editor of the *Silver World*, who was living in Montrose, offered to find accommodations for anyone from Lake City who wanted to attend the event. Over 100 people took the train to Montrose and brought a seven and one-half pound dressed trout and fifty pounds of small native and brook trout for the President. Unfortunately a Montrose lawyer presented the fish and took credit for the gift.[593]

Ex-editor Blair was also an avid baseball fan at a time when almost every town in Colorado had its own team, many members of which were semi-professionals. Blair would often pay for the Lake City team to play in Montrose and then would bet on the game.[594] Lake City's team practiced in the area of Lake City that is still called "Ball Flats."

Even in the twentieth century, Lake City still had a Wild West flavor. On April 1, 1901, John Addington and Alexander Surtee had a gunfight over a girl of questionable character. They met on Silver Street between the bank and the Hough building and both were able to fire a shot and strike their opponent. Surtee died immediately and Addington passed away two days later. Both men were married and Addington had children. Dr. Benjamin Cummings, who ran into the street when he heard shots, was hit in the buttocks and had to find another doctor to operate on him. The bullet was not found in his flesh, but later when Dr. Cummings pulled his silk handkerchief out of his rear pocket, the bullet came out with it!

A photo of Lake City about 1908, looking to the south. Pete's Lake is simply a wet area and the creek exits through a completely different route than the route followed after the present-day dam was built. Note the railroad's "one mile bridge" crossing the Lake Fork at center left. (Whitman Cross, USGS Photo)

In another event, a young doctor, R.O. Lacy, walked into a saloon, while already drinking heavily, and fatally shot his best friend, Henry Vittle, evidently for no reason at all. Because he was drunk at the time, Lacy was sentenced to only one year in the Lake City jail, during which time he could still call on patients. Then Patrick Doneley, who was a saloon keeper in Capitol City, shot and killed Anton Nickole because he had started an argument in his saloon.[595] Another man was shot in Lake City while trying to stop a man from beating his wife. Several election shootings also occurred during the early 1900s, and at least one was fatal.[596]

In an election fight in 1908, Dr. Cummings was shot by Steve Kinsey in a pool room. Kinsey was convicted of assault with a deadly weapon and, while in custody, was given whiskey and a gun by a drunk being housed for the night in the jail. In an attempt to escape, Kinsey shot the jail deputy in the hip. The drunk, a man by the name of Kit Carter, and Kinsey were both given additional time to serve because of the attempted escape, and Carter burned to death in the jail, evidently starting the fire when he kicked over a lamp.[597]

By 1913, Lake City was beginning to enjoy a few more tourists each summer, most of whom gravitated to Lake San Cristobal, which was a big draw for Lake City and Hinsdale County. The Lake City *Times* got really excited about only a trickle of people, and boasted that:

More than one hundred tourists visited Lake San Cristobal this summer, and we expect more than three hundred next year. Lake City is an ideal resort, and Lake City people exhibit the spirit of hospitality.[598]

In 1917, the Grand Junction *Sentinel* carried a long, detailed article containing the newspaper editor's impressions of Lake City after he spent a two week vacation at Lake San Cristobal. It was entitled "A Story of a Paradise in the Land of the Sky."[599] Horseback riding in the nearby mountains has always been popular with Lake City residents and tourists, and burros were a major part of early Lake City tourism. In the days before mining almost disappeared, prospectors would often let their burros roam in town in the winter or in the nearby hills, especially if the prospectors left for good. Burros were a part of Lake City life, much like the deer that now roam around town.

Most of the white picket fences seen in the historical district were originally built to keep grazing burros out of people's yards, and especially to keep them away from flower beds, but usually to no avail. Before automobiles and four-wheel drive vehicles, the women and children liked to ride burros because they were close to the ground, hard to spook, and passengers were much less likely to get hurt if they fell off. It was especially important for the women, most of whom rode side saddle in those days. Women, children, and tourists would often have parties or picnics where they would all ride burros into the nearby mountains. Local women and children often had little two wheeled carts that were pulled by burros, so as to not have the dangers of a runaway horse. Even with the problems that burros often caused, most of the women and children in Lake City loved them dearly. For a boy, having a burro was like getting a first car today. And best of all, burros could be taken in from the strays roaming around town without having to pay for them; and since they would eat almost anything, it made their upkeep very inexpensive.

Alex Carey wrote of "Old Sid," who he said stood out from all the rest of the burros that roamed around Lake City in the 1930s and 1940s because of that particular burro's tenacity.[600]

When the mines shut down (the burros) put in their time running around town getting into all kinds of mischief, getting into people's gardens, eating up the flowers, and braying their heads off. They took a very special delight in getting under your bedroom window in the early morning hours and braying like the dickens....

(Old Sid) traveled alone. With his years of experience, "Old Sid" was the smoothest gate opener of them all. A large white donkey

About 1900 a small crowd gathered outside the Occidental Hotel with two women and a child on burros. The reason is unknown, but since they got their photo taken, it is highly likely they were tourists going for a ride. (Author's Collection).

Views are not as common of southern Gunnison Avenue as they are of south Silver Street, but there were plenty of commercial buildings on Gunnison. (Author's Collection)

with great long ears and large soulful eyes, always with a look of complete innocence on his face. Many the cussin' he received but his abilities were respected by all. If anyone from the outside tried to steal him the whole town would have risen up in wrath.

Every day "Old Sid" made his rounds from gate to gate, the other donkeys often standing back watching, they respected his abilities too, and when he got a gate opened they would follow him in. When they had gained an entrance, it was just too bad for the garden if the people who lived there were not at home to chase them out. They would eat their fill and what they didn't eat they would trample into the ground. "Old Sid" was good also at opening shed doors. One time, so the story goes, Joe Hunt had a nice bunch of chickens which were fed wheat that he kept in a shed with a good latch on it. None of the other donkeys try as they would, could get into it. It was duck soup for "Old Sid!" He made it several times, eating up all the wheat, which donkeys love, and scattering the rest around just for the heck of it. Joe went up to town and bought more wheat every time and finally in desperation purchased a strong hasp and padlock. He put that on the door, locking it tight, and probably saying to himself, 'Let's see you get into that, you old so and so.' That evening as Joe and his wife were eating their evening meal, he happened to look out the window…. 'Look at that,' Joe shouted to his wife, pointing at Old Sid. 'Look at that damned donkey trying to find where I hid the key!'[601]

Colorado voted to go dry in 1914. Most of the Colorado farming and ranching communities voted to be dry, but the mining communities, and especially the San Juans, voted to stay wet. The result was widespread bootlegging and illegal stills throughout the San Juans, with Hinsdale County being no exception. Adding to the desire to produce liquor was the ease in which a still could be hidden in the rugged nearby mountains, and the fact that most mountain communities were warned by others when the federal authorities were on their way, invariably by train, to look for stills or illegal liquor.

In the summer of 1915, a fire destroyed two Lake City saloons; but rather than rebuild with prohibition looming, the owners were reported to set up drinks at the armory. In December of that year Colorado went dry. The Lake City *Times* announced that:

> *While not in sympathy with temperance by legislation, the* Times *urges everybody to help everybody else to respect and obey the law. Swat the bootlegger and the hypocrite.*[602]

Then in the last issue of that year it announced:

> *Everybody will now please rise and sing that touching little ditty entitled "How Dry I Am: How Dry I Am: Nobody Knows How Dry I Am."*

In the spring of 1917, as the United States neared entry into World War I, the Lake City *Times* had cautioned its readers to not be caught up in a prevailing national outcry against U.S. citizens of German origin. Then on April 5, 1917 the editor wrote:

> *Now that we have committed to the fray, we must carry it to a successful (conclusion).... Money, food, and men we must furnish to the limit of our abilities.*[603]

The Ute-Ulay Mine was reopened and producing in 1918, probably for the base metals (mainly copper, lead, and zinc) needed in World War I, but production soon stopped again. The first few decades of the twentieth century were a critical time for Lake City. As the mines closed and merchants left, the population of Lake City fell dramatically. The year-round census dropped from 2,000 in 1900, to an estimated 1,000 in 1908, to 405 in 1910; and in 1940 it was only 185.

Although the major wars were good for local mining because of the demand for base metals, the activity was short-lived; and some of the local boys went to war and never came back. Lake City has a monument in Memorial Park (between Gunnison Avenue and the Hinsdale Courthouse) to remember the local men who died in all of our nations wars. Veterans are not forgotten in Lake City. Gold production was totally shut down during the two World Wars and silver production was limited. What the United States needed were base metals, and Lake City helped provide a great deal of them, but much more out of a sense of patriotism than a desire to make a profit.

The 1929 Great Depression and Stock Market Crash hurt Lake City and Hinsdale County, but not as much as most of the country. The little production left in the mines dried up, but one consolation was that Ma and Pa hard rock mining operations, as well as some placer mining, allowed locals to make a little money, while many of the residents in the big cities had no good way to make a living. Some of the dumps of the bigger mines were reworked for a little profit; and, of course, Lake City was used to hard times, as it had been depressed for several decades. The Great Depression did not change matters that much. The New Deal did not offer much help for mining, but there were a few projects in Hinsdale and nearby counties conducted by the Civilian Conservation Corps (CCC).

Matters were bad enough during the Great Depression that the D&RG railroad could justify stopping service to the town. When that happened, as one resident described it, "Everything went down the drain."[604] The D&RG rails were ripped up in 1937. As Perk Vickers put it:

In order to understand life around here during the 1920s and 1930s, you have to realize that there were not too many of us here. We were rather isolated and nobody had much money.[605]

The third Occidental Hotel, always Lake City's finest, had its photo taken in 1935 by famous ghost town author Muriel Wolle. The hotel burned down in 1937. It was located at the southeast corner of 4th and Silver Streets. (Denver Public Library X-32)

The main hotel in Lake City, the Occidental, burned in 1937. The Golden Fleece was sold in 1943 for taxes. Lake City seemed to be heading for ghost town status. Buildings ran down, grass grew in the streets, and the population of the town proper sank to below 100. But the isolation that Perk talked about became a draw, along with a new recognition of the beautiful scenery and good fishing of Hinsdale County. People heard that Lake City was a beautiful place; and, just as in the 1880s, Lake City became popular for its natural attractions. People from Texas, Oklahoma, Kansas, and other nearby states; built simple little "fishing cabins" in Ball Flats or bought and refurbished small Victorian cottages along Silver Street.

However the permanent population continued to fall. In 1970, only ninety-one brave Lake City souls spent the winter in the settlement. The only reason that it was not totally vacated was that more and more tourists were coming to enjoy the summertime recreational facilities, and a few dedicated residents were bound and determined that Lake City would continue to exist without relying on just mining. The *Silver World* newspaper closed in 1938, and the town did not have a paper again until 1948, when the Lake City *Tribune* was started. Many times there was no banking facility and the only medical provider of any kind was Theo French, a registered surgical nurse.[606] With the road to Gunnison still being dirt, it meant a two-hour trip each way to shop for items and services that were not available in Lake City. The times were indeed bleak, but Lake City's citizens held on.

As in most of the United States, after WWII, many Western Slope young people started gravitating to the big cities, but in a strange twist, quite a few of the people from the large cities decided to move to, or at least have a second home in, the mountains. The influx was gradual in the late 1940s, but picked up in the 1950s and 1960s, and became a definite trend in the 1970s and 1980s. Lodges and then tourist cabins began to appear in town and returned to being built around Lake San Cristobal. By 1980, the year-round population of Hinsdale County rebounded, although the summer population had started rebounding soon after World War II. Christian camps for young people appeared. The local arts were expanded. Yes, Lake City still had a sense of class. Tourism picked up throughout all of Colorado during this time, and it soon became one of Colorado's top three industries. In Lake City, the tourists, second home owners, and the arrival of more permanent residents spurred building construction and home maintenance businesses, which are two of the largest industries in the town today, other than tourism and governmental work such as schools, city, county, and state jobs. The real estate business has also become an important trade in the county.[607]

In recent years, Lake City had been a pretty quiet town and major crime was virtually non-existent. The horrible exception came on November 18, 1994, when Sheriff Roger Coursey was killed by outsiders, thirty-eight year old Mark Vredenburg and thirty-one year old Ruth Slater. Sheriff Coursey and Undersheriff Ray Blaum (the town's entire police force at the time) were on the lookout on Slumgullion Pass for a brown pickup truck that was involved in a botched bank robbery. They had been notified that the two fugitives were possibly headed toward Lake City. When the officers stopped a brown truck, Coursey walked up to the vehicle and told the occupants to get out. He was answered by gunfire from a .44 magnum revolver and was immediately killed. Blaum, who had been in the passenger seat of the patrol car and told Coursey they should wait for backup, emptied his gun at the fleeing truck, which was found abandoned about a mile from the scene of the crime. A nationwide manhunt ensued, but with no results for almost a month. Then, on December 17, a search by dogs around the area where the pickup was found led to the bodies of the murderers about a mile and a half from the abandoned truck. They had used the same .44 magnum revolver to kill themselves as they lay under a brown sleeping bag. The FBI reasoned that they had never left the Slumgullion area.[608]

Lake City was pretty well deserted about 1940 when this photo was taken. The Lake City Garage still had the old fashioned gas pumps outside, where you manually pumped the gas up into the glass container at the top and then let it drain by gravity into the car. (Denver Public Library, Western History Department)

The west side of Silver Street between 2nd and 3rd looks pretty much like it does today in the early 1950s, although the Masonic Lodge didn't make it into the photograph. (Denver Public Library X-21, Muriel Wolle Photo)

The event shook the quiet Lake City community to its core. This was a town where people did not lock their doors, young children played in the streets at night in the summer, and keys were left in residents' cars. Although the town now recognizes the added danger that can be presented from occasional outside criminals, it has somewhat returned to normal after all these years; but, similar to 9/11 — those living in Lake City at the time of Sheriff Coursey's death will always remember and know exactly where they were when they heard what had happened. They will also tell you that Lake City has never quite been the same since the event occurred.

After World War II, the used army jeep played a very important part in Lake City's growth, as surplus jeeps could master the mountain roads originally built for access to the mines, almost all of which are now out of business. The four-wheel drive vehicle allowed many people, who were not physically able to hike or ride horseback, to enjoy recreation in the high country. This is now a major past time in Lake City in the summer, with four wheel drive vehicles being joined by even more versatile ATVs and OHVs. At first, these newer vehicles caused a fair amount of damage in the high country, but it seems that a little more respect for the beauty of our area is coming into play. Large mines pretty well disappeared in Hinsdale County in the 1970s, because of ecological concerns and government regulations; but a few small mines, with only a few, if any, employees and, therefore, exempt from much of the mining regulations, have sprouted up and are doing well in Hinsdale County. One twist is that "designer minerals," like smoky quartz and rhodocrosite, are sometimes worth more than the ore of some of the local mines. The Golden Wonder did well enough in recent years that its gold production probably exceeded that of all the previous mining of any kind done in Hinsdale County in terms of dollars; but it was nowhere close in terms of ounces of silver and gold.

However, it is tourism that seems at present to be Lake City's biggest hope for the future. Tourism has always been present in Hinsdale County to some extent, but now it has become critical. However a rush of tourists to Hinsdale County could potentially destroy the very resources that have kept Hinsdale County alive for the last century. So the development of tourism must be done with care. We will discuss those issues in Chapter Ten.

Ute Trail was one of many Christian camps in Hinsdale County in the last half of the twentieth century. This is a photo postcard the camp supplied to campers (including the author) to let their parents know they were still alive. (Author's Collection)

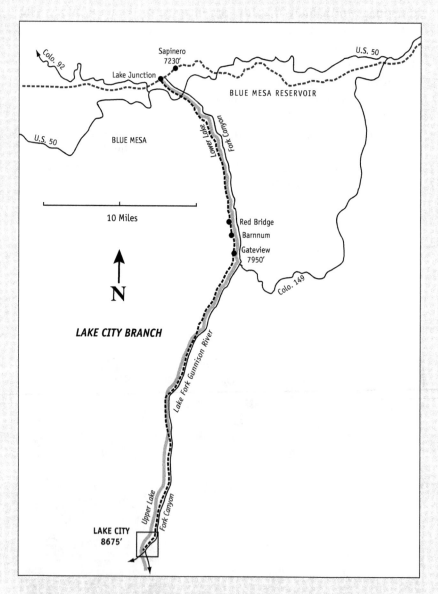

Railroad Map (Western Reflections Publishing)

CHAPTER 7

THE RAILROAD FINALLY COMES

·──⬦──·

A lmost from its founding, Lake City badly needed a railroad. The *Silver World* as early as September 30, 1876, explained why:

The position which Lake City has conquered as one of the most thriving, bustling, growing towns in any mining country and the most promising town ever sustained in an exclusively silver mining country, puts her far in advance of her neighbors in the race for supremacy and control of the business of the San Juan country. Her geographical position places her where the energy and activity of her citizens if rightly directed can make her the depot of the vast supplies which must be brought from abroad to sustain the thousands who will be in this country to develop the abundant resources of the mines of the several districts....

While we must not forsake or overlook the benefits conferred by the toll roads leading to this place from Saguache and Del Norte yet it becomes us to look beyond for communication by railroads direct and the number of railroads now projected in this direction by the different companies gives us hope that before long the shrill whistle of the locomotive will be heard in the canyons and valleys of this country. We feel that the consumption and production of this country will soon be great enough to sustain the expansion of one line and in a short time will be sufficient to pay a good profit to any honestly managed railroad to say nothing of the way business between here and say Denver or Pueblo. At the present time the Denver and San Juan, and the Atchison, Topeka, and Santa Fe roads seem the ones most likely to reach here first. Whether either of them will come to Lake City or pass by her to some other point is yet undecided....

That there will be a railroad in this country within two years, hardly anybody who knows anything about the matter doubts, the question being as to the line and the direction.

William's Tourist Guide and Map of the San Juan Mines of Colorado quoted the Lake City *Silver World* on a possible route in 1877:

> It is not probable, for many years to come, that any other railroad project (other than the D&RG) will be prosecuted into this mining region. All routes thither are nearly impracticable, except (those two) already chosen by the Rio Grande Railway.... From Garland via Saguache and Cochetopa Pass, will be the only reliable and the easiest way of travel to all of this mining field. It will have a natural road bed up the Rio Grande Valley to Clear Creek....
>
> We are justified in hoping that within two years the whistle of the iron horse will wake the echoes of the grand old hills, and our town (Lake City), so fitly named the "Queen of the Mountains," be linked to the bands of steel to the cities by the seas.[609]

As it became evident that most of Lake City's ore was low grade, it also became obvious that cheap railroad transportation was needed if the local mines would ever be successful or even operational. A railroad was also a less expensive form of transportation for bringing in goods, equipment and supplies from the outside world. For example, in 1880, Lake City merchants spent half a million dollars to bring in fifteen million pounds of freight by wagon. That expense could have been cut to a small fraction with railroad transportation. Yet another good reason that a railroad was needed was that winters' snow and ice slowed down the wagon traffic and often brought it to a complete standstill. A railroad would be immensely quicker and usually be a year-round route into Lake City.

Over the years, *The Silver World* constantly brought up the need for a railroad. At one time, in the summer of 1876, the newspaper even predicted that Lake City would have three railroads — the Denver and South Park, the Atchison, Topeka and Santa Fe, and the Denver and Rio Grande. All looked like real possibilities at the time. What a very different future Lake City would have had if any one of the three railroads had come in the 1870s.[610] Instead it was 1889 before a D&RG locomotive blew the first train whistle to be heard in Lake City.

The Denver and Rio Grande Railroad had been incorporated in October, 1870, by William Jackson Palmer and others, and construction crews headed south out of Denver in July, 1871. General Palmer was a far reaching visionary, who wanted to connect the intermountain West with the rest of the United States and Mexico. He believed that a narrow gauge railroad (three feet between the rails) would help him do this. A narrow gauge was cheaper to build and maintain and could take the sharp curves necessitated by the mountains. It could also handle a grade almost twice that of broad gauge. The narrow gauge allowed for smaller rails and ties, cheaper equipment such as locomotives and cars, and lower operating costs. Palmer had good connections in eastern financial circles which helped him raise the money to build the railroad; and he had the vision to realize that narrow gauge railroads could operate hand in hand with Colorado's gold and silver mines. As he began to build the railroad, he further quickly realized the tourism possibilities of the Denver and Rio Grande.

Palmer's original plan for the route of his railroad was to go south from Denver down to Colorado Springs and Pueblo, then go west up the Arkansas River, south over Poncha Pass, and down through the San Luis Valley on the eastern side of the San Juans to the Rio Grande River. Then he planned to go up the Rio Grande into the San Juans as well as down the Rio Grande from the San Luis Valley to El Paso, Texas. Along the way there would be feeder lines built into various mining camps. His railroad soon gained the nickname of "the biggest little railroad in the world."[611] After a wicked and expensive battle (crews were actually shooting at each other) with the Santa Fe Railroad through the Royal Gorge, Palmer decided to change his route and to head south from Pueblo to La Veta Pass, over which he would enter the San Luis Valley at Ft. Garland.

Williams Guide to the San Juan Mountains in 1877 listed the route from Ft. Garland to the San Juans at that time:

The Denver and Rio Grande Railway is being rapidly built from LaVeta, across the Sangre de Cristo range, into the San Luis Valley, to "Wagon Creek," nine miles east of Fort Garland, the contract being to complete it by June 10, 1877. From Garland the main line will probably be built westward to the Rio Grande Valley to Santa Fe and old Mexico. Negotiations are pending and likely to be consummated, for the building of a branch of this railroad westward from the Rio Grande, crossing to and via Del Norte, up the valley of the Rio Grande, via Antelope Park, to Lake City.[612]

However the D&RG Railroad was now really struggling financially to move on from Ft. Garland to Del Norte or at least to the new town of Alamosa. In an effort to help financially, Palmer was offered a half-interest in the valuable Trinchera Estates property, a fifty-foot right of way on either side of the proposed track, and six acres for a depot. Despite the financial help, the D&RG temporarily stopped at Ft. Garland and its surrounding settlement of Garland City, which was over a hundred miles from its goal of the San Juan mines. The D&RG became so insolvent that it even passed into Atchison, Topeka, and Santa

Fe receivership in 1878; however the D&RG, within a year, got control of its line again and track laying resumed to the west from Ft. Garland. The company managed to get the railroad to the new town of Alamosa, which had been founded just two months before the railroad arrived in July, 1878.

For whatever reason the D&RG line stopped in Alamosa for two years, perhaps because Palmer thought he had control of the San Juan Mountains and the Lake City railroad business, or perhaps Palmer thought it was time to slow down and see just how the mines on the Western Slope would develop, but probably because they had no money to continue.[613]

As usual, freighters and the Barlow and Sanderson stage line set up offices at the end of the line at Alamosa and began hauling freight and passengers into the San Juans and across the Continental Divide to the Western Slope of Colorado. However everyone agreed that a railroad was needed on the Western Slope, which no one knew much about at this early date. As Duane Smith put it:

The coming of the railroad to the Western Slope was like a key unlocking a previously unopened door. Who knew what riches

This photo shows one of the reasons that Lake City needed a railroad to get large machinery into the town, but even after the railroad the heavy equipment went to the mines in the mountains in this manner. (Author's Collection)

*would be unearthed? ... Previously weather, isolation, and distance
had defeated every attempt. The railroad meant that supplies could
be brought in more safely and at less expense than by burro train or
mule wagon. More important, ore, cattle, and farm produce could
be shipped out in bulk and with much greater speed than on the
backs of burros or mule wagon.*[614]

There had been talk of possibly building a railroad over Marshall
Pass, with a branch to Ouray and Lake City as early as 1879, when Otto
Mears started his toll road from Poncha Springs to Gunnison.[615] The
mining boom to the north of Gunnison was just starting to materialize,
and Palmer eventually decided that the railroad needed to go through
the Gunnison country. From there he would place his railroad in
between the Gunnison and the San Juan mining booms. Since the D&RG
generally would follow the route of the toll road, construction would go
quickly. Work started feverishly, as there were two other railroads that
had decided they would also build to Gunnison.

As soon as the Marshall Pass track was nearing Gunnison, the D&RG
also gave attention to the Lake City branch. In fact, on August 6, 1881,
even before the D&RG actually made it to Gunnison, surveyors were
laying out the Lake City route and construction crews were moving to
the site and planning to start grading by fall. The news raced around
Lake City that the railroad was finally coming! The mines and the town
got ready to shift gears into another great boom. The D&RG survey of
the branch line followed the Lake Fork of the Gunnison very closely
from Sapinero to Lake City.[616] The surveyors reported that the branch
would be feasible along the thirty-six mile route, and contractors
began working on the grade. There was also work on a wagon road
above the cliffs of the Lake Fork to bring in supplies and equipment
for the contractors. The official starting point of the railroad was not
to be Sapinero, but rather a mile west at a location to be named "Lake
Junction."[617]

The construction firm of McGavock and Tate was given the contract
to build the grade from the mouth of the Lake Fork to Barnum.
Tarkington and May did the grading in the Lake City area, and the firm
of Myers and Simmons did the work in the middle of the route. Three
to five hundred men worked on various sections of the track bed; but as
the winter of 1881-82 approached, there were concerns that the grading
would not be complete before heavy winter snows shut construction
down for the winter. The people of Lake City thought that once the
lower Canyon of the Lake Fork was conquered that track laying would
begin, but it did not, probably because rails were a major portion of the
construction costs of any railroad.

The time spent on blasting a route out of solid rock in the lower Lake Fork Canyon was not only expensive and time consuming, but also very dangerous work. Men died during the construction of this stretch of rail. Black powder was used for blasting, which was dangerous in itself. Work continued on the railroad grade during the fall of 1881; but by the late fall, there were rumors that the D&RG might reduce its number of workers on the branch line. When the D&RG sent officials to Lake City to select a spot for the depot and engine house, they reassured the locals that all was well, and the D&RG was committed to building into Lake City. As fall turned to winter, the railroad crews worked hard to finish the grade before the heavy snows, but by November they had only completed two-thirds of the total grade. Then some of the workers were assigned to work in the Black Canyon, and work on the Lake City Branch soon came to a complete halt with the onset of winter. Word had come to lay off all men working on the Lake City Branch and wait for the spring thaws before resuming construction.

At the same time, a branch line was being built by the D&RG to the coal mines in Crested Butte. The company was again being stretched financially thin between the cost of the Crested Butte and Lake City branches, and building the main line headed west toward the Black Canyon. Unfortunately, Lake City received the lowest priority of the three. By late November 1881, the *Silver World* reported that hopes were fading for the line to be finished before the next summer.[618] It was evident that Palmer's first priority was to get through the Black Canyon; and the Lake City branch, although not abandoned, was neglected.[619] Building through the Black Canyon proved to be terribly expensive and very hard work, so the track was not finished to Cimarron, Colorado (where the track exited the Black Canyon) until August, 1882.[620]

In 1881 as the Gunnison-Black Canyon extension of the D&RG main line, the company continued its construction in the San Luis Valley by heading south out of Alamosa. The company announced that instead of going up the Rio Grande to Lake City, it was shifting its efforts to a route that would go south completely through the San Luis Valley to Antonito, west over 10,015 foot Cumbres Pass, through the Toltec Gorge to Chama, New Mexico and then the Animas River. Near the spot where the Animas River came out of the San Juans, the railroad founded the new town of "Durango," Colorado, and then followed the Animas River north to Silverton, where very rich mineral discoveries had been made at Red Mountain. The main route was supposed to continue from Durango to the West Coast plus another route was to eventually follow the Rio Grande River south to Mexico. Plans to go up the Rio Grande to Lake City were completely dropped.

The section of D&RG track into Silverton was finished in July, 1882. The Denver and Rio Grande had reached the center of the San Juans from the south. The plans to build south to El Paso and west from Durango never happened, as money was running short again.

Otto Mears realized the branch line from Sapinero would not be completed any time soon, and in September of 1881, he began work on a toll road from the D&RG depot at Sapinero to his existing toll road at Barnum, where travelers could then go on to Lake City on the Saguache to Lake City Toll Road. Mears' new toll road shortened the wagon road from Lake City to the railroad by about ten miles, but it was only a stop gap measure. Even though there were rich new mining discoveries in Hinsdale County, the mining excitement dwindled because of lack of cheap transportation on the railroad.

Then in the spring of 1882, the fear of the people of Lake City came true. The D&RG did not continue work on the Lake City branch, and its construction crews were moved to other jobs, mainly in the Black Canyon.[621] The local Lake City papers remained optimistic that the branch would be finished — probably by the end of that year. As spring turned to the summer of 1882, nothing had happened. Then the official word came — the Denver and Rio Grande would not complete the Lake City branch any time in the near future because of the financial reversals it had suffered because of the railroad's push to get to Utah and Silverton.

When the railroad had announced it was not coming to Lake City from the San Luis Valley in 1881, and then later stopped work on the branch line from Gunnison to Lake City, another bust occurred. The situation was made only slightly better by good gold ore being found at the Ute-Ulay and Golden Fleece. The Lake City economy continued to sputter on as it had in the late 1870s. During the winter of 1885, over 5,000 tons of concentrates piled up at the mills and smelters at Lake City, because they could not be shipped in wagons due to the heavy snow.[622] To make matters worse, it was realized that many Hinsdale's silver ores were complex, and that they needed the treatment of experienced smelter operators in Pueblo and Denver.

This left Lake City with only the vague hope of a railroad building at some unknown time from Sapinero or the San Luis Valley, and even that hope seemed to be slipping away fast. Even more of a disaster was that the D&RG's change of plans meant Lake City would not be on a main line. That meant a great loss in the amount of railroad freight, passengers, and especially tourists. The new route to the south also meant that much of the ore in the San Juans would now be shipped out via Silverton and much of the San Juan freight would be shipped in by the same route. When the D&RG owners announced that they and other partners were going to build mills and smelters in their new town of Durango that could treat most of the complex San Juan ore, much of the ore stopped coming to Lake City's mills and smelters from along the upper Animas River and from Ouray, since at the lower altitude and with inexpensive railroad transportation, Durango smelters were cheaper and yielded better results on the San Juan ores than Lake City. The actions of the D&RG Railroad had forever ended Lake City's dreams of becoming the "Metropolis of the San Juans." Now it was hoped that Lake City could just get a branch to ship out its low grade ore.

Even before the D&RG stopped laying track in the San Luis Valley, there were several railroads that had been organized with the intention of building into the San Juans. A railroad called the Mt. Carbon, Gunnison, and Lake City Railroad and Coal Company had been incorporated on November 17, 1877. Eighty miles of track were to be laid from Richardson's coal mine near Crested Butte to Lake City, but no rails were ever put on the ground for this company; instead the D&RG built to Crested Butte from Gunnison.[623] Another proposal was the San Juan Railroad Company, which was to build to Lake City on basically the same route that today's U.S. 149 follows from Gunnison. The proposers of this railroad wanted to go north down the Lake Fork from Lake City, then west down the Gunnison River, and on to Utah. The Miners and Merchants Bank of Lake City, owned by the Thatcher Brothers of Pueblo, was part of this group. It was a good route, the Thatcher brothers could have financed it, and it would have been very beneficial to Lake City, but it never materialized. The Del Norte and Alamosa Railroad was also proposed to be built along the Del Norte-Lake City toll road during the two years the D&RG was not building in the San Luis Valley,[624] but again nothing had happened.

Much of Lake City's hopes for a railroad disappeared. The only consolation was that it was learned that several of the D&RG officers had supposedly stated that whatever route was taken to Silverton that the railroad somehow needed to continue to Lake City. The D&RG did build a branch from Alamosa to Del Norte in 1881, and extended it to the hot springs at Wagon Wheel Gap in 1883. It would have been relatively easy for the D&RG to continue on to Lake City, but the line stopped at Wagon Wheel Gap until it was extended to Creede during that area's boom in the 1890s. The line never proceeded past Creede.

The Ute-Ulay shut completely down in the fall of 1883 after the Crookes announced they were selling their interests and leaving the San Juans. This obviously came from disgust at the railroad not coming and was instead opening new smelters in Durango that the Crookes could not compete with. The Ute-Ulay Mine would be closed until 1887, but a new owner was found when hopes from the D&RG coming to Lake

City were renewed. In just eight years Lake City had gone through two major booms and busts, but it gave the town a foundation that ensured its longevity during the slow decline in the third bust (1902 to 1970) and helped to mold the hardy character its citizens' exhibit today.[625]

The population of Lake City had plummeted from 3,000 to 1,000 in just months after the D&RG announcement in 1882. Many of the businesses and mines closed. To make matters even worse, Lake City joined the rest of the nation as it slid into the major recession of 1883-1884. About this time General Palmer decided to step down as head of the D&RG Railroad; but his replacement Frederick Lovejoy, who was later described as "bungling, inefficient management," caused an even greater financial disaster that brought about the cessation of all new construction on the railroad between 1884 and 1886. During 1885, the well-respected banker, mining developer, and railroad builder, David Moffat was appointed to replace Lovejoy, but the poor financial condition of the railroad forced him to wait for a year on any new construction; and then he had to move very slowly, as he had to take care of many existing problems before new projects could be undertaken.[626]

The D&RG Railroad and David Moffat acknowledged that, with the grade almost completed, Lake City would be the logical first place to resume work when construction began again. By 1886, Lake City's economy was at an all-time low, and its citizens started looking for a railroad company other than the D&RG to complete the work. By the end of 1886, the national recession had ended, and both Lake City and the railroad were doing a little better. In the spring of 1887, Moffat asked the Lake City Board of Trade to give him information on Lake City's and Hinsdale County's financial situations and a close estimate on how much business the railroad might expect from them. Hopes were again raised among the town people, but nothing happened. In 1888, more information was requested by the D&RG and the possibility of the railroad again starting the branch line looked better. The people of Lake City were understandably beginning to have a "we will believe it when we see it attitude," however the town had one good advantage. The D&RG was in a crunch because it would forfeit its right of way from Sapinero to Lake City under its original contract if it did not build to Lake City in 1889, and several other railroad companies were beginning to eye the branch.

Not only would the D&RG lose all the money it had already invested on grading, planning, and surveying, which they estimated at $300,000 (this was definitely a high figure); but failure to act also meant another railroad could be offered the grade for free as an inducement to come to Lake City. The D&RG had always made it clear that it wanted to be in sole control of the San Juans, but after all the delays, the people of Lake

City were ready to offer the grade inducement to another railroad. The *Lake City Phonograph* of October 19, 1888, stated the town's position:

Lake City must have a railroad. It is becoming an imperative necessity, both for the influence it will have in restoring confidence in our mine owners, and its effect in giving us an important reduction in freight rates…. We must have a railroad connection, and if the Denver and Rio Grande does not supply that necessity soon, Lake City influence and friendship, small though it be considered, will be given to the road that will first move to build here.

By 1888, J. J. Abbott, who had always been a firm supporter of the D&RG Railroad for the Lake City Board of Trade, started mentioning to other railroads that the D&RG's right of way expired in 1889. Several railroads, such as the Atchison, Topeka and Santa Fe and the Denver, South Park and Pacific, were evidently ready to accept the offer. This seemed to be the momentum that got the D&RG Railroad going again. When asked, Lake City officially agreed to secure a right of way for the D&RG through town at no cost to the railroad. The town also agreed to secure all the money and the ground needed for track, the depot, and all the other functions that the railroad needed inside the city limits, at no cost to the D&RG. In November 1888, the board of the D&RG voted to continue construction on the Lake City branch. The city did not have to wait long to see actual results. On November 30, 1888, the D&RG officially authorized and budgeted the construction of the Lake City Branch for an additional cost of $206,698. By December 21 construction was actually underway again.

It was interesting that the D&RG was beginning construction again even though the Lake City Board of Trade was now estimating that the town would be shipping only about 100 tons of freight and ore per day, down from a 675 ton a day estimate in 1887.[627] Obviously competition between the railroads of the era was fierce and was one of the main reasons driving the D&RG to finish off the branch to Lake City.

Much of the original grading on the Lake City Branch had been damaged or eroded, so it was almost like starting over again. Work started first at the mouth of the Lake Fork and 200 workers, mainly Italians, tackled the blasting work that still needed to be done in the lower Lake Fork Canyon. The lower Lake Fork Canyon was so tight that there was a need for many small bridges to be built along the side or actually over parts of the river. The first four miles into the canyon were 200-foot perpendicular cliffs, and it was obvious the job would take a while. Some geologists even compared the lower Lake Fork Canyon to the Black Canyon of the Gunnison.[628] The rails ran one mile west from Sapinero to

Lake Junction, and then turned south for twelve miles through the lower Lake Fork Canyon with its towering mountains on each side of the river. By the end of April, five miles of track had been laid from Sapinero and near the middle of the branch construction workers were building the Elk Creek and High Bridges — two major undertakings.

Although the town had agreed to provide the railroad's right of way inside the city limits, it was not an easy task. It would require vacating several streets and alleys, as well as buying property previously purchased by private citizens that would now be in the railroad's right of way.

The distance to build from Lake Junction near Sapinero to Lake City was 35.7 miles with an average 1.4% grade and with curves up to 24 degrees.[629] As Lake City entered its third boom in 1889, the railroad spurred on all kinds of business for the new branch; so much so, that after Moffatt made the decision to build the line, it was profitable even during the 1893 Silver Panic and continued so until well after the turn of the century. Even more important to the D&RG was it kept the Denver and South Park Railroad, which also ran a main line to Gunnison, out of Lake City and the San Juans.[630]

As construction of the actual railroad began in January 1889, a major mining and construction boom started in Hinsdale County; not only because of the promise of inexpensive transportation, but also because the railroad had many construction jobs and building contracts to negotiate with the locals. Businesses in the area were hiring again, anticipating the boom but also to help fill the needs of the railroad and its construction workers.

A 150-foot steel truss bridge had to be built over the Gunnison River and then an eighty-six foot wooden bridge was constructed over the Lake Fork. These were the first of ten bridges on the Lake City route depending on whether some of the small ones are counted. About 200 men were initially assigned to work on the Lake City Branch, but eventually there were many more. The ties and lumber needed by the contractors were all cut by locals from the great forests along the Lake Fork and the Cebolla Rivers. As with most of the early Colorado mountain narrow gauge railroads, the Lake City branch's ties were six feet long and not treated with a preservative. This would necessitate the replacement of the ties in the near future.

By summer the construction crews were close to Lake City and would sometimes come to town. The *Hinsdale Phonograph* of June 22, 1889 stated:

> *In the space of one short week Lake City has been transformed from a quiet, peaceful town into a perfect sheol[631] of brawling graders, the streets disgusting with a carousing crowd, many of its members*

making one almost ashamed to be called a human being. We suppose it is a necessary evil, but it is a relief to believe that it will last only until the grading camps have moved away.

Track layers arrived at the Lake City town limits on June 15, but they still had to lay tracks to the depot, make the balloon loop to reverse the engine, lay track for several sidings and to the engine house, and build the water tower, scales, and coaling facilities. On June 24, 1889, the two work locomotives coming into town blew their whistles "long and vigorously." Some of the people of Lake City set off black powder in response. The celebration went on into the evening. The work continued in the town at the site of the depot at Second Street. Lake City citizens were ready to hold a large celebration on June 24, 1884, when the main line was finally finished in Lake City; but rather than start service, it seemed to the locals that the D&RG took some time in doing the finishing work.

At the beginning of the Lake City line, the D&RG's main line was on the north (left) bank of the Gunnison River and the branch therefore had to cross both the Gunnison and the Lake Fork at this spot using two different bridges on the lower level. The new highway also crossed the Lake Fork on the big steel arch bridge, far above the other bridges. Three bridges in one spot were very unusual and many photos and post cards were taken of the spot. (D&RG Archives, Author's Collection)

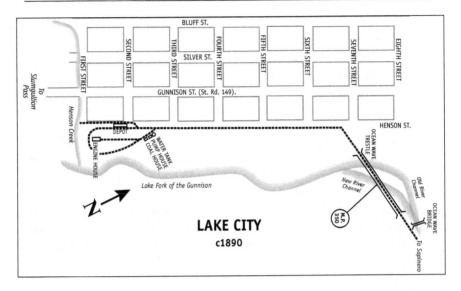

The railroad yard in Lake City managed to get a lot into basically a two block area. Note the river channel was changed for the Ocean Wave Trestle (also called The One Mile Trestle). (Western Reflections Publishing Co. Map)

Even after the grade was finished, the track was laid, and the bridges built, there actually was plenty of construction that still needed to be done on the railroad facilities in Lake City proper and along the branch line. The Lake City depot complex was a structure 200 feet long and 50 feet wide, with a deck around the building. The depot proper was a two-story 24 by 48 foot building, and the connected express baggage and freight section was 60 by 20 feet. It was initially planned for there to be a two stall, 36 by 64 foot engine house in the center of the loop where the locomotive was kept out of the weather after being restocked with coal and water. The engine house could also hold two cars if their load needed to be kept from freezing or out of the weather. It was a typical D&RG depot, with pot-bellied stoves, long oak benches, and a ticket counter. There were side tracks for freight to be loaded and unloaded into freight cars that extended north from the depot almost to Fifth Street, and also a siding extending south from the west side of the depot to Henson Creek.

The local paper was jubilant:

This coming of the railroad to (Lake City) means revival of hope, revival of business in all its branches, revival of the development of the hidden treasures which have been sleeping in the recesses of our rugged mountains for so many years, waiting for the arm of the sturdy miner to bring them to the surface.... At the beginning of our business relations we meet as friends and not rivals.... Welcome thou agent of a higher civilization to our humble mountain city, and may each arrival and departure bring nothing but increased friendship between us.[632]

Three 30 x 40 foot section houses needed to be constructed along the Lake City route, as well as several sidings. Sidings were built for scheduled stops at Madera near Barnum, Gateview, and Youmans near present-day Sky Ranch - Ute Trail. Each stop had an outhouse. The line had four water towers and a watchman's house was built at the High Bridge to look for fires after a train passed. Inspection parties had to come to make sure all of the new construction was in order. W. M. Fuller was hired as station agent and four other men were hired to work below him.

Dr. B. F. Cummings of Lake City was made the official D&RG doctor for the third division. All in all, the cost of the branch line was said to be $770,996, including the interest the D&RG was paying on bonds and loans connected with the project since 1881. The line never produced its anticipated revenues, but it did operate at a profit for many years.[633] Because of anticipated revenue now being lower, a few cuts had been made in the initial plans.

It was August 15, 1889, at 10:00 a.m. before the first official regularly scheduled passenger train of the Lake City Branch of the D&RG Railroad reached Lake City from Sapinero (now underwater at Blue Mesa).[634] The depot at Lake City opened that same day. It was almost an anti-climax. As lifetime resident Joel Swank put it in his book:

After plans and promises, struggles and disappointments over a period of fourteen years, the Lake City branch line of the Denver and Rio Grande Western Railroad (the D&RG added "Western" to its name after its reorganization) finally became a reality.[635]

The railroad did not solve all of Lake City's problems, but it did give its citizens easy access to the outside world and inexpensive transportation rates for locally mined ore.[636] The early 1890s were the busiest years for the Lake City branch, with 1895 being the peak. The 1893 Silver Panic took a toll and slowed down activity in Lake City, Colorado, and all over the West, but because of gold discoveries in Hinsdale County, Lake City was almost untouched, except that some of its lower grade silver mines had to close.

The D&RG's narrow gauge tracks continued west from Sapinero to Montrose and east to Salida, thereby connecting Lake City by rail

The Lake City depot was the standard Denver and Rio Grande Railroad version. The station agent lived on the second floor. (Author's Collection)

to the outside world. From Salida, the tracks switched to broad gauge. The Lake City to Sapinero trip took about three hours each way. It can now be made in one hour by car by a slightly longer route. Lake City's D&RG depot is no longer standing, but the town's fire station is very reminiscent of what it looked like. The train crossed the Lake Fork in town on the "One Mile Bridge"[637] from the east side of the Lake Fork near today's 8 ½ Street bridge and today's Medical Center on the west side, then followed today's Henson Street to the station.

The trains were usually small — the narrow gauge locomotive, its tender, two or three passenger or combine cars (sometimes only one) and a caboose. Usually there was a freight car and also ore cars, if the mines were shipping. The train would be filled with water from the wooden water tank, stocked up on coal, and then backed into the engine house. The next day it would travel north a few hundred feet, then back up to the station, load passengers and freight, and start the trip to Sapinero.[638] The route followed by the new branch line to Lake City was spectacular. The town of Sapinero was the logical end of the line, although the official end was at Lake Junction, which only had one 8 by 8 foot structure to house telephone facilities.[639]

Between Sapinero and Lake City, there were several sidings for loading timber and livestock. The High Bridge, eight miles north of Lake City, was the engineering masterpiece of the branch. The bridges and sidings, as well as regular stops along the branch, all had names. Two miles upriver from Sapinero in the Lake Fork Canyon was Grabiola, which was originally a construction camp (there were as many as fifty construction camps in the lower Lake Fork Canyon alone),[640] but later it was used by gold miners after prospectors found gold near Grabiola in 1899. Hundreds of prospectors were soon in the area hoping to strike it rich. The Lake Fork Placer Mining Company was organized but soon disbanded for lack of gold. Much of the mining was originally placer, but it eventually turned to lode mining. It was a short-lived, but very big, rush.

As the railroad's workers, most of whom were Italian, constructed the right of way and laid track, more camps were established along the grade. The workers ate and slept at these camps. The cooks made small stone or brick ovens to bake bread for the hungry men. Some of these ovens are still standing along the old right of way, which is now a dead end road at Blue Mesa Reservoir. After the men had worked past one camp, another camp and another oven would be built.

Six miles further north, in the Lake Fork Canyon, was another construction camp later turned mining camp named Marion for the Marion Mining Company. This spot, which had a siding, was also called Vanguard for another mining company. Once again, the mining activity was very short-lived.

Two or three miles further south, as the tracks came out of the lower Lake Fork Canyon, is the "Red Bridge," which is not red today. For centuries before the railroad, this was a major crossing of the Lake Fork by Native Americans. The original red bridge was replaced and is no longer painted red, but locals still call it by that name. A lumber camp named "Madera" was established just south of the bridge at Johnson Gulch. Madera means "lumber" in Spanish.

A little further at the lower end of Indian Creek (the canyon where Highway 149 now runs between the Blue Mesa and Sapinero Cutoffs) was the location of a small settlement called Barnum. The station was named for Lou Barnum, a division superintendent of the Barlow and Sanderson Stage Company who died in 1876.[641] Barnum was a major stop for several toll roads, as it was on Otto Mears' road from Saguache to Lake City, his toll road from Sapinero to Lake City, and his toll road from Ouray to Gunnison or Saguache. It was also on the Crookes' toll road to Crested Butte from Lake City. This made it the perfect place for an early day post office. When B. F. Allen bought the Barnum stage station and surrounding ranch, the name was changed to Allen. Then F.M. Mendenhall bought the ranch and changed the name of the stop to Gateview. Jack Carr bought the ranch in 1934, and in 1996 it was sold through a conservation fund to the BLM.[642] The BLM then traded the land to a private individual but reserved public fishing rights along the river.[643]

The stop was a popular way to get from the train to the ranches around Powderhorn; and, later, to the short-lived but large gold boom northwest of Powderhorn in what was called "The Gunnison Gold Belt." Several large camps were built along the Gold Belt, including Spencer, Dubois, Telefario, and Vulcan; and some of the Gold Belt's traffic moved through Barnum. However the gold never amounted to a bonanza and the boom was over in just six to eight years.

The actual small settlement of Gateview was two miles further south of Barnum near "The Gate." The Gate is a natural landmark — a narrow passage through steep cliffs, which most Hinsdale County residents consider to be the official entry into "Lake City Country," even though the Hinsdale County line is about eight miles further south. Gateview had a post office and was a stop for travelers on the Mears toll road from Saguache; it was a place where passengers could eat and sleep. Besides a big house, it had a large barn, corrals, and pasture for travelers' horses.

About a mile upriver from Gateview was Dayton, which had a post office but not much else for many years. About a mile past Dayton was the Spruce Lumber siding and a sawmill owned by J. H. Kellogg. About fifteen sawmill workers lived in Dayton in a large boardinghouse and three bunkhouses while working at the Spruce Lumber saw mill. Most people do not realize it now; but Hinsdale County and especially the lower Lake Fork, were once very heavily wooded, and Kellogg ran a major sawmill that furnished lumber all over the Western Slope of Colorado. Basically all signs of these small settlements are now gone.

Besides making railroad ties for the D&RG's entire line, the lumber industry took up some of the slack from the loss of mining. Besides Spruce Lumber, several

This view is labeled "Barnum, on the toll road to Lake City," but the terrain does not match the location where most people think Barnum was located (the Carr Ranch). (Author's Collection)

other sawmills flourished along the Lake City Branch from about 1904 to 1916. The Lake City Branch was built through the middle of several large forests that ran almost continuously along twenty miles of pine, spruce, and other commercial trees. In one week in September 1910, forty carloads of lumber were shipped from the Gateview Mill alone.[644] J. H. Kellogg at one times had sawmills at both Youmans and Gateview. The sheep and cattle industries later thrived along the railroad and helped the Hinsdale economy for a few more decades.

Making railroad ties was an industry that employed many locals, especially in the winter, for several decades after the railroad was built. The work was hard — all by hand, using axes, handsaws, and broadaxes. The shaped trees were pulled out by horses and cut into the proper lengths at the tracks. Most of the ties were narrow gauge. Anyone who owned timber could sell ties to the railroad, but they had to be piled near the tracks in a way that they could be inspected for quality and grade. This system was used all over Colorado, and D&RG inspectors were often on the trains looking for piles of ties for sale. Many of the original ties for the Lake City Branch came from the Powderhorn area. Approximately 25,000 ties were floated down the Cebolla to the Gunnison River, where they were loaded on a construction train and taken up the Lake Fork. Ties for the railroad were an important source of income for locals in

Notice the huge size of the first growth logs cut in the 1880s and 1890s. Fewer horses were needed in the winter when sleds were used instead of wagons. Or if the snow was deep enough the horses just pulled the individual logs without a wagon. (Author's Collection)

the winter. After the Lake City Branch was running, many of the ties continued to be floated down the Cebolla to spots near the Gunnison River, where thousands and thousands of ties were stashed to await the railroad picking them up. The D&RG estimated there were enough trees close to the Lake City Branch right-of-way and along the Cebolla that they could obtain over 5 million ties.

A lot of hard work went into making these ties, yet they were sold in the old days for 30 cents for a first class pine or spruce tie. Second class was mostly ties from other woods and brought 25 cents apiece. Later the price was raised to about 50 cents each, as wood became scarcer and located further away from the track. Two hard-working men could cut thirty to fifty ties a day,[645] so it was a good paying job for the time.

Another six miles or so south, and eleven miles before reaching Lake City, was a stop called "Youmans", which was named for Harry Youmans and his original 160-acre homesteader of the property. As described earlier, Youmans was a very early pioneer whose ranch adjoined the little camp where the Kellogg Lumber Company had another sawmill.[646] A small one-room school, called Belmont, as well as several small houses, were on or near Youman's ranch. Besides these buildings, there was a D&RG water tank, a large section house, a siding, large corrals, and a loading chute for cattle being shipped out on the train.[647]

The first major bridge along the line, after the two at Lake Junction, was the Elk Creek Bridge, which[648] was located just south of today's Sky Ranch Ute Trail. Elk Creek would become the second highest (it missed being the highest by one foot) and second longest bridge on the line, at 206-feet long and 112-feet high. On most railroads it would have been the star trestle of the line, but the "High Bridge" was just a few mile south. By April 1889 work was proceeding rapidly on at the highest bridge on the branch, located three miles south of the Elk Creek Bridge. The High Bridge was 800-feet long and 113 feet tall. It took 350,000 board feet of lumber to build the bridge, and it was also used by wagons to get across the canyon. It was built with 10 x 10 and 12 x 12 inch timbers. It turned out to be the most photographed spot along the route. In fact it was probably the most photographed bridge on the D&RG Railroad and was reported by some to be the largest bridge in the entire system.[649]

The D&RG locomotive's engineer would often stop in the middle of the High Bridge to let some passengers enjoy the view and others freak out from the height.[650] In 1921, a flood pushed the High Bridge slightly out of alignment, and it probably would have collapsed if volunteers from Lake City had not helped remove the large amount of debris that was backing up against the pilings. The pilings were then replaced with cement footers.

The locals took the High Bridge in stride. Lillian Smoot remembered:

The High Bridge was said to be at that time the highest of all the wooden railroad structures in the world. I have ridden on the little train over the High Bridge many times. However the height of the bridge is nothing compared to some of the winding wagon roads further up.[651]

For many years, a watchman named Bailey lived in a small company house north of the High Bridge and would check both the High Bridge and the Elk Creek Bridge for sparks that might have started a fire when a train passed over the bridges. His job was no longer needed when the tops of the bridges were covered with gravel to prevent fires. The last major bridge (long but low), located in Lake City near the Ocean Wave Bridge and mill, was built in May and early June, 1889.

The immediate boom in Lake City that everyone expected after the railroad's arrival did not materialize; however, the railroad did help to turn the Lake City economy around substantially and it created a good economy for the next ten to fifteen years. For example, in 1889, before the arrival of the railroad, Hinsdale mines produced about $30,000. The next year production was up to $130,000, and then ore production went over $500,000 in 1892. The peak year for the third boom was 1895, but the mining economy continued to be good into the early 1900s.[652]

The four level, wooden High Bridge trestle was the wonder of the Lake City Branch, both because it was so big but also because it was so expensive. This photo was shot in the 1900s, and note the train is pulling only one car. (E.W.S. Photo Courtesy of Burton and Nora Smith)

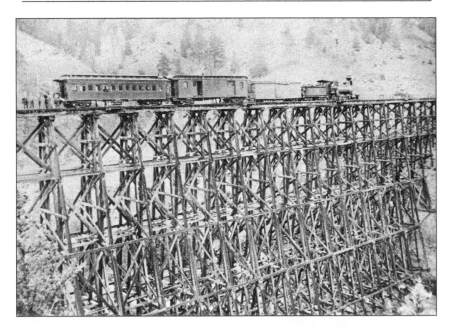

The High Bridge deserves two photos. In this one the train has stopped on the bridge and the conductor and several passengers have gotten out for a better view. (Author's Collection)

The positive effect of the train was felt immediately; and, as well as ore being shipped out, many cars of mining machinery and equipment were brought in to Lake City by train in the early 1890s to help handle the expected mining boom.

For the first few years of its operation, the Lake City train ran with two or three passenger cars, but after 1894, the passenger cars were replaced by combination or combine cars, that carried baggage, express, and mail as well as passengers. From 1889 to 1893 there were usually two to four freight cars and/or cars filled with coal, which was used by the smelters, the train's locomotives, and by Lake City locals in the winter for heating. At this time the freight cars were usually full, as well as the passenger cars, and often it was standing room only. Times were good in the early 1890s. Many full trains left Lake City pulling carloads of concentrates and high grade ore. The Lake City *Times*, in its January 22, 1891 issue, reported on passenger traffic:

Passenger traffic on the Lake City branch of the Denver and Rio Grande is increasing in a very satisfactory manner, and freight business is becoming quite heavy. All this bespeaks the steady progress being made in all branches of business here, and particularly mining, and is a sure and certain forerunner of the rush that will come in still greater volume with the opening of the early spring.

After the railroad arrived, traveling shows and circuses would often come to Lake City via the railroad. The circus always included an elephant or two, and during one show the animals had to cross the Lake Fork to the circus tent in Ball Flats. When they got to the center of the river they started spraying each other with their trunks and then spraying the crowd. Everyone had a great time until the trainers waded into the river and forced the elephants out. Stage plays were held in Lake City at the Opera House (the Armory), as well as dog and pony shows that contained extraordinarily trained animals.

As mentioned, Lake City fared better than many Colorado mining camps during the Silver Panic of 1893, as rich deposits of gold had been discovered and were being mined at the Golden Fleece and the Golden Wonder Mines earlier in 1893. The Gunnison Gold Belt also opened up soon after this time. Gold, of course, was not affected by the Silver Panic. Business from the Gold Belt went to both Gunnison and Lake City, as it was located between the two towns and was in Gunnison County, but the Gold Belt was closer and more easily accessed from the Lake City Branch of the railroad. Dubois, located on Goose Creek, eight miles from Gateway, had well over a hundred buildings and a population of about 500. South of Dubois by three miles was Taliafaro. Then gold was discovered at Spencer, eight miles northeast of Gateview. Spencer had a population of 500 by 1896. All of these towns had short lives, except Spencer, which lasted until about 1920.

However, despite some of the Gold Belt ore being shipped out on the Lake City Branch, Gold Belt ore production continued to slowly drop, and the Ute-Ulay was forced to close. By July 30, 1896, the Lake City *Times* reported that "the business of the railroad has fallen about half since the Ute-Ulay Mine and Mill shut down."

Since gold was at a premium after the Silver Panic of 1893, the Golden Fleece was sold to new owners who had the capital to get the gold out. On the other hand, the Ute-Ulay Mine's output was still mainly silver, but it was producing enough silver and base metals (copper, lead, zinc) that it somehow struggled on, although it was forced to occasionally shut down. Between 1892 and 1897, Hinsdale County mines produced $3.2 million in gold, silver, and other metals, and the railroad was kept very busy.

Meanwhile, the little narrow gauge engine on the Lake City branch kept chugging along. In the winter, snow was usually not a great problem, but ice freezing on the track and switches was. The ice had to be hammered off by workers, and on occasion the tracks had to be plowed or shoveled out so the train could get through the snow.[653] Although a few snow blockades were days long, most were only a matter of hours. Heavy winter snows, ice, and avalanches were always a terrible winter obstacle for the railroad, but summer washouts of the track by flash floods were perhaps the most devastating and a constant problem. On a couple of occasions the route was blocked for twenty or thirty days while the roadbed was repaired and track replaced. The sharp curves of the Lake City branch restricted vision and were considered dangerous enough that trains traveled the branch very slowly, averaging only about ten to twelve miles an hour, so that the engineer would have time spot problems and stop if the track was blocked or washed out around the curve. A man on a horse could keep up with the train for several miles.

Another interesting railroad project, but one on which construction was never started, was an effort in the early 1900s to connect one of Silverton's three small railroad lines (The Silverton, The Silverton Northerly, and The Silverton, Gladstone and Northern) to the D&RG at Lake City. This would have cut 153 miles off the trip to Denver from Silverton and reduced the time of travel between the two towns from about twenty-four to fourteen hours. The savings in time and money would have been enormous, if only the rugged seventeen miles from the terminus of the Silverton Northern at Animas Forks, the terminus of The Silverton, Gladstone and Northern at Gladstone, or even the Silverton Railroad at Red Mountain could have been built to bridge the gap. Considerable talk, time, and money were spent looking for a solution, but to no avail.[654] Probably the best route would have been from Animas Forks over to Cottonwood Creek to Sherman. After reaching Sherman, the going would have been very easy, but even this route would have been a nightmare to construct.

Despite a decrease in ore shipped, The Lake City *Times* was able to report, on May 26, 1904, that the Golden Fleece had sent the richest carload of ore ever to the smelter. It netted $49,800 (over two million dollars in terms of today's currency). But as time went by, these types of reports became more and more infrequent.

As the mining business slowed, it was not long before the D&RG began publicizing what they called "The Circle Route," which was a trip that circled the San Juans to Ouray, Silverton, Durango, Alamosa, and Lake City.[655] Although successful, the Lake City branch was obviously a side trip and Lake City did not do nearly as well as the towns that were actually on "The Circle." A 1905 railroad travel book called *Over the Range* gave considerable space to the natural wonders of the Lake City branch:

This extension is thirty-six miles in length, and has its terminus at Lake City. The line turns to the left (south) about a mile west of Sapinero, and passes through the remarkable Lake Fork Cañon en route.

This cañon is a most attractive bit of scenery. It is noted for its narrowness, and the height and grandeur of its walls. For thirteen miles the railroad winds through the tortuous chasm, the walls rising on each hand to a height varying from eight hundred to thirteen hundred feet. The river claims the right of way but the railroad also asserts its rights, and by exercising engineering skill has forced a passage. In many places the solid wall of granite has been blasted away, and from the fallen blocks a solid embankment

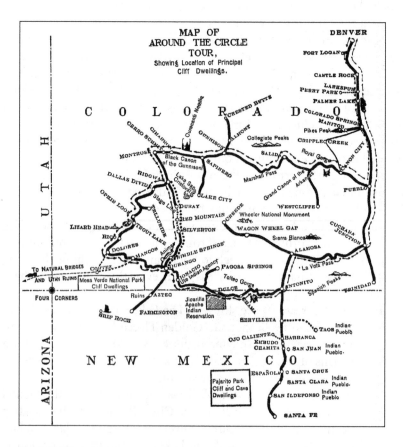

The D&RG Circle Route map of their tour includes all the side trips, such as Lake City and Creede, and an optional trip from Ouray to Silverton by stagecoach, as no railroad ever bridged that gap. (Around the Circle Route, Author's Collection)

constructed upon which the rails have been laid. The Lake Fork is a rapid and tumultuous stream, abounding in rapids and presenting a most interesting, varied, and exhilarating panorama to the eye. Emerging from the cañon and gaining a greater altitude, the view is one of magnificent extent and grandeur. Northward the peaks of the range form a long line of well-separated summits. Northeastward, the vista between nearer hills is filled with the clustered height of the Continental Divide....

The book only describes the Town of Lake City as "substantial and pretty," but then shifts to Hinsdale County's mines and the county's abundant wildlife:

Mines of marvelous value surround the town, and give life and energy to all the commercial and speculative projects of the people. The development of her mining resources has been carried on steadily, and the shipment of precious ores has reached a very heavy tonnage. It will not be long before Lake City's mines will become as famous as those of her fortunate sisters in the wide circle of the San Juan silver region. The romance surrounding this pretty town — the lovely lake, San Cristoval, from which it takes its characteristic name, the grand mountains, and the grassy parks — has made it a favorite for the lovers of nature in the past, and will still attract them in the future. This is a paradise for a sportsman. Over these rolling uplands, among the aspen groves, upon the foothills and along the willow bordered creek deer now throng, and even an occasional elk and antelope are to be seen. In the rocky fastness (sic), the bear and panther find refuge, and every little park is enlivened by the flitting forms of timid hares and the whirring escape of the grouse disturbed by our passing.[656]

In 1913 the *Around the Circle* pamphlet, which was printed by the D&RG to promote tourism in the San Juans, described the Lake City Branch as follows;

Lake City is reached by the Lake Fork Branch of the Denver & Rio Grande, and is about 350 miles from Denver on the "Around the Circle" tour. The track skirts the tumultuous Lake Fork tributary of the Gunnison through the narrow, deep, Lake Fork Canyon. The view from the farther end of the cañon is most impressive, embracing a wide sweep of snowy ranges. Lake City is a thriving place of 450 people, with mining the chief interest. It is one of the prettiest towns in the state. Here is charming Lake San Cristoval, named by a Spanish monk of the seventeenth century.[657] *From Lake City the summit of Uncompahgre Peak, 14,289 feet, may be attained. The altitude of the town is 8,686 feet.*

When in the early 1900s, it became obvious that the Lake City Branch was no longer profitable, the D&RG constantly changed schedules to see if that would help. Then it started running shorter trains and reducing service. At the same time, the county's 1900 population of 1,609 fell to 646 in 1910.

As mining continued to drop, the Lake City Branch did benefit from both rising lumber prices and a booming cattle business in the area. In 1918 sixty carloads of cattle were shipped to Denver from along the Lake Fork. Yet it was not enough. The growing numbers of wrecks, washouts, derailments, and other problems along the route showed that the branch was suffering greatly from deferred maintenance during its hard times. Winter travel and summer floods were especially difficult and costly. By 1920 Lake City was down to just 317 residents and there were only 538 people in Hinsdale County.

From the time of the arrival of the first train, Engineer Pete Ready was running most of the locomotives on the Lake City Branch. He was extremely careful and had only two accidents in the thirty-two years he operated the locomotive out of the forty-three the Lake City Branch was open. Pete knew every inch of the track and most of the residents of the ranches along the way. He was dearly beloved. When Pete's train from Sapinero reached the Blue Cut, about a quarter of a mile north of town, he blew the locomotive's whistle long and hard, so all the townspeople knew the train was arriving. Pete Ready outlasted several locomotives, and was so well thought of by the D&RG that he was allowed to mount his own personal whistle on the locomotives from Sapinero to Lake City.

One day Pete pulled into town without any of the cars that were supposed to be behind the locomotive's tender. They had come loose

Youman was the railroad stop at today's Sky Ranch Ute Trail. Center left is the school house, center on the siding to the right of the mainline is the saw mill. Youman's Ranch house was where buildings are still located in the trees at upper right. (Author's Collection)

Rather than hire men to shovel snow for hours, Pete Ready or someone with the railroad decided to go "full steam ahead" and to push through the snow out of the Lake City rail yard. A derailment in Ball Flats was the result. The Ocean Wave Mill is in the background. (Photo from Tiny Hinsdale of the Silvery San Juan.)

along the way, but the brakeman got them stopped and waited patiently for Pete to come back and pick them up. Pete never did live that down.

Pete was always ready to accommodate the residents along his route. Probably the extreme example is detailed in J. Henry Benson's book, *Pioneer Ranching in the Rockies*:

> *My mother would flag down Pete's train and ask him to deliver small packages of vegetables, butter, cream and eggs to friends in Lake City. One day my mother flagged down the train and told Pete Ready that she wanted to send a dozen eggs to Mrs. Myers but noticed that she only had eleven. However, there was a hen on the nest, and if Pete would hold the train a few minutes, she was certain there would soon be another egg to even out the dozen. Good-natured Pete agreed, and the train waited until the 12th egg was laid. Now where else, but on a sleepy country railroad like the Lake City branch could you get service like that?*[658]

Pete Ready waited for people to get married in Lake Fork Canyon, he took men to their favorite fishing hole, and he stopped on the High Bridge so that passengers could take photographs or just admire the view. He was like a well-loved king when he took his seat in the Lake City Branch locomotive. On cold nights another D&RG employee, Johnny Benson, would come to the engine house well before Pete arrived to stoke the boiler and build up engine pressure no matter how low the thermometer had fallen during the night. Johnny Benson loved to fire up the engine on New Year's Eve; and, from 11:55 a.m. to 12:05 p.m., he would blow the whistle continuously to welcome in the New Year. He loved the shrill, loud sound and the town loved it too, but Johnny would be temporarily deaf for a while after the event.[659]

When Pete left Lake City, he estimated he had made more than 10,000 runs on the Lake City Branch. Long after he left, Pete told stories about the train. One joke was that the long time conductor, Pete Gallagher, when he knew the train was ready to leave, would yell to Pete in the locomotive:

"Ready Pete?" The engineer flashed a grin and called back, as he had done so many times before, "Nope I'm Pete Ready! Let'r go Gallagher!" And with that, his big gloved fist slowly inched the throttle open as the drivers began to turn for another trip through the Canyon of the Lake Fork.[660]

Between June 3 and June 10, 1921, Hinsdale County had a week of torrential rains that totaled over seven inches. There was also an unusually high spring runoff going on at the time. The resulting flash flood damaged the station house, swept away several small D&RG buildings, and tore up the right-of-way and track. Lake Junction and Sapinero were also badly damaged. Four miles of rail were swept away just north of town, and the town itself was in great danger and had some severe damage. Citizens built dikes wherever they were needed. Several railroad and all the wagon road bridges were badly damaged along the route. This meant repair crews could not get to Lake City to repair the track. It took almost a month to repair the damage, during which time the mail came in on horseback.[661]

Most of the industries that supported the railroad were now gone or shrinking fast. Tourism was growing, but most tourists now came by automobile instead of by train. Lake City's population was only 259 in 1930.[662] A few tourists would ride the train to secluded fishing spots or maybe a family would go on a picnic or berry picking adventure, but as early as 1895 the D&RG had let the Public Utilities Commission know they were not meeting expenses and asked to be allowed to run a train only two days per week. The protest was loud enough that the change was denied. Nothing improved with the economy as Lake City residents were sure would happen, so on October 2, 1927 the D&RG renewed its request for twice a week service. It was averaging only five passengers a day and less than $200 revenue per week. The request was granted.

Severe floods occurred again in the summer of 1929, and destroyed much of the bedding for the track along the line. The railroad wanted to take the opportunity to shut down the line, but it was necessary for the D&RG to do the repairs because of the U. S. mail contract they had signed. By 1931, with the Great Depression going strong, a hearing was held to abandon the line. The outcry from Lake City residents was so great that the line was given a second chance, but once again revenues still did not increase.

At the end of 1931, the D&RG offered to give or lease the line to any interested person who wanted to keep the branch operating. The taxes were running over $20,000 a year, but the estimated revenue from a salvage operation was only $8,400. One newspaperman wrote of the line:

> If you haven't enough trouble of your own, here is a chance to get an operating railroad free of charge. The (D&RG Railroad) has notified the State Public Utilities Commission that it will give its thirty-nine mile branch between Sapinero and Lake City to anyone who will agree to operate it and pay the taxes, or if you do not care to take on that much responsibility the railroad will lease you the branch for $480 a year and throw in the free use of a locomotive and coach.
>
> In the bustling '90s the Lake City branch was one of the thriving feeders of the Rio Grande system. Hundreds of travelers were going in and out of the booming mining camp and hundreds of tons of rich ore were being transported to the smelters but 1932 finds the branch such a burden that it is willing to give it away to stop the expenses of taxes and operation.[663]

There were no takers on the offer, and then, six months later, the railroad received permission to close the depot. On May 5, 1932, the D&RG petitioned to abandon the line completely. Mike Burke, who had bought the Ute-Ulay Mine in 1925, told the PUC he would supply enough ore to keep the branch running. The railroad countered that it would cost them $250,000 in repairs to keep the line safe. The railroad, in its petition, declared that the Lake City branch had:

> ...furnished little traffic to the branch for at least 5.5 years and has been at a low ebb for a much longer period.... It may be that production could be increased when the demand for metals improves, but there is no assurance of production on a scale

sufficient to support the cost of operating the line or to warrant the expenditure necessary for rehabilitation... [664]

The PUC passed the decision on to the ICC which declared the line could be abandoned. The final D&RG train ran May 25, 1933. Abandonment was to begin in August 1933; but Mike Burke stepped forward again. He felt so strongly that a railroad was needed for his mining operation that he decided to start his own railroad operation on the line. Burke asked that the tearing up of the track be delayed, so he could negotiate a sale with the D&RG. His new railroad was named the "San Christobal" (sic) Railroad Company. Burke misspelled the lake's name, but the name for the railroad stuck anyway. Burke bought the right of way for $16,000. He was to pay the D&RG $1,000 down and $15,000 over three years for ownership of the track and right of way. He also agreed to pay the 1933 taxes in the amount of $20,000. Under the terms of the deal, Burke could not dismantle or change the track or any of the bridges in any way, and no stops were to be made along the route.

Burke had no locomotive or any freight cars, so he built a Galloping Goose to carry ore and bring in supplies. A Galloping Goose was half auto and half freight car, which had been pioneered by the Rio Grande Southern (RGS) Railroad, which ran between Ridgway and Durango. Burke had some income from the train because he had received the mail contract when he bought the line from the D&RG. He used a Galloping Goose with a gasoline powered motor, which unfortunately was very unreliable, so he soon lost the mail contract. In Burke's version of the Goose, he used his own 1928 Pierce Arrow automobile with an 80 horsepower gasoline engine. The Galloping Goose was built by McFarland-Eggers of Denver, in a similar way to the Rio Grande Southern had built its "Goose" fleet (they had seven). Burke's Goose ran on the Lake City Branch with only a few incidents between February 28, 1934, and mid-August of the same year. Then the Goose spent months being remodeled at the RGS shops, only to run a very few additional runs. In 1937 Burke gave up. Burke's railroad never came near showing a profit. The traffic just was not there; not only because of the major downturn in the Hinsdale economy but also because automobiles and trucks now carried most of the local freight, passengers, and tourists. Burke's Goose sat in the RGS shops for many years afterwards with the name "San Christobal Railroad" still painted on its side.

Muriel Lee Burke, in her book *Ghosts of the Lake Fork*, gives a little different ending to this story. She states that in mid-August, 1934, Burke decided to have his Galloping Goose rebuilt in the Rio Grande Southern (RGS) shops in Ridgway, Colorado. The cost would be about $2,000, but it meant no service on the Lake City Branch during the down time.

Final cost after many delays was $2,337.87, and the rebuilt Goose now looked very similar to Goose No. 7 of the RGS. It was not until July of 1935 that the Goose was finished, and by this time there were major sections of Lake City Branch track that had to be repaired or replaced before the rebuilt vehicle would be back running on the Lake City line. To make matters worse, the country was now in the middle of the Great Depression. By late 1935, the depression had caused Burke to close the Ute-Ulay and his railroad. By 1937 Burke realized that the Ute-Ulay would probably be closed for good, and he gave up the Lake City rails and right-of-way, and his Goose was sold to the Rio Grande Southern.[665]

After the railroad closed, Lake City had yet another time of great despair that could perhaps be called a bust within a bust. The town truly began to look like a ghost town. Weeds grew in the streets. Many houses were in total disrepair. It was said that some houses could be bought at the time for as little as twenty-five dollars. The rails of the Lake City branch were pulled during the summer of 1937. The railroad's depot was sold for salvage and the bridges were dismantled for their huge timbers. The Lake City branch was officially gone, but it has not been forgotten by the few people still living at the time of this writing who traveled over it or by railroad historians.

The last train from Lake City. (From *Lake City Railroad Memories*.)

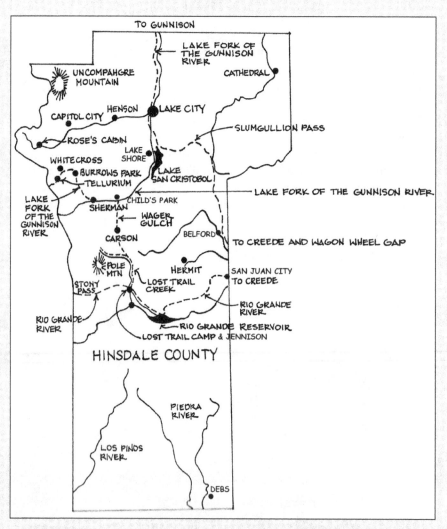

Hinsdale County Map Showing Former Settlements. (Basic sketch by Steven M. Burke, *Ghosts of the Lake Fork Region* — Western Reflections Map)

CHAPTER 8

THE OTHER HINSDALE COUNTY TOWNS AND CAMPS

A t the present time, Lake City is the only town located in Hinsdale County, but from 1874 to the 1920s, there were many other settlements in the county. Most of the larger local mines had post offices; and when there were workers' cabins scattered around the mine, these settlements were usually considered to be a "town" or at least a mining camp. If virtually all the people in these "towns" worked for the mine, the settlement was called a "company town." The history of the larger mines and their company towns usually need to be considered together, as their histories are so interwoven. If there were others living in the town besides mine employees, then the camp was usually considered to be a true town. Although almost all evidence of most of these settlements and company towns is now gone, they were important in the growth and history of Lake City and Hinsdale County.

Almost all the towns in Hinsdale County were established along its major rivers and creeks; most of the exceptions being camps that are now in Mineral County after Hinsdale County was split into two counties in 1893. Most of the camps now in Mineral County were small; none had more than two dozen inhabitants. Several settlements that were still located in Hinsdale County after the split had more than 500 residents for a brief time — making them as big in terms of a permanent population as the present Town of Lake City.

ENGINEER CITY, near the top of Engineer Pass, was one of the most transient and short-lived settlements in Hinsdale County; but during the summer, it had a large population. It was located at the Frank Hough Mine, just short of the divide with Ouray County at Engineer Pass, and was basically a company town that flourished in the early 1880s. In 1882, the newspaper correspondent from Engineer City to the Lake City's *Silver World* noted:

271

Engineer City looks awfully cold in this photograph taken by someone going over Engineer Pass in the dead of winter. The camp was known as the largest town in Colorado without a saloon. (Author's Collection)

> *Engineer City can boast more inhabitants than Mineral City, Animas Forks, or Capitol City, yet we have no saloon and the boys openly declare that with the grub up at Davidson's Hotel that they can very well do without any.*[666]

Much of the town was composed of tents that were used only in the summer. In the winter the "town" was basically non-existent. Jack Davidson, mentioned above, erected a huge tent that the *Silver World* referred to as a "hotel," which served as a boarding house and could comfortably hold fifty men. The "town" reappeared every summer, but was gone for good by 1900.

ROSE'S CABIN was an early-day stagecoach stop and settlement located near the headwaters of Henson Creek about half way between Lake City and Ouray or Silverton. Rose's Cabin was on the north side of Henson Creek, just below Schafer (sometimes spelled Shafer) Gulch (named for the second of the proprietors of Rose's Cabin, Charles Schafer). At an altitude of approximately 11,000 feet, it was located just below tree line, and there was usually snow on the ground at Rose's Cabin for seven or eight months of the year.

Rose was not a woman, but rather Corydon Rose (also called Charles), who was one of the very earliest San Juan pioneers. Charles Schafer, Theodore Dick, and Theodore Schoch had come from the Animas drainage to this area in 1872 to prospect, and they had fairly good results. After the Brunot Treaty was ratified in 1874, Corydon Rose, Gus Sorenson, and Harry Chamberlain were also in the area, and Rose decided to stay and build a cabin. Soon, Schoch, Schafer, and Dick were also living there, hauling freight and supplies across the divide to Animas Forks and Mineral Point out of Rose's Cabin. By 1876, Rose had enlarged his home and opened a small "hotel" and bar.[667] Theodore Dick helped with the running of the hotel, and George Meritt helped with the cooking.

William Booth, who had a store at Mineral Point, also opened a general store in Rose's Cabin when the operation was purchased by Charles Schafer in 1878 and moved to a newer and larger log structure. Food was said to be served at Rose's Cabin at any hour of the day. Shafer may have even received a few tourists, as the *Lake City Mining Review* reported Schaffer "has the principal depot for the shipment of supplies, and conducts a hotel, which is a famous resort." However more likely the writer was just kidding.[668] The distance was too far for a traveler to make it from Lake City to Ouray or Silverton in one day, even on horseback, so travelers usually stopped for the night at Mineral Point or Rose's Cabin. From Rose's Cabin, it was fifteen miles to Lake City, about ten miles to Ouray, and about fifteen miles to Howardsville. Ouray was closer, but the trail was steeper on the Ouray side of the divide; so the time taken to travel between the towns was about the same. In the summers after 1877, Rose's Cabin was also a stop along the Henson Creek Toll Road for stages going to and from Silverton, Mineral Point, Lake City, and Ouray. Later, the stage service to Rose's Cabin was only to and from Lake City.

After Rose sold out to Schafer, Dick continued to run the forwarding business from Rose's, taking freight at the end of the wagon road

One of, if not the earliest photograph of Rose's Cabin, which was taken about 1876. Rose's Cabin was expanded, moved, and remodeled many times over the years but was owned by Charles Schafer for most of the time it was a hotel and restaurant, as well as the center of a small mining camp. Rose probably still was the owner when this photo was taken. (Author's Collection)

by mules to the upper Animas drainage towns of Mineral Point and Animas Forks.[669] Schafer and Dick kept sixty mules at Rose's Cabin to transport goods to the Animas or to the local mines. Their mule team was said to be in almost constant use from 1880 to 1884.

Schafer ran the post office at Rose's Cabin, which operated between June, 1878 and September, 1887. While he was there, Rose and Schafer worked the nearby Moltke Mine. A snow slide hit their little cabin at the mine in the winter of 1877-78, injuring both men, but Rose almost fatally. This is probably why Rose sold to Schafer and moved away.

Until 1879, and the founding of Capitol City, Rose's Cabin was the only commercial spot to stop for meals, lodging, and perhaps most importantly liquor, between Mineral Point and Lake City. However the local mines and residences along Henson Creek were usually open to a traveler for a night's sleep and were good for a hot meal. Rose's Cabin also served as a place to leave messages, letters, and packages for the wandering prospectors in the area.

In 1882, something went wrong in an all-night poker game at Rose's Cabin and Joe Nevins, who had a reputation as a very bad character, hit Andy MacLaughlin in the head with a hatchet. Mac Laughlin responded by shooting Nevins dead, but he was quickly acquitted at a trial in Lake City with a verdict of self-defense.[670]

This scene at Rose's Cabin was taken about 1920 when the place was ending its use as a hotel, saloon, or barns for a forwarding company. A few of the additions over the years are very evident. (Author's Collection)

That same year Schafer built a larger two-story cabin (eventually expanded into two and a half stories) and took another ex-prospector as a partner. Schafer was also an assayer and a small assayer's oven was located at Rose's Cabin (which some more recent visitors misidentify as a smelter). About 125 miners or prospectors were living and working in the area of Rose's Cabin during the summer of 1885, and by that time Crofutt called the spot a "mining camp." Shafer had twenty-two small bedrooms upstairs, a restaurant, and a saloon with a bar that ran along the entire side of one wall on the first floor. Schafer married in 1884 and moved to Lake City not long after his marriage to become a full-time assayer.[671]

The camp was said to have been surrounded by 100 good claims and several dozen cabins, the Palmetto and Dolly Varden being the best of the local mines.[672] Rose's Cabin would have been at its peak about 1880 to 1885, but the small settlement lasted for many more years afterwards.

In 1920, the barns and buildings at Rose's Cabin were remodeled by the Golconda Mining Company; and the cabin even had some modern plumbing, a huge fireplace, and propane heat. The little camp prospered again during this time. The Golconda Mine tried to stay open all winter in 1920, but the weather was just too harsh. Like so many San Juan mining structures, the main building at Rose's Cabin was torn down in 1950 to salvage its building materials. Only the partial remains of the hotel's fireplace, the assay oven, and the sixty-mule stable are still visible.

When Muriel Wolle, author of the famous ghost town book, *Stampede to Timberline*, saw Rose's Cabin, it had been "remodeled" again by the Golconda Mine and used for offices and a staging area before the steep climb to the mine on the Hurricane Basin Road. Wolle, who saw almost all of Colorado's ghost towns while doing research for her classic ghost town book, wrote:

> *Even in its remodeled state Rose's Cabin is a symbol of the enterprise and determination of the pioneers, who let neither Indians nor mountain ranges hinder their progress into uncharted mineral territory.*[673]

About six or eight miles toward Lake City from Rose's Cabin, a large valley opens up that was the site of CAPITOL CITY. The odd spelling of Capitol City is correct, although some residents claim the town's name was at first spelled "Capital City." The land on which the town was laid out was originally a smelter and concentrator site owned by George Greene, who was also the owner of the first smelter in Silverton.[674] Both of Greene's operations were unfortunately very inefficient. When George S. Lee arrived from Central City in May, 1877, the Greene concentrating mill was already operating about a mile upstream from Greene's town site, which he had named "Galena City" because it was located in the Galena Mining District. However there were not more than a few cabins on Greene's site, even though it was obviously a very good place for a town with flat ground, two creeks running through the town, and many operating mines in the immediate area.

Capitol City was the dream of George S. Lee, who was one of the driving forces in Hinsdale County in the late 1870s and early 1880s. Lee purchased the 200 acre site in 1877. The new name of Capitol City appeared in July, 1877, in a Del Norte *San Juan Prospector* article, which also stated that the town already had 100 houses and 100 people; but it is highly likely that the housing figure was a gross exaggeration. The article said that there "....were only three or four women, two stores, a post office, but no regular mail service."[675] This would not have been the case if there were a hundred houses at the time.

Galena City was renamed "Capitol City" because the U. S. post office department already had another Galena City in Colorado. It is very likely that the town's new name came from the nearby Capitol Mountain, located to the northwest of the town site, which early miners named because it looked like a capitol building. (Some authorities state

Capitol City doesn't look too large about 1885 when this photo was taken but the photo only shows about a third of the town. George Lee's house would be out of the photo to the right. (Author's Collection)

George Lee's pretentious brick "mansion" in Capitol City was quite grand. The etching shows that it had a large complex around the house as well as elegant furnishings and decorations inside. (From Croffut's Gripsack Guide to Colorado)

the name came from a desire by Lee for the town to be the capital of Colorado, but the name was misspelled; others state the name may have been by consensus of the residents.) Fossett was probably the first to write that Lee hoped Capitol City would one day become the capital of Colorado, although Fossett's statement was probably made in jest. Lee did, however, have high hopes for his town and the local mines in the area. The name of the mountain from which the town got its name was changed to Uncompahgre, as it can be seen from the Uncompahgre River (which means red, hot springs in Ute), and was considered by some at the time to be the highest mountain in Colorado or the "Uncompahgre Range."

In 1878 Lee started building his own smelter because major discoveries had been found in the mines around Capitol City. Lee's smelter was 36 by 80 feet in dimension and required 150,000 bricks. The bricks for Lee's smelter and mansion were reportedly mailed to the site, as mail was cheaper than the local freight rates. Lee also eventually bought the Greene concentrating mill and smelter. The town received its post office May 18, 1877, and continued to receive mail until October 30, 1920. Lee built his brick house in 1879 and called it the "Mountain House Hotel." Lee's home (hotel) in Capitol City had a glass conservatory, where beautiful tropical plants were grown. Lee's house even had a ballroom with a small orchestra pit. It was two stories, with high ceilings and a small theater. He had a large fenced and well-groomed yard, and large lamp posts stood on either side of the entrance to his residence. He drove a beautiful coach with four horses and had a number of servants. The hotel also had a brick carriage house and even a four-hole brick outhouse. The home faced Henson Creek and was located between the main town site and Lee's smelter. Lee was said to have always had an American flag flying from a pole attached to the top of his house.[676]

Fossett wrote:

> *(The town is) located at the junction of the forks of Hensen (sic) Creek... where the almost perpendicular peaks and ranges open out into a level valley called Capitol City, most of which is embraced in the Lee's town site patent. All around this enclosure are numerous silver-bearing veins, and Capitol itself seems destined to become an important smelting center. Paying ores are plentiful and so are lead, iron, and other flux materials. And right here among these rugged mountains of faraway San Juan, where one would least expect to find it is the most elegantly furnished house in Southern Colorado. The handsome brick residence of George S. Lee and lady, distinguished for their hospitality, is the landmark of this locality. The scenic attractions, delightful atmosphere and the hunting, fishing, and boating facilities make this a popular summer resort, while the pleasure seekers and traveler will find the best accommodations that San Juan affords.*[677]

Lee also built a saw and planing mill in the middle of town and delivered shingles and lumber to Lake City. He built his Henson Creek Smelting Works a mile below town. The smelter and concentrating mill that he bought from Greene was at the other (upper) end of town. Lee, obviously a very brave man, brought his wife to Capitol City for the first time on October 25, 1877 — their tenth wedding anniversary.[678]

Capitol City was incorporated March 15, 1879, and it was the only incorporated settlement in the county in the 1800s other than the much larger Lake City.[679] Capitol City's elevation was 9,500 feet, and it had a reported population in 1881 of 400 miners, women, and prospectors. The *Lake City Mining Review* reported:

> *The camp is favorably situated for all purposes, having ample water power, an abundance of timber, a good wagon road to Lake City, and surrounded by immense veins of precious metals.... A mile below town (Capitol City), on Henson Creek, the Lee Smelter Works, is now idle. A mile above are the works of the Henson Creek Reduction Works Co., almost finished. Within town is Lee's saw and planing mill.*[680]

Capitol City's school house didn't look like much and evidently had only seven children, but they and the teachers posed with the Lake City stage about 1900. (Author's Collection, Photo by Morse and Bielser)

Until about 1893, the town had grown rapidly because of the arrival of the railroad at Lake City; and, at this time, Capitol City had saloons, numerous homes, hotels, restaurants, and a big, white school house built in 1883 at a cost $1,511. Sadly though, the residents didn't realize that Capitol City's population of about 800 was at its peak, and the town would quickly diminish in size after the Silver Panic of 1893, as virtually all of the nearby mines at the time produced silver with little or no gold.[681]

Capitol City's population fluctuated over the years because of new mining discoveries, but the local mines, unfortunately, almost always proved to be low grade. Many of the mining claims in the Capitol City area also overlapped; and as early as 1880, litigation was holding up production from many of the mines. Lee renamed Greene's mill "The Henson Creek Reduction Company." Lee himself moved away from Capitol City in 1882, after it was clear that the railroad was not coming to Lake City any time soon and the local mine owners were fighting over the ownership of their mines to the point that the two smelters in town were regularly sitting idle.

Muriel Wolle quotes information she gleaned from one of the last residents of Capitol City:

I heard too of the grand ball they held here in May, 1877, in the Capitol Saloon. About fifteen couples went. My father was the fiddler for the dance and he kept the newspaper write-up of it.... (Quoting the paper) — 'The music of the violin and guitar swayed the feet of the gay dancers until the morning light invaded the hall of revelry, and presented the claims of the coming day, when the happy crowd dispersed.' This place was planned to be big, but it over built itself. The boys found silver on the surface and before they found how deep the veins ran they built on a big scale.... There were plenty of paying properties too, but the best got tied up in litigation, and the owners got fighting over boundary lines and overlapping claims.

Lee also built the Rose Lime Kiln about two miles up Henson Creek at a limestone deposit that he used for mortar and cement in his hotel and kilns, and for the roasting process in the kilns at Capitol City. One of Lee's kilns at Capitol City and the chimney of the Rose Lime Kiln are both still standing, although they are located several miles apart. Only the settlements of Lake City, Capitol City, and Henson (which was located between these former mentioned towns) ever had daily service

Muriel Wolle took this photo in the late 1930s when the Lee Mansion was definitely showing its age but was basically all still there. The home was still partially remaining in 1960 when it was deemed a safety hazard and torn down shortly afterwards. (Denver Public Library, X-4002)

of mail and daily stagecoach service. The other settlements in Hinsdale County had service every other day or twice a week, and in both cases, their service was for summertime only.

Just how much the population fluctuated can be seen from George Crofutt, who in 1880 and 1885 gave Capitol City a population of about 100. Bancroft gave it 125 to 200 in the late 1880s. Muriel Wolle wrote:

During the nineties there were nearly 700 people here and there was plenty of room for a thousand more. In 1900 when they found gold here there was another boom and a lot of prospectors began picking at the hills again or reopening old properties. That's when the Ajax and Moro lodes produced hundreds of tons of high grade gold and copper ore and shipped it.[682]

By 1910 the town had a population of 30, but by 1911, it supposedly held 105 persons, most probably working at one of the nearby mines.[683]

Capitol City's first boom was based on the train coming to Lake City with resulting cheap transportation for the low grade, but plentiful, ores, in the area. Its second boom was based on gold discoveries by the Ajax and Moro Mines, which struck large amounts of gold and copper. Yet, once again, the pockets were small and the majority of the ore proved to be low-grade.[684]

Many of Capitol City's buildings were later salvaged by locals for their materials — a fate of many of the mining camps in the San Juans when structures were abandoned, especially during the Great Depression. Because it was made of brick, Lee's mansion lasted until the 1960s, when it was found to be a safety hazard after a tourist fell through a hole for the absent staircase from the second floor. The old log cabin that still stands in the park (it has been restored several times by the Hinsdale County Historical Society) was the post office, and the remains of a few smaller, older outbuildings, and one of the kilns are scattered amongst newer homes in the area.

PIKE SNOWDEN'S CABIN is located in a small park on the Henson Creek Road near the Nellie Creek turnoff. It was never really the site of a town or even a mining camp, but it is included in this book because for many years it was a spot for lodging on the Engineer Road. Snowden built the cabin in the late 1870s, and his door was always open to any traveler. He was one of the very earliest pioneers of the San Juans and was known by just about everyone. He was also one of the founding fathers of Silverton, but lived in his Hinsdale County cabin until about 1915, all the while doing prospecting near his cabin. One of Pike's best mines, at least according to him, was located just above the cabin.[685] Pike

Pike Snowden posed in front of his house. (From *Tiny Hinsdale of the Silvery San Juan*)

came to live permanently in Hinsdale County about 1880, after having prospected for years all over the San Juans. He was a loner, but loved to talk with travelers.

The bars that you will note on some of the cabin's windows were installed by Snowden after he won a small fortune in a poker game in Creede and became worried that someone might try to steal the money from him. The meadow around his cabin was a favorite picnic spot for Lake City residents around the turn of the century. He was such a well-liked person that the Wrights give him an entire chapter in their book *Tiny Hinsdale of the Silvery San Juan*.

Pike was described as a "short, rather heavy-set little man with twinkling blue eyes." He would often stop the Lake City stage on its way to Capitol City on the Henson Creek Road to send or receive an order he had made. "He always had a story to tell, no matter what subject came up." One of the best of his tales was when Pike would explain to listeners that he had no hair because he had been scalped by Indians. Another was that if he got drunk his dog would come find him and put him in bed; then in the morning his dog would put on coffee, and start the fire to help sober him up. Clarence Wright wrote about a story Pike told when the two were hunting deer with dogs. Pike said that on another hunt, just as the dogs were about to catch a deer, it climbed a tree. Wright said, "Hold on Pike, you know deer can't climb trees" Pike' answer: "This one had to."[686]

HENSON was a company town located at the Ute-Ulay Mine, which is discussed in Chapter 9. The town and the creek are named for Henry Henson, one of the three prospectors that discovered the mine in August, 1871, when the area still belonged to the Ute Indians. The town was above the lower workings and mill that are along the present road (County Road 20). It lay alongside Ute (also called Finley) Creek. Henson was also at one time reportedly called "Crookes' Town" or just "Crookes," although another settlement near Lake City was called "Crookesville." Henson was formed about 1880 after the mine sold for $1,200,000 and hired many more employees. In 1882, a concentrating mill was built at the mine and about 300 men lived in Henson. In 1893, right before the Silver Crash, the Ute-Ulay was reportedly the largest mine in the San Juans.[687] There were a lot of brawls and accidents in the company town of Henson. So many that it was said (although it was certainly an exaggeration) that at one time the little company town had eight doctors on the payroll, who were kept busy day and night, and averaged eight to ten operations a day.[688]

One of the largest mining disasters in San Juan mining history— a large explosion of gas— occurred when the Ute-Ulay and the Hidden Treasure drove their tunnels together, discovering that they had been working different branches of the same vein. The explosion killed or injured twenty men at the Ute and sixteen at the Hidden Treasure.[689] In 1910, Henson still had 100 residents, including some miners who had their families with them. They received mail six times a week in the

Some of the mine's houses at Henson and perhaps a saloon, as many men are standing in front of it, on the right. (Author's Collection)

summer and once a week in the winter.[690] The dates of the Henson post office are confusing. Ray Newburn states postal records show that a post office was established at the mine May 7, 1883, and ran continuously until November 30, 1913. However the Wrights say the post office was not opened until 1894 and ran to 1910. These are both good sources, but Newburn supposedly used the official U. S. Post Office records. More than likely the postal service was actually discontinued every time the mine shut down and was started again when the mine reopened.

About one mile south of Lake City on Highway 149 was the location of CROOKESVILLE, basically just a company town located on the west side of the Lake Fork of the Gunnison. It housed the employees of the Crooke Mill and Smelter and some of the management of the Ute-Ulay Mine, while that mine was owned by the Crookes. However, since it was so close to Lake City, and since there was a real shortage of lots and houses in Lake City in its early years, there were people living and working in Crookesville who did not work for the Crookes or the Ute-Ulay Mine or Mill. Crookesville is still not a part of Lake City. The 1879 business directory listed a post office at Crookesville with C. E. Kaufman serving as postmaster in his general store. H. David and H. Wooley also owned saloons in the town.[691]

Crookesville was basically the part of Lake City between the town and Crookes' Mill on the hill at far left center. (Author's Collection)

Traveling south from Lake City and Crookesville, at the paved fork in Highway 149, we will first take the left fork and go on a trip on Highway 149 to the county line between Hinsdale and Mineral Counties. PENNINGTON (PENNISTON) PARK never was a camp, little less a town, but it was a stage stop on the Slumgullion Pass Road; and, like Pike Snowden's Cabin, has always been a wonderful place to get away from it all. It is the big flat area about two or three miles up Slumgullion from the Dawn of Hope Bridge over the Lake Fork. It is named after Renzi Pennington (Penniston), who operated the stage stop on the upper end of the park for many years.[692] However the park was evidently originally called Sparling's Ranch after being homesteaded by Oen Noland for a couple of years. Noland grew hay and kept a freighting and storage business at the spot. Noland got into the storage business when a freighter carrying machinery and supplies for a local mine could not get any further toward the mine in late fall of 1875 and made a deal with Noland to watch the freight for the winter. Noland could not get to Lake City for several months that winter and ended up eating all of the food in the freighter's shipment.[693] The park was formed when the early Slumgullion Earthflow blocked a tributary valley (through which Highway 149 crosses), and formed a small lake and swampy area. Then, over time, the lake filled partially with silt.

SAN JUAN CITY, not Lake City, was the first settlement in Hinsdale County, but the small camp may possibly now be located in Mineral County. Although it was never very large, it was the first county seat of Hinsdale County. It was located in Antelope Park at a good spot on the eastern side of the Continental Divide near the division of a very old Indian path that ran from the San Luis Valley and split at this point. One of the trails led over Weminuche Pass to the Pagosa Springs area or over Stony Pass to the future Silverton area. The other trail at the fork led over Spring Creek and Slumgullion Passes to Lake San Cristobal or the Cebolla River.

In 1873, a man by the name of Harry Franklin staked out a ranch on the Rio Grande River about twenty miles upstream from the future Creede. Since this spot is east of the Continental Divide it was not considered to be part of the Ute Reservation at the time. He then platted and staked out a town site within his ranch. A cabin owned by W. H. Greene was near the spot that was selected as the county seat of Hinsdale County when it was formed almost a year later in 1874, but on February 23, 1875, the citizens of Hinsdale County voted to move the county seat to Lake City. San Juan City was listed in the *Handbook of Colorado* as a mining camp, even though it was not near the mines and had only one merchant, who was also the postmaster. George Crofutt had the following to say about San Juan City in 1885:

This cabin is identified as being part of San Juan City in Hinsdale County, but the terrain looks like it was further up the trail to Silverton. (Author's Collection)

The site of San Juan City has been presumed to be on the San Juan Ranch, shown in this photo. Five cabins have been built together at this spot. (Author's Collection)

San Juan (City) — Hinsdale County, on the Rio Grande, and the stage road from Alamosa to Silverton, five miles northwest of Antelope Springs. It is a station and post office, 8,900 feet altitude, surrounded by mountains filled with game of all kinds, and the Rio Grande with trout.[694]

Although San Juan City did have a platted town site, it was never a town, and when it was at its largest, it was said to have only six cabins. Later on, San Juan City became a stage stop on the Lake City route from Del Norte. San Juan City had daily mail service in its very early days, since it was located at the split in the road between the future Lake City and Silverton. The nearby Galloway Ranch cornered the early freight market to the future Lake City and Silverton because from 1873 to 1875 freight had to be transferred from wagons to mules and burros at Galloways or San Juan City in order to proceed past this point.[695]

San Juan City was located near at the present Hinsdale-Mineral County line, but there is still some debate over which county it is now located in. Newburn's postal history[696] and several other sources state it was on the San Juan Ranch and is still a couple of hundred feet in Hinsdale County, but some early maps show, and some historians state, that it was in southern Antelope Park, which is now in Mineral County.[697] One historian locates it on the north side of Crooked Creek, about a mile above its junction with Spring Creek. Later on it was known as "Officer's Ranch."

Going back north to Lake San Cristobal near the Golden Fleece Mine, there was a settlement called LAKESHORE (often written LAKE SHORE) on the western bank and at the north end of Lake San Cristobal. Lakeshore was the location of the beginnings of Lake City's tourism business, as Lake San Cristobal was a very popular attraction for even the earliest of tourists. It was small, but it had stage service and a post office from October 19, 1896 to May 14, 1904. It was served later by a postal Star Route, which came from Lake City during non-winter months. Star Routes were given to private contractors making the lowest bid for delivering mail reliably and securely. They were abolished in 1970.[698] The main mines in the area were the Golden Fleece, Hiawasse, Black Crooke, Contention, General Sherman, and a few other smaller mines. Since it was very near the Golden Fleece, it also served as a supply point for that and other nearby mines and their workers, as well as for fishermen at the lake. A few miners' families lived close by, so there was even a school at the spot for a while. This area will be covered more in Chapter 10.

This postcard photo shows a part of Lake Shore pretty much at its peak. (Burton and Nora Smith Collection)

Lake Shore can be seen on the opposite side of the lake. The Golden Fleece was near enough that some of its workers with families lived here. They were close enough together that Lake Shore served as a supply point for lodging for both the mine and for local tourists and fishermen. (U. S. G. S. Survey photo.)

About six miles upstream from Lake San Cristobal, a four-wheel drive road leads to the left and up Wager Gulch to the ghost town of Carson. The point where the Carson and Cinnamon roads intersect was called CHILDS' PARK and it had a post office, but it really was more of a stop for mail and supplies than a town. M. L. Childs bought most of the big mines in Carson City in 1902, but it is not known for sure if that is the source of the name of the park. The Wrights, who are considered to be good Lake City historians, wrote there was no post office, but rather a Mr. Stephens, who lived there, always had stamps and would use a pen to postmark letters "Childs' Park," then send them with someone to Lake City to be mailed. This practice ended in 1918. Ray Newburn, author of the unpublished manuscript *Postal History of the Colorado San Juans,* writes that Childs' Park had an official post office from May 9, 1912 to February 28, 1919.

CARSON CITY is one of the best preserved ghost towns in Colorado and is well worth the side trip, but only in dry weather as rain or snow makes the road extremely slippery. It was established in 1882,[699] and was probably named for J. E. Carson, although other writers argue vehemently that the settlement was named for Christopher J. Carson, who was a nephew of Kit Carson. Kit Carson was known to trap in the area in the 1830s, fifty years before the discovery of silver at Carson. J.E. Carson discovered his mine on the north side of the Divide in 1881, some sixteen miles from Lake City, on Wager Creek, and right at the Continental Divide. The Carson mining district was organized in 1882.

One author writes that, like a cavalry saddle, Carson City was thrown on the Continental Divide at an elevation of 12,300 feet with

Carson City was described as "like a cavalry saddle thrown over the Continental Divide." This view shows the mines on the north side. (U.S.G.S. Photo)

part of the camp on the Pacific Slope and the other part on the Atlantic Slope.[700] Access was through Wager Gulch on the Lake City side and along Lost Trail on the Rio Grande side. Carson was also called "Carson City," although some people apply the name "Carson" to the settlement of the south side of the Continental Divide and "Carson City" to that on the north. Carson City was nowhere close to the size of a city, but putting the word "city" in the name of what was really just a small town or camp was popular at the time.

Ray Newburn is insistent in his postal history[701] that Carson is named for Christopher J. Carson and not J. E. Carson. Muriel Wolle also writes that Christopher J. Carson discovered the prospects in the area, then staked the Bonanza King. Supposedly J. E. Carson, who most believe the camp is named after, told Ed Cannon in the winter of 1881-1882 that he had found gold in the area that came to be named Carson City. They came back in the spring of 1882 and sent the ore they mined to Del Norte, which was the easiest way out at the time; but because Del Norte was seventy miles away, they sent only the richest handpicked ore to the mills.[702]

By 1883, hundreds of men were at Carson, and part of the town had been built down to tree line in Wager Gulch. In the first few years of its existence there was no real road to Carson, but a fair road was built south from Carson towards the future Creede in the mid-1880s. This "road" from Del Norte was upgraded in 1887, although trails had been built on both sides of the Divide since 1882. The "road" — really only a trail—from Lake City was originally impassable by wagons.

We have few existing photos of the buildings on the south side of Carson, but this recent photo shows the camp on the north side is still in pretty good shape. Most of these buildings still exist today because of restoration. (Author's Photo)

In 1883, many more people had heard of Carson and came to the district. There was no true town yet, but there were buildings at five or six of the mines.[703] Again, because of transportation costs, only the richest ore was shipped to Del Norte and the rest was stockpiled. Still it was reported that capitalists were at Carson looking for mines to buy by 1883.[704] Assays of the mines' high grade ore from pockets in the area were running 150 to 4800 ounces in silver and .1 to 20 ounces in gold, with ten to twenty-nine percent copper. In 1889 a road was constructed down to Lake City, upgrading the previous trail, for use by the Vermont and the Bonanza King Mines near Carson. For the first time Lake City was well connected with the mining camp, although the road was steep and slippery in spots.

Carson had a log post office from September of 1889 to October 15, 1903.[705] Carson was basically a summer-only camp but was open all winter from 1897 to 1902.[706]

Only twenty hopeful mine owners or prospectors lived in Carson in 1910.[707] R.E. Townsend and his son Harry kept the camp alive from 1930 to 1958. They owned fifty-eight claims, plus the Hays Placer. A very small amount of production, exploration, and core drilling was done at Carson City in the 1990s.[708]

The south side of Carson has almost disappeared, with only the bottom row of one or two log cabins still visible. The Carson mines produced gold, ruby silver, and copper; and the local ores sometimes ran as high as $2,000 a ton. However this was usually the high grade ore from pockets with perhaps $40,000 in ore in each large rich pocket.[709] The group of buildings that still remain on the north side of the divide thanks to partial reclamation on several occasions through the years, were later called the "Bachelor Cabins" after the nearby Bachelor Mine.[710]

Back on the Cinnamon Pass Road, at the junction of Cottonwood Creek and the Lake Fork, the town of SHERMAN had a few cabins by 1875. It was founded and platted in 1877 by A. D. Freeman and others, who laid it out with sixty foot wide streets and also alleys, which were twenty feet wide. A rich strike was originally made in nearby Cuba Gulch, but the town did not get busy until 1880, and the town's nicest hotel, the Sherman House, was built in 1881. It advertised "Good Accommodations for Travelers, Liquors, Wines, St. Louis Beer, and Cigars."[711] Sherman had a big building at Main and Sixth Street that was used as a warehouse and forwarding station for the mines further up the Cinnamon Pass Road in Burrows Park; but the building also had a butcher shop, bakery, and a grocery store. Sherman got a post office in 1877, with Benton Fraley being the first postmaster.

Some say Sherman was named for General William Sherman of Civil War fame (or infamy depending on what side you were on), but the town was more likely named for F. S. Sherman, an early prospector and settler in the area.[712] During its first years of existence, Sherman had a population of about fifty. The town was never incorporated, although it sits at a nice level spot near where the Cinnamon Pass Road starts to climb steeply up to Burrows Park.

Sherman had a lot of trouble with flooding almost every spring. A dam was built above the town shortly after the turn of the century, and it later failed and buried a good part of the town. Even today the devastating results of the flood can be seen. There were many mines around the town; but Sherman's fortune rose and fell with that of its biggest mine, the Black Wonder. The town was in a good location for prospectors, as Cataract Gulch, Cottonwood Gulch, Cuba Gulch, and Burrows Park were all close by.

At its height, Sherman contained several stores, saloons, and restaurants. The large Black Wonder Mill dominated the town. Crofutt gave Sherman a population of 100 in 1880; and the next year spoke highly of the new Sherman House Hotel, which also contained "a store full of merchandise (that) tempted the 100 citizens to spend their money at home... This is a mining camp of both placer and lode claims." A

Sherman had sixty-foot-wide streets but not much of a road. The Black Wonder Mill is at the center of the photo. The two men are probably looking at the mine. (Colorado Historical Society Photo, CHS-B305)

The general store was located right next to the Black Wonder Mill, which was probably the largest single mill in Hinsdale County, but was originally built in Burrows Park, then dismantled and brought to Sherman in 1895. (From Croffut's Grip Sac Guide of Colorado)

post office was present at Sherman from 1877 to 1898.[713] The summer population might have been as high as 300, but slipped to only forty or fifty in the winter.[714]

An eastern company took over the Black Wonder in 1897, and spent over $200,000 in improvements. When the Black Wonder Mill was bought in 1897, the dam was built as part of a rejuvenation project. In 1900, the Black Wonder Mill was reworked and powered by boilers using firewood for fuel. The mill soon shut down and for the next several decades, the town had only three or four old timers living there; but in 1925, the mine was reopened and Sherman was actually a town again. The water pipeline that can be seen below the jeep road climbing to Burrows Park (especially at the suspension bridge, about half way up to Burrows Park) brought water to turn a Pelton Wheel for electricity at the mill. The houses in town were also electrified at the time, as well as street lights that were placed on the main street. Sherman even had a baseball team for a while.[715] One man told Muriel Wolle:

I put in the dam up there over forty years ago for a company that was working the mines…. The dam was to be 147 feet high, but

293

by the time I built it sixty-nine feet high the company was broke. Another company took over and wanted the dam raised. They had the work done, and then a cloudburst took out the dam and most of the town, and left it the way it is today.[716]

By 1930, the town was again in decline. Although Sherman was at 9,600 feet in elevation, besides mining it had a brick kiln. 40,000 bricks were supposedly made there for use at the local mill and smelter.

There was a small town named GARDEN CITY or GARDNER CITY about two miles up Cottonwood Creek from Sherman, but little is known about it.

BURROWS PARK, which is located above the Sherman town site on the Cinnamon Pass Road, has confused historians for ages. Within a two or three mile distance, generally at the west (upper) end of Burrows Park, there were five towns named Whitecross, Sterling, Argentum, Tellurium, and a settlement called Burrows Park.[717] Considerable confusion exists as to exactly where each of the towns was located; and several times the post office was moved from one settlement to another nearby with the name of the former town being kept. For example, the town of Burrows Park is generally conceded to have been located at the present trailheads to Redcloud and Handies Peaks, but the area was also called Argentum (a local ore) at one time. Nine families wintered somewhere in Burrows Park in 1878, and a few families were there in the winter for several decades thereafter, as the weather outside really did not affect the men working in the mines.[718]

Burrows Park is named for Albert W. Burrows, who led a party that explored the park in 1873 when the land was still owned by the Ute Indians. Burrows came from the Los Piños Agency, up the Lake Fork of the Gunnison, and eventually went over Cinnamon, thereby following the route of the original Baker party. However, the group then came

The Burrows Park post office in 1893 was located in Whitecross. (Author's Collection)

back to Burrows Park and staked many claims in the park as well as in the Mineral Point area, where they constructed a few rough log cabins in 1873.[719]

The TOWN OF BURROWS PARK was located just above the point where Silver Creek joins the Lake Fork in Burrows Park. In 1881, the population according to Crofutt was between 50 and 100. By 1885, it was said to vary between 100 and 10 (presumably the first in summer, the second in the winter). Mail was delivered by buckboard from Lake City once or twice a week in the summer and by skiers going over Cinnamon in the winter.[720] The camp of Burrows Park had the park's second post office (Tellurium had the first), which was established September 26, 1876. James W. Stewart was the first postmaster, but there were three different postmasters in 1877. The park did not really have a big enough population for two post offices located only a couple of miles apart; but

The town of Burrows Park was pretty spread out. The two buildings near the center of the photo and close to the trail are still standing and were the stage stop/hotel and the post office/general store. Sunshine Peak is in the background. (USGS Photo)

the creation of the second post office was probably due in large part to an already existing mail route from Lake City to Silverton going along the Mears toll road through Burrows Park, making it easy to drop off letters or packages along the existing route. The Burrows Park post office was eventually changed to White Cross in 1882, and the Tellurium post office was closed for good in 1880.[721]

ARGENTUM was the first true town to be located in Burrows Park and was located basically at the same spot as the town of Burrows Park.[722] J. H. Sloan built a cabin there in 1876. Argentum and the town of Burrows Park were the largest of the small towns located in the park, and at one time had several small hotels, two stores, a blacksmith's shop, a post office, and a dozen log cabin residences. The smaller of the two cabins still located there today was the post office (built in the late 1870s), and the other was used as a hotel and the stage stop. The Napoleon, Undine, and Ouida were some of the local mines. Argentum had its post office from September 26, 1876 to September 28, 1882; then, to make matters even more confusing, the post office that had been called both Burrows Park and Argentum was moved to Whitecross, but at least the *Silver World* announced in 1882 that the name of the post office had been changed to Whitecross. The post office continued at Whitecross from 1882 to 1912.

The town of WHITECROSS was named for Whitecross Mountain, which is located across the canyon from the town. The mountain was named for a slanting white cross of quartz in a gully near the top of the mountain. The cross lies on its side and some people think it looks more like an "X".[723] Whitecross was first located in 1880. The Hotel de Clauson (also spelled Clawson) was a popular part of the camp, as well as several other businesses being located in the area. The town's population was small, as most of the local miners lived at the mines at which they were employed. The population of Whitecross fell drastically in 1895, when its mill was moved to Sherman, but rose again when the Tabasco (sometimes spelled Tobasco) Mill was built in 1901. The Hotel de Clauson was the best hotel in Burrows Park and the social center of the area.[724] The mines in Burrows Park always had problems with getting their ore out. In 1898, the Premier and Tabasco "settled down to systematic work on two of the best groups of mines in the park...."[725] The Tabasco, Bon Homme, and Champion were considered the best mines in the area in the early 1900s.[726]

With the opening of the Tabasco Mine and the building of the Tabasco Mill and tram in 1900-1902, Whitecross became very active about 1900, and had a post office, store, saloon, hotel, and a boarding

Whitecross was named for the white quartz cross (sometimes called an "x" as it leans) that is near the top of the highest pinnacle in the upper right part of the photo. It is hard to see even with the naked eye. This little string of cabins was much of the town but there were a few more nearby. (U.S.G.S. Photo)

house, thirteen cabins, two stables, and two freighters. At this time, its population was touted to reach almost 300 men, women, and children, but many of them were temporary construction workers that left after the mill was completed.

Whitecross had a post office from September 28, 1882 to May 15, 1912. At least as early as 1878, families were wintering there. The Wrights called the Tabasco operation (which was owned by the Tabasco Sauce family) a "promotion" that hurt the better mines in the county. Perk Vickers is quoted as saying the owners of the Tabasco simply got the cart (the mill) before the horse (the mine).[727] The Wrights report that equipment from the Tabasco was being hauled away by anyone who wanted it by 1906.[728]

When Muriel Wolle was in Burrows Park in the 1950s, it was already hard to tell where each of the many camps was located. She admits that the locations were a problem, but wrote that Whitecross was one quarter of a mile above Burrows Park, Tellurium was just above Whitecross, and Sterling was just above Tellurium. She further mentions that Argentum was six miles above Sherman.

The town of TELLURIUM was at the junction of Adams Creek and the Lake Fork. Tellurium was named because the local mine owner had hopes of finding a gold ore of the same name at the location, but unfortunately none was found. Henry Linton and Frank Barnes were operating a saloon and restaurant in the camp of Tellurium by the spring of 1876.[729] By 1878, a few people were spending the winter in the camp. Tellurium had delusions of grandeur and a large town site was laid out in the mid-seventies and a mill built just a little later; but most of the town did not get beyond the paper stage, and the mill was often not running.[730]

George Crofutt found Tellurium:

A small mining camp, of a dozen persons, situated in Burrows Park, near the headwaters of the Lake Fork of the Gunnison River. The place was named for a kind of mineral that certain parties hoped to discover nearby, but up to this time, have failed in their efforts. Nearby is an expensive mill standing idle when we passed through the town in October, 1880. It is twenty two miles west from Lake City, fare $3.25...[731]

Tellurium was in the upper end of the park and was one of the earliest camps in Hinsdale County. There was usually a woman or two at the camp at this time.[732] Five adjoining cabins made up the heart of the camp, but several other cabins were in the area. The vacant mill referred to by Crofutt was operated for a short time after 1880 for the nearby Gunnison Mine. Tellurium received the first post office in Burrows Park on August 24, 1875, and it continued to October 4, 1880. The Wrights noted that Tellurium received the mail for thirteen cabins in 1900, but only two of those cabins were actually in Tellurium. Tellurium and Whitecross (also spelled White Cross) had a post office named Whitecross from 1885 to 1907, but with summer only service.

The Wrights verified that there were 300 people getting mail in Whitecross in 1902, while the Tabasco Mill and tram to the mine was being built.[733] Tellurium and Whitecross were close enough together that the post office shifted from one camp to the other. The cabins of both towns were actually scattered along the road for about half a mile. Tellurium gained the Whitecross post office from 1887 to 1912, mainly because it was slightly closer to the mines like the Tabasco that were working only a little further up the Cinnamon Pass Road.

Somewhere along the Cinnamon road above Whitecross was the camp called "Sterling," which probably was never more than a tent city.

There were OTHER HINSDALE SETTLEMENTS, but they were so small, and sometimes so short-lived, that very little is known about them. Several of them were at one time located in Hinsdale County, but their sites became part of Mineral County when it was created from part of Hinsdale. Most were stage stops, if there was a stage, most had a school, and some had a store.

BEARTOWN was located about four miles to the south of the Stony Pass cutoff on Lost Trail. Some mining was done in the area in the 1870s, but it was not until 1893 that a rich strike at the Sylvanite Mine at Kite Lake brought 400 prospectors to the area, which is slightly in San Juan County, although separated from direct access to Silverton by the Continental Divide. Most prospectors were so excited about the local ore that they lived in tents until they were absolutely forced to build cabins in the winter of 1893. Beartown did well enough in 1893 that many Creede merchants soon built stores there. The mines had good ore and there was a lot of activity in the area until the first part of the twentieth century. The Sylvanite Mine's ore was worth as much as $4,000 per ton, making that mine one of the big producer of the area.[734] The town was also called Gold Run, Sylvanite, and Silvertip at various times.[735]

BELFORD had a post office from December 10, 1879 to November 21, 1881. It was located on the Del Norte-Lake City stage road on the east side of North Clear Creek, near the confluence of North Clear Creek and Big Springs Creek. It was probably named for James Belford, a judge of the Colorado Territory Supreme Court.

CATHEDRAL was located on the upper Cebolla at its junction with Spring Creek and had a post office from July 18, 1898 to September 30, 1921. It served the local ranches and the stage on the Otto Mears toll road. There is a rock formation called Cathedral Rocks on Cathedral Creek, but this spot is about two miles above the town. The population of Cathedral was twenty-seven in 1910, and it had a school until it was combined with Lake City in 1960. Mining Engineer T. A. Rickard, in 1902, commented:

> At noon we pulled into a spot marked in large letters on the map "Cathedral," and found a solitary log cabin with a hospitable woman in command, who gave us dinner. Subsequently, when smoking a soothing pipe, we could appreciate the simple grandeur of the granite forms, sculptured by Time and chiseled by the heat of the day and the frost of the night into buttresses and pinnacles simulating all the stern magnificence of a Gothic ruin—of a cathedral not made by hands, domed by the sky, and aisled with the green of the peaceful valley.[736]

DEBS had a post office from September 10, 1915 to January 31, 1925. Debs, located on a bluff just south of the East Fork of the Piedra River and just above its junction with the Middle Fork, was close to the far southern border of Hinsdale County. There was a Hinsdale County school at Debs that later became part of the Archuleta School District.

HERMIT had a post office from July 6, 1904 to September 15, 1920. It was located on the south side of North Clear Creek, where it leaves the lower part of Hermit Lakes. Access was from a short road up Clear Creek from where it crosses the Spring Creek Pass Road. It had a school but little else is known of it.

JENNISON was probably on or near the site of the earlier Carr's Cabin (built in 1872), although no one is exactly sure of the exact location of Carr's Cabin. It was in the area of the upper Rio Grande River a little more than three miles above Lost Trail Creek.[737] Carr's Cabin was named for B. F. Carr, a very early San Juan prospector. The spot was a place where travelers and freighters often, in the spring, had to stop on the east side of the Continental Divide to wait for the snow to melt on Stony Pass, so as to make it passable to Silverton. William Henry Jackson visited the spot in 1874, and called it "a very primitive structure."[738] For some reason Carr abandoned his cabin, and it is generally believed that Charles and Irene Jennison remodeled it, moved in, and it was later renamed Jennison, after the couple. The Jennisons called their ranch "Chemiso" (Spanish for a small ranch). Charlie Jennison soon died and his wife Irene sold the cabin to Joel Brewster in early summer of 1876.

Jennison had a post office from January 15, 1875 to December 20, 1875; April 11, 1877 to December 10, 1877; and then finally from May 20, 1878 to April 25, 1879. Until 1878, Jennison was the only post office between San Juan City and Howardsville. Since the post office was closed for two of the three winters of its existence, the Jennisons may not have stayed at the ranch during that time of year. They had a great place for a ranch in the summer, as it was located right where the Rio Grande branches into many small tributaries. The Jennisons had a small store and freighting operation, and when Irene sold out in 1876, Joel Brewster kept the Jennison name and opened a lodge, boarding house, storage building, and had a freighting business for items brought in to Jennison by wagons that were going over Stony Pass by mule or burro train, because Stony Pass was very difficult for wagon traffic. The Brewsters had a family operation involving all of their eight children. The large park that Jennison was located in is now called Brewster Park. One visitor to Brewster's early hotel noted that the interior of the cabin had only stud walls with tarps nailed to the studs to separate it into rooms.[739]

JUNCTION CITY was another camp that got ahead of itself. Some ore was found there in 1894, a town was platted, and a few cabins were built. But then everyone got disgusted and left. Only one cabin is left near the junction of Bear and Pole Creeks and the Rio Grande River. Bear Creek was originally named Hines Creek after the photographer that traveled with Lt. Ruffner's expedition.[740]

LOST TRAIL had a post office from January 28, 1878 to September 30, 1879; then May 14, 1883 to August 14, 1884; and finally June 27, 1892 to May 10, 1894. It was located on the north bank of the upper Rio Grande at its junction with Lost Trail Creek. Crofutt describes it as "a post office and a ranch hotel." He suggested that travelers camp out near the "hotel" rather than stay there. Later tourists enjoyed Lost Trail and still do. There was a ranch office, post office, store, saloon, and several cabins. Most activity declined in the 1890s.[741] It is now the site of a campground, so people are still camping there.

TIMBER HILL opened in 1878 and had a post office from April 25, 1879 to January 31, 1881. The post office was considered only a name change for Jennison, although the site was probably not in exactly the same place. William D. Watson was the owner, and the name came from a nearby bluff called Timber Hill. It was located at the first really steep place on the Stony Pass Road. Crofutt writes that it was just a ranch and a post office, but the Greene Smelter in Silverton had a small warehouse at the spot. The Brewsters eventually moved from Carr's Cabin (Jennison) to Timber Hill. There were so many little stops on the last part of the Stony Pass road on the eastern side of the Divide because it was a long uphill haul of many miles and a steep climb from this point to the top. Because it was so isolated, it was also a favorite spot for robberies on the road from Silverton to Del Norte. One time, three rich ore wagons accompanied by three guards who rode ahead of the wagon, were attacked by robbers, and two of the three guards were killed at Timber Hill near what some now call Bandit Rock. The last guard raced back to warn the wagons, and the wagon crews dumped two of the wagon's contents in a nearby hiding place. The robbers took the third wagon and killed the third guard. The other two wagon loads of ore are supposedly still hidden somewhere along the trail.

Most of the settlements along the upper Rio Grande were abandoned after the railroad came to Silverton from Durango in 1882 as there was really no further need to use the Stony Pass Road. Hinsdale County's little settlements are all gone, but it is important to remember that early pioneers lived and worked at these spots and that more than a few of these individuals are buried near their one-time homes, although most lie in unmarked graves.

STAKING CLAIMS.

Many early prospectors were so anxious to file a claim that they would do so in the snow next to an existing claim, hoping that they would find something when the snow melted. (Harper's Weekly *drawing, Author's Collection*)

CHAPTER 9

HINSDALE COUNTY MINES AND MINING

From 1875 to 1920, Hinsdale County mines produced well more than 30 million dollars' of gold, silver, lead, zinc, and copper, worth perhaps over a half billion dollars in today's values. There are even a few mines still working off and on, but on a small scale, at the time of this writing. Other areas of the San Juans have produced more gold and silver than Hinsdale County, but Hinsdale led the early San Juan mining production in silver ore, although many of its mines soon produced only low grade ore. As early as 1918, Wilbur Stone wrote in his *History of Colorado* that:

> *The San Juan is a great mining country, being ribbed with heavy deposits. Many a time the prospector "stuck it rich" in the '80s and '90s. Often he was disappointed when, instead of a fortune, he found a mass of low grade ore.*[742]

Although there were some exceptions, unfortunately for Hinsdale County there were many more discoveries of large deposits of low grade ore than local prospectors "striking it rich." However there was a never ending optimism among the Hinsdale County prospectors, brought on by rich high grade ore pockets discovered in otherwise low grade ore. Local long-time resident, Perk Vickers, who mined in the area off and on for all of his life, described in his book, *Coming Home*, why the prospectors kept looking:

> *There's a drive; there's a hope; there's a belief that this is going to be the big one. If you go in just a little further, a little bit deeper, you're going to hit gold. Really hit the Mother Lode....*
>
> *(Local prospectors) had a sense of optimism that kept them going. It produced a drive to keep on digging, long after most people would have given up....*

It seems like those of us who like it here are always looking for some outsider to put up some bucks, so we can go on with various projects. (Outsiders) can't realize how many people from so many different parts of the country have had a hand in most of these mining developments.[743]

There are literally thousands of mining claims and hundreds of mines in Hinsdale County. By 1897 there would be 8,566 claims recorded in Hinsdale County, and there are even more today; but we will examine only a few of the biggest, best, and most interesting. As George Crofutt mentioned in 1885:

To name all the mines in this region, where the records show the existence of over 5,000 (in 1880), would require a large volume; and disclaiming any desire to make individual distinctions, we shall only mention a few of those that have obtained more than local fame.[744]

THE SAN JUAN TRIANGLE

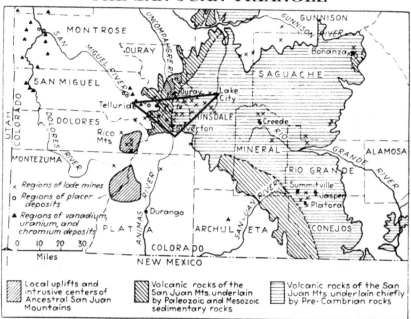

The San Juan Triangle covered most of the rich mines in the San Juans, although there were exceptions such as Creede, Rico, and Summitville. This particular map also shows a few other locations of mines but 90% of the value of San Juan minerals were within the triangle shown on this map. (Western Reflections map adapted from Burbank, Engineering and Mining Journal)

In Hinsdale County, precious minerals are usually found at the northeastern part of the San Juan Triangle. Most of the mines in the Lake City area were discovered in four areas — along almost the entire length of Henson Creek; along the Lake Fork of the Gunnison, mainly above the Town of Lake City and including Lake San Cristobal; at Carson on the Continental Divide, and in Burrows Park near Cinnamon Pass. From a geologic point of view, the locations along these two main rivers of the county make sense, as the lower areas that contain streams are often the edges of volcanic calderas or are softer earth associated with the formation of metallic veins that erode quicker than the harder surrounding granite rock. These areas are generally extremely steep due to the action of glaciers, and to a much lesser extent, streams and water.

In the earlier history of these mountains they were bolder than they are now, and when, at the close of the volcanic activity, earthquakes supervened, then landslides occurred on a colossal scale and were accompanied by a shattering of the rocks, covering areas extending over many square miles.[745]

Most early San Juan discoveries were found at timberline or higher (11,000 to 13,000 feet). The rule in the San Juans was generally that the higher up that the ore was found, the more valuable it would be. However this was not necessarily true in Hinsdale County. Trails to the mines were incredibly rough and steep, and the first prospectors lived only in canvas tents covered with linseed oil for rain-proofing. It was a hard life, but one of utter freedom with the promise of striking it rich every new day.[746] However instead of hard work and suffering, many good discoveries were made entirely by accident. As John Bell wrote in *The Pilgrim and the Pioneer*:

Quite often the discovery is made by mere accident. One claim here (Hinsdale County), which was sold for more than a hundred thousand dollars, was discovered by an Irishman falling over a cliff and kicking off a piece of the brilliant silver-bearing rock; and another that was sold equally high was discovered by a little boy shooting at a jack rabbit while it was sitting near a crag—going up to where the bullet struck, he found he had chipped off a piece of glittering gold; and similar incidents are reported from all the principal camps.[747]

Since the San Juans were a giant 26,000 foot high dome before millions of years of wind and water erosion and glacial action, it is of no surprise that the streams in the northern San Juans generally head north. Henson Creek which travels around the north side of the Lake City Caldera is one exception, running mostly east, following the caldera's edge rather than the San Juan dome's slope.

Geologists Irving and Bancroft describe the uniqueness of the Lake and Galena Mining Districts:

> *Hinsdale County was divided into two main mining districts — the Galena and the Lake Districts. The history of Lake City mining has been one of alternations — of general depression and of excessive activity — which have rendered its existence a little more eventful than that of the neighboring towns in the San Juan Mountains. These alternations have been due to several causes, but chiefly to the extreme richness of part of a few of the ore bodies discovered and the poverty of the rest.... Similar variant conditions have prevailed to a greater or less extent in almost all mining centers, but in few places in Colorado have they been so pronounced as at Lake City.*[748]

Minerals that are found in the Lake City ores include gold, silver, lead, copper, and zinc. They are usually found in galena, pyrites, argentiferous, sphalerite, and tetrahedrite ores. Silver is usually much more common in Hinsdale County than gold with a few major exceptions like the Golden Fleece and Golden Wonder Mines. Because most people want to know something about the types and amounts of precious minerals that the Hinsdale area produced, this book will answer a few of those questions. However a few factors need to be considered first. Gold and silver amounts are usually stated in ounces per ton of ore. Other minerals, such as lead, zinc, and copper, are usually given as percentages of weight of the ore in which they were contained. Ore is defined as any rock that contains enough valuable minerals of any kind to make it economical to mine and separate. Sometimes mines reported their values by using sorted ore, which would be much more valuable than the average of the ore body. Some values were given after the ore was crushed and milled. Since the early concentrating mills often lost a good deal of the precious metals, these values were sometimes much less than the actual amount of precious metals in the veins. So mine production figures have to be taken with a grain of salt, but will give some indication of what the mine was producing and some indication of how rich the vein was.

Hinsdale County ores generally appear in fissure veins, which are cracks or crevices in the rock caused by faults and volcanic eruptions. These cracks were later filled with mineral-bearing waters and gases that evaporated and left valuable minerals behind. A tunnel, or "adit" in mining terminology, needs to be at least three feet wide and five feet tall to access these veins, so the width of the vein is very important.

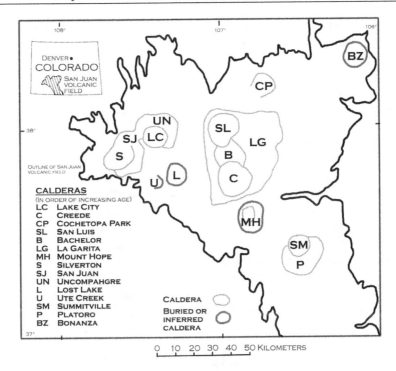

Note from this U.S.G.S. map of the San Juan Calderas that the Lake City Caldera (LC) is the youngest, although millions of years old. (Adapted from USGS Professional Paper 958)

The wider the vein, the less waste rock that has to be mined to get the ore out. Another factor in the value of the ore was how easy it could be smelted. Some ores required very expensive and complicated techniques to remove the gold and silver; and some veins could be processed fairly simply. Hinsdale County was mainly a silver area and silver has properties that can make it very difficult to extract silver from the ore. Hinsdale County mines therefore became the province of chemists, geologists, metallurgists, and engineers.

The San Juans also contain replacement ores, where minerals were forced into and replaced other rock. Generally this occurred when rich minerals at the top of veins seeped into the lower rock. Replacement ore mining could cause great "rooms" in the mines, but the roofs of these rooms needed rock columns of ore to be left to support their ceilings. There is one such place as this in the Ute-Ulay.

Few of the richer veins discovered in Hinsdale County are above 12,000 feet and the lowest veins in the county are at about 8,500 feet. In the lower areas, near streams, falling rock debris has generally covered the outcrop of veins. The veins are usually there, but they are covered by broken barren rock. Therefore many of the Hinsdale County mines, like the Ute-Ulay, were discovered on the surface at higher elevations (but still below many of the rich discoveries in other parts of the San Juans) and then mined downward through a shaft until an adit was eventually opened into the vein at a lower level. Sometimes this was unsuccessful, because the vein could not be found, or because many of the veins in Hinsdale split into smaller branches and headed in every direction. Many of these smaller branches were not worth mining.

The Hinsdale County veins also tended to become richer with depth for a short distance (perhaps 10 to 30 feet) and then decreased in value with further depth and eventually were not worth mining; although, sometimes a different vein might be struck at the lower level.[749] The lower adits usually meant that the vein would be longer at that point, as the steep terrain often meant that glaciers and other erosion had washed away the upper part of the veins. If it was possible, using a lower adit made mining much more economical than using a shaft, as water was drained by gravity instead of using pumps, and fresh air would flow naturally into the mine. Also it was easier to haul the rock out in an ore car by gravity than to try to fight gravity by lifting it to the surface using a winch.[750]

The Hinsdale County veins averaged about 1,000 to 1,200 feet in length, however some of the exceptionally wide veins like the Black Crooke, Golden Fleece, Ute Ulay, and Hidden Treasure ran for nearly 3,000 feet. The width of the pay-streak part of the veins in the Hinsdale

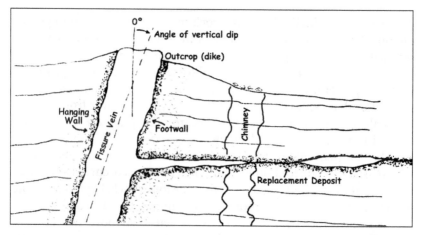

This cross section shows some of the terminology and geological formations involved with mining. A fissure vein might run for miles. A chimney is usually oval and might be a few feet in radius or some were hundreds of feet. Replacement ores were usually mined in "rooms" with pillars left to hold up the ceiling. (Western Reflections Drawing)

A drawing from Frank Fossett's Colorado *shows a vein being followed and being "stoped" (dug out). The bottom area is a tunnel dug for access but not containing ore. (Author's Collection)*

area usually ran from a few inches to twenty inches, but those veins that were worked extensively averaged about eighteen inches. Many veins were wider in their upper reaches and narrower with depth. Almost all veins eventually pinched out to nothing at extreme depth. Typically the entire vein would be quite a bit wider than the pay streak, sometimes being many feet wide. The area outside the pay streak was only worth mining because of the much higher values in the pay streak. A few areas of very rich ore did extend to twenty feet wide or more, but most of these were pockets that played out after fairly short distances, sometimes just a few feet. The Ute-Ulay, Golden Fleece, and Black Crooke had pockets of rich ore that were eight or ten feet in width in certain portions of the vein.[751]

Veins hardly ever go in a straight line, but rather twist and turn along what is called the "strike." Most veins in Hinsdale County run northeast-southwest or northwest-southeast. Veins can also intersect with each other, which caused much richer ore at that point than in either of the separate veins. This was evidently what happened when the Golden Fleece hit an extremely rich gold ore "chute." As mentioned earlier, water solution can also filter down from the upper parts of the vein causing replacement ore or increasing the presence of valuable minerals in the vein. Hinsdale County ores that are formed by mineral waters include quartz, pyrite, galena, rhodochrosite, sphalerite, tetrahydrite, barite, chalcopyrite, and other sulphide enriched minerals. Telluride and hinsdalite (an ore named for Hinsdale County, where hinsdalite was first discovered) are also examples. Both silver and gold can be found in these ores separately, but are usually found together in various proportions. Silver and gold were found in hinsdalite in the Golden Fleece in almost equal parts, which was a much higher ratio of gold than in most of the other local mines.

Telluride gold ore was found in the Golden Fleece, Gallic-Vulcan, Golden Wonder, and possibly the Isolde. Except for the Golden Wonder, it was found in fairly small quantities, but contained good gold and some silver. In summing up their evaluation of Lake City ores, geologists Irving and Bancroft bring up the point mentioned elsewhere in this book that there were great excesses of costly expenditures in the boom periods of Hinsdale County, which hurt local mining, but also meant that many mines ran out of money before much development was done.

Much of the loss which has been sustained in mining in this (the Lake) district has arisen from unjustified excessive initial expenses. There have been some startling examples of reckless expenditures in the district, which tend to weaken the confidence of the mining public and to destroy any chance of obtaining funds for judicious exploitation.[752]

On the other hand, the early closure of many of the mines meant that although they were abandoned, they might still someday prove to be profitable if worked again, as metal prices have increased immensely over the past century. Virtually all geologists agree that there is still considerable ore in the mountains of Hinsdale County.

All of the land on which mines were first discovered in Hinsdale County was, of course, public property. How did a prospector get title to his discovery? The process was controlled by federal and state law, as well as the rules and regulations of the particular mining district in which the mine was located. Unpatented claims could be filed until fairly recently by simply staking the corners and the sides of a 300 by 1,500

Dimensions of Lake City lodes.			
	Length.	Depth.	Width.a
	Feet.	*Feet.*	*Feet.*
Lellie	720+	700	0. 5–4
Ulay	380+	1,600	5
Ute-Hidden Treasure	2,700+	1,400+	4
Pelican	900+	275+	0. 3–4
Missouri Favourite	350+	400+	0. 8–2
Nellie M.	700+	500+	2
Monte Queen	950+	600+	3
Black Crook	1,965	1,300	1. 5–8
Contention	700+	700	1. 5
Golden Fleece	1,300	1,464	0. 5–10
Moro-Hendrison	2,000	500	1. 2–3

a These figures represent rough estimates. They cover vein filling only, not altered or replaced parts of vein walls.

A table from Geology and Ore Deposits Near Lake City, Colorado, *shows the width, depth, and length of veins of some of the major mines in Hinsdale County. (Author's Collection)* foot claim (which was about 10.3 acres) and filing a location certificate that showed where the vein was located with the county clerk. However an unpatented claim required "assessment work" of at least $100 each year, which could be done by labor or materials. In the late 1800s this required the owner to work on the claim for about a month each year, or a shorter time if more than one man was doing the work or money was being spent on improvements. Otherwise the unpatented claim was lost and could be filed on by another prospector, who would go through the same process.

After five years of assessment work, a fee could be paid and the land purchased from the federal government, which issued a "patent" or original deed to the claim. If the assessment work was not done on an unpatented claim or not done on time, the claim was "on the market" again, but could be relocated by the original discoverer or by another person by what prospectors called "legal claim jumping." If the assessment work had been done, a survey done, the fees paid, and a patent issued, then the claim was the legal property of the claimant just like any other land in private ownership in the United States. This was called a "patented claim" and could only be lost if the owner did not pay his taxes or a mortgage was foreclosed on.

In Colorado, the size of a lode claim varied a little. Some of the earlier claims were 150 by 1500 or 1500 by 600 feet, but later, the size of a lode was standardized at 300 by 1500 feet. However, the original stakes on the claim controlled over the legal distance when the stakes were a shorter distance than 300 and 1500 feet. Also, the first location had title if two claims overlapped each other, which many did. Therefore some claims were less than 10.3 acres. The side lines of the claim were supposed to be equal distance from the center of the vein, but a rough guess usually seemed to be good enough.

The first requirement for a lode claim was that its minerals had to be part of a vein, and not "float" or placer minerals like gold, which could be part of a placer claim. Title to a lode claim relates back to the time of discovery, but the original discovery work had to be done; and, within six months, a notice of such filed with the county clerk. Also the assessment work had to be done during the calendar year starting with the year of the location. The location certificate needed to have the name of the claimant, the name of the claim, the approximate direction of the vein, and the size of the claim up to 300 by 1,500 feet; but it could be smaller. The discovery shaft, trench, or tunnel had to be located on a map of the claim; and the outside boundaries needed to be shown on the ground by posts, piles of rocks, or blazes on trees at the corners or bends in a side line. The cost in the early days was $5 per acre to buy the land and its minerals. Placer mines were $2.50 per acre and covered twenty acres. Mill sites could be filed on and patented on five acres of non-mineral land at $5 per acre.[753]

Any three miners could create their own mining district and make such laws as were required. They could change the size of claims after the district was formed, but could not affect those located before the change. They filed their rules with the county recorder and described the area encompassed by the district.[754] Hinsdale County was originally just the Lake District, but was ultimately divided into six mining districts; however one, the Cimarron District, has so few mines (only two at present) that it is often not counted. The other five are the Galena (sometimes called Henson), which extends to the top of Engineer and includes mines on both sides of Henson Creek); Park (Burrows Park); Lake (Lake City to southern Lake San Cristobal); Sherman (upper Lake Fork and the area around the town of Sherman); and Carson (City). The Lake District was the biggest district, extending three miles west and nine miles south of Lake City.[755]

The State of Colorado also made mining laws:

The mining laws were generally known and understood like common law, except in the matter of local rules in different districts. In 1881 R.S. Morrison and Jacob Fillious, lawyers in Denver, published a volume on Mining Rights containing all the Colorado statutes on mining, including the rules adopted by the provisional government, and all successive regulations with the U. S. laws on the subject. The law to which reference was had above required a discovery shaft to be ten feet deep and $100 worth of assessment work to be performed annually to hold it; or, if $500 worth was done, a patent might be obtained.[756]

In Hinsdale County's earliest days, little actual production was done on most mining claims, as the area was full of prospectors and speculators, but capitalists (people with money to invest) had not yet arrived. The prospectors would locate the claim, the speculator would buy many of the better claims in the hopes of eventually selling them for much more money, and the capitalist would put up the money to hire workers, buy machinery, and start active production. Perk Vickers noted:

You know Mark Twain once said that a mine is nothing but a hole in the ground owned by a liar. To my knowledge he never was in Lake City, but his description certainly fit many who were here in the olden days. I don't know that a lot of them were liars really — it's just that they were driven to dream of hitting it big....

So both what they believed, and what they told others — whether buying or selling — reflected an exaggerated sense of optimism; no outright lies really, just unbridled and undaunted optimism....

It's hard today to realize the kind of wheeling and dealing that went on around here with these mines.[757]

As mentioned earlier, the first valid mineral locations could not be made until the spring of 1874, but after transportation routes were established and it was verified that the Utes had left the San Juans, a heavy rush to the San Juans through Hinsdale County began in the spring of 1875. This caused the first mining boom of 1875 to 1878, with a peak about 1876 and 1877.[758] Most of the early discoveries were in the Henson or Lake Districts. *Williams Guide to the San Juans* in 1877 printed:

(The Lake District) is the most accessible and one of the best developed districts in the San Juans. It has the best roads leading

Early reports from the San Juans indicated there was gold and silver for the picking. An 1874 article in Harper's Weekly included this drawing which definitely exaggerates just how plentiful the mines were, and in 1874 most prospectors were merely locating a vein with stakes and doing enough assessment work to hold it. (Author's Collection)

Early San Juan prospectors panned for gold with little success. Then they learned to follow hardrock veins, which usually required they dig a shaft as the veins were usually leeched at the surface and would be richer a short distance down. These men are examining the ore to see if they have struck it rich. (Harper's Weekly, Author's Collection)

to all the principal portions of the country. Its mines, which are second to no other district, carry galena with gray copper and black sulphurets, while it has one mine at least carrying both gold and silver with tellurium, sylvanite, and calavarite — the Hotchkiss....

A large number of locations have been made in the district, yet the mountains have been run over—not carefully and closely prospected. It is believed that there are hundreds of veins undiscovered as rich as any yet found.[759]

In 1880, Robert Strahorn reported that:

(Hinsdale County) contains nearly 1,000 located veins, most of them silver, a few very rich in gold, and has thus far furnished the bulk of southwest Colorado's bullion output. [760]

William's Guide to the San Juan Mountains also reported in 1877 that:

At Lake City is located the concentrating works of Crookes Bros., having a capacity of fifty tons a day. It is the intention of the proprietors to increase their facilities, and they are now arranging to add chlorination machinery.... About the first of December, 1876, W. H. Van Gieson's lixiviation works were completed and made a successful run.... These works are operated by steam power, and have a capacity of thirty tons a day.... G. B. Greene has arranged to put up a smelter at the forks of Henson Creek, the machinery for which is on the ground.[761]

A second mining boom occurred in 1880 to 1882, with the development of the outlying mining camps, the Crookes building mills and smelters, and the announcement of the coming of the railroad (which unfortunately fell through). One report was that the Crookes were doing most of the smelting for all the San Juan mines at this time. The Crookes' Mill and Smelter production in 1882 was 600 tons of lead and 75,000 ounces of silver. The Polar Star and Ute-Ulay made up the majority of their production to this time and pushed the Crookes' works almost to their full capacity. The Palmetto had a fifteen stamp mill capable of concentrating 25 tons per day. Four hundred tons of ore yielded $28,000 in 1882. In 1883, Hinsdale County produced $20,000 in gold and $250,000 in silver. In 1884, production fell off considerably because of the closing of Crooke's Mining and Smelting Company after just three months of production that year.[762] Reduction works and concentrating mills helped with transportation to the smelters. However it has been estimated that early concentrating mills such as the Crookes were only about sixty percent successful in capturing the

Metallic production of Hinsdale County from 1884 to 1906.

[Figures derived from United States Mint reports, 1884 to 1896, inclusive; from reports of State Bureau of Mines, Colorado, 1897 to 1903; from Mineral Resources of the United States, published by the United States Geological Survey, 1904 to 1908.]

Years.	Gold.	Silver.	Copper.	Lead.	Zinc.	Total value.
		Fine ounces.	Pounds.	Pounds.	Pounds.	
1884	$2,500	156,967				$180,317
1885						
1886	2,060	18,586		30,435		23,743
1887	5,214	94,546	13,545	657,400		128,432
1888	2,667	110,433	1,815	1,495,614		172,586
1889	1,680	18,673	40,000	244,500		33,849
1890	3,577	61,023	40,950	546,920		96,112
1891	20,594	186,841	3,636	441,380		442,384
1892	13,529	418,422	20,182	6,'25,747		653,107
1893	88,279	340,774	(a)	(a)		354,754
1894	95,293	404,750	(a)	(a)		350,286
1895	274,421	466,836		3,676,733		689,577
1896	215,648	465,598	13,006	6,934,099		726,668
1897	168,171	243,437	8,085	3,550,058		501,822
1898	51,282	186,456	104,038	9,828,482		529,151
1899	38,343	155,902	49,676	10,572,353		612,561
1900	56,470	155,485	29,180	9,377,062		600,309
1901	76,148	152,122	12,532	7,588,675		496,792
1902	98,348	117,177	8,314	6,213,763		428,733
1903	16,515	33,139	11,263	459,462	106,000	60,910
1904	7,692	39,283	10,530	1,054,421	75,815	81,416
1905	11,991	54,419	84,485	767,681	2,085	94,244
1906	24,510	87,940	63,261	753,950	30,475	140,543
1907	7,520	50,109	99,410	1,204,628	23,034	125,678
1908	2,454	29,498	188,698	280,465		54,776
Total	1,284,906	4,047,416	802,606	78,903,828	237,409	7,577,750

a No figures for lead and copper available.

This graph shows ore production in Hinsdale County in terms of dollars during the third boom and the busts on each side. It was a long boom (almost fourteen years with several peaks over $600,000 in a year), but after 1902 mining was pretty well dead. (From Geology and Ore Deposits near Lake City, Colorado) precious metals until floatation mills were later invented and used, and the recovery went to about ninety percent.[763]

Ore mills in Hinsdale County in 1879 included Lake City Mining and Smelting, incorporated in February of 1876, which had several owners; The Lake City Sampling Works owned by Titus and McClelland and having an 8 ton capacity; The Lee Mining and Smelting Works, incorporated in August of 1878; Henson Creek Reduction Works; Van Gieson Lixiviation Works, with a capacity of 10 tons and located in Lake City; Ocean Wave Mining and Smelting Co. Inc., incorporated in May of 1877 with a 20-ton capacity per day and a main building measuring 48 by 64 feet; and Crooke Concentrating Works Inc., incorporated March of 1877, located near Lake City, with a total capacity of 75 tons.[764]

Crofutt predicted correctly in 1885 that a third boom would happen when the railroad came:

> *With the completion of the railroad to Lake City a new impetus will be given to all kinds of mining business; capital, the greatest need for the first development of all mines, will find its way to this country.... And trains will be loaded with minerals daily for shipment to eastern establishments for treatment.[765]*

Crofutt also mentioned, somewhat optimistically, that the county's wagon roads were open almost all year with only a few exceptions.[766] The

A good example of the large amount of space needed for the extremely high temperature created by a large smelting furnace. Men fed wood and coal on the right while the molten metal is poured out near the center of the sketch. (Harper's Weekly, May 30, 1874, Author's Collection)

third boom, which was the longest, occurred when the railroad actually arrived in 1889, and some of the low grade ores could be shipped out on the railroad. After the railroad's arrival, there were eighteen producing mines in Hinsdale County by the end of 1890. Fifty-six "active" mines and 229 mine employees were also reported that year. The Ute-Ulay now had its own mill with a capacity of sixty tons a day.[767] The Silver Panic of 1893 should have put Hinsdale County into another bust, but several gold discoveries and some extremely rich silver discoveries kept mining going well into the early 1900s. Some historians subdivide the third boom into 1887 to 1890 (the time when the mines were gearing up for the coming of the railroad), and the late 1890s until 1902 or 1903 (the time when mines were actually shipping ore, much of it gold, out on the railroad).

By the year 1897, the peak of the third boom, an average of 493 men was employed in mining, and 108 mines and prospects were being operated.[768] Due to the presence of the railroad, Hinsdale County in 1897 shipped $501,822 in gold, silver, copper and lead. All in all, over $13 million was produced in Hinsdale County by 1900. Much more than that figure has been estimated to have been mined from 1990 to 2014 in gold alone from one mine— the Golden Wonder. However the price of gold is now much higher. Translating all years into 2015 values would make Hinsdale County's total historical production about $500 million.[769]

Looking at the individual Lake City mines, we will start at the top of Henson Creek at Engineer Pass and work our way back to Lake City, and then we will move up the Lake Fork to the top of Cinnamon Pass with a side trip to Carson City.

Engineer Mountain was first named in 1873 for Lt. E. H. Rufner, but he later asked that the name be changed to honor the entire U. S. Army Engineer Corps. Although originally located just on the other side of 13,218 foot Engineer Pass, the POLAR STAR has always been associated with Lake City, and eventually had a tunnel all the way through Engineer Mountain, so that the mine could be accessed from either side. The Polar Star was located in March of 1875 by H. A. Woods. He was in Howardsville, near present-day Silverton, and overheard other prospectors, who were drinking heavily, talking about going to an extremely rich spot. Woods had several claims on Engineer Pass and knew the prospectors were talking of a claim that had been located, but had not had the necessary assessment work done. That night he took off ahead of the others, arrived at the claim at 6:00 a.m., and beat the other men by a few hours. It was very cold at the time of his arrival and the presence of the morning star in the sky gave rise to the name of the mine. By 1882, the mine was owned by Woods and the Crooke brothers, and the ore was shipped to the Crooke Smelter at Lake City for processing. Twenty men worked the mine, which produced good amounts of silver for many years. In 1882, a solid streak of pure silver, which eventually totaled 600 pounds, was discovered at the mine.[770]

Near the Polar Star, on the Hinsdale County side of the Engineer Divide, was the FRANK HOUGH (pronounced "Huff"). This mine was located in the high basin near the top of Engineer Mountain, just inside Hinsdale County. The mine was discovered by John Hough, who named the claim for his son, Frank. It produced gray copper, copper pyrites, and iron pyrites with silver running up to 50 or 60 ounces per ton. The ore also contained 20 to 25 percent copper and traces of gold running up to one ounce per ton. The mine started producing in January of 1881, and late that year it shipped 60 tons of high-grade copper-silver ore with an average value of $125 per ton. In 1882, a large quantity of copper-silver ore was also shipped.[771] In 1883, the Frank Hough shipped 800 tons of ore, but management was having trouble figuring out the true formation of the mine's ores and much of the ore's value was being lost at their mill. In 1884, the Frank Hough produced 700 tons of ore valued at $52,500.

The Frank Hough vein was large — two to seven feet wide — and by the early 1890s the mine had produced over $250,000. In the 1890s, Lake City touted the Frank Hough as the largest and richest silver and copper mine in southern Colorado. By the late 1890s the mine was owned by A. E. Reynolds, J. H. Maughan, and the Thatcher Brothers, all very famous and wealthy Colorado mining men, but the mine was not being worked. By 1900, the mine was shut down and the area basically deserted, probably in large part because of Reynolds' vow to see the day when grass would grow in Lake City's streets after he was denied to right to build a tall dam at Lake San Cristobal to power his mining interests.[772] The Frank Hough's dump was recently reclaimed and not much of the mine is still visible.

In this same area the INEZ produced decomposed sulphurets, running about $150 a ton; and the MAMMOTH had a four foot pay streak with $1200 to $1500 per ton of sorted ore. Its second class ore was said to contain 277 ounces in silver and 1.5 ounces of gold,[773] making it worth $300 per ton. However, this very rich ore did not last for long.

Another big producing mine in the Galena District in the 1880s was the PALMETTO GULCH MINING AND MILLING COMPANY, which was operated in the gulch by the same name about a mile below the Frank Hough. In 1879, the Palmetto Mine was said to have a 3 foot vein with an 8 inch pay streak producing gray copper and brittle silver that averaged 100 ounces of silver per ton.[774] In the early 1880s it produced many 40-ton lots running $200 to $400 per ton. Its vein was 12 to 24

This view catches the Palmetto Mill at left center, a shaft house, right center, and a little of the Frank Hough Mine, far in the distance at upper left. (Author's Collection)

inches of ruby, wire, and brittle silver.[775] The many shafts and dumps that can still be seen in the area were all part of the mine. The remains of the Palmetto Mill are still faintly visible at the bottom of the gulch. In 1880, a great deal of work was done on the mine and its fifteen-stamp mill was built at this time. The mill processed about 25 tons of ore a day. It was a concentrating mill, separating out the barren rock and concentrating the ore for shipment. The Palmetto Mine, like the Frank Hough, produced mainly silver, copper, and iron. In 1881, 400 tons of ore yielded $28,000 worth of silver and 600 tons of ore brought $18,480. However, by 1882, the ore was running only about $50 a ton. By 1898, the mill was said to have produced over $200,000, mainly in ruby and brittle silver.[776] The company always had problems with its concentrating mill and evidently only about forty percent of the valuable minerals were being recovered.

Other mines in the upper Henson Creek area included the WYOMING, VARDEN BELLE, BOB INGERSOL, DEWEY, NEWPORT, KENTUCKY BOY, INDEPENDENCE, and many others that never became big producers.

THE DOLLY VARDEN is on the mountain of the same name north of Rose's Cabin. The Dolly Varden ore was sphalerite and galena with some chalcopyrite. For a while it carried very high silver values.[777] The Dolly Varden was discovered in 1874, and its vein was four feet wide with a ten inch pay streak of gray copper and copper pyrites with 300 ounces of silver per ton. Two early shafts, one 50 feet deep and the other 30 feet deep yielded $6,000.[778] At one time the vein was so rich with silver that it was pronounced to be the "highest grade silver ore of any mine in Hinsdale County." During 1878, considerable ore was sold that ran $225 to $1,100 per ton. Later, one railroad car of silver ore was said to bring $60,000, about a million dollars in today's values.[779]

Just below Rose's Cabin, but on the other side of the creek, was the BONANZA TUNNEL AND MILL. Mining engineer T. A. Rickard was only slightly impressed with its ore in 1892, but was very unimpressed with the electric drills being tried out at the mine. Rickard mentioned it was a good idea if only they would work!

The Empire Chief Mill was hit by an avalanche in 1929 and was closed, but it was partially rebuilt for the tourists using lottery funds, only to be hit again by an avalanche in 2007, and was once again pretty well destroyed. (Bob Stigall Photo)

About a mile further downhill was the EMPIRE CHIEF MINE AND MILL. The mill was constructed in 1927-28 and began operating in 1929. The mine produced lead, silver, and zinc ore but was hit by an avalanche only two months after it opened and four men were killed. It never fully recovered and closed in 1929 or 1930. The mill was partially restored around 2007 by the BLM and then was hit by a slide in the same path that destroyed it eighty years earlier.

The GOLCONDA is located high up in upper Hurricane Basin, which is one of the roughest places for a mine in the San Juans, but the mine's headquarters were located at Rose's Cabin for a while. The mine's main portal is at 12,600 feet. The two-story log boarding house at the mine proper was recently restored, as well as the power house, and it is well worth the one mile trip up the narrow, rough road from near Rose's Cabin to see it. The Galconda produced silver and gold, and also lead, zinc, and antimony. Its ore included galena, pyrite, sphalerite, chalcopyrite, and argentite.

With only a few exceptions, the mine was worked steadily from 1916 to 1977.

There were quite a few mines around Capitol City. The dumps of a few are still visible in the surrounding mountains. THE CAPITOL CITY, YELLOW MEDICINE, GREAT EASTERN, SAN BRUNO, HANNAH, MORNING STAR, EXCELSIOR, BROKER, SILVER CORD, AJAX, MORO, and CZAR are just a few. It is fairly rare to find so many mines so close together, working several good veins; but the ore was not extremely rich and transportation costs were always a problem. The local mines did however keep the town of Capitol City alive for fifty years. Only three of Capitol City's fifty or so surrounding mines had their own mills — the Hannah, Moro, and Yellow Medicine.[780] The rest of the mines had their ore processed in Capitol City or Lake City.

The EXCELSIOR is on the slopes just north of Capitol City. Its ore was hauled to Lake City, ten miles away, for processing. The Excelsior was discovered in 1878, and the first shipment of ore was two carloads averaging $65 a ton with 59 ounces of silver and 10 to 12 percent copper. In 1885, 200 tons of ore were shipped that averaged about the same. After that, only one to five cars were shipped each year from 1896 to October, 1908. There are no records after that time. A contiguous mine on the same vein, the Broker, tied in with the Excelsior. Its ore was galena, sphalerite, pyrite, gray and yellow copper, and chalcopyrite. A large amount of native copper and some native silver were also found.[781]

The CZAR is located about half a mile from Capitol City on

The crew at the Excelsior Mine is still working on the surface buildings in this photo taken about 1880. The large unfinished building was probably a boarding house, while the low shed probably houses tools and perhaps the entry to the mine. The shed is built into the hillside so that a possible avalanche would pass over it. (Denver Public Library, Western History Collection, X-61910)

the eastern slope of Yellowstone Gulch. It is reported to have at first shipped two carloads to a smelter in Cañon City that yielded 22 percent lead, 26 percent zinc, 3 percent copper, 9 to 14 ounces of silver and $3 in gold per ton. A third carload later gave only slightly better results. There are two veins, one on the upper level and another on the lower. Both at first were narrow, not over two feet wide in any place, eight inches in other places and down to a half inch in some places.[782] Later the Czar had a 6 foot vein with an 18 inch pay streak that averaged 100 ounces of silver per ton. The Czarina had a 3 foot vein and 14 inch pay streak with 80 ounces of silver in 1880.[783]

The CAPITOL CITY MINE is on the west side of Yellowstone Gulch and has three levels. The Capitol City Mill was operated in connection with the mine, but was torn down in 1900. The ore body is very similar to the Excelsior and Czar, and the pay streak varies from 9 to 12 inches.[784]

The YELLOW MEDICINE is in Yellowstone Gulch, a little more than a mile from Capitol City. About 500 tons of ore were shipped before 1892, and another 500 tons were shipped in 1896. There were three levels to the mine. A mill was built in 1897 and was located on the lower level. A blacksmith's shop was built on the second level. The Yellow Medicine ore was mainly galena with sphalerite, pyrite, and chalcopyrite.[785]

The SILVER CHORD is on the east side of Yellowstone Gulch and had ore similar to the Czar. The vein is 6 to 8 inches wide and the pay streak from 1 to 3 inches. Some ore was shipped, but most details are not known. The Chord, Silver Chord, and Czarina are all next to each other. The Silver Chord had a vein of 4 feet and a pay streak of 14 inches in 1879 producing 97 ounces of silver per ton.

The SILVER CHORD EXTENSION is on the east side of Yellowstone Gulch and was not worked much. Its ore is similar to the mines around it. The Silver Chord Extension had a 4 foot vein and a 6 to 20 inch pay streak in 1880, with gray copper ore containing 300 ounces of silver, but the vein then narrowed. The WOODSTOCK is also in Yellowstone Gulch and shipped a small amount of native wire gold found about 40 feet down the shaft. The nearby TOBY was mainly iron ores.[786]

The LUCKY STRIKE TUNNEL was run in hopes of cutting the Czar, Excelsior and other mines in the area at a lower depth. "Tunnels" in mining are used for access only unless unknown ore is struck while driving the tunnel. Irving states a lot of unnecessary work was done and that only small veins were discovered at the low level.[787]

There were several good mines up the South Fork of Henson Creek (also called simply "Henson Creek." (South Henson Creek ends near Engineer Pass and North Henson at American Flats.) The MORO is about one and a half miles from Capitol City. A wire tram connected the mine and its 100-ton capacity mill, which was at the creek level, 1200 feet below the mine. The Moro Mill also treated ore from other mines in the Capitol City area. The vein was worked from three tunnels and was strong on the first level, but had many stringers on the second and third levels. The vein was worked on both sides of the gulch in which the mine is located. The ore included sphalerite, chalcopyrite, pyrite, and tetrahedrite, but galena was by far the most abundant ore. The mine had many vugs lined with beautiful crystals of quartz and barite. The low grade ore from the upper level contained 10 to 17 ounces of silver, 10 to 15 percent lead, 4.4 percent copper, and 6 to 15 percent zinc, giving a total value of about $30 per ton. Ore at the lower third level was about the same but also contained .5 to 3 ounces of gold.

There were also many mines along the North Fork of Henson Creek in the Capitol City area. The GALLIC and VULCAN were two of the best. The Vulcan was discovered in 1883, and the Gallic a few years

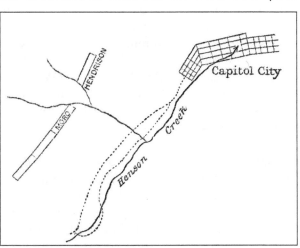

The Moro Mine was one of Capitol City's best and was worked on three different levels as shown by this cross section. A tram ran from the mine down to its mill on North Henson Creek. (Geology and Ore Deposits Near Lake City, Colorado)

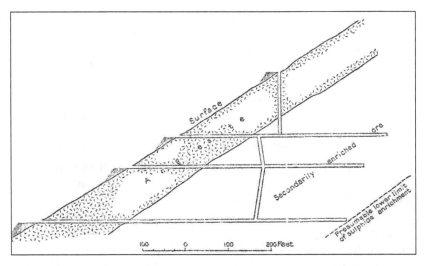

A longitudinal section of the Moro shows it was being worked on many levels. Its secondary enriched ore covered a large area but was not very rich. (Irving and Bancroft, Geology and Ore Deposits Near Lake City, Colorado)

later. Both mines were only a mile or so from Capitol City, but on the south side of North Henson Creek. The ore ran an average of .2 ounces of gold, 10 ounces of silver, and 50 percent lead with some zinc and iron. The Wrights called this operation a scam, stating that the mill and buildings were torn down just five years after being built.[788] The claims were operated early on by the members of a family, and the mine never had more than half a dozen miners working at a time. Total production was small, and its ore was hand sorted and crushed at a small mill at the mine. The two claims joined 800 feet in and were worked as one mine. The ore was soft and blasting was not usually needed. The ore was mainly galena, sphalerite, and pyrite.

There are many small mines all along both sides of Henson Creek between Lake City and Capitol City, including the BIG AND LITTLE CASINOS, SCOTIA, PEARL, FAIRVIEW, VERMONT, and the ALABAMA. There are also some of the bigger Hinsdale County mines on this section of Henson Creek, like the Ocean Wave, the Ute-Ulay, and the Hidden Treasure.

The PRIDE OF AMERICA and the BIG CASINO had two veins, one about 2 feet wide and the other smaller. Both veins were galena with silver bearing tetrahedrite. The tetrahedrite at some places carried very high values in silver, but the galena had only about 12 ounces of silver per ton. There were unverified statements from the owner that the tetrahedrite carried 200 to 412 ounces of silver per ton. Irving wrote he tended to believe him.[789] The Pride of America was discovered in 1875 and produced gray copper and galena with 65 ounces of silver per ton. The Big Casino was also said to have lead ore with a vein of 1 to 4 feet in width in places. The Big Casino was discovered in 1875, was the first claim filed in Hinsdale County, and in 1879 had a 3 foot vein of gray copper and galena with 65 ounces of silver.[790] In 1883 the Big Casino and Pride of America shipped 234 tons of ore that averaged 45 ounces of silver and 55 percent lead. At that time, the vein was 7 feet wide with a 3 foot pay streak of galena and gray copper.

The LESLIE and RED ROVER are located on a steep bluff on the west side of Henson Creek about a mile west of the mouth of Pole Creek. Some say the Leslie was never a very heavy producer, but mint reports in 1899 show that it was producing four railroad cars a week and netting about $800 per car. However its further production seems to be limited to that amount a year, as it was worked only intermittently afterwards. The mine had a boarding house, machine shops, and a fifty ton per day concentrating mill. The vein ran from 1 to 4 feet at higher levels and 8 to 14 inches at lower levels. The ore was quartz, rhodochrosite, barite, pyrite, galena, sphalerite and tetrahedrite, most of the valuable minerals in the latter, although short sections of galena could be very valuable.

Some of the chalcopyrite also carried gold that could be valuable for short distances. Some of the richest ore after concentrating was 200 to 1,000 ounces of silver, 12% copper, and 1.5 ounces of gold.[791] The Red Rover was owned by the Crookes in 1879 and had a 4 foot vein with an 8 to 20 inch pay streak. Its gray copper and galena ore averaged 150 ounces of silver per ton.[792]

The Vermont is located west of El Paso Creek about one-half mile north of Henson Creek and about two miles back toward Lake City from Capitol City. The VERMONT, SCOTIA, OCEAN WAVE, LILLIE, and WAVE OF THE OCEAN were all probably end to end on the same vein. The mines are all about 500 feet in elevation above Henson Creek. The upper workings had been abandoned by 1899, but the Vermont did at one time produce a considerable amount of ore. It was reported to have produced $70,000 by the end of the nineteenth century in silver, gray and yellow copper, and some gold and lead.[793] The managers attempted a lower tunnel at Henson Creek, which was driven for 1500 feet and then abandoned. Work at the mine ended in 1906. The ore was chiefly argentiferous tetrahedrite and galena, as were the other claims in the group. In the upper workings, 4,100 tons yielded 84.53 ounces of silver per ton with 27.96 percent lead. Ores from the lower working averaged $44.80 in silver and $12.06 in lead.

The OCEAN WAVE, which was one of Lake City's biggest mines, was eight miles from its smelter in Lake City and two or so miles down the Henson Creek road from Capitol City. It was discovered a little later

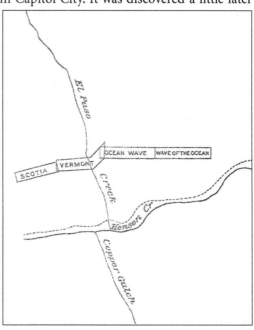

As shown on this claim map, the Ocean Wave, Wave-of-the-Ocean, Vermont and Scotia were all on the same vein. The Ocean Wave produced the best early on but the Vermont produced better later. Both mines produced silver and lead ores. (From *Geology and Ore Deposits Near Lake City, Colorado*)

(January 18, 1877) than many of the mines in its area by William R. Bernard and Zeno Snowden. They also discovered the J. J. CROOKE LODE nearby. The road up Henson Creek was originally upgraded from a trail because of this early mine.[794] The Ocean Wave had a 4 foot vein by 1879. Its galena and gray copper ore was averaging $200 per ton. Its vein was 3 ½ feet wide with a 10 to 12 inch pay streak of gray copper and galena.

Williams, in his guide book *Tourist Guide and Map of the San Juan Mines*, wrote in 1877:

> *The Ocean Wave, eight miles from Lake City up Henson Creek, is a five foot vein of fine galena, showing a great deal of gray copper. It is probably the best developed mine in the district.*[795]

Up to the year 1880, total production from the Ocean Wave was 110,000 ounces of silver, but then the mine was idle for a few years.[796]

The UTE-ULAY was actually two separate end to end claims, but they were usually worked together and, as it turned out, they were probably on branches of the same vein.[797] They were discovered in 1871 by Henry Henson, Joseph K. (J. K.) Mullin (also spelled Mullen), Albert Meade, and Charles Godwin. The four men that discovered the Ute and Ulay knew they could not legally file on the claim, so they waited for the Utes to be removed from the area before officially filing. As soon as the Brunot Treaty was ratified, they returned in 1874 and staked and worked a little on the claim. Then they sold the operation to the Crookes in 1876. Williams wrote of the Ute-Ulay in 1877:

> *Three miles up from Lake City, on Henson Creek, are the Ute and Ule' mines, having a clear and well-defined vein of solid galena three feet wide. The Ute shows gray copper.*[798]

Note the spelling of "Ule." The Utes had no written language, so the Spanish and Americans spelled the name phonetically. In Spanish (a language that Ouray spoke well, besides Ute), Ouray's name would be spelled "Ule." In English it was spelled either Ula or Ulay. That was because the Ute had troubled producing an "r" sound. Then the Ute chief said "Ou-lay was a sound he made as a kid, but final settled on Ouray being the closest sound in English.

The Ute Mine is located far up the mountain on the north side of Henson Creek. The Ulay or Ule' was located below the Ute and was much closer to the creek. The earliest work was done on the Ulay, which crosses Henson Creek and was actually worked at one time below the creek level. Both claims got richer as development occurred, which was normal for most San Juan mines for a while, but was not normal

The Ute-Ulay was one of the great mines of the San Juans. This shot was taken about 1885. The structure in the foreground is a flume for bringing water to the mill. The early shaft house was at the upper left above the waste dump and the surface tram's route can be seen below the shaft. Everything in the right lower quarter pertains to the mill, which is mining from the lower tunnel connected by a trestle. (Author's Collection)

for many Hinsdale mines, where the richest ore usually lay near the surface. The mines assays went from 20 ounces of silver to 40 to 90 as development proceeded in the 1870s. Some gold was also found, as well as 30 percent or 40 percent lead and a few rich pockets of silver that assayed as high as $550 per ton.[799] The Ute vein averaged about 4 feet in width, and the Ulay had eleven levels.

This mine is one of the greatest of the San Juans. In most years, it was the leading mine in Hinsdale County in terms of tons of ore mined. The Ute and Ulay claims actually encompass four veins — the Ute, Ulay, Annie, and an unnamed vein. Although work was done on the Ulay vein on the level of Henson Creek, there was very little ore shipped from this level.

The original discoverers sold the Ute-Ulay Mine for $125,000 in 1876 to the Crooke brothers, who built reduction works on the site. Their plant originally had fifteen stamps. In 1878, a lead smelter and chlorination mill were added. The mill was extremely important for the mine because, in the 1880s, the concentrated ore had to be transported to near Gunnison by wagon to the D&RG Railroad at a cost of $25 to $30 a ton to get it to a smelter.[800]

The Ute-Ulay Mine had a double tramway (actually an incline) to the mill. Two tram cars were tied together, loaded with ore, and sent down the tram rails from the mine to the mill. Using gravity, the weight of the two loaded cars pulled the two unloaded cars back up to the adit. The smelter also processed ore from the Polar Star Mine near the top of Engineer Pass. The Crooke brothers, after doing extensive development work, sold the mine in 1880 for $1.2 million and the mine was sold again two years later to English investors. In 1883, the Ute-Ulay was reported to be "the most extensively developed mine in the San Juan." Its ore then ran 60 to 70 percent lead, 15 to 50 ounces of silver, and about .3 ounces of gold.

The Ute-Ulay in 1882 had a concentrating mill at the site with a 150 ton per day capacity. While the Crookes owned the mine they also had the Granite Falls Mill with a 35 to 40 ton capacity per day. The mine produced 8,100 tons of ore in 1882, but only 3,750 tons were treated that year. By 1883, the Ulay had 4,000 feet of development and the Ute had 3,000 feet and had struck a rich ore body 20 feet wide. The mine was producing 1,000 tons of concentrated ore a month. The COMPROMISE

The blacksmith's shop (left part of building) was always a busy place at a big mine. This photo was probably taken about the same time as the previous (about 1885) and the shop can be seen at middle left in the previous photo. Some of the men look like they are carpenters building the addition to the right. (Author's Collection)

LODE, which was the northeast extension of the Ute, had ore similar to the Ute but was not being worked in 1883. In the fall of 1885, the Ute-Ulay shut down production and only shipped a little of its stockpiled ore the next year.

By 1886, the Crookes' home company in New York had to be sold to pay debts — a sad ending for a company that the Lake City paper wrote was "the chief engineer of (Lake City's) prosperity."[801] But, the Ute-Ulay was sold again and reopened. In 1888, the mine produced $2,500 in gold, $84,038 in silver, and $52,800 in lead. The ore in the Ute was galena, pyrite, barite, and tetrahedrite. There were eleven levels to the mine, but most production came from the upper three.

During the late 1880s and 1890s, there were usually 200 to 300 men employed at the mine and mill. The promised high tonnage from the Ute-Ulay was one of the main reasons the D&RG Railroad finally built into Lake City from Sapinero. In 1901, the Auric Mining and Milling Company installed modern equipment, supposedly better than any in Colorado except for one mill in Leadville. The mine was then worked efficiently for many years.

Many different offshoots branched off the main Ute-Ulay vein. Like most Hinsdale County mines, the largest production and highest values came from the upper workings. The mine was extensively stoped (dug out) with only a few pillars of lead ore to hold up the roof (the ceiling of the area that was excavated).

In the early 1920s, the Ute-Ulay closed but soon reopened under the ownership of Michael Burke, a wealthy mining promoter. Burke brought in modern mining equipment, built a new 100 ton flotation mill, constructed a 60-foot high dam on Henson Creek, and installed a hydroelectric generating plant.[802] Even more important to Lake City, Burke kept the D&RG running regular trains. However in 1929, the Great Depression hit, metal prices fell, and Burke never made his promised shipments of ore. The Ute-Ulay was always one of the biggest employers of miners in Hinsdale County, and when it was not operating mining in the county was considered dead.[803]

The total Ute-Ulay production of all the years it operated was about $14,000,000, which made it one of the greatest of the San Juan mines, even though its early concentrating plant did not work well. In 1943, the great Ute-Ulay was sold for taxes.[804]

The HIDDEN TREASURE is about a half mile northeast of the Ute-Ulay, but one of the Hidden Treasure's veins runs roughly parallel to the Ute-Ulay and part of a branch runs towards it. It was worked on four levels. The portal of the Hidden Treasure is about three miles above Lake City, and it had a small company town named Treasureville. The Hidden Treasure was later worked in connection with the Ute-Ulay. Its ore ran 20 to 90 ounces of silver and 40 percent lead. There were also large quantities of gray copper. In 1879, the tunnel was 340 feet in gray copper and galena, averaging 75 ounces of silver per ton.[805] The mine consisted originally of five claims, the Hidden Treasure, Invincible, Protector, Don Quixote, and Crystal Crown. The mine was discovered in 1874, but not much work was done there until the 1890s. A 100-ton a day concentrator mill was built in 1898, and was connected to the mine by a 3,800-foot tram. It was worked extensively from 1897 to 1930. The

The Hidden Treasure's mills, offices and bunkhouse took up a lot of space near the bottom of the area they were mining, but most of the mining was done through a shaft, way up on the mountain. The Ute-Ulay and the Hidden Treasure eventually proved to be on the same vein and were worked together in later times. (Stope Map from Geology and Ore Deposits Near Lake City, Colorado. Photo from Tiny Hinsdale of the Silvery San Juan.)

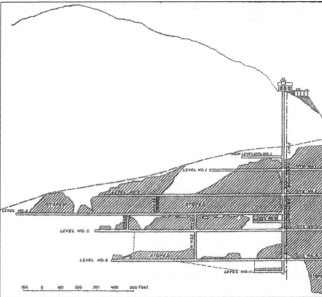

bulk of the ore was low-grade, averaging about $40 a ton, so the ore was concentrated before being shipped. Eight levels were eventually run from a 265 foot shaft. The mine produced about $1.2 million between 1897 and 1930.

About a mile from Lake City above the Henson Creek road was the PELICAN MINE AND MILL. The mine is 875 feet above the north side of Henson Creek and only a few pieces of foundation identify the mill site along the road today. It produced a little gold and a fair amount of silver (165 ounces a ton at one time). It did not produce much total ore, but had considerable development work done. It had two shafts and two levels. The ore body varied from a few inches to 4 feet in width. Barite, galena, ruby silver, freibergite, pyrite, and sphalerite were some of its minerals. Although not valuable minerals, its vein reportedly contained many vugs filled with beautiful quartz crystals. It also contained some rhodochrosite. At one time, it had a 5 foot vein with an 18 inch pay in gray copper averaging 59 ounces of silver.

The FANNY FERN MINE is also about a mile above Lake City on the opposite side of Henson Creek from the Pelican. Its ore appeared to be a mixture of tetrahedrite and galena in barite and quartz. Its veins run in all directions and are very irregular. It had an aerial tram that connected it to the Pelican Mill.

There were also many mines along the Lake Fork of the Gunnison, mainly to the south (upriver) from Lake City. Almost within the present town limits of Lake City was the CROOKE MILL AND SMELTER, located at Granite Falls (later called Crooke Falls after their mill was built) about one mile south of Lake City. There was no mine at the site, but the 75 foot drop of Granite Falls powered the original 15 stamp Crooke Reduction Works, which was established in August, 1876. More crushers and a smelting works were added in 1878. Frank Fossett, in 1879, described the Crookes' smelting and milling operations as follows:

> (The Crookes were) the first eastern capitalists that showed their appreciation of the region by putting their money in it.
>
> Up to this time (1879) Crooke and Co. had expended over $400,000 on their mines, works, and other properties of this locality.[806]

Between the Crookes' mill and smelter and Lake San Cristobal were the Belle of the West and the Belle of the East, Monte Queen, Golden Wonder, and another of the Crookes' mines, the Black Crooke.

The BELLE OF THE EAST and BELLE OF THE WEST are about three miles southeast of Lake City on the road to Creede. The two mines follow veins that seem to be parallel. The ore was tetrahedrite, sphalerite,

The Crooke's mill site at Crookes (Granite) Falls as shown in an engraving from Frank Fossett's, Colorado about 1879, The smoke is coming from all the different smelters at the site. The lower engraving is of the interior of a smelter. They used coke, which burns even hotter than coal to reduce to ore. (Smelter engraving from Harper's Weekly, Author's Collection)

galena, and small amounts of chalcopyrite in quartz and barite.[807] Two carloads of ore shipped in 1907 were said to average $70 a ton in just gold, but several richer pockets were also mined. Most of the gold values were evidently brought in by secondary replacement of pyrites.[808] The Belle of the East was well developed, but only had a 2 to 15 inch pay streak. The Belle of the West had a 5 foot vein and 10 inch pay streak of gray copper and galena averaging 85 ounces of silver. The Belle of the West was very well developed in 1879 and had produced $50,000 by that year. Otto Mears owned part of both mines at this time. The mines were later owned by A. E. Reynolds and produced over $100,000 in gold and silver.[809]

The MONTE QUEEN lies south of Lake City on the west side of the Lake Fork, 300 feet above the river. The ore was in pockets or "shoots," enclosed with quartz. Some of these shoots contained up to 2,000 ounces of silver and 20 percent bismuth.[810]

Perhaps the most talked about mine in the Lake City area in 1878 and 1879 was the GOLDEN WONDER. It was filed on by Percy Fisher on August 6, 1880, and sold less than a month later, on September 3, 1880, for $100,000. At one time it was said to be "the richest gold property in Colorado."[811] The Belle of the West, the Belle of the East, and the Golden Wonder are located on what is called "Gold Hill," on or near the present-day Vickers Ranch. At the point where the road to Creede intersects the road over Cinnamon Pass, the Golden Wonder Mine is across the river to the east on the hillside. A young boy supposedly picked up a pretty rock on the spot and his employer later saw it and recognized it as containing gold. The boy took the employer to the spot where he had found the rock and the prospect was staked. Some of the ore that the mine shipped ran over $40,000 per ton — close to a million dollars per ton today.

Perk Vickers owned the Golden Wonder at one time and wrote:

The patent on the Golden Wonder is one of the oldest in Hinsdale County. Back in the early years... a fellow by the name of Tom

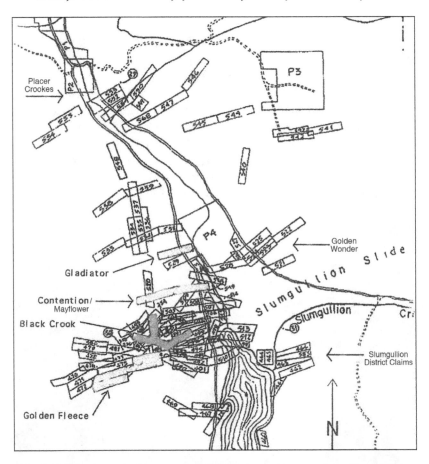

This claim map shows the large number of claims located between Lake City and Lake San Cristobal, including several of Hinsdale County's best. The area was as mineralized as it is at the eastern edge of the Lake City Caldera, and it was the site of a lot of early mining but also some great late discoveries like the Golden Wonder. (Courtesy of Hall Realty)

Beam found a boulder (of ore) right on the surface. J. W. Vickers said that Beam started digging around this thing and it turned out to be the size of a Model T Ford.

When the ore was processed, I think gold was $20.00 an ounce. They got $35,000 from that one boulder. Can you imagine how a guy like that must have felt? He came into this area after fighting in the Civil War and then hit into that rich find. As far as I know that was the only hunk that he and his partner—a fellow by the name McClellan Fisher—ever found....

For some reason, old man Beam sold out to a guy named Sowers around 1900 or so. He did quite a bit of work up there, but all of it was on the surface.[812]

Beam sold the property about 1900 for $60,000 cash, a lot of money in those days — enough for most people to retire on.[813] By 1932 the ownership of the mine was in the Vickers' family

The CONTENTION MINE includes the MAYFLOWER claim and is located about 1,000 feet north of the north end of Lake San Cristobal. It had a small community at its base. For a short period of time the mine produced a considerable amount of silver from its upper workings. However these ore bodies turned out to be small, and the mine produced only $230 in gold and $8,148 in silver over a later four year period. Yet at one time one pocket of rich ore had yielded $60,000 in silver (a million

A view to the south of Lake City shows the many mines in that area, although there were few mines to the north of the city. (U.S.G.S. Photo)

dollars in today's values). Some of the original miners reported large amounts of native silver in the upper workings, assaying as high as 1,000 ounces per ton. The mine further reported many vugs with beautiful quartz crystals.[814] A large mill was erected in 1904 and was evidently very successful; management claimed they were saving about 90 percent of the gold and silver at a time when 70 to 80 percent was considered a very good recovery. Some local mills were only recovering half of the gold and silver in their ores. The vein varied from 14 inches to 2 feet. The Contention ore was silver bearing gray copper or freibergite, sphalerite, chalcopyrite, pyrite, barite, and rhodochrosite. The gray copper ore produced the bulk of the gold and silver and made up most of the ore in the upper levels.

The Wrights wrote that the mine was only a stock scheme, but it had twenty men employed, so the Wrights seem to be wrong in their assertion. In 1900, it was written that the mine showed a full 400 feet of stoping with a pay streak running from 12 to 20 inches.

The BLACK CROOKE lies north of and adjacent to the upper workings of the Golden Fleece and was composed of five claims. In 1884, in just three months, the mine produced 1,277 tons of ore worth $124,447, an average of $97.21 per ton. This came from about 21 ounces of silver and 3 ounces of gold per ton. Evidently a large amount of very high grade ore from pockets was included in these figures. With increasing depth, the ore value fell off, much of it only $35 per ton in gold and silver.[815] The mine was worked intermittingly from 1891 to 1903. A long tunnel was necessary down low, part of which was shared with the Golden Fleece. This allowed the vein to be tapped 1200 feet below the outcrop. Like many of the mines in the district, this much lower part of the vein was not nearly as rich as that higher, so an upward shaft called a raise was driven to get to the richer ore. The two main veins were called the Ilma and Gold King. The Ilma was by far the richer of the two, and most production was taken from it. The vein had many branches, but the main mineralized zone had a width of 4 to 8 feet. However the ore often was of such low value it was not even worth sending to the concentrating mill and it became waste rock on the dump. The ore was sphalerite, galena, tetrahedrite, chalcopyrite, barite, and rhodochrosite. Sphalerite contains considerable zinc, which could not be economically recovered by smelters before 1903, so a penalty was often charged at the smelters for this ore. The silver was mainly in the galena and tetrahedrite. Some high grade tellurium was also taken from all five claims.

The GOLDEN FLEECE is located about four miles south of Lake City, about a half mile up the hillside on the west side of Lake San Cristobal near the northern end of the lake. The mine was noted for high grade telluride and tellurium gold ores.[816] The Golden Fleece was originally

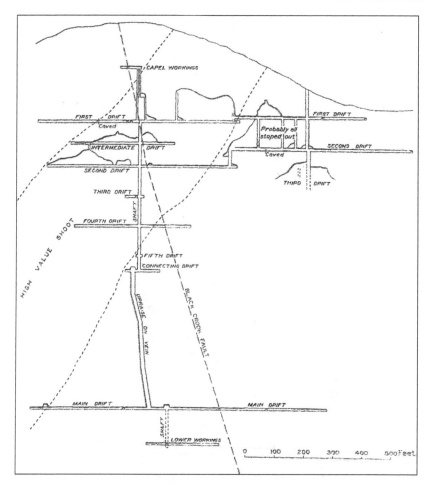

This cross section shows all the various levels on the Black Crooke and the areas of good ore that were stoped out. (From *Geology and Ore Deposits Near Lake City, Colorado*)

filed on by Enos Hotchkiss, and was at that time called the "Hotchkiss Mine." Later owners, George Wilson and Chris Johnson, used the name "Golden Fleece" after the sheepskin used to catch small gold flakes in Homer's Odyssey. Although some pockets in the mine were extremely rich, the initial results were averaging $150 to $180 per ton. Esteemed geologist and mining engineer, Thomas A. Rickard, reported on the Golden Fleece at length:

> *In 1874 Enos F. Hotchkiss, connected with a ... surveying party which was laying out a toll road from Saguache to Lake City, caught sight of the outcrop of the Golden Fleece standing conspicuously above*

the hill-slope, and examined it. He located it as the "Hotchkiss" mine and had some assessment work done while he was engaged in his survey work in the vicinity. A year later, when Hotchkiss had abandoned his claim, it was relocated by George Wilson and Chris Johnson, under the name "The "Golden Fleece."[817] *They began what is now known as the No. 1 Tunnel, but finding only little stringers of rich ore, they ceased work. Others did similar desultory prospecting. O. P. Posey found a very rich bunch of ore in the croppings above the No. 1 Tunnel and took out several hundred pounds, which were packed to Del Norte and sent to the Pueblo Smelter. Then John J. Crooke took a lease and bond; he also extracted about $30,000*

If we could see through the earth, this drawing would be an aerial view of the underground workings of the Black Crooke and the Golden Fleece. The upper cluster of tunnels and drifts is the Black Crooke and the lower is the Golden Fleece. Later in their operations the Black Crooke and the Golden Fleece were both accessed from the Golden Fleece Tunnel at the right. (From Geology and Ore Deposits Near Lake City, Colorado)

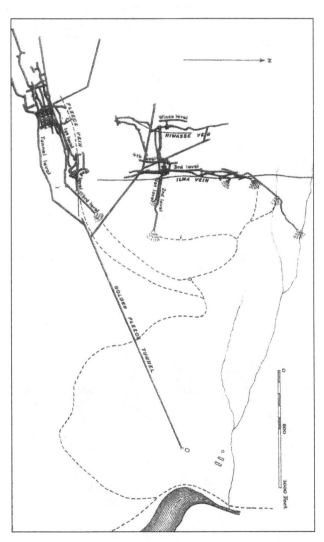

from the outcrop above the No. 1 Tunnel, which had been extended a little further without results. This was between 1876 and 1878. In 1889 Charles Davis took a lease and bond; he did a good deal of work along the high croppings and finally sunk a shaft 30 feet deep, which struck a body of ore yielding $40,000 in a very short time. Later in that year, 1889, George W. Pierce bought the mine for $50,000 and commenced extensive explorations. He found out very soon indeed that Davis had extracted all the ore in sight, and the outlook was not cheerful. All the work up to that this time had been to the north on the supposition that the vein had been faulted in that direction. The new owner crosscut south at the No. 2 Tunnel which had been previously extended a little way, but had found nothing. The vein was picked up, but not much ore was encountered at first. They persisted, however, and within a year rich ore was cut on No. 2, and it was traced upward until it became easy to intersect the same body at No. 1. It was discovered that the former owners had been within ten feet of the main ore body of the mine, which from that time until 1897 was very profitable.[818]

The Hotchkiss Mine's initial assay of float (rock that had crumbled off the vein naturally) was $40,000 a ton. It was staked in the names of Enos Hotchkiss, D.P. Church, and Henry Finley on November 2, 1874 and filed February 22, 1875. The location certificate was amended May 10, 1875, but the Hotchkiss book authors, Mary Hotchkiss Farmer and Lee McMurtry Farmer, do not say why Hotchkiss did not do the original

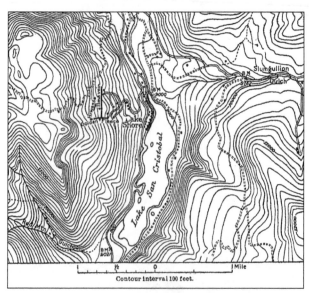

Contour interval 100 feet.

A topographic map shows the steepness of the area around the Golden Fleece Mine as well as a few of the cabins in the town of Lake Shore on Lake San Cristobal. (From Geology and Ore Deposits Near Lake City, Colorado)

The Golden Fleece cooks came out to get their photo taken at the right. They were a very important part of any mine's operation, because if the food was bad many miners would quit and move to another mine. (Author's Collection)

assessment work. In 1875, 18 tons of ore were shipped worth $1,319 a ton and 75 tons remained on the dump that were valued at $150 per ton. However Hotchkiss had his accident in the mine in November of 1876 and work came to an abrupt halt. Early on there was an ore zone in the mine where ore assayed from $17,000 to $20,000 per ton,[819] then the Hotchkiss ran out of ore in that pocket and closed.[820]

The Hotchkiss Mine did little in the way of production between 1876 and 1878.[821] The mine was idle for months, then sold at a Sheriff's sale to Chris Johnson, George E. Wilson, and Samuel Wendell. It was at this time that the mine was probably renamed as the Golden Fleece.[822] In 1879, the Hotchkiss was no longer owned by Hotchkiss but was showing gray copper and tellurium with 400 ounces of silver per ton.[823]

In 1880, Strahorn wrote:

> *It was reported that the Lake Fork veins usually ran straight into the mountain eliminating costly shafts and crosscuts. The Hotchkiss vein was reported to be 7 feet wide and yielding high grade tellurium ore. The Golden Wonder had just been discovered. Seventy mines are around Lake San Cristobal, all showing good ore, but some worked more than other. Smelters are also close by.*[824]

As mentioned, the Hotchkiss lost its main vein; but, in 1883, it was rediscovered, and the mine announced at this time that it expected to be hiring a large force of men to work it. In 1885 Crofutt reported the average Golden Fleece ore was running $1,000 per ton. Only small pockets of such rich ore were found until 1889, when the value of the ore picked up even more significantly. In 1891, a large amount of valuable tellurium ore was discovered. However, the mine was so hit and miss that Charles Davis only received $75,000 when he sold the mine in 1891. Some locals thought the new owner had been swindled; but, by 1895, shipments from the mine were averaging $24,000 per month.

Rickard mentions that the Golden Fleece outcrop was honeycombed with patches of extremely rich ore.[825] Rickard also wrote that the mine milled only low-grade ore in its mill and that it was a very inefficient mill, recovering only 45 to 60 percent of the gold and silver.

> *A good deal of money has been obtained from isolated pockets all the way down to the main tunnel or about 700 feet below the third level. Several larger bodies of low-grade ore have also been encountered in the deeper workings.*[826]

From 1889 to 1897, and then again in 1902, the Golden Fleece did very well and was worked with a sixty stamp mill. Most geologists agree that it was late in the summer of 1891, when the real potential of the mine was recognized. The main vein of the mine is now considered to be one of the most celebrated in all of Colorado. The most productive ore was found about 1,000 feet above Lake San Cristobal and about 2,600 feet west of the north end of the lake. Shipments in 1895 ran $288,000 for an average of $24,000 per month. About 100 men worked at the mine at that time.[827]

In 1896, the mine was still working 100 men and shipped nine railroads cars of ore that brought $33,000 to $49,000 per car. At today's

The miners, cooks, and other employees of the Golden Fleece paused from a meal to let the photographer get this photo. The men with high boots are geologists and engineers. (Author's Collection)

prices that is almost a million dollars a car for a total of $9 million! In just a few months the mine shipped $1.6 million in ore, worth about $25 million at today's prices. The richest shipment of ore from the Golden Fleece was reported to run 25 percent gold and 45 percent silver and was shipped straight to the smelter without concentrating.

Nearly all the ore of merchantable grade was taken from above the third level, but a few small pockets of extremely rich ore were found down as low as the main tunnel. One pocket gave an unbelievable assay of 125 ounces of gold and 1,255 ounces of silver per ton. The rich ore of the Golden Fleece did much to stimulate prospecting in the Lake City area, leading to other discoveries. The main Golden Fleece vein was 8 to 10 feet wide and filled with hard minerals which made the outcrop stand quite a bit higher than the surrounding ground. The outcrop is a brilliant yellow with some red and is quite visible even today. It is now honeycombed underground with the work of many lessors who were looking for high grade pockets within the vein (and there were many, usually near the surface).[828]

Golden Fleece ore consists mainly of petzite (a gold telluride ore), pyrite, argentiferous tetrahedrite, galena, hinsdalite, and pyrargite. Petzite carried the most in gold values. Telluride ores in the form of petzite occurred at the Hotchkiss/Golden Fleece associated with zinc, lead, iron, and copper. Petzite is 25.5 percent gold, 40 percent silver and 34.5 percent other components. The richer ore was shipped directly to the smelter, while lower grades were first concentrated by the mill at the mine.[829] Gray copper was fairly abundant, but rarely carried more than 60 ounces of silver.

Later in 1918-20, the Golden Fleece Mine was owned by Colorado-Ute Mines, but the mine lay idle during that time. In 1922, the mine was owned by Golden Fleece Mining and Milling Co., and was then purchased by H. E. Moore in 1944, but no great amount of production was done during either of these times. Altogether the mine probably shipped $15 or $16 million in ore, worth perhaps $300 million today.[830]

Many people do not realize there was mining for five or six miles up the Slumgullion Earth Flow from Lake San Cristobal. In fact, some of the earliest mines in Hinsdale County were in this area.[831] Most of the minerals were found mixed in with the slide's clay as float — some small parts of which assayed up to $76,000 per ton in gold and silver, if the prospectors had been able to find a ton of the ore. Even after almost twenty years, none of the prospectors had a real mine. However the early prospectors had great hopes for what they called the "SLUMGULLION DISTRICT."[832]

The CARSON CITY MINING DISTRICT is at the top of Wager Gulch. Carson had many mines surrounding it on both sides of the

Continental Divide. The area was discovered by J. E. Carson in 1881, but most prospecting did not start until the following year when the Carson Mining District was formed. J. E. Carson and Ed Cannon came back in the spring of 1882 and located the ST. JACOB and the KING GEORGE III, which were the most prominent of the Carson District Mines in the early 1880s. Joel Swank said Christopher J. Carson discovered the BACHELOR MINE in 1881, and that it was first mine in Carson area. By 1883 there were over a hundred prospectors in the area, working about 150 claims, all started on "float," as rich minerals were found lying all over the surface of the area. The mines south of the Continental Divide produced mainly silver, and those north of the Divide consisted mainly of gold ores. The best mines in the area in the 1880s were the ST. JACOB, MAID OF CARSON, BLIZZARD, WEST LOST TRAIL GROUP, RAVEN, SILVER SPRAY, TOBINSON GROUP, and JESS. Ore was originally shipped to Del Norte for milling as there was no easy way off the mountain toward Lake City. The St. Jacobs Mine, on the north side of the Continental Divide, was the biggest mine in the area and eventually produced over a million dollars in gold. The BONANZA KING was also a big producer. Other mines included the CHANDLER, LEGAL TENDER, KIT CARSON, GEORGE II, DUNDERBERG, CRESCO, IRON MASK, ST. JOHNS, and many others. At one time

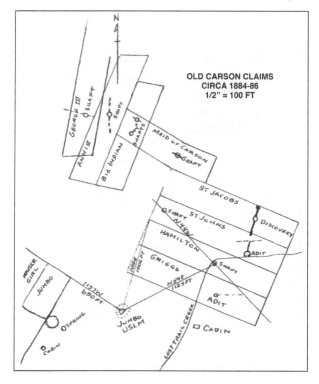

Old Carson Claim Map - This claim map from about 1884 shows the relationship of the St. Jacobs and St. Johns to several of the other large mines of the Carson City District. (Author Collection)

there were a dozen producing mines and 150 claims within a few miles of Carson City.

The Maid of Carson, which was part of the St. Jacobs Mine, was very rich and had a vein of 6 to 8 feet width with up to 1600 ounces of silver and eighteen ounces of gold. The St. Jacobs got on to the Maid of Carson vein and the lawsuit that resulted showed a pay streak 7 ½ feet wide with 1600 ounces of silver and 20 ounces of gold per ton.[833]

The Carson City mines continued to do well in the early 1890s until the Silver Panic of 1893. In 1889, about 450 people were in the area and sixty claims had been patented. Ten mining companies in the area went public with their stock selling from $1 to $10 dollars a share, but they soon fell to 50 cents or less with the demonetization of silver in 1893, and all the stock companies soon folded.[834] The camp was quiet until larger quantities of gold were discovered in 1896, and then mining picked back up, mainly for gold on the northern side of the Continental Divide. In 1898, the St. Jacobs Mine was working three shifts and was the best gold property in the area that year with $190,000 in production. A new boarding house and smelter were erected at the mine.

About 400 people lived in Carson between 1900 and 1902, but production went down quickly at the end of 1902, when Carson's biggest mine owner Col. C. F. Meek sold his holdings.[835] In 1905, the ANNIE and ST. JACOBS were the big mines in the Carson area, but almost all the other mines had stopped producing.

Back down on the Cinnamon Pass Road, the principal mine of the Sherman District was the BLACK WONDER, but the GEORGE WASHINGTON, NEW HOPE, COME UP, STERLING, MOUNTAIN VIEW, CLINTON, SMILE OF FORTUNE, THE MONSTER, MINNIE LEE, IRISH WORLD, ADELAIDE, and IXL (mine names are almost as much fun as burro names) did okay. The Black Wonder was just above the shelf road to Burrows Park and the mill was in town. The Black Wonder Mill, one of the largest in the San Juans, was re-built in Sherman after it was moved from its original location in Burrows Park in 1895. Unfortunately the mill was originally a roasting mill at Whitecross, designed to extract gold, but the Black Wonder had mainly silver. The Black Wonder Mine and Mill were connected after 1895 by a two bucket tram operation — the bucket full of ore going down pulled the empty bucket back up.

The Black Wonder had very rich selected ore that ran $167 in gold and $17,174 in silver per ton. That quantity of silver is ore that had a content of almost half silver, an amazingly high amount. The gold came from copper pyrites and the silver was in ruby or brittle form. The mill was reworked in 1920, and the town again prospered for a while. The last mining near Sherman was in 1925.

BURROWS PARK is full of mines, but none of them was a bonanza. Burrows Park had good veins, but because of its extreme remoteness, only assessment work or a small amount of production was done until the end of the nineteenth century. Yet the park was full of small cabins, saloons, hotels, stores, sawmills, and burros from 1875 to 1910. *The Silver World* (June 17, 1875) complained that there were enough of the little animals braying in the park as "to make the night hideous."

In Burrows Park, the ores were essentially of three types: sphalerite-galena ore, chalcopyrite ore, and gold-silver ore with small amounts of zinc and lead.[836] The ores were deposited from deep within the earth and are deposited in zones. In the east half of Burrows Park and extending down (east) to Sherman are copper ores. This area includes the CHAMPION, J.B, DANVILLE, and BLACK WONDER mines. The far west of this zone is the lead-zinc zone, and then to the northeast is a gold, silver, lead, and zinc zone. Mines in the middle zone include the MONTICELLO, ILLINOIS BOY, PARK VIEW, and the BON HOMME. The last (upper) zone includes the GOLCONDA in Hurricane Basin, which is accessed from Henson Creek, but is located right at the ridge between

Henson Creek and the Lake Fork of the Gunnison. There is also the BOURBON COUNTY in Horse-shoe Basin, east of Hurricane. The ISOLDE and the CLEVELAND are on the Lake Fork side of the gold zone.

The TABASCO MILL AND MINE were above the small settlements of Tellurium and Whitecross. The mill was connected to the

The Black Wonder Mill is shown with the mine behind it below the high cliffs. (George Beam Photo, Author's Collection)

mine by a tram that ran about two miles uphill and then just over the crest of Cinnamon Pass. The Tabasco and the nearby Premier produced well shortly after starting production in 1898. The mill was built in 1901, and was powered by electricity produced in Sherman. Other mines in the area included the LABELLE, BALTIMORE, PHILADELPHIA, GREAT OHIO, JAPANESE, and PREMIERE. The Tabasco Mill and tram were under construction about 1902, using a power plant at Sherman to generate electric power that was carried by three lines to the mill and mines. However by 1905, the Tabasco was abandoned. The mill had a 100 ton capacity but only operated for four years.

Most Hinsdale County mines are now shut down, but some day they may reopen. In 1926 noted geologist Charles Henderson[837] mentions that there were still large amounts of low grade ore left in Hinsdale County. Little mining has been done since that time, and much of that "low-grade" ore is now high grade and would be worth mining, but many mine owners and operators do not wish to put up with the regulations and what they feel is a hassle from the federal government and conservation groups. There is also a belief that tourism and mining do not go together, but we will explore that further in Chapter 10.

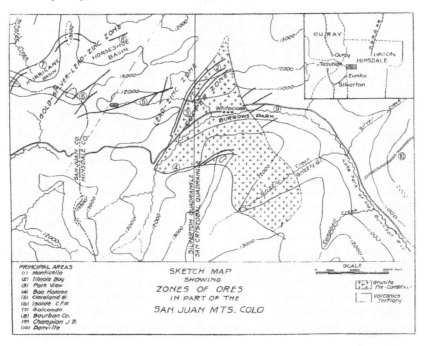

This geological map shows the three mineral zones in Burrows Park as well as some of the principal mines. The Golconda was actually in Henson Creek drainage as well as the Lake Fork. (Colorado School of Mines Map)

Tourism started early in Hinsdale County and included this couple taking a ride on the Ute-Ulay's tram bucket in 1906. (Author's Collection)

CHAPTER 10

Good Times at the Lake
(and Rivers)
Tourism 1905 to Present

═══◎═══

Lake City has always had other ways to draw people to Hinsdale
County besides its mines. It may not be as rewarding monetarily
as a successful gold mine, but the area's scenery is priceless and
hunting and fishing have always been excellent in the area — even if
Alferd Packer said it was not so. With five fourteeners, including the
highest mountain in the San Juans (Uncompahgre), our numerous
waterfalls, and pristine Lake San Cristobal, tourism has always been a
factor in the Lake City economy. Although tourism had begun by 1876
and continued strong through the rest of the nineteenth century, it was
not firmly establish as Hinsdale County's number one industry until the
twentieth century after large scale mining disappeared.

Lake San Cristobal has consistently been one of the main draws of
Hinsdale County. It is known by many as the queen of all the natural lakes
in Colorado. It is Colorado's largest natural lake, depending on whether
Grand Lake, which is hour-glass shaped and connected in the center by
a short stream, is considered to be one or two lakes. San Cristobal is two
and a half miles long, about three-quarters of a mile at its widest, covers
324 acres when full, and is about 90 feet at its deepest.[838]

Over the years changes have been seen in the lake, as it has been
viewed not just as a natural beauty, but also a natural resource in terms
of developing power and water for the town and the mining industry.
In 1899, Albert Eugene Reynolds, Colorado mining magnate, planned
to create a seventy-five foot high dam that would have added fifteen to
fifty feet to the lake level. He then planned to use the water to generate
electric power for the Frank Hough mine near the top of Engineer
Mountain. The proposal was denied by Hinsdale commissioners, who
were worried about public safety and damage to private property.
However the main reason was that there was also a huge public outcry
against building any type of dam.[839] Reynolds, in retaliation, shut down
his substantial mining interests in Hinsdale County and vowed to see

the day when grass would grow in the streets of Lake City. It was, in fact, just a few years after this event that Hinsdale County's mining virtually disappeared and grass did grow in the streets, but the town persevered.

Later the Golden Fleece Mine also wanted to use water from the lake to power a mill near Argenta Falls (about a half mile below the lake),[840] but the project was eventually abandoned because of low metal prices at the time. Then in 1930, yet another mining plan was to raise the water level of the lake sixty-nine feet to generate power for D.R. Webb's mine, but the Great Depression killed that idea. Lately several projects at the outlet have increased the height of the lake by 2 to 5 feet for extra water storage for Hinsdale County and Lake City residents and for flooding safety.[841]

The very first white men to venture into Hinsdale County reported that Lake San Cristobal had no fish.[842] Granite (Crookes) and Argenta Falls kept the fish from naturally getting to Lake San Cristobal, but fish were soon planted by locals, who netted them below the falls and brought them in barrels to the lake. They placed a screen across the outlet of the lake to keep the fish in, and the trout grew fast and large, feasting on the waterdogs (a type of salamander that grows up to a foot long)

Hinsdale County and Lake City advertised fishing and a natural environment, starting in the early 1900s. (Author's Collection)

that infested the lake. Early visitors to Hinsdale County soon noted the good fishing of all kinds in the area, but fishing in Lake San Cristobal became the favorite spot, and fishermen were soon reported to be at the lake day and night during the summer. The meat of the early trout was red because they fed on fresh water shrimp and they were reported to be especially delicious. Evidently, some of the early mining in Burrows Park polluted the upper Lake Fork so badly that fish could not live above the lake for a while.[843]

Early residents learned that stocking the beaver ponds helped the creeks and streams, as the fish would thrive in the ponds and then move into the streams. However, the fishing was only marginally good after about 1885 until the twentieth century. The beaver being trapped out was another part of the problem at this time. The dams they built backed up water deep enough to allow the trout to live through the winter. When the beaver were gone, the ponds eventually washed out and were no longer available to the fish. When the beaver started making a comeback in the mid-twentieth century, fish were stocked and thrived again in the high streams. Locals many of the streams and small alpine lakes (many times with native cutthroat) and sometimes even packed in fresh water shrimp to make sure the trout in the many small lakes in the county had food. Even though the quality of the fishing had dropped a little, fishing was king in Hinsdale County in the 1890s. For example an 1894 newspaper announced that:

J. E. Kamm, of Highland, Ill. is at the Pueblo House. Mr Kamm is spending a few days here fishing. Jas. A. Briggs, New York City, was a Lake City visitor this week. Mr. Briggs will remain some time and try his luck after the speckled beauties in Lake San Cristobal. A party composed of Mr. and Mrs. Sheppard, Mr. and Mrs. J. H. Purdy ... and Mr. Luther Burns of Wichita, Kansas arrived in Lake City Wednesday evening on a fishing and site seeing tour.

Because the late 1800s also saw massive overfishing, there were soon very few fish in the streams of Hinsdale County or in Lake San Cristobal. Limits were placed on the number of fish in possession as some early tourists caught and kept a hundred trout a day, just for the photograph, and a catch and release mentality was encouraged.

In the twentieth century Lake San Cristobal became one of the prime spots for obtaining trout eggs for the private and government hatcheries that were being opened. Tom French worked for the federal Fish and Game agency as a boy, then graduated from Columbia as a fish culturist. He was superintendent of the Creede hatchery and later became superintendent of the Leadville hatchery.[844] During his time in

Hinsdale and Mineral Counties the fish were netted, stripped of their eggs, and the eggs quickly sent to the federal hatchery at Creede on the Rio Grande.[845]

The lake was federal property until 1953 when it was turned over to the State of Colorado. Until that time half of the lake spawn came back to Lake San Cristobal and the other half was split among other Colorado hatcheries. During the spawn the federal fish and wildlife had limited fishing and tried to protect the Lake San Cristobal spawning beds. Lake San Cristobal was federal property until 1953 when Hinsdale County placed logs and rocks in the lake immediately above the lower bridge. This caused the course of the river to change and destroyed the rainbow and brook trout spawning beds.[846] Once Lake San Cristobal had no spawn to speak of, Hinsdale County was basically ignored for many years, as it was too remote and the areas that were populated with the most tourists in the summer tended to get the most, or all, of the hatchery grown fish.

It is now necessary for the lake to be heavily stocked, but the fishing is still good. After 1953, Colorado Fish and Game started to plant fish in small lakes they built on creeks and in the high country streams all over Hinsdale County. Fresh water shrimp were again often packed in to many of the small Alpine lakes and made it possible for trout to live in most of them year-round. Some of these public lakes were "leased" by locals and used as hatcheries, with fish shipped to restaurants and used to stock other lakes and streams.

Besides being eaten by the local fishermen, many of the early privately stocked trout were shipped to restaurants. At that time, residents tried to catch and eat the larger fish, as they were hard to sell to the restaurants and the big fish ate numerous smaller fish. Today many Hinsdale lakes, ponds, rivers, streams, creeks, and even irrigation ditches provide some of the best fishing in Colorado.

Fishing starts about mid-March, which is a good time for the big browns in the Lake Fork, which come upstream from Blue Mesa Reservoir. About mid-April, a few huge lake trout can be caught out of Lake San Cristobal as the ice melts from the lake, and some good-size trout are also caught during ice fishing season. Then, except during the heaviest of the spring snow melt (usually the first half of June but often as late as July 1), the fishing is good all summer. During heavy spring runoff most fishermen switch to small creeks, beaver ponds, and the high country's small lakes that are just losing their ice. Fall is a great time for brookies, as they will hit on almost any fly or lure. Brook trout are usually spawning in the fall so please use catch and release.[847] If you are not used to fishing small streams, check out *Luck Has Nothing to Do With It*, published by Western Reflections, which is specifically about fishing the high country around Hinsdale County.

Do not forget that the great Rio Grande River, third largest in the United States, has its headwaters in Hinsdale County and runs through a large part of the southern part of the county.[848] The Rio Grande eventually drains all the rivers on the eastern slope of the San Juans.[849] Going upstream, the Rio Grande branches into many smaller streams. Guided fishing is available out of Lake City and Creede to take you to some of those "secret sweet spots."

As early as 1876, E.F. Bennett built and was using a six-person skiff on the lake. The boat was also made available as a rental to the public and was often used. In June, 1877, the Jones and Tremble Company announced the availability at the lake of three boats and a picnic area with fire pits and tables.[850] By June, 1879, a restaurant was opened at the lake and additional boats were available.

Boating remains a favorite past time in the Lake City area; including fishing and pontoon boats on Lake San Cristobal, as well as canoes, kayaks, and sailboats. Rafting is also popular on the Lake Fork of the Gunnison in the spring and early summer, when the river is high enough but not dangerously fast. There are seven different boat rentals businesses at the time of this writing, although they are not all located at the lake. Ask at the fly shops or the chamber of commerce for more details.

Besides fishing, Lake San Cristobal was from an early date very popular with boaters. Rowboats, sailboats, and canoes were all used, and some early photographs show as many as ten or fifteen boats just on one end of the lake or the other, simply boating and not fishing. Just like

Boating was very popular on Lake San Cristobal from 1876 on. However it seems the man should be rowing. (Author's Collection)

today, there were also many people who would come to the lake merely for the atmosphere.

Before 1900 many of these people going to the lake would stay at houses that rented a room or two to tourists and which were close to the lake. Buggies were rented by tourists to go to the lake, and in 1879 there was regular "buggy service" to and from the lake. A four-horse team transported visitors from Lake City to the lake at a charge of fifty cents a person.[851]

Lake City and Hinsdale County's beautiful scenery were written up by many tourist guides starting as early as 1879 and continuing into the 1920s. Traveling up the Lake Fork by train, Frank Hall wrote in his 1895 *History of Colorado*:

> *The visitor is lost in wonder at the variety and general magnificence of the scenery (in Hinsdale County), the fantastic rock formations, the marvelously picturesque contour of the ranges on either side, and the loveliness of the entire valley. In many respects it surpasses any other section traversed by the Rio Grande Railroad.... There are pictures here well calculated to set a great landscape painter wild with desire to reproduce them on canvas.*
>
> *The town under consideration (Lake City) is prettily nestled in a broad amphitheater of the mountains, is well laid out with wide, shaded streets, and quite substantially built of frame, brick, and stone....*
>
> *A trip to Lake San Cristobal, originally named Lake Chrystobal (sic), by Mr. H.G. Proutt (of the Ruffner Expedition) ... in 1873) is delightful in summer; it would be hard to find a lovelier spot in the Rocky Mountains... This lake is a beautiful sheet of water, clear and transparent, two and a half miles long and one mile wide; it is studded with fairy-like islets, where boating parties go to enjoy a picnic. The variety of scenery along its borders is the wonder and delight of the artist.*[852]

Lake City holds the honor of being the earliest tourist spot in the San Juans, in great part because of an attempt by locals to try to take up the economically slack times when Hinsdale County was in one of its many mining busts. As mentioned at the beginning of this book, even the very earliest American explorers recognized the beauty of the area and the abundance and variety of its wildlife.

Tourism picked up greatly with the arrival of the railroad in 1889 and the advent of the "Circle Tour," mentioned in Chapter Seven. The ease of getting to Lake City by railroad, combined with all of the railroads' extensive promotion of Colorado's mountain towns and

Rodeos were held in the early 1900s at Ball Flats. Although there were grandstands there was no fencing for the animals. (Nora and Burton Smith Collection)

scenery, definitely helped keep Lake City alive after mining started its great decline in 1903. Special trains between 1898 and 1933 brought in scores of tourists to Lake City.[853]

Color postcards helped promote the area, as well as the use of the then new Kodak camera by the general population. To keep the town looking good, Lake City started fining residents who did not remove their rubbish.

As the cattle industry blossomed in Hinsdale County, the residents started a local rodeo, which was popular with both locals and tourists. The event was usually held in what is now called Ball Flats, but there was no stadium or corrals. The events were just held in the open fields, but were always well attended. The rodeo died out with the cattle industry in the 1940s and 1950s, but the ranches continued to provide horses, mules, and burros for those tourists that wanted to go into the mountains to see the sights. The women and children preferred burros, but the men always chose a horse or mule in order to maintain their masculine image. In 1800s and early 1900s many of the trips into the mountains were made by large parties of twenty to forty people. Burro riding was also great fun for local children. If a Lake City child did not own a burro, he could usually catch one grazing in the local hills or along the town streets. One tradition for the school children was to ride burros to the Golden Fleece Mine, where they were given a tour of the mine and a free specimen of Golden Fleece ore. The children also liked to play around Crooke's (Granite) Falls and watch the molten slag at the Crooke Smelter being poured and carried to the dumps. Once in a while they could see bars of silver and gold.[854]

Lake City's tourist industry was helped by the fact that in the first half of the twentieth century, the entire United States was fascinated with the

Locals advertised the rodeo by having calf roping and bronco busting at the intersection of Silver and Third Streets. (Nora and Burton Smith Collection)

American West. Tourists loved to come to Colorado and ride burros, visit the old mines and the ghost towns, or ride in a real stagecoach. As Duane Vandenbusche put it:

> *They came to view the magnificent scenery (and) to partake of the "vanishing" frontier.*[855]

As tourists rediscovered Lake City in the 1920s and 1930s, Margaret Bates wrote:

> *The quality of Lake City people never diminished even though quantity did. They discovered a nucleus of dedicated townspeople, who along with other Coloradoans, were eager to put Lake City back on the road to prosperity....*

As mentioned, in the late nineteenth and the first four decades of the twentieth century, tourism centered on Lake San Cristobal, and a small community grew up on the banks of the lake called "Lake Shore." Eventually there were perhaps twenty or thirty buildings on the site, ranging from small "fishermen cabins" to the large Lake Shore Inn that had over thirty-six sleeping rooms and a ballroom. There were also several small stores and some of the families of men working at the Golden Fleece or Black Crooke lived at or near Lake Shore.

In the 1920s, 1930s and even the early 1940s, one of the foremost tourist developments at Lake San Cristobal was the famous Lake Shore Inn and the related resort development surrounding it. The Lake Shore was owned, developed, and operated by Colonel F. C. French and his wife Theo. The Inn was an impressive two-story, thirty-six room, log structure, which provided meals and lodging in a beautiful setting just a few dozen feet from the lake's shore. It had electricity provided by a large generator (lights out was at ten p.m.) and water was piped in. The lodge was started when the Frenches bought and added to a cabin owned by Mary Croft in 1917. The couple filed on the water rights and engineered the resort. Some of the surrounding miners' cabins were refurbished to become additional lakefront rentals besides the lodge. Impressive marketing materials were developed and the area was advertised nationwide, promoting not only the lake and its fishing, but also the fabulous scenery of Hinsdale County, as well as hiking, boat rentals, and sightseeing. Later a writing academy was even established at the Inn. The famous Kellogg family of Kellogg's cereal fame was listed in the Inn's guest register.

F. C. French, an engineer and college professor and dean at Marquette Engineering School, also helped to bring in and establish other resorts around the lake. Some of the many lodges or rental cabins at the lake included The All States Inn and the Turtle Island Lodge (located near today's public boat ramp on what is not really an island). Tragically the Lake Shore Inn burned in 1938, but a second Lake Shore Inn with surrounding cabins was built near the first in the 1940s and continued into the mid- 1950s.[856] At the same time (the late 1940s and 1950s) many tourist courts, cabins and resorts started opening in Lake City.

The Inn at Lake Shore was large and comfortable for its time. (Nora and Burton Smith Collection)

One major problem eventually occurred at the lake in the 1940s. Many of the buildings there were built on mining claims that had no minerals. Most people realized that they owned the surface rights if they owned a mining claim, but did not realize they could not patent the claim unless it had minerals. The federal government learned of the situation in the late 1930s and 1940s and started moving people off the land, claiming that they did not own it even though they had a patent and that they were merely squatters. Some of these people had lived on this land for decades but the "feds" were pretty ruthless in moving people out — sometimes tearing down cabins while owners were away and once even setting fire to a cabin, although the feds stated that they didn't mean to do so. Then, after the fire at the Lake Shore Inn, which was built on homesteaded property and was patented, the buildings on the western shore of San Cristobal were pretty well eliminated and the town of Lake Shore disappeared. The area is only just now starting to come back to life.

The late 1940s, after World War II, is when the rest of America began to discover Lake City, although it took a little longer for the year-round population of the town and county to rebound. Hinsdale County's population was 209 in 1970 — the lowest since the year the county was founded in 1874.

In an effort to get more people to Lake City and to combat its isolation, an air strip was built by Joel Swank on Henson Street in 1947. Henson Street had been the right of way for the railroad and was now used for a different form of transportation. Governor Lee Knous (a San Juan Mountain native) attended the dedication of the "airport." One of the first advantages was the weekly transport of a doctor to town.[857]

Joel Swank also helped to usher in snowmobiling to Hinsdale County in the 1950s. There are many great trails and large, flat and open areas in the county for the use by those who enjoy the sport. Joel took credit for building the first snowmobile, although it was similar to an airboat on skis and it is unclear if he meant the first in Hinsdale, Colorado, or even the United States.

Automobiles and the advent of better roads for their use had opened up the mountains of Colorado to tourists by 1920, but tourism shifted into an even busier time in Hinsdale County with the advent of automobiles with bigger engines and better cooling systems that could make it through the mountainous terrain without too much difficulty. The author can still remember that in 1950 my father had to stop twice while going over Monarch Pass to fill up the car's radiator with water. Some of the older cars of that time simply did not have the power to make it at all. The formation and promotion of National Parks and Forests also helped to spur the nation's tourist industry. Towns, counties, and states began tourist advertising, almost exclusively the province of railroad companies before this time. Lake City was no exception.

As summer tourists began to arrive in Lake City, little tourist cabins became popular rentals, as well as RV parks and campgrounds, both public and private. John and Emma Liska started the first tourist cabins in the actual town of Lake City in the 1920s. The Liskas brought five cabins from Sherman and located them on the site of the former Van Geison Lixiviation Works, which had burned in a fire in July, 1900.[858]

The moving of cabins or their lumber to town from the outlying settlements to be used for tourists is one reason that little remains of the other Hinsdale County settlements.

By 1972, Lake City had about twenty tourist lodging facilities. Only three were motels, the rest were lodges and resorts sometimes with small cabins for the visitors. Since that time, many of the small cabins have been sold to individuals, some of whom still rent them out, but many have become second homes. Some of the ranches in Hinsdale County have also been subdivided into small tracts. This has meant that the number of lodging units (also called number of beds for rent) has gone

For decades the people of Lake City have plowed snow and graded roads to make more of the high country accessible to tourists. (Author's Collection)

down. There is at present a move to convert some large building into rental units, but only one new hotel or motel has been built in Lake City in the last half century.

Some of the other interesting tourist spots in Hinsdale County are a little difficult to fully understand. For example, the Slumgullion Earthflow, located at the base of Cannibal Plateau, is not as spectacular to look at as our mountains or Lake San Cristobal, but it is one of the geologic wonders of the world. It is actually two earthflows;[859] the oldest flow runs for four and a half miles down the east and southeast sides of Mesa Seco, to the east shore of the lake, blocking the Lake Fork of the Gunnison about 770 years ago (about 1250 A.D.) and has become basically stable. The newer earthflow began about 400 years ago (about 1620 A.D.) and is still moving. The older earthflow starts at 11,400 feet in elevation and stops at 8,800 feet at the lake. The active earthflow is now about half way down the older earthflow. The earthflows are composed mainly of a clay material called "montmorillonite," which expands when saturated with water. This makes the new earthflow move with a very slow wave-like motion, but it is still moving about an inch a day in some places. The earthflow is therefore, geologically speaking, very new and moving fairly fast.

Movement of the new earthflow is not constant along its entire length, as some areas are moving at 15 to 20 feet per year (near the middle of the new earthflow), and some areas are moving only 2.5 feet a year (near the toe or the bottom of the new earthflow). Some geologists feel that the movement could be as much as 300 feet a year in some places at the top of the earthflow.[860] The bottom of the moving earthflow can be seen at a well-marked observation point with descriptive signs, which is about three or four miles up the Slumgullion Pass Road (Highway 149). The moving earthflow is very obvious because of the lack of most vegetation and the leaning and crooked configuration of the few trees growing on it. The trees and some vegetation are growing normally on the old earthflow.[861]

The earthflow is "almost unequalled by any such event in the history of the United States."[862] The earthflow was probably named after a miner's stew of the time that was the yellowish color of the earthflow, although it has also been speculated that it looks like the remains of whale blubber or looks like a stew made from it. Possibly it is both — an ex-whaler who prospected in the area and made a stew that reminded him of the whales.[863] The part of the earthflow that is running is very slippery and does not smell very good either, so be warned if you walk on the active earthflow.

Although tourists had always come to Lake City from its founding, especially later as part of the D&RG railroad excursions, tourism as an industry began to form in Hinsdale County about 1910. Fishermen and hunters were the mainstay of tourism at this time, but families began to come to the area also. Texans and Oklahomans were especially interested in escaping the heat and spending a few weeks or months in the beautiful, cool San Juans.

However, there was a negative side to increased tourism in Colorado. In some places, like ski areas, former mining towns were overrun by tourists, changing, for better or worse, the atmosphere of the place drastically. This type of growth is something that has never appealed to most Lake City residents and visitors, so being overrun by tourists has never been a problem, although a better economy was and is definitely needed.

The construction industry was born again in Lake City because of the demand for summer rentals and second homes. It was not easy to get to Lake City in the mid-1900s, as there was no railroad and the sixty-mile dirt road was the last leading to a county seat in Colorado to obtain a paved road (it was 1964 before it was completely finished). The upgrade of Colorado's mountain roads in the 1920s helped tourism in many places in Colorado, but the roads from Gunnison to Lake City was one of the last in Colorado to be upgraded to asphalt. The process was done in sections, beginning in 1954 and continuing for several years. The upgrade of the road to Creede in the mid-1980s was held up by

The Slumgullion Earthflow, which starts on Mesa Seco, 4 ½ miles away, is huge and caused the Lake Fork to back up and form Lake San Cristobal. (U.S.G.S. Photo)

the Forest Service which controlled six miles of public land that the road ran through. They were worried about how they would pay for the maintenance cost of their part of the road if it was asphalted. The problem was soon solved by making what is now Highway 149 a state road. Lake City was no longer at the end of a dead end road for most of the year.[864]

In the 1970s, people started to move to Lake City to live in this special part of the San Juans year-round. There was something they liked in Lake City— a way of life and an outlook on living life that made sense in the hustle and bustle of the modern world. This trend continues to gain momentum at the time this book is written.

Hunting seems to be slowing down in Hinsdale County as it has become more and more expensive. In the 1960s to 1980s, the Lake City bars were crammed with hunters, but as regulations have tightened, license fee have risen, and more people seem to like to shoot photos of rather than bullets at our animals, hunting has become much less of an economic impact. There have been many other recreational opportunities over the years, most of which are still enjoyed by residents and visitors. In the winter, ice skating, ice fishing, cross country skiing, snowshoeing, downhill skiing at the small local ski hill, and sledding have always been favorite winter sports. In the past, sleigh rides were popular; but in more recent times snowmobiling and ice climbing have become major winter activities. In the old days, miners in the high country used ten foot skis (then called snow shoes) for travel to and from the high country mines and mining camps in the deep snow, but they also used them for recreation. A large pole was carried to help balance and to act as a brake and help turn the unwieldy skis.

Winter in Hinsdale County is a special time for most full-time residents, as life slows down and another aspect of nature opens up. The solar heat of unpolluted skies, lack of humidity, and generally calm winds make winter temperatures in the sun feel much warmer than they actually are. Nights are cool even in the summer, but locals adapt to the cold and many of them sleep with windows open until temperatures drop below freezing. One surprising fact is that it is usually colder in the valleys than in the high mountains in the winter, as cold air sinks and air circulation is more stagnant in the valleys, causing inversions.

One problem for Lake City has been winter tourism, since a major ski area has never received the support of local residents. Not many locals regret this decision, but attempts at promoting snowmobiling, ice-climbing, and cross country skiing have had only limited successful. Another limitation is that Lake City is a "family town," but with schooling, families with children have only set times when they can come to Lake City in the winter.[865]

If they do not already own a four-wheel drive vehicle, today's summer tourists can rent a jeep or an Off-Highway Vehicle (OHV), a boat, a mountain bike or a horse. You can camp or stay in an RV in a lovely private or public campsite overlooking Lake San Cristobal or along any one of Hinsdale County's many streams and high country lakes; stay in a log cabin or spend your time in a nice motel or a luxury home. You may enjoy one of the largest display of wildflowers in the United States during what is the heat of the summer at lower elevations; hunt our abundant wild game with your camera, bow or muzzleloader, shop at one of the local gift stores, attend one of the many different "shows" or enjoy an ice cream cone at the local Soda Shop; explore the ruins of old mining camps or mines (especially the Ute-Ulay and the Hard Tack); study unique geological formations; dine in excellent restaurants; have a good time at any one of the several nice "saloons"; picnic in the three town parks or in the wilderness; and enjoy the companionship of some of the "friendliest people in the U.S.A."[866]

Although the Ute-Ulay Mine and its buildings are still being restored at the time of this writing, eleven-acres of the site are now under public ownership. Plans to restore many of the buildings at this mine are already

Lake City Weather Statistics

Month	Avg. High (°F)	Avg. Low (°F)	Avg. Precip. (inches)
January	34	-3	.85
February	38	1	.80
March	44	12	.99
April	53	22	1.12
May	62	30	1.04
June	73	38	.80
July	77	44	2.07
August	75	43	2.10
September	69	35	1.24
October	60	25	1.24
November	40	7	.99
December	35	0	1.05

Average Median High	55°F
Average Median Low	21°F
Average Total Precipitation	14.29 inches
Average Snowfall (approx.)	84 inches

Data provided by Zorba and the U. S. Weather Service. Based on forty years of climatological information.

Lake City's Weather

underway, and it is hoped that it will become a major heritage tourist destination and very unique historic display for local mining. The Hard Tack Mine Tour, about a half mile before reaching the Ute-Ulay, will also give you a great idea of what underground hard rock mining was like a hundred years or more ago. It is located three miles southwest of town on Henson Creek.

In the summer, hiking is and has always been, very popular; especially when climbing the five 14,000 foot peaks located a short distance from Lake City or trekking into the five spectacular Federal Wilderness areas in the area. Some people like to do this in the winter. For those wanting a "peak" experience, Hinsdale County's and Lake City's official Vacation Guide at the time of this writing will give plenty of information. They can be found all over town. Uncompahgre (14,301 feet) seems to be the favorite peak, as it is the tallest in the San Juans, but there are also Red Cloud (14,050), Handies (14, 049), Sunshine (14,018) and Wetterhorn (14,017). Redcloud and Sunshine are close enough together that they can be climbed in one day by the energetic.

However, four wheeling is the favorite summer sport. It became very popular throughout the San Juans after World War II with the availability of the army surplus jeep with four-wheel drive and low ratio gears. Our jeep roads are generally old wagon roads created over 100 years ago and still maintained to some extent. Our hiking trails are often old pack trails used by mules and burros, and both roads and trails generally lead to a historic mine, camp, or other "landmark" places. Over sixty-five years ago, local volunteers cleared and rebuilt many of the old wagon roads, making them passable by four wheel drive vehicles. The sport opened up the San Juan high country to people who otherwise could never have seen such beauty. Unfortunately, this also allowed many people to thoughtlessly take souvenirs home until there were very few historic man-made objects left to see. Please do not cause our "history" to deteriorate and disappear any faster than it already is because of harsh winters and other natural reasons.

Local "must-see" four-wheeling spots include the two main jeep roads, Engineer and Cinnamon Pass Roads. A long one-day loop can be made by going up one and coming back on the other. A side trip to Silverton could also be included. These roads are known to virtually every person who enjoys four-wheeling in the high country of the San Juans. However Hinsdale County has several other shorter trips that are also spectacular but not as well known. Off the Engineer Pass Road, you will see Nellie Creek, North Henson, and the Golconda boarding house roads. These are all dead end roads, but are very interesting short trips. Nellie Creek (well-marked) features a lovely waterfall and at it end a public campground with a trailhead to climb Uncompahgre Peak; but since it is a rough road, so people sometimes hike the four miles to the trailhead. North Henson has many old mines and beautiful aspen forests and is a little easier. The Golconda road can be a little scary because of a steep drop off along it, but the mine's recently restored boarding house and power house are very interesting.

Off Highway 149 going to Creede is the four-wheel drive Sawmill Road that loops around and comes out after several hours to Highway 149 at Spring Creek Pass or on a fork leads to the communications tower on 71 Mountain. It was once part of Horsethief Trail, which linked Utah and the Colorado Front Range and was used by outlaws and Native Americans who stole horses. Sawmill Park gets its name from a sawmill that operated in the park before 1900.[867] True to Horsethief Trail's name, in July, 1879, Marshall J. P. Galloway was taking a horse thief, William Thomas, from Antelope Park to Lake City over this part of the trail when they stopped at a spring to get water. Thomas tried to escape and Galloway shot him dead with one shot at sixty feet. After the coroner

Four-wheeling opened the San Juans to all people and Lake City and Hinsdale County wasted no time in getting photos like this into publications. (Colorado Department of Public Relations)

inquest at the spot, Thomas was buried along the trail that goes up Hill 71.[868] When a local boy later took some of the horse thief's bones home, he was forced to return them to the spot where they were found, rebury them, and mark the spot; but no one has found it.[869] Let the historical society know if you do.

If you would rather not go four wheeling, you might just want to drive along Highway 149 to Creede or go up Henson Creek (CR20) to Capitol City. If taking the Creede route, be sure to stop at the lake overlook, the Slumgullion slide information sign, and Penniston (but some locals call it Pennington) Park.[870] This is a good place to spot moose. Further on, Windy Point gives an absolutely fantastic view of the San Juan mountains and many of the Hinsdale County Fourteeners and high Thirteeners. The view changes constantly depending on the weather, the time of day, and the time of year. Get your camera ready! Next, near the top of Slumgullion Pass, is the Cebolla ("onion" in Spanish) Loop and Deer Lakes. It is about twenty minutes to Deer Lakes, but about a two hour trip if you travel down the Mill Creek Road to the Cebolla and on to Powderhorn. This dirt road is a little rough, but no problem for a passenger car if you go slow. Deer Lakes is marked on the main road and is a favorite spot to take children fishing, as worms or salmon eggs are allowed. Be aware that there are three lakes — one about a mile hike above the middle lake after going across the dam and another that is lower with only a small part of the lake visible from the middle lake dam. This is also a good spot to see moose.

After crossing Slumgullion Pass (12,580 feet) and then the Continental Divide at Spring Creek Pass (actually a lower pass than "Slum"), the country is wide open. Many people do not realize they are still in Hinsdale County for many more miles. Many lakes and streams are accessed off Highway 149, which is a part of the Silver Thread Historic and Scenic Byway. A favorite, "must-see" waterfall is North Clear Creek Falls. It cannot be seen from the road, but is only a half mile or less off the highway. Many feel that North Clear Creek Falls is in the top three of the most beautiful waterfalls in all of Colorado, if not the *most* beautiful. You can continue down this dirt road (the original highway to Creede) for a few miles, and it will tie back in with the highway as it continues to Creede.

Now back to the fork in the paved road just a few miles south of Lake City. The Cinnamon Pass and Lake San Cristobal Road (CR30) passes several of the mills and waste rock dumps of old mines until it reaches the lake. If you go over the bridge when you first see the lake, there is a dirt road (County Road 33 and accessible to regular cars) that goes around the lake on its east side. There are several campgrounds overlooking the lake on this side. If you stay on the paved road, there is a public boat ramp for boats, canoes, and kayaks on what is called Turtle Island, which is actually a peninsula. There is also a nice, well-marked, day-use picnic area at the base of the south side of Red Mountain. When you come to another bridge at the other end of the lake, by going straight it takes you back around the lake or going to the right at the bridge takes you on the dirt Cinnamon Pass Road, which is still usable by regular passenger cars for about twenty more miles. At Castle Lakes (private and originally called Old Stevens Ranch[871] start looking for the Wager Gulch or Carson Road on your left. This road is a fairly easy four wheel drive unless it is wet, in which case it should be considered undriveable because of slick clay along the route.

There are several campgrounds further along the Cinnamon road and also many good hiking trails. Eventually the road becomes four-wheel drive at the ghost town of Sherman, which is hard to see in the dense aspen forest near the road. If you go left through Sherman, there is a dead end, four wheel drive road up Cottonwood Creek, which also has some good and well-marked trails and the little that is left of Garden City. The main road to Cinnamon Pass gets tougher as you ascend it, but eventually comes into flat and level Burrows Park, which has the remains of several small ghost towns and the trailheads to three nearby fourteeners. Most people climbing the Fourteeners camp in the park and leave for their climb early the next morning, so as to avoid thunderstorms. Just after you start leaving the park is the short, but rough road to American Basin, where the wildflowers are unbelievably lush, diverse, and beautiful in late June and July (sometimes even in August). American Basin is one of the best reasons the San Juans are called the "wildflower capital of Colorado," although Crested Butte and Cataract Gulch also try to claim that title. The Cinnamon Pass Road continues to get rougher; but in about two more miles, you reach the top of the pass.

Back in town, if you go north on Highway 149 out of Lake City toward Gunnison there are many good Silver Thread information signs at pullouts that describe the local scenery and history. These are well worth a stop. Just outside Hinsdale County, about ten or eleven miles from Lake City, is the Big Blue Cuttoff. This road will eventually take you into true wilderness, at which the road dead ends, like a stick pointing the way to go. This is an easy four wheel drive or a somewhat difficult road for a regular car, which should not be driven while the road is wet. Near the top of the pass, a somewhat difficult auto road called the Alpine Plateau Road takes you north to Arrowhead near Cimarron and Montrose, but it takes a while, so do not use this as a short cut to Montrose. The Alpine Ranger station on Big Blue Creek has been restored by the Historic Corps.

Please stay on the roads and trails, as our alpine tundra is fragile and if damaged can take hundreds of years to completely grow back. When four-wheeling remember to go slow and be careful. The average speed on a jeep trail is five miles an hour or less, so leave plenty of time for your trip. People here gauge distance in hours, not miles. These warnings are meant to help keep you safe while enjoying the beauty of our mountains; but if you are hurt or if your vehicle breaks down, we have rescue teams, EMTs, and four wheel drive tow trucks to come after you, just get word back to town.

By the 1970s, the cross country motorcycle had become a popular way to travel in the mountains, and in recent years four wheel drive all-terrain vehicles (ATVs or OHVs) have become one of the favorite ways to see the high country. Besides the amazing natural scenery of the San Juan Mountains, there are still mills, mines, and ghost towns to be seen, but remember these are all private property. The history of most of these historic spots can be found in the author's book *Exploring the Historic San Juan Triangle*. When you travel into the high country, try to not be alone and be sure to tell someone where you are going and when you should be back. Even in the summer, be sure to take adequate provisions, especially water because of our low humidity), have proper maps, and do not be afraid to ask the locals for information or directions. Be sure to take a coat or heavy sweater and rain gear while enjoying the high country. Our climate can change quickly and varies radically. Almost daily, rain will fall in July and August (it is called the "Monsoon Season").

Autumn is usually fairly dry and hot during the day and chilly at night. The normally low humidity, solar heat, and lack of wind makes it feel warmer than it really is; but this can change quickly in a rainstorm, when night falls, or with the winds of an approaching storm. Remember there is only about half the oxygen here as at sea level, so give your body a chance to adjust. Allow two or three days to acclimate before doing strenuous exercise.

If camping, please be especially careful of regulations, and determine if a campfire is allowed. This depends on how dry the forest is (there is information on a board in front of the visitor's center). If allowed, be sure your campfire is fully extinguished with water poured on it as an extra safety precaution. Also remember to pack out your garbage; and, if you find the garbage of less considerate others, take it with you. Please remember that the mines and structures you will find in the high country are all on private property and that you should not pick the wildflowers. "Take nothing with you but memories and photos and leave only footprints." If hiking or camping, please be careful of bears, especially if they have cubs or you have food with you; we have many of them in Hinsdale County. Moose should also be considered especially dangerous.

Now let's explore the Town of Lake City. Perry Eberhart referred to Lake City in 1959 as follows:

> *Lake City is a lovely old lady now, but she had a rich and boisterous past. In her day, she was one the busiest cities in Colorado. She was the queen bee in a rich beehive of activity and she has grown old gracefully.*[872]

The town still has that "lovely old lady" feeling. Some of the "must see" spots in Lake City proper are the old First National Bank building (Community Bank at this time); and the Hinsdale County Courthouse, where Alferd Packer was tried for murder. (The courthouse at the time of this writing is under restoration.) The Baptist church is on Bluff Street and the Presbyterian and Episcopal churches below it on Fifth Street. The Saint Rose of Lima Catholic church is accessed through the trailer park just south of the Henson bridge. These historical sites give a wide span of the architecture used in the town over the last century and a half and are well worth a visit. Another interesting site is the recently restored brick Armory. The armory has served many purposes and provided many activities over the years — an armory, "opera house", the first fire house,[873] a basketball court, climbing walls, and community center to name a few.

At the time this book is being written, the Ute-Ulay Mine is undergoing a transformation into a "heritage tourism destination." It should be open in the summer of 2017 and will be a wonderful example of mining and milling in the San Juans. Unfortunately, it is too early to give many details.

Many tourists can be seen driving slowly around Lake City in the summer enjoying the beautifully restored Victorian homes and commercial buildings. There are too many Victorian houses to list here, but many are on Silver Street and Gunnison Avenue. One very good reference for these homes is *Historic Homes of Lake City*, the Hinsdale County Historical Society's official guide to vintage residences in the Lake City Historical District, researched by Grant Houston. Lake City is a National Historic District and plaques are placed in front of many of the homes to describe their past history, as well as information about some of the owners. Lake City contains one of the largest and best controlled Historic Districts in Colorado. Every facet of our history is considered. About 2010, the town received a grant to stabilize several of the old outhouses, sheds, and outbuildings in the town. This sounds sort of silly, but if you really want to see some of the original buildings in Lake City, then drive down an alley, almost any alley. The Historic District covers twenty-eight blocks and contains over 200 designated structures.

If you are interested in local history, then the Hinsdale County Museum at 130 Silver Street is a must see for a small fee. One third of the exhibits are changed every two years, so even if you have been there before, you will probably still see plenty of interesting new items. The Finley building was originally a general merchandise store, then a hardware store, grocery store, saloon, and the International Order of Odd Fellows (IOOF) Silver Star #37 lodge. The Hinsdale County Historical Society bought the building in 1989, and the well restored Smith-Grantham house was moved next door in 1993.

Visits to Lake City's two cemeteries are popular. The Hinsdale County Historical Museum gives guided tours of the cemeteries and homes, and a ghost tour in the summer. Check with them about times for the tours. The 1877 IOOF Cemetery is above the old cemetery near the top of the first rise (called Greenfield Hill) and at the toe of the Lake City Landslide.[874] The old (1876) cemetery is below Highway 149 (the paved road to Gunnison) at the north end of town.

With all the amazing scenery in the area, it is no surprise that photography, water color, and oil painting are very popular in Hinsdale County; especially in the fall. The colors start to change in late August in the high country and then work down to Lake City where the colors

Muriel Wolle took many photos of Lake City and Hinsdale County from the late 1930s until the 1960s, including this family plot in the lower cemetery. (Muriel Wolle Photo, Denver Public Library, X-54)

are usually at their peak the first part of October. There are even classes in Lake City in the summer meant for locals and tourists, children and adult. One popular spot is the Sweety's Wildlife Zoo where children can see all sorts of "animals" and "adopt" and paint "pet" rocks. Between the spectacular mountains, thought provoking ghost towns, waterfalls, snowfields, and unusual rock formations, it is hard to not start taking photographs. Area wildlife is varied and often quite comfortable around humans, but the bears need to be treated very cautiously.

If you like waterfalls, there are some beauties in Hinsdale County. Whitmore Falls on the Engineer Road (CR20) is worth the short but steep hike to where it can be seen. Lake City's two most famous waterfalls, Crooke (Granite) Falls and Argenta Falls, are both on the Lake Fork of the Gunnison, but are hard to get to because of private property either at the falls or in their vicinities. North Clear Creek Falls on the east side of the Continental Divide is perhaps the most dramatic, but South Clear Creek Falls, accessed from the campground of the same name, is also very nice. Nellie Creek Falls, about a mile up the Nellie Creek Jeep Road, is very peaceful and a local favorite. Also Cataract Creek Falls south of Sherman, Lake Fork Falls west of Sherman, and Henson Falls below the Hidden Treasure, but not visible from the road, are very enjoyable. There are also many seasonal waterfalls along the Engineer Road in the early summer.

Lake City is known as a family town and one regular late afternoon stop at the time of this writing is at the ice cream shop on Silver Street. The downtown park also contains a public restroom. All ages of children enjoy playing games and sports at the Lake City Town Park — usually until dark. There are also two other parks in Lake City. Do not miss Memorial Park, which has skateboarding, handicap fishing, restrooms, picnic gazebo, a "beach," and a baseball field. In the summer Lake City also has many films, shows, and other events for children.

Animals you might see while jeeping or hiking (and sometimes even right in town) include deer and marmots. Moose, can usually be seen at Lake San Cristobal, the Lake Fork above Williams Creek Campground, and around Deer Lakes. Bighorn sheep can sometimes be seen on the upper Cinnamon Road beyond Sherman, but they can also be found along Highway 149 around the Hinsdale and Mineral County line. Lynx, bear, bobcats, and mountain lions are local predators. All but the bear stay pretty well hidden. Bear are everywhere, including in town on many occasions. Moose are perhaps even more dangerous than bears. They may charge and even stalk a person for long distances.[875]

Other animals common to the area include chipmunks, golden mantle ground squirrels (often mistaken for chipmunks, but their stripes do not extend to the heads), cottontail, snowshoe, and jack

Marmots are unique to the high country, but many tourists mistake them for beaver or ground hogs. This one seems to enjoy smelling the flowers. (Edna Mason Photo)

rabbits, weasels, tree martins, coyote, fox, beaver, mule deer, elk, pika, and yellow-bellied marmots. Big horn sheep and elk were abundant in the early days, but were killed off. They both were restocked during the mid-twentieth century. The elk were imported from Wyoming after Colorado's elk were all killed, and inhabit the higher country in the summer, but can be seen in the fields near Lake City in the winter.

Migratory birds like ducks, geese, pelicans, peregrine falcons, and herons spend much time here in spring and fall. Owls, golden eagles, hawks and bald eagles live at the lake a large part of the year. Birds that are common include the great heron, Lusby grouse, American goldfinch, belted kingfish, American dipper, a variety of hummingbirds, mountain bluebird, stellar jay, red-tailed hawk, eagles,, cassin's finch, stellar jay, great horned owl, dark-eyed junco, mountain chickadee, pine siskin, evening grosbeak, western tanager, and the lark bunting (the Colorado State Bird). Birds in Hinsdale County also include blue and sage grouse and Gunnison grouse and its relative the ptarmigan, which are white in winter and brown in the summer, and hundreds of varieties of song birds and other smaller birds that enjoy the area in the summer.

If you are interested in geology, in the Lake City area there are three different ages of volcanic activity that are visible. In the immediate vicinity of town is the volcanic debris of the second period. North of town, the rocks are older, being mainly the debris of the first volcanic stage. The third phase, or most recent, is southwest of town. The Lake Fork of the Gunnison is the south and east boundary of the Lake City Caldera. Henson Creek forms the north boundary. A caldera is where a volcano eventually collapses upon itself after spewing out much of the material below it. Most caldera's rims contain rivers because they are lower than the surrounding territory.[876]

Perhaps most importantly to those of us who live here, the locals have always appreciated their quality of life and the special type of freedom, individualism, and ruggedness that prevails. Lake City has most of those qualities in spades. It is more than that but it is hard to describe, but maybe an attempt might be a law-abiding, educated, artistic, and religious (or at least moral) atmosphere combined with a slower, family way of life. The locals include a wide variety of lifestyles and know that our home does not appeal to some people, and it is okay with them; as it has been for almost a century and a half.

To wind up this book, this author has thought long and hard about how to describe the "Lake City indomitable spirit of "hanging in there" that made and makes people stay in Lake City even through bad economic times? What is it that makes this place so special to those who live here year-round or come back year after year? The author was able to come up with some ideas, but soon discovered that Lyn Lampert, long time Lake City resident, had already put a lot of thought into describing this

Big Horn sheep are always a nice surprise. (Edna Mason Photo)

special lifestyle in a small book called *Lake City Serendipity*. Graciously, Lyn agreed to let the author quote parts of his book.

If you are thinking of living here permanently or buying a second home, you should read Lyn's three books. If you want to enjoy all the San Juans offers, you should read this book. They will help you realize what makes life here so very special, or it may help you realize that this way of life may not be for you.

Whether religious or not, many people seem to recognize a greatness and feel closer to God when they are in the mountains, but what is really amazing are the "special" times that people who live here year-round or that are here every summer experience. Lyn Lampert, who is also a minister, tells us:

Life in the mountains is delightfully unpredictable fertile ground for experiencing a lifetime of what I call San Juan Serendipity.... I know of no better locale for exercising the talent of serendipity (the facility of making happy chance discoveries) than right here in the San Juans, where some very delightful discoveries are served up daily simply for the taking.... The unexpected invades your routine little world and suddenly, for a brief moment at least, life is boundlessly joyful.... I have come to realize that although a certain element of serendipity is beyond your control, it is possible to put yourself in

How majestic are the big birds of the San Juans – eagles, hawks, herons, and many more. This is a golden eagle. (Edna Mason Photo)

The pika wins the prize for the cutest animal in the San Juans. It is endangered but still lives in our high country, where you will probably hear its squeaks but may not be able to find the animal. (Edna Mason Photo)

a position of experiencing it more often. Learn to look. Learn to see.... Curiosity and wonder are close relatives of serendipity.... When all is said and done, though, I think serendipity must be grace, a precious gift freely bestowed by our creator for no other reason than to give us joy through the unexpected surprises of life.

There is something in the makeup of man that craves exploration.... The joy of exploration, with its attendant joy of discovery, causes the human soul to cry out with the thrill of being someplace new, of finding something unexpected.... The San Juans are an explorer's paradise.... The San Juans offer an incredible variety of exploring adventures.

Lyn then goes on to describe some of his priceless time in the San Juan Mountains. A few of those experiences I have also enjoyed, but since each person gets his own "once in a lifetime experience," there are many others that I relish. You too can have your own special surprises. Many of these surprises happen right here within the city limits of Lake City, some happen on streams, some happen in the high country; but they happen almost every day, if we pay attention to the blessings around us. Lyn tells us to watch the heavens at night, soak in the stillness and starkness of winter, to slow down to watch, to research and plan some of your trips but let others be totally spontaneous, and to soak in the abundant and great variety of wildlife in Hinsdale County. The people of

Lake City could tell you thousands of stories, most of them different, of what has happened to them while living here — all experiences that they probably would not have had in the big city. One such person is Karen Hurd, who is totally in tune with the animals. Her book on living with the wildlife in the Lake City area is called *My Sweetie* and is a must read.

Lyn Lampert also tells us, after pointing out what past generations endured in these mountains, that:

> *Even today, though the edge is not as raw as it once was, life in the San Juans coexists unavoidably with raw nature, in both its glory and its terror.... Living on the raw edge can be eminently character-building. First it is a lifestyle that can be superbly exhilarating... Those who think heating with wood is too much work will probably never live in Lake City, but those who love life on the raw edge feel more alive after swinging a maul, making a cord of firewood.... There is something profoundly humbling in knowing that in the San Juans you really could be swept away by an avalanche, frostbitten by a winter storm, or even eaten by a mountain lion.... For many who have found in the San Juans an incredibly exhilarating and humbling environment, living on the slightly raw edge of life beats not living on the edge at all.*

Edna Mason calls this photograph "The Old Man In the Tree." Just one of those surprises! (Edna Mason Photo)

Lyn calls for the need for a secret place and that the San Juans are full of them:

> *For many Lake City itself is just such a secret place, seemingly far removed from the mad rush of business, traffic and pollution, and in one sense it is....*

The stream is a secret place because it is separate in the best sense from my everyday world, even separate from the twentieth century... Secret places give the opportunity to see through a child's eyes once again the mystery and beauty of all life.... Creation is full of mysteries.... which can overwhelm with sheer wonder.... Wonder is not analysis and wonder is not demanding an explanation. Wonder is beholding a mystery and not demanding an explanation, but being both humbled and fulfilled in the knowledge that there are things beyond our knowledge and in Someone else's control....

Since their reintroduction into Hinsdale and Mineral Counties many years ago, the moose are doing well and are now seen on many occasions; but be careful – they can be dangerous. (Edna Mason Photo)

Being simply rich is finding treasure in that which is free. There is joy in knowing that you and those you love don't require the acquisition of things to make them happy or to feel wealthy. There is joy unspeakable in being "simply rich." Being simply rich means nothing other than placing value on those things that will never be found in the pages of a catalog and finding treasure in what is free.... Living in the San Juans has taught me volumes about what it means to be "simply rich...." I believe that I am the richest man on earth.

Lyn gives many examples of what it means to be "simply rich," but I would like to give you just a few examples from my own life. I wish I had kept a diary of the thousands of times in the forty years I have lived in the San Juans during which I have felt the awe, the mystery, life on the edge, the natural art and music — the San Juan Serendipity that Lyn talks about. John Denver touched me with it in his song "Rocky Mountain High." He knew what being "simply rich" means. There are also many poets in the San Juans that can describe it. I will give you only a few examples as you really have to experience the awe and magnificence yourself to fully understand:

• While fishing, noting a beautiful and very colorful cliff at the edge of the water that had lavish green ferns growing out of it. Then I noticed the bird's nest, with three small chicks, tucked into a crevice.

• The first time I clearly saw the Milky Way with its gorgeous colors on a cold, clear winter's night.

• A bear and two cubs, sitting on our front porch at night and the squalling of one of the cubs when left behind by his mother.

• A friend who showed me a chipmunk he had trained to do tricks when offered a peanut.

• A very large brown trout that rolled right next to me in the middle of the Lake Fork. I truthfully thought for a few seconds that it was a porpoise.

• The smell of a campfire on a crisp summer night and the smell of your clothes for days afterwards.

• The taste of freshly-picked wild raspberries or homemade choke cherry or dandelion wine.

• The feel of a deer's nose.

• The buzz of a hummingbird.

• The sound of wind blowing through the evergreens with a storm approaching.

• Ptarmigan in the high country that let three of us get so close that we were afraid we would step on them.

Edna calls this photo "porcupine rock." Can you see it? (Edna Mason Photo)

This field of full-blooming columbines was certainly a surprise to the author when he came upon them. (Author's Photo)

• Seeing hundreds of elk on a Mineral Point hillside, so many that it looked like the ground was moving.

• Having a lynx sit and watch us for many minutes from his perch on a rock just a few feet away.

• Three bobcats running through the snow in my front yard, and finding the tracks that proved they were indeed there (they have huge paws).

• Or a simple pack rat that I had to write a five page essay about — they are amazing and very smart creature.

What will your surprises be — a newborn fawn you did not see until you almost stepped on it, a small area of a canyon with especially beautiful rock, a wolf (which isn't supposed to live in the San Juans, but I and several others have seen one up close), a bald eagle catching a trout? What will your explorations reveal—an old bottle, a flower, a shiny stone shaped like a heart? I cannot tell you what they will be. These "surprises" are why those oldtimers stayed here even when the mines closed. It is why the locals have fought so hard to keep Lake City from becoming a ghost town. It is why people who have experienced it always come back year after year.

Some of what I experienced I could only write down in poetry, which I start doing while I was just visiting before I lived in the San

Juans permanently. This is not a book of poetry, but I would like to end with my first, written in 1975, when I started to realize what is here:

Nature
Have you ever seen a mountain take a cloud, divide it into parts,
and put it back together again?
Have you ever seen a night so clear that there were no stars, just galaxies?
Have you ever seen a flower bud open to the rising sun,
then shrink in terror when you touched it?
Well I have! And it is my hope that you see such things too!

Can you see the grouchy old man's face at the right of the photo? (Edna Mason Photo)

LAKE CITY IN THE 21ST CENTURY

L ake City hit the low point in its entire history in the 1950s and 1960s. There was no mining, no newspaper, radio or television, and even the *Silver World* building was sold in 1950 and its equipment later moved to Oklahoma.[877] During this time, Lake City had no bank, and for the most part no doctors, dentists, or lawyers and often no law enforcement officer. The firemen were all volunteers and they used very antiquated equipment. However, local residents were determined their community would not become a ghost town. Many of the folks from this era still live in Lake City, although they have started to die off fast. They exemplified that Lake City Spirit discussed in the introduction; and, thanks to them, Lake City seems to have turned another corner.

Even in 1956, when Lake City was at its low point in population, it still received favorable publicity. *Colorado Wonderlands* Magazine had this to say:

> *Your adventure starts in deeply isolated Lake City, 8,681 feet high near the source of the rippling waters of the Lake Fork of the Gunnison. You may have heard of this tiny town, 260 miles southwest of Denver, with 141 persons, the seat of Hinsdale County, the smallest population in Colorado's 63 (counties).*
>
> *You must know that it is 47 miles from the nearest paved road, U.S. 50 at Iola, and that it lies at the foot of that pass with the rich and flavorful name, Slumgullion.... What you may not know is that Lake City lies on the edge of one of Colorado's wildest areas of unconquered mountain fastness (sic).*

When Thomas Gray Thompson wrote his Master's Thesis in 1961 on Lake City's Social and Cultural history he wrote:

> *When the last tourist leaves, Lake City does not become a stagnant, isolated town waiting for the next vacation season. Those who*

remain revert to those pleasures of uninterrupted reading, quiet, leisurely visits with friends and neighbors of long standing, small club activities, and church services, all in the pattern of their pioneer background. The radio and television have finally been intruded, but they have not replaced the pleasure of playing the piano, the pump-organ and the violin, nor the joys of singing together familiar songs of the past.[878]

Thompson's observations still apply today, although we do enjoy a few winter tourists. Those who use Lake City as a summer home and leave for the winter are sorely missed until they return. The town is still not quite big enough to continue the social and economic joys of summer on through the long, hard winters. Yet many locals do not want to see the town change much. It would destroy why they live here in the first place. Lake City is civilized, artistic, and peaceful. People wave to you from their cars. Residents may give you a few dollars to complete your purchase at the grocery store if you are short on money. Lake Citians may talk your ear off or invite you to dinner or a bonfire. In other words Lake City's residents are very friendly.

There will still be challenges for Lake City in the future. One will be to make sure we do not let this special type of life be destroyed by a large influx of outsiders who have their own ideas of what is best for Lake City. Another challenge may be pressure in the future to restart mining. Although it is more expensive to mine and there are many more regulations to follow, there just might still be prospectors out there who want to strike it rich. Some feel that mining in Hinsdale County is dead and should stay that way. Mining has never been totally eliminated in Hinsdale County and the severance taxes and grants that come with mining have been very useful to Hinsdale County. A significant part of our population was once miners or connected with the mining industry. When gold, silver, or base metals rise high enough in dollar value, the pressure will be back on to mine them. Mining and tourism have always been a very important part of Lake City life. Both should be allowed to continue, but slowly and cautiously and with controls to make sure Lake City does not end up with a ski area or a very visible strip mine.

Perhaps it is a good thing that Hinsdale County did not prosper throughout the twentieth century. The town's very remoteness has enabled Lake City to retain much of its early-day charm. Its tree-lined streets are dotted with attractive Victorian frame houses and log structures.[879]

Joel Swank wrote that the "Let's keep it like it is" movement evidently started about 1930.[880] It is still alive and well, but if one looks closely, it is obvious that the town has changed a lot since that time, and almost all of the change has been for the better. Yet many of the retired residents and second home owners want to continue to keep it "Just like it has been." The problem is that the working people have to be able to make a living — something that is simply not possible for most unless the town grows.

Lake City, as recent as 1970, had a population of only ninety-one, although by 1980 it was 206. As this book is written, the population for Lake City in 2015 is estimated on line to be about fifty persons smaller than 2010; not much of a drop in numbers, but a fifteen percent decrease in population. Hinsdale County's population is much smaller now than it was in 1900, but so are almost all San Juan towns.[881]

With a 2010 population of 843 in Hinsdale County (third smallest in Colorado and estimated in 2014 by Wikipedia (Hinsdale_County_Colorado) to be only 786 in 2015, there is a density of three-quarters of a person per square mile, the least dense in Colorado. However, the county is one of the largest in terms of acres per resident of public land and contains one of the largest roadless areas (generally the same as Wilderness areas) in the United States. The county was 95 percent public land in 1980 and 97 percent in 2015.[882]

Planning for the future by the people who live here and not just the local, state, and federal authorities becomes more important in these mountains, both in terms of preserving the environment and figuring out how to keep a balance between the different desires of different residents. We have a great advantage that so much of our county is public land that cannot be developed. Many of the year-round locals and most of those involved with the governmental agencies are coming to realize this situation, but many summer residents feel strongly they

Historical population		
Census	**Pop.**	**%±**
1880	1,487	—
1890	862	−42.0%
1900	1,609	86.7%
1910	646	−59.9%
1920	538	−16.7%
1930	449	−16.5%
1940	349	−22.3%
1950	263	−24.6%
1960	208	−20.9%
1970	202	−2.9%
1980	408	102.0%
1990	467	14.5%
2000	790	69.2%
2010	843	6.7%
Est. 2014	786 [6]	−6.8%

Historic Population of Hinsdale County

want to keep Hinsdale County "just like it is." But Hinsdale County and Lake City have and will continue to change even with that attitude.

Change will happen — even if there is a formal no growth policy in Hinsdale County. If wealthy people want to live here, they will, no matter what the cost; but eventually only the super-rich will find it affordable to live in Hinsdale County, instead of the great cross section of our society that now lives here. Wilderness and National Forests are great draws for tourists, but perhaps the local economy could be helped more if there were more private, trained guides and facilities for making sure that those tourists really see and understand what is here and are motivated to protect it. Fall is a time when our San Juan Mountains are at their best. The nights are cool and the days are warm, but not too warm. The rivers are low, the fishing is good, there often is a dusting of new snow on the mountains making them even more beautiful, and the roads are usually still open in most of the high country. One can enjoy a fire at night; and the animals are at their physical peak after the rejuvenation of the summer foliage and warm days. It is a very special time and yet there are only a fraction of the tourists here in the fall compared to the summer. Perhaps just education could bring more tourists in the fall, or maybe something else is needed.

Keeping our history alive is very important. A rural feeling and old-fashioned values are important draws, and both rely heavily on the past. Keep the historic buildings looking old, but not as a pile of scrap lumber lying on the ground. Let us point out the secluded places to winter and summer tourists, instead of reserving them for the locals. If we make sure that the visitors understand what we have here, then they and their families will keep coming back for generations, just as they have since the 1950s and before. Let us try to keep control of our environment in a way that the locals understand and agree with and not relying simply on federal and state governments. Duane Vandenbusche wrote:

> *With proper planning and courageous leadership, growth can be accommodated in almost all areas where energy and recreation have an impact.*[883]

We need to identify what we want to keep and what we wish to change and then plan for those goals. Recently the local governments have done a very good job of this. Let's make sure it continues. So how do we keep the way of life we have in Lake City? First we need to identify it, then we need to protect it as we change to make Lake City and Hinsdale County even better, and "Keep it just like it is" is not an answer.

BIBLIOGRAPHY

Athearn, Robert G., *The Coloradans*, University of New Mexico Press, Albuquerque, New México, 1976.

Baggs, Mae Lacy, *Colorado: The Queen Jewel of the Rockies*, The Page Company, Boston, Mass., 1918.

Bancroft, Hubert Howe, *History of Colorado*, Western Reflections Publishing, Lake City, Colorado, 2008. (A Reprint of a portion of *History of the Pacific States of North America, 1540 to 1880*. Printed in 1888).

Banks, James E., *Alferd Packer Wilderness Cookbook*, Filter Press, Palmer Lake, Colorado, 1998.

Bauer, William H., Ozment, James L., Wilard, John H., *Colorado Post Offices, 1859-1989*, Colorado Railroad Museum, Golden, Colorado, 1990.

Bell, John C., *The Pilgrim and the Pioneer*, Self-Published, Montrose, Colorado, 1906.

Benson, J. Henry, *Pioneer Ranching in the Rockies*, World Publishing Co., Apache Junction, Arizona, 1999.

Blair, Rob, Editor, *The Western San Juan Mountains*, University Press of Colorado, Durango, Colorado, 1996.

Brown, Robert L., *An Empire of Silver*, Sundance Books, Denver, Colorado, 1984.

Bryant, Stewart, *Freemont's Failed Fourth Expedition 1848-49, A Modern Trail Guide*, Self-Published, Del Norte, Colorado, 2012.

Burke, Marril Lee, *A Bumpy Ride*, Western Reflections Publishing Co., Lake City, Colorado, 2007

Burke, Marril Lee, *Ghosts of the Lake Fork*, Western Reflections Publishing Company, Lake City, Colorado, 2009.

Carhart, Arthur H., *Colorado*, Coward-McCann, New York, 1932.

Crofutt, George R., *Crofutt's Grip-Sack Guide to Colorado*, The Overland Publishing Co, Omaha, Nebraska, 1885.

Cross, Whitman and Larsen, Esper S., *A Brief Review of the Geology of the San Juan Region of Southwestern Colorado*, USGS Bulletin 843, Washington, D.C., 1933.

Crouter, George, *Colorado's Highest*, Sundance Books, Silverton, Colorado, 1977.

Dallas, Sandra, *Gaslights and Gingerbread*, Sage Books, Chicago, 1965.

Darley, George M., *Pioneering in the San Juan*, Reprint of 1899 original by Western Reflections Publishing Company, Lake City, Colorado.

Eberhart, Perry, *Guide to the Colorado Ghost Towns and Mining Camps*, Sage Books, Denver, Colorado, 1959.

Enss, Chris, *The Lady was a Gambler*, Twodot Press, Helena, Montana, 2006.

Fandrich, J. W., *The Slumgullion Earthflow*, Self-Published, Lake City, Colorado, 1968.

Farmer, Mary Hotchkiss and Farmer, Lee McMurray, *In the Footsteps of the Hotchkiss Brothers*, Self-Published, 2009.

Felts, Kenneth, *Oen Edgar Noland*, Western Reflections Publishing Co., Lake City, Colorado, 2013.

Fossett, Frank, *Colorado, Its Gold and Silver Mines... Tourists Guide to the Rocky Mountains*, Self Published, New York, 1879.

Gantt, Paul H., *The Case of Alfred Packer, The Man-Eater*, University of Denver Press, Denver, Colorado, 1952.

Gibbons, Rev. J.J., *In the San Juans*, St. Daniels Church, Calumet Book and Engraving Co., 1898, reprinted by Western Reflections Publishing Co., Lake City, Colorado, 2008.

Griffiths, Mel, *San Juan Country*, Pruett Publishing Co., Boulder, Colorado, 1984

Griswold, Don and Jean, *Colorado's Century of "Cities,"* Published by Authors, Denver, Colorado, 1958.

Hafen, LeRoy R. and Ann, *The Colorado Story*, The Old West Publishing Co., Denver, Colorado, 1953.

Hall, Frank, *History of Colorado*, Vols, II and IV, Chicago 1890 and 1895, Reprinted by Western Reflections Publishing Company, Lake City, Colorado, 2008.

Henderson, Charles W., *Mining in Colorado*, U.S.G.S. Professional Paper 138, Washington, D. C., 1926.

Hinshaw, Glen, *Crusaders for Wildlife*, Western Reflections Publishing Co., Ouray, Colorado, 2000.

Houston, Grant, *Lake City Reflections*, Self-Published, Lake City, Colorado, No Date.

Howard, George, *Howard's Diary 1872-73*, original diary at Montrose County Library, unpublished.

Huston, Richard, *A Gold Camp Called Summitville*, Western Reflections Publishing Co., Lake City, Colorado, 2012.

Ingersoll, Ernest, *Crest of the Continent*, R.R. Donnelley and Son, Chicago, 1885 (Reprinted by Western Reflections, Publishing Co., Lake City, Colorado, 2010.

Irving, John and Bancroft, Howland, *Geology and Ore Deposits Near Lake City, Colorado*, A Reprint of USGS Bulletin 478, Western Reflections Publishing Co., Lake City, Colorado, 2010.

Jocknick, Sidney, *Early Days on the Western Slope of Colorado*, The Carson-Harper Co., Denver, Colorado, 1913, Reprinted by Western Reflections Publishing Co., Montrose, Colorado, 1998.

Kaplan, Michael, *Otto Mears, Paradoxical Pathfinder*, San Juan County Book Company, Silverton, Colorado, 1982.

Kinquist, Kathy, *Stony Pass*, San Juan County Book Company, Silverton, Colorado, 1987.

Kushner, Ervan, *Alferd Packer, Cannibal! Victim?,*, Platte and Press, Frederick, Colorado, 1980.

LaMassena, Robert A., *Colorado's Mountain Railroads*, Sundance Books, Denver, Colorado, 1984.

Lampert, Lynn, *Lakes City Places*, Golden Stone Press, Lake City, Colorado, 1999.

Lampert, Lynn, *Lake City Serendipity*, Golden Stone Press, Lake City, Colorado, 2004.

Lawrence, John, *Frontier Eyewitness*, Saguache County Museum, 1990.

Martin, MaryJoy, *Something in the Wind*, Pruett Publishing Co., Boulder, CO, 2001.

Mazzula, Fred and Jo, *Al Packer, A Colorado Cannibal*, Self-Published, Denver, Colorado, 1968.

Monroe, Arthur, *San Juan Silver*, A Reprint by Western Reflections Publishing Co., Lake City, Colorado, 2009.

Morse, Milo Z. and Bielser, Faye, *A Brief History of Mining in Hinsdale County*, Published by Authors, 2000.

Newburn, Ray L., *Postal History of the Colorado San Juan*, Unpublished Manuscript, copy in author's possession.

Nichols, Jack, *Under the Sun at Lake City*, Cannibal Publishing Co., Lake City, Colorado, 1995.

Nosserman, Allen, *Many More Mountains, Vols. I*, II, and III, Sundance Books, Denver, Colorado, 1989, 1993, 1998.

O'Rourke, Paul M., *Frontier in Transition*, Bureau of Land Management Colorado, Cultural Resources Series, No. 10, 1980.

Oldham, Ann, *Alferd G. Packer, Soldier, Prospector and Cannibal*, Published by Author, 2005.

Rawson, Downing O., *Carson Country*, Self-Published, no date.

Reyher, Ken, *Silver and Sawdust, Life in the San Juans*, Western Reflections Publishing Co., Ouray, Colorado, 2000.

Reyher, Ken, *Through the Valley of the Shadow of Death*, Western Reflections Publishing, Lake City, Colorado, 2009.

Rhoda, Franklin, *Summits to Reach, Reports on the Topography of the San Juan Country*, Edited and Comments by Mike Foster, Pruett Publishing, Boulder, Colorado, 1984.

Rickard, T. A., *Across the San Juan Mountains*, Denver Publishing Co., San Francisco, California (Reprinted from *Journeys of Observation*, 1907).

Rockwell, Wilson, *Sunset Slope*, Reprinted by Western Reflections Publishing Co, Ouray, Colorado, 1999.

Ruffner, Lt. E. H., *Reconnaissance of the Ute Country, Made in the Year 1873*, Government Printing Office, Washington, D.C., 1874.

Sammons, Judy Buffington, *Keepin' the Peace*, Western Reflections Publishing Co., Lake City, Colorado, 2010.

Saguache County @ Saguache.html

Sarah Platte Decker Chapter, N.S.D.A.R., *Pioneers of the San Juan Country, Vols. I-IV*, Out West Printing, Colorado Springs, Colorado, 1942, 1946, 1954, 1961.

Scamehorn, *Albert Eugene Reynolds, Colorado's Mining King*, University of Oklahoma Press, Norman, Oklahoma, 1995.

Shores, "Doc" Cyrus, *Memoirs of a Lawman*, edited by Wilson Rockwell, Sage Books, Denver, Colorado, reprinted by Western Reflections Publishing Company.

Simmons, Virginia McConnell, *The San Luis Valley*, University Press opf Colorado, Boulder, Colorado, 1999.

Sloan, Robert E. and Skowronski, Carl A., *The Rainbow Route*, Sundance Publications, Denver, Colorado, 1975.

Smith, Duane A., *Rocky Mountain Mining Camps*, Reprint by Western Reflections Publishing Company, Lake City, Colorado, 2009.

Smith, Duane, *San Juan Gold*, Western Reflections Publishing Company, Montrose, Colorado, 2002.

Smith, Duane A., *Sisters in Sin*, Western Reflections Publishing Co., Lake City, Colorado, 2011.

Smith, Duane, *Song of the Hammer and Drill*, Colorado School of Mines Press, Golden, Colorado, 1982.

Smith, P. David, *Exploring the Historic San Juan Triangle*, Wayfinder Press, Ridgway, Colorado, 2004.

Smith, P. David, *Ouray: Chief of the Utes*, Wayfinder Press, Ouray, Colorado, 1986.

Smith, P. David, *The San Juan Mountain of Southwestern Colorado, Calderas, Mastadons, Conquistadors, and Gold*, Western Reflections Publishing Co., Lake City, Colorado, 2013.

Smith, P. David and Bezek, Lyn, *On the Backs of Burros*, Western Reflections Publishing Company, Lake City, Colorado, 2010.

Spencer, Frank C., *The Story of the San Luis Valley*, San Luis Valley Historical Society, Alamosa, Colorado, 1975.

Sprague, Marshall, *The Great Gates*, Little, Brown and Company, Boston, 1964.

Steele, Joe M., *Lake City Geology*, Self-Published, Lake City, Colorado, 2002.

Stigall, Mary, *Up Here*, Western Reflections Publishing, Montrose, Colorado, 2002.

Stiger, Mark, *Archeological Investigations of the Tenderfoot Site*, Western State College, Gunnison, Colorado, 1993.

Stiger, Mark, *Hunter-Gatherer Archeology of the Colorado High Country*, University Press of Colorado, Boulder, Colorado, 2001.

Stone, Wilbur Fisk, *History of Colorado*, Vol. 1, The S. J. Clarke Publishing Co., Chicago, 1918.

Strahorn, Robert Edmund, *Gunnison and the San Juans*, 1880, Reprint by Western Reflections Publishing Co., Lake City, Colorado, 2012.

Swank, Joel, Mountain Memories, Mennonite Press, North Newton, Kansas.

Thomas, D. B., *From Fort Massachusetts to the Rio Grande*, Self-Published, 2002.

Thompson, Thomas Gray, *The Social and Cultural History of Lake City, Colorado, 1876 to 1900*, University of Oklahoma Master of Arts Thesis, Norman Oklahoma, 1961 (also Self-published, Oklahoma City, Oklahoma, 1974.

Tucker, E.F., *Otto Mears and the San Juans*, Western Reflections Publishing Co., Montrose, Colorado, 2003.

Vandenbusche, Duane and Smith, Duane, *A Land Alone: Colorado's Western Slope*, Pruett Publishing, Boulder, Colorado, 1981.

Vandenbusche, Duane, *Early Days in the Gunnison Country*, Self-Published, Gunnison, Colorado, 1974.

Vandenbusche, Duane, *The Gunnison Country*, Self-Published, Gunnison, Colorado, 1980.

Vickers, Purk, *Welcome Home, The Story of the Vickers Ranch*, Self-Published, Lake City, Colorado, 1989.

Vinton, L. A. & Co., *Resources and Mineral Wealth of Hinsdale County*, Lake City, self published, 1900.

Wallace, Betty, *Epitaph for an Editor*, Self-Published, Gunnison, Colorado, 1987.

Wallace, Betty, *Gunnison Country*, Sage Books, Denver, 1961.

Wallace, Betty, *History with the Hide Off*, Sage Books, Denver, Colorado, 1964.

Westermeier, Clifford P., *Colorado's First Portrait: Scenes by Early Artists*, University of New Mexico Press, Albuquerque, New Mexico, 1970.

Wickerman, Laurel Michele and LeBaron, Rawlene, *Mine Owners and Mines of the Colorado Gold Rush*, Heritage Books, Westminister, Maryland, 2004.

Wilkins, Tivis E., *Colorado Railroads*, Self Published, Boulder, Colorado, 1974.

William's Tourists Guide and Map of the San Juan Mines of Colorado, Cubar Reprint, 1965 of 1877 Original.

Williams, Ruby, *Otto Mears, Pathfinder of the San Juans*, Self-Published, 1985.

Wise, Joe, *A Sense of Place*, Western Reflections Publishing Co., Montrose, Colorado, 2003.

Wolle, Muriel Sibell, *Stampede to Timberline*, Published by Author, Denver, Colorado, 1949.

Wolle, Muriel, *Timberline Tailings*, Sage Books, Chicago, Illinois, 1977.

Womack, Linda R., *Our Ladies of the Tenderloin, Colorado's Legends in Lace*, Caxton Press, Caldwell, Idaho, 2005.

Wood, Frances and Dorothy, *I Hauled These Mountains in Here*, Caxton Printers, Caldwell, Idaho, 1977.

Wood, Stanley, *Over the Range to the Golden Gate*, R.R. Donnelley & Sons, Chicago, Illinois, 1905.

Wright, Carolyn and Clarence, *Tiny Hinsdale of the Silvery San Juan*, Western Reflections Publishing Co., Lake City, Colorado, 2012 (Reprint with additional material, 1964).

Wyman, Mark, *Hard Rock Epic*, University of California Press, Berkley, California, 1979.

PAMPHLETS, MAGAZINES, AND NEWSPAPER ARTICLES

Bancroft, Caroline, *Unique Ghost Towns and Mountain Spots*, Johnson Publishing Co, Boulder, Colorado, 1961.

Bates, Margaret, *A Quick History of Lake City, Colorado*, Little London Press, Colorado Springs, Colorado, 1973.

Battles, Rodney, "Banking in Lake City," no date, self-published.

Brenneman, Bill, "Take the Jeep Trails," *Colorado Wonderland Magazine*, June 1956.

Borland, Dr. Lois, "Sale of the San Juans," *The Colorado Magazine*, Vol. 28, No. 2, April, 1951.

Brown, W. Horatio, "The Mineral Zones of the Whitecross District and Neighboring Deposits in Hinsdale County, Colorado," *The Colorado School of Mines Magazine*, Vol. XV, Number 11, March, 1926.

Chavez, Lorenzo, "Hinsdale Home to Hunting and Fishing," *Colorado History News*, Colorado Historical Society, July 1996.

Churchill, E. Richard, *Doc Holiday, Bat Masterson & Wyatt Earp – Their Colorado Careers*, Western Reflections Publishing Co., Ouray, CO, undated.

Collman, Russ, "The Lake City Branch," *Trails Among the Columbine*, Sundance Publications, pgs. 166-192, Denver, Colorado, 1988.

Curry, Andrew, "Case of the Colorado Cannibal," *Archeology Magazine*, May/June 2002.

Dunlee, Edward V., "Colorado Cannibalism," *1946 Denver Brand Book*, The Westerners, Denver, Colorado, 1946.

Fenwick, Robert W., *Alfred Packer – The True Story of the Maneater*, Publishers Press, Denver, Colorado, 1963.

Foster, Mike, "Mapping Mountains – A.D. Wilson, Nineteenth Century Colorado Cartographer," *Colorado Heritage Magazine*, 1988, Issue 4, Colorado Historical Society, Denver, Colorado.

Gray, John S., "Young Fur Trapper," *Colorado Heritage Magazine*, Denver, Colorado.

Harvey, Mark W. T., "Misguided Reformer, *Colorado Heritage Magazine*, Issue 1, Denver, Colorado, 1982.

Houston, Grant, *Historic Homes of Lake City, Colorado*, Hinsdale County Hitorical Museum, Lake City, Colorado, 2002.

Houston, "Lake City's Meoldy of the Past," *Trails Among the Columbine*, Pgs. 135-165, Sundance Publications, Denver, Colorado, 1988.

Kaplan, Michael, "Colorado's Big Little Man: The Early Career of Otto Mears, 1840-1881," *Western States Jewish Quarterly*, Vol. IV, Number 3, April, 1972.

Mason, Edna, "Peeking Through the Aspen", *Trails Among the Columbine*, Sundance Publications, Denver, Colorado, 1988, Pgs. 166-192.

McConell, Virginia, "Baker and the San Juan Humbug," *Colorado Historical Society Magazine*, Issue 1, 1982Vol. 48, No. 1, 1971.

Pitney, Margaret Rawson, *My Lake City Railroad Memories*, Hinsdale County Historical Museum, Lake City, Colorado, 2005.

Ruhoff, Ron, "Back Country Adventures in Mineral and Hinsdale Counties," *Trails Among the Columbine*, Pgs. 104-135, Sundance Publications, Denver, Colorado, 1988.

Sabin, Edward L., *Around the Circle, A Thousand Miles Through the Rockies*, Passenger Department of the Denver & Rio Grande Railroad, 1913.

Saguache County@saguache.html.

Silver World Newspaper, Various issues.

Smith, Duane, *Ho for the San Juans*, Center for Southwest Studies, No Date

Smith, Duane, "The San Juaner: A Computerized Portrait," *Colorado Magazine*, Colorado Historical Society, Spring 1975, Vol. 52, Issue 2, Denver, Colorado.

Smith, Duane A., "My Profit, Your Land, Colorado Mining and the Environment, 1858-1900, in *A Taste of the West*, Pruett Publishing Co., Boulder, Colorado, 1983.

Stanfield, E. E., *Souvenir Song of the San Juan,* Self Published, 1949.

Thompson, Thomas Gray, "Early Development of Lake City, *The Colorado Magazine,* April, 1963, Vol. XL, Number 2.

Vandenbusche, Duane and Borneman, Walter, "The D&RG Lake City Branch and a Galloping Goose," *Colorado Rail Annual No. 14,* Pgs. 25-110, Colorado Railroad Museum, Golden, CO 1979.

ENDNOTES

1   Griswold, *Colorado's Century of "Cities,"* pg. 231.
2   Irving and Bancroft, *Geology and Ore Deposits Near Lake City, Colorado,* pgs. 12-13.
3   Thompson, *The Social and Cultural History of Lake City, Colorado, 1876-1900,* pg. v.
4   Thompson quoting from D.A.R., "At Telluride and Lake City," *Pioneers of the San Juan Country, Vol. II,* pg. 94.
5   Vandenbusche, *A Land Alone: Colorado's Western Slope,* pg. 1.
6   Thompson, *The Social and Cultural History of Lake City, Colorado, 1876 to 1900,* pg. 1 of thesis.
7   Mazzula, *Al Packer, A Colorado Cannibal,* pg. 496.
8   Only a few very small remnants of glaciers exist in the San Juan Mountains today.
9   Nichols, *Under the Sun at Lake City,* pg. 6.
10   Bancroft, *History of Colorado,* pg. 496.
11   Burke, *Ghosts of the Lake Fork,* pgs. 6-7.
12   See Stiger, *Hunter-Gatherer Archeology of the Colorado High Country,* and Stiger, *Archeological Investigations of the Tenderfoot Site.*
13   For information on early Native Americans see Smith, *The San Juan Mountains of Southwestern Colorado: Calderas, Mastodons, Conquistadors and Gold,* Chapter 3.
14   Burton Smith from Ft. Union map. Burton also relates that the Utes called the Gunnison "The Eagle Tail."
15   Burke, *Ghosts of the Lake Fork,* pg. 13.
16   Vandenbusche, *A Land Alone: Colorado's Western Slope,* pg. 12.
17   Vandenbusche, *A Land Alone: Colorado's Western Slope,* pg. 14.
18   The Shoshone, relatives of the Utes, lived in the north and were generally friendly. The Ute territory blended into their much poorer relatives the Piutes in the Great Basin to the west. See Smith, *Exploring the Historic San Juan Triangle,* pg. 217.
19   Spanish prospecting in the San Juans could have even occurred as early as a Coronado subgroup in 1540.
20   Burton Smith reports rocks with Spanish symbols or words in the Weminuche Wilderness.
21   See Smith, *The San Juan Mountains of Southwestern Colorado: Calderas, Mastodons, Conquistadors and Gold,* Chapters 7-9 for Spanish occupation of the San Juans.
22   Kinquist, *Stony Pass,* pg. 17.
23   Houston, *Lake City Reflections,* pg. 11.
24   Historians still argue about the exact route of Fremont's party, although every few

years someone declares they have found the "real" route.

25 Burke, *Ghosts of the Lake Fork,* pg. 15.

26 Simmons, "Captain Baker and the San Juan Humbug," pg. 61, footnote 91.

27 Simmons, "Captain Baker and the San Juan Humbug," footnote 13.

28 Nosserman, *Many More Mountains, Vol. I,* pg. 37, and Sprague, *The Great Gates,* pgs. 177-178.

29 Nosserman, *Many More Mountains, Vol. I,* pgs. 65-66.

30 January 21, 1861.

31 McConnell, "Captain Baker and the San Juan Humbug," *The Colorado Magazine,* pg. 61.

32 Nosserman, *Many More Mountains, Vol. I* Pg. 63 for a fairly complete list of people in the party.

33 Vandenbusche, *A Land Alone: Colorado's Western Slope,* pg. 45.

34 *Rocky Mountain News,* January 2, 1861.

35 Bancroft, *History of Colorado,* pg. 497.

36 Jocknick, *Early Days on the Western Slope of Colorado,* pg. 348.

37 Jocknick, *Early Days on the Western Slope of Colorado,* pg. 354.

38 For information on early Native Americans see Smith, *The San Juan Mountains of Southwestern Colorado: Calderas, Mastodons, Conquistadors and Gold,* Chapter 3.

39 It has been estimated that at this time approximately 60,000 Americans, mostly young men, were in Colorado as opposed to 8,000 Utes, many of whom were women and children.

40 Brown, *An Empire of Silver,* pg. 27.

41 Simmons, "Captain Baker and the San Juan Humbug," pg. 13.

42 Brown, *An Empire of Silver,* pg. 27.

43 Huston, *A Gold Camp Called Summitville,* pg. 27.

44 Huston, *A Gold Camp Called Summitville,* pg.30.

45 Huston, *A Gold Camp Called Summitville,* pgs. 28-29.

46 Huston, *A Gold Camp Called Summitville,* pg. 26.

47 Howard, *Howard's Diary.*

48 Hafen, *The Colorado Story,* pgs. 24-25.

49 The Ute had trouble pronouncing the English "r," and therefore Ouray's name was initially spelled "Ure" in Spanish and Ulay in English.

50 Author's search of courthouse records.

51 Author's search of courthouse records.

52 The higher mining location figure probably included those filed at Summitville.

53 Nosserman, *Many More Mountains, Vol. I,* pg. 137.

54 Morse, *A Brief History of Mining in Hinsdale County,* pg. 25.

55 Recorded in D.A.R. *Pioneers of the San Juan Country,* Vol. II, pgs. 36-38.

56 Recorded in D.A.R. *Pioneers of the San Juan Country,* Vol. II, pgs. 36-38.

57 Kaplan, "Colorado's Big Little Man: The Early Career of Otto Mears, 1840-1881," pg. 119.

58 This was not the same Loutsenhizer who was with the Alfred Packer party, although O. D. Loutzenhizer was in the area shortly after Youmans left for Saguache in December with 100 pounds of furs. Wallace, *History with the Hide Off,* pg. 190.

59 Both men were also later Hinsdale County Sheriffs, according to ex-Sheriff Burton Smith.

60 Hall, *History of Colorado, Vol. II,* pg. 192.

61 Hall, *History of Colorado, Vol. II,* pg. 191.

62 Jocknick, *Early Days on the Western Slope of Colorado,* pg. 368.

63 Rufner, *Reconnaissance of the Ute Country,* pgs. 2-3.

64 Rufner, *Reconnaissance of the Ute Country,* pgs. 11-12.

65 Kinquist, *Stony Pass,* pg. 35.

66 Rufner, *Reconnaissance of the Ute Country,* pg. 27.

67   Rufner, *Reconnaissance of the Ute Country*, pg. 29.
68   Lampert, *Lake City Places*, pg. 11. Burton Smith notes that the lake was still spelled "San Cristoval" by a *New York Times* reporter in 1921, but from this point we will use the current day spelling.
69   Rufner, *Reconnaissance of the Ute Country*, pg. 30.
70   Rufner, *Reconnaissance of the Ute Country*, pg. 31.
71   This last name is probably where Capitol City actually received its name, even though the mountain cannot be seen from there. Another possibility was that there was a Capitol Mine in that area before the town was named.
72   Rufner, *Reconnaissance of the Ute Country*, pg. 32.
73   Rufner, *Reconnaissance of the Ute Country*, pg. 32.
74   Rufner, *Reconnaissance of the Ute Country*, pg. 33.
75   Rufner, *Reconnaissance of the Ute Country*, pg. 34.
76   Rufner, *Reconnaissance of the Ute Country*, pg. 35.
77   Shortly thereafter this was no longer necessary as Indian tribes were not considered to be nations, in great part because they had no concept of the private ownership of land.
78   *Silver World*, May 22, 1880.
79   Nosserman, *Many More Mountains, Vol. I*, pg. 229.
80   Kinquist, *Stony Pass*, pg. 29.
81   Kushner, *Alferd Packer, Cannibal! Victim?,*, pg. 19.
82   O'Rourke, "Frontier in Transition," pg. 62.
83   Nosserman, *Many More Mountains, Vol. I*, pg. 148.
84   Nosserman, *Many More Mountains, Vol. I*, pg. 188.
85   Rhoda, *Summits to Reach, Reports on the Topography of the San Juan Country*, pgs. 12-16.
86   Rhoda, *Summits to Reach, Reports on the Topography of the San Juan Country*, pg. 17.
87   Burton Smith.
88   Rhoda, *Summits to Reach, Reports on the Topography of the San Juan Country*, pgs. 20-26.
89   Rhoda, *Summits to Reach, Reports on the Topography of the San Juan Country*, pgs. 20-25.
90   Rhoda, *Summits to Reach, Reports on the Topography of the San Juan Country*, pgs. 29-30.
91   Rhoda, *Summits to Reach, Reports on the Topography of the San Juan Country*, pgs. 32 & 46.
92   Chavez, "Hinsdale Home to Hunting and Fishing," pg. 9.
93   Fenwick, *Alfred Packer – The True Story of the Maneater*, pg. 50.
94   He was convicted of manslaughter not cannibalism.
95   Gantt, *The Case of Alfred Packer, The Man-Eater*, pg. 57.
96   Some authors report that he was born on January 21, 1842. Local Packer authority Michelle Pierce cites census records that show he was born in Indiana.
97   He used the age twenty-four at the time of this story, although he was actually thirty-one.
98   Kushner, *Alferd Packer, Cannibal! Victim?*, pgs. 13-14.
99   April 4, 1862 to December, 1862.
100   Oldham, *Alferd, Soldier, Prospector and Cannibal*, pg. 4.
101   Kushner, *Alferd Packer, Cannibal! Victim?,*, pg. 16.
102   Oldham, *Alferd Packer, Soldier, Prospector and Cannibal*, pg. 8.
103   Some authorities say Provo, Utah.
104   Kushner, *Alferd Packer, Cannibal! Victim?*, pg. 18.
105   Jocknick, *Early Days on the Western Slope of Colorado*, pgs. 60-62.
106   Jocknick, *Early Days on the Western Slope of Colorado*, pg. 60.

107   In fact he was 31 or 32.

108   Kushner, *Alferd Packer, Cannibal! Victim?*, pg. 17.

109   Kushner, *Alferd Packer, Cannibal! Victim?*, pg. 19.

110   Gantt, *The Case of Alfred Packer, The Man-Eater*, pg. 234.

111   Gantt, *The Case of Alfred Packer, The Man-Eater*, pg. 240.

112   Kushner, *Alferd Packer, Cannibal! Victim?*, pg. 19.

113   Jocknick, *Early Days on the Western Slope of Colorado*, pg. 63.

114   Kushner, *Alferd Packer, Cannibal! Victim?*, pg. 19.

115   They originally had two pistols, but the barrel of one exploded and they threw it away. Huston, *A Gold Camp Called Summitville*, pg. 112.

116   Oldham, *Alfred, Soldier, Prospector and Cannibal*, pg. 12.

117   Jocknick, *Early Days on the Western Slope of Colorado*, pgs. 55-56.

118   Gantt, *The Case of Alfred Packer, The Man-Eater*, pg. 26.

119   Jocknick, *Early Days on the Western Slope of Colorado*, pg. 57.

120   Some writers say three weeks, Jocknick says nine. Jocknick, *Early Days on the Western Slope of Colorado*, pg. 65.

121   Vandenbusche, *The Gunnison Country*, pg. 36.

122   Oldham, *Alfred, Soldier, Prospector and Cannibal*, pg. 12.

123   Jocknick, *Early Days on the Western Slope of Colorado*, pg. 65.

124   Rockwell, *Sunset Slope*, pg. 104.

125   Smith, *Ouray, Chief of the Utes*, pg. 120.

126   Kushner, *Alferd Packer, Cannibal! Victim?*, pg. 20.

127   Fenwick, *Alfred Packer: The True Story of the Maneater*, pg. 4.

128   The store was started as a trading post with the Utes in 1868 but had recently been expanded into a full mercantile business.

129   Kushner, *Alferd Packer, Cannibal! Victim?*, pg. 20.

130   Kushner, *Alferd Packer, Cannibal! Victim?*, pg. 98.

131   Cross and Larsen, *A Brief Review of the Geology of the San Juan Region of Southwestern Colorado*, pg. 99.

132   Oldham, *Alfred, Soldier, Prospector and Cannibal*, pg. 18.

133   Jocknick, *Early Days on the Western Slope of Colorado*, pg. 74.

134   Actually this was questionable as no one knew for sure where the crime, if any, had occurred.

135   Wright, *Tiny Hinsdale of the Silvery San Juan*, pg. 128, and Jocknick, *Early Days on the Western Slope of Colorado*, pg. 73, among others.

136   Jocknick, *Early Days on the Western Slope of Colorado*, pg. 74.

137   Kushner, *Alferd Packer, Cannibal! Victim?*, pg. 21.

138   Gantt, *The Case of Alfred Packer, The Man-Eater*, pg. 36.

139   Kushner, *Alferd Packer, Cannibal! Victim?*, pgs. 24-25.

140   Kushner, *Alferd Packer, Cannibal! Victim?*, pg. 76.

141   Gantt, *The Case of Alfred Packer, The Man-Eater*, pg. 39.

142   There is some evidence that the party might have been on the Cebolla and that Packer was telling the truth, but Nutter later testified that the search party went down the Cebolla to Powderhorn Creek, then over to and down Indian Creek, and it was on the Lake Fork that Packer said he was lost. Kushner, *Alferd Packer, Cannibal! Victim?*, pg. 69.

143   Gantt, *The Case of Alfred Packer, The Man-Eater*, pg. 39.

144   Gantt, *The Case of Alfred Packer, The Man-Eater*, pg. 240.

145   The Graham party could not have made it to the agency and had the Del Norte paper report on their discovery in just two days, so they obviously found the bodies before Randolph. Michelle Pierce pointed this out to this author.

146   O'Rourke, "Frontier in Transition," pg. 61.

147   Fenwick, *Alfred Packer – The True Story of the Maneater*, pg. 50.

148   Kushner, *Alferd Packer, Cannibal! Victim?*, pg. 245.

149 Oldham, *Alfred, Soldier, Prospector and Cannibal*, pg. 22.

150 Oldham, *Alfred, Soldier, Prospector and Cannibal*, pg. 24.

151 Kaplan, *Otto Mears, Paradoxical Pathfinder*, pg. 66.

152 Dunlee, "Colorado Cannibalism," pg. 101.

153 Kushner, *Alferd Packer, Cannibal! Victim?*, pg. 31.

154 Gantt, *The Case of Alfred Packer, The Man-Eater*, pg. 132.

155 Kushner, *Alferd Packer, Cannibal! Victim?*, pg. 247.

156 Gantt, *The Case of Alfred Packer, The Man-Eater*, pg. 51.

157 Kushner, *Alferd Packer, Cannibal! Victim?*, pg. 31.

158 Kushner, *Alferd Packer, Cannibal! Victim?*, pg. 238.

159 Gantt, *The Case of Alfred Packer, The Man-Eater*, pg. 57.

160 It was true that Lake San Cristobal had no fish at this time due to the two giant waterfalls just downstream.

161 If he went, he would have gone up today's Slumgullion Pass. Smith, *Ouray, Chief of the Utes*, pg. 126.

162 Kushner, *Alferd Packer, Cannibal! Victim?*, pgs. 80 & 82.

163 Jocknick, *Early Days on the Western Slope of Colorado*, pgs. 45 & 114.

164 Gantt, *The Case of Alfred Packer, The Man-Eater*, pg. 57.

165 Hinsdale County had probably been created by the time of the crime, but Colorado did not become a state until 1876.

166 Dunlee, "Colorado Cannibalism," pg. 102.

167 Wallace, *History with the Hide Off*, pg. 180.

168 Michelle Pierce believes this part of Packer's story is plausible, as he was obviously going up the Lake Fork towards Lake San Cristobal, instead of downstream. Perhaps with snow and ice over the river he truly couldn't tell. Michelle believes it is possible the "lake" was actually the present-day Vickers ranch. Packer said he believed it a lake because there was no vegetation, but there might or might not have been vegetation there in 1874, and he said they continued upstream from the "lake" to camp. The camps that were later found were downstream from the lake and upstream from the Vicker's ranch.

169 Wright, *Tiny Hinsdale of the Silvery San Juan*, pg. 131.

170 Wallace, *History with the Hide Off*, pg. 180.

171 Kushner believes Packer stole over $6,000.

172 Morse and Bielser, *A Brief History of the Colorado San Juan*, pg. 13.

173 Packer was never charged with cannibalism.

174 Burton Smith points out that it was highly unlikely that Packer would have caught beaver in a lake frozen with up to three feet of ice.

175 Gantt, *The Case of Alfred Packer, The Man-Eater*, pg. 59. The jury should not have used their own information in the case.

176 Dunlee, *Colorado Cannibalism*, pg. 32.

177 Judge Gerry's sentence appears in print in several books, but with minor differences. This version is the most grammatically correct.

178 Dunlee, *Colorado Cannibalism*, pg. 32.

179 Wallace, *Epitaph for an Editor*, pg. 99.

180 Wallace, *History with the Hide Off*, pg. 182.

181 Gantt, *The Case of Alfred Packer, The Man-Eater*, pg. 166. One of these can be seen today at the Hinsdale County Museum.

182 Shores, "Doc" Cyrus, pg. 341.

183 Gantt, *The Case of Alfred Packer, The Man-Eater*, pg. 167.

184 Shores, "Doc" Cyrus, pg. 343.

185 Shores, "Doc" Cyrus, pg. 341.

186 Shores, "Doc" Cyrus, pg. 343.

187 Shores, "Doc" Cyrus, pg. 340.

188 Gantt, *The Case of Alfred Packer, The Man-Eater*, pg. 84.

189 Kushner, *Alferd Packer, Cannibal! Victim?*, pg. 48.
190 Kushner, *Alferd Packer, Cannibal! Victim?*, pg. 50.
191 Oldham, *Alferd, Soldier, Prospector and Cannibal*, pg. 42.
192 Dunlee, *Colorado Cannibalism*, pg. 33.
193 Gantt, *The Case of Alfred Packer, The Man-Eater*, pg. 83.
194 Nosserman, *Many More Mountains, Vol. I*, pg. 114.
195 Gantt, *The Case of Alfred Packer, The Man-Eater*, pg. 85.
196 Gantt, *The Case of Alfred Packer, The Man-Eater*, pgs. 252 &256.
197 Gantt, *The Case of Alfred Packer, The Man-Eater*, pg. 257.
198 Gantt, *The Case of Alfred Packer, The Man-Eater*, pg. 281.
199 Dunlee, *Colorado Cannibalism*, pgs. 105-351.
200 May 5, 1900.
201 Dunlee, *Colorado Cannibalism*, pg. 39.
202 Wallace, *Epitaph for an Editor*, pg. 98.
203 Oldham, *Alferd, Soldier, Prospector and Cannibal*, pg. 133.
204 Gantt, *The Case of Alfred Packer, The Man-Eater*, pg. 290. The Mazzolas, very credible Colorado historians, write that he died August 23, 1907.
205 Fenwick, *Alfred Packer – The True Story of the Maneater*, pg. 52.
206 DAR Vol. II, pg.92
207 Fenwick, *Alfred Packer – The True Story of the Maneater*, pg. 52.
208   This latter conclusion does not agree with the *Harper's Weekly* drawing done at the time, the testimony of many witnesses, or the Lawrence affidavits.
209 Fenwick, *Alfred Packer – The True Story of the Maneater*, pg. 53.
210 This may or may not have been the "pepperbox" pistol, a very different type pistol, with three bullets still in the chamber that was found at the site of the massacre ten years after the event.
211 This is not quite correct but they were buried nearby.
212 This plaque was donated by Eddie Burke, later owner of the Ute-Ulay Mine and owner of the "San Christobal" (sic) Railroad. The site was proposed by the Lake City Women's Club and became a favorite picnic spot for the locals. Information from Burton Smith.
213 See Tucker, *Otto Mears and the San Juans*, for the entire Mears story.
214 Tucker, *Otto Mears and the San Juans*, pg. 27.
215 Tucker, *Otto Mears and the San Juans*, pg. 28.
216 Kaplan, "Colorado's Big Little Man: The Early Career of Otto Mears, 1840-1881," pg. 122.
217 Burke, *Ghosts of the Lake Fork*, pg. 65.
218 SaguacheCounty@saguache.html.
219 Famous newspaper editor and Mears' good friend, David F. Day, coined the title.
220 Ripley, *The Handclasp of the East and West*, pg. 95.
221 Kaplan, "Colorado's Big Little Man: The Early Career of Otto Mears, 1840-1881," pg. 119.
222 Lawrence, *Frontier Eyewitness*, pg. 52, and Simmons, *The San Luis Valley*, pg. 135.
223 Lawrence, *Frontier Eyewitness*, pg. 53.
224 Jocknick, *Early Days on the Western Slope of Colorado*.
225 Lawrence, *Frontier Eyewitness*, pg. 52.
226 Smith wrote an entire book on this premise – *Rocky Mountain Mining Camps*.
227 Griffiths, *San Juan Country*, pg. 133.
228 Kaplan, "Colorado's Big Little Man: The Early Career of Otto Mears, 1840-1881," pg. 122.
229 Jocknick, *Early Days on the Western Slope of Colorado*, pg. 238; Farmer and Farmer, *In the Footsteps of the Hotchkiss Brothers*, pg. 49; D.A.R., *Pioneers of the San Juan Country*, pg. 94.
230 Tucker, *Otto Mears and the San Juans*, pg. 34.

231 Michael Kaplan in his small book on Otto Mears (Kaplan, "Colorado's Big Little Man: The Early Career of Otto Mears, 1840-1881," pg. 128) states Mears paid Hotchkiss to survey and build the Saguache and San Juan Toll Road. That source also states that Mears financed the townsite of Lake City, but goes on to claim Mears paid Hotchkiss to build the Antelope Park- Lake City toll road, which is not correct.

232 Kaplan, "Colorado's Big Little Man: The Early Career of Otto Mears, 1840-1881," pgs. 117-127.

233 Vandenbusche, *The Gunnison Country*, pg. 64

234 *Silver World*, August 14,1875.

235 Kushner, *Alferd Packer, Cannibal! Victim?*, pg. 243.

236 Kushner, *Alferd Packer, Cannibal! Victim?*, pg. 244.

237 Kushner, *Alferd Packer, Cannibal! Victim?*, pgs. 244-245.

238 Nosserman, *Many More Mountains, Vol. II*, pg. 95.

239 Nosserman, *Many More Mountains, Vol. I*, pg. 213.

240 Nosserman, *Many More Mountains, Vol. II*, pg. 95.

241 Kushner, *Alferd Packer, Cannibal! Victim?*, pg. 240.

242 Williams, *Otto Mears, Pathfinder of the San Juans*, pg. 7.

243 Kinquist, *Stony Pass*, pg. 56.

244 Vandenbusche, *The Gunnison Country*, pg. 64.

245 Tucker, *Otto Mears and the San Juans*, pg. 34.

246 Wallace, *Epitaph for an Editor*, pg. 41.

247 Jocknick, *Early Days on the Western Slope of Colorado*, pg. 122.

248 *Silver World*, January 5, 1978.

249 Farmer and Farmer, *In the Footsteps of the Hotchkiss Brothers*, pg. 53.

250 Farmer and Farmer, *In the Footsteps of the Hotchkiss Brothers*, pg. 50.

251 Wallace, *History with the Hide Off*, pg. 17; Vandenbusche, *The Gunnison Country*, pg. 42.

252 Houston, "Lake City's Melody of the Past," pg. 146.

253 Author search of Hinsdale County records.

254 Vandenbusche and Smith, *A Land Alone: Colorado's Western Slope*, pg. 54.

255 Athearn, *The Coloradans*, pg. 129.

256 Some authors' claim Hotchkiss found the rich float himself.

257 Robert Brown.

258 Monroe, *San Juan Silver*, pg. 29.

259 Monroe, *San Juan Silver*, pg. 29.

260 Monroe, *San Juan Silver*, pg. 30.

261 Monroe, *San Juan Silver*, pg. 30.

262 Kushner, *Alferd Packer, Cannibal! Victim?*, Pgs. 247-248.

263 Farmer and Farmer, *In the Footsteps of the Hotchkiss Brothers*, pg. 53.

264 *Brief History of Mining* notes the name Hotchkiss Mine was used until November 1883 and by that time the original vein was lost and the mine was working a totally different nearby vein.

265 Hinsdale County Records.

266 Monroe, *San Juan Silver*, pg. 15.

267 Monroe, *San Juan Silver*, pg. 16.

268 Farmer and Farmer, *In the Footsteps of the Hotchkiss Brothers*, pg. 52.

269 Some authors claim the sale was only a lease for 100 feet of the mine.

270 Farmer and Farmer, *In the Footsteps of the Hotchkiss Brothers*, pg. 56.

271 Halls, Colorado, Vol. IV, pg. 155.

272 Farmer and Farmer, *In the Footsteps of the Hotchkiss Brothers*, pg. 50.

273 Burke, *Ghosts of the Lake Fork*, pg. 68.

274 Wallace, *Epitaph for an Editor*, pg. 2.

275 Morse and Bielser, *A Brief History of Mining in Hinsdale County*, pg. 26.

276 Author search of Hinsdale County records.
277 Jocknick, *Early Days on the Western Slope of Colorado*, pg. 311; Stone, *History of Colorado*, Vol. 1, Pg. 156.
278 Bancroft, *History of Colorado*, pg. 50.
279 Houston, "Lake City's Melody of the Past," pg. 153.
280 Wallace, *Epitaph for an Editor*, pg. 4
281 *Silver World,* 6/19/1875.
282 Nosserman, *Many More Mountains,* Vol 1, pg 298.
283 Reyher, *Silver and Sawdust*, pg. 35.
284 *Silver World,* 6/26/75.
285 See Burke, *A Bumpy Ride.*
286 Bell, *The Pilgrim and the Pioneer,* pg. 177.
287 Newburn, *Postal History of the Colorado San Juan*, pg. 13.
288 D.A.R., *Pioneers of the San Juan Country*, Vol. II, pg. 90.
289 Spencer, *The Story of the San Luis Valley*, pg. 56.
290 Wallace, *Gunnison Country*, pg. 65.
291 Kinquest, *Stony Pass*, pg. 38.
292 Kinquest, *Stony Pass*, pg. 40.
293 Houston, *Historic Homes of Lake City, Colorado.*
294 Houston, *Lake City Reflections,* pgs. 41-42.
295 Pitney, "My Lake City Railroad Memories," pgs. 2-11.
296 Pitney, "My Lake City Railroad Memories," pg. 12..
297 Pitney, "My Lake City Railroad Memories," pg. 17.
298 *Silver World,* June 19, 1875.
299 Reyher, *Silver and Sawdust, Life in the San Juans,* pg. 17.
300 *Silver World*, October 1, 1875.
301 Nosserman, *Many More Mountains, Vol. I,* pg. 253.
302 *Silver World*, July 3, 1875.
303 *Silver World*, July 3, 1875.
304 Fossett, *Colorado, Its Gold and Silver Mines,* pg. 515
305 Nosserman, *Many More Mountains, Vol. I,* pg. 213.
306 Vandenbusche and Borneman, "The D. & R. G. Lake City Branch and a Galloping Goose," pg. 31.
307 *Silver World,* June 19, 1875.
308 Jocknick, *Early Days on the Western Slope of Colorado,* pg. 239.
309 Wagon Wheel Gap and Powderhorn, *Silver World,* July 3, 1875.
310 Thompson, "Early Development of Lake City," pg. 95.
311 D.A.R., *Pioneers of the San Juan Country, Vol. II,* pg. 20.
312 *Silver World,* June 19, 1875.
313 At this time many people thought Uncompahgre the highest in Colorado, but it was later discovered to be fifth highest.
314 *Silver World*, January 19, 1875.
315 Thompson, *The Social and Cultural History of Lake City, Colorado, 1876 to 1900,* pg. 16.
316 D.A.R., *Pioneers of the San Juan Country, Vol. II,* pg. 88.
317 Bates, *A Quick History of Lake City,* pg. 8.
318 *Silver World*, January 29, 1876.
319 D.A.R., *Pioneers of the San Juan Country, Vol. II,* pg 58.
320 See Wright, *Tiny Hinsdale of the Silvery San Juan,* pg. 32 for details on post office locations in town and in the county's other settlements.
321 Smith, *Rocky Mountain Mining Camps,* pg. 81.
322 *Silver World,* July 10, 1875.
323 *Silver World,* August 7, 1875.
324 *Silver World,* August 14, 1875.

325 Vandenbusche, *Early days in the Gunnison Country,* pg. 37.

326 Vandenbusche, *Early days in the Gunnison Country,* pg. 67.

327 D.A.R., "Pioneers of the San Juan Country," *Vol. II,* Pioneers of Hinsdale County; Thompson, "Early Development of Lake City," pg. 95; and Wright, *Tiny Hinsdale of the Silvery San Juan,* pg. 12.

328 Houston, *Lake City Reflections,* pg. 28.

329 *Silver World,* December 25, 1875.

330 Quoted from Martin, *Something in the Wind,* pg. 30.

331 O'Rourke, *Frontier in Transition,* pg. 64.

332 Henderson, *Mining in Colorado,* pg. 51.

333 Various sources say the interest was 3/4, 11/16, and 15/16ths.

334 Darley, *Pioneering in the San Juan,* pgs. 16- 17.

335 D.A.R., *Pioneers of the San Juan Country, Vol. II,* pg. 56.

336 Fossett, *Colorado, Its Gold and Silver Mines,* pg. 53.

337 Wright, *Tiny Hinsdale of the Silvery San Juan,* pg. 12.

338 Burke, *Ghosts of the Lake Fork,* pg. 56.

339 One source states August 1, 1876.

340 *Silver World,* January 5, 1878.

341 *Rocky Mountain News,* June 28, 1876.

342 *Rocky Mountain News,* June 28, 1876.

343 *Silver World,* June 24, 1876.

344 Houston, *Lake City Reflections,* pg. 53.

345 Reyher, *Silver and Sawdust,* pg. 20.

346 Battles, *Banking in Lake City.*

347 Battles, *Banking in Lake City,* pg. 6.

348 Wright, *Tiny Hinsdale of the Silvery San Juan,* pg. 106.

349 Wolle, *Stampede to Timberline,* pg. 342.

350 Burton Smith.

351 Athearn, *The Coloradans,* pg. 87.

352 Smith, *San Juan Gold.*

353 Darley, Pioneering in the San Juans.

354 *Silver World,* February 2, 1876.

355 Thompson, *The Social and Cultural History of Lake City, Colorado, 1876-1900.* Some historians claim it was "Hell's Half Acre."

356 Nichols, *Under the Sun at Lake City,* pg. 53.

357 *Silver World,* September 2, 1876.

358 Thompson, *The Social and Cultural History of Lake City, Colorado, 1876-1900,* pg. 143.

359 Smith, *Rocky Mountain Mining Camps,* pg. 81.

360 Nosserman, *Many More Mountains, Vol. II,* pg. 145.

361 Thompson, *The Social and Cultural History of Lake City, Colorado,* pg. 51.

362 For more details on churches see Thompson, *The Social and Cultural History of Lake City, Colorado,* All of Chapter V.

363 Nosserman, *Many More Mountains, Vol. II,* pg. 63.

364 Darley, *Pioneering in the San Juan,* pgs. 16-17.

365 Burton Smith reports that the 1880 census shows George as a resident of Henson at the Ute-Ulay Mine.

366 Smith, *Ho for the San Juans,* pg. 15.

367 Quoted in Nosserman, *Many More Mountains, Vol. 2,* page 63.

368 Darley, *Pioneering in the San Juan,* pgs. 17-18.

369 Darley, *Pioneering in the San Juan,* pg. 122.

370 Darley, *Pioneering in the San Juan,* pg. 38.

371 Darley, *Pioneering in the San Juan,* pg.38.

372 Burton Smith.

373   Darley, *Pioneering in the San Juan*, pg.83.
374   Houston, *Lake City Reflections*, pg. 109.
375   Reyher, *Silver and Sawdust*, pg. 170.
376   D.A.R., *Pioneers of the San Juan Country, Vol. III*, pgs 113-114. Darley's account is in Darley, *Pioneering in the San Juan*, Pg. 27-31.
377   Darley, *Pioneering in the San Juan*, pgs. 57 & 59.
378   Wright, *Tiny Hinsdale of the Silvery San Juan*, pg. 71.
379   Reyher, *Silver and Sawdust*, pg. 166.
380   Wallace, *Epitaph for an Editor*, pg. 18 says January, 1877.
381   Wright, *Tiny Hinsdale of the Silvery San Juan*, pg. 72.
382   Wright, *Tiny Hinsdale of the Silvery San Juan*, pg. 74.
383   Wright, *Tiny Hinsdale of the Silvery San Juan*, pg. 72 says they disbanded in 1878.
384   *Silver World*, March 11, 1882.
385   Eberhart, *Guide to the Colorado Ghost Towns and Mining Camps*, pg. 388.
386   *Silver World*, November 30, 1876.
387   Thompson, *The Social and Cultural History of Lake City, Colorado, 1876-1900*, pg. 28.
388   Wallace, *Epitaph for an Editor*, pgs. 25-30.
389   *William's Tourists Guide and Map of the San Juan Mines of Colorado*, pg. 8.
390   *William's Tourists Guide and Map of the San Juan Mines of Colorado*, pg. 10.
391   *William's Tourists Guide and Map of the San Juan Mines of Colorado*, pg. 19.
392   *William's Tourists Guide and Map of the San Juan Mines of Colorado*, pg. 20.
393   *Silver World*, September 9, 1875.
394   Thompson, *The Social and Cultural History of Lake City, Colorado, 1876 to 1900*, writes that T. H. Cannon started the school.
395   Burton Smith reports the cornerstone is now at the Masonic Lodge.
396   *Silver World*, January 8, 1881.
397   Reyher, *Silver and Sawdust*, pg. 106.
398   Wright, *Tiny Hinsdale of the Silvery San Juan*, pgs. 62-68.
399   Kushner, *Alferd Packer, Cannibal! Victim?*, Pg. 34.
400   Wood, *I Hauled These Mountains in Here*, pgs. 42-44.
401   *Silver World*, August 18, 1877.
402   Wood, *I Hauled These Mountains in Here*, pg. 58.
403   Vandenbusche, *The Gunnison Country*, pg. 75.
404   Quoted in Wood, *I Hauled These Mountains in Here*, pg.157.
405   Wood, *I Hauled These Mountains in Here*, pg.154.
406   Thompson, *The Social and Cultural History of Lake City, Colorado, 1876 to 1900*, pg. 4.
407   May 17, 1877.
408   Thompson, *The Social and Cultural History of Lake City, Colorado, 1876 to 1900*, pg. 90.
409   Thompson, *The Social and Cultural History of Lake City, Colorado, 1876 to 1900*, pgs. 90-91.
410   Thompson, *The Social and Cultural History of Lake City, Colorado, 1876 to 1900*, pg. 88.
411   Martin, *Something in the Wind*, pg. 37.
412   Brown, *An Empire of Silver*, pg. 33.
413   Nosserman, *Many More Mountains, Vol. II*, pg. 133.
414   Thompson, *The Social and Cultural History of Lake City, Colorado, 1876 to 1900*, pg. 86.
415   Smith, *San Juan Gold*, pg. 5.
416   Thompson, "Early Development of Lake City," pg. 96.
417   Nosserman, *Many More Mountains, Vol. II*, pg. 252.

418 Wright, *Tiny Hinsdale of the Silvery San Juan*, pg. 171; Houston, "Lake City's Melody of the Past."

419 Vandenbusche and Borneman, "The D. & R. G. Lake City Branch and a Galloping Goose," pg. 29.

420 Morse, *A Brief History of Mining in Hinsdale County*, pg. 29.

421 D.A.R., *Pioneers of the San Juan Country, Vol. II*, pg. 94.

422 Nosserman, *Many More Mountains, Vol. II*, pg. 145.

423 Burton Smith.

424 Nosserman, *Many More Mountains, Vol. II*, pg. 234.

425 Smith, *San Juan Gold*, pg. 5.

426 Thompson, "Early Development of Lake City," pg. 96.

427 Halls, *History of Colorado, Vol. IV*, pg. 156.

428 Wright, *Tiny Hinsdale of the Silvery San Juan*, pg. 171.

429 Bell, *The Pilgrim and the Pioneer*, pg. 99.

430 Bell, *The Pilgrim and the Pioneer*, pgs. 99, 104, 105, 145, & 232.

431 Bell, *The Pilgrim and the Pioneer*, pg. 189.

432 Bell, *The Pilgrim and the Pioneer*, pg. 189.

433 Henry Woods reports that Hough regularly showed off one of several shirts.

434 Wright, *Tiny Hinsdale of the Silvery San Juan*, pg. 182.

435 Burke, *Ghosts of the Lake Fork*, pg. 156.

436 Reyher, *Through the Valley of the Shadow of Death*, pg. 63.

437 Reyher, *Through the Valley of the Shadow of Death*, pg. 30.

438 Kushner, *Alferd Packer, Cannibal! Victim?*, Pg. 10.

439 Churchill, *Doc Holliday, Bat Masterson & Wyatt Earp – Their Colorado Careers*, pg. 18.

440 Churchill, *Doc Holliday, Bat Masterson & Wyatt Earp – Their Colorado Careers*, pgs. 30-31.

441 Enss, *The Lady Was A Gambler*, pgs. 21-29.

442 Wood, *Over the Range to the Golden Gate*, pg. 141.

443 *Silver World*, April 14, 1877 and April 21, 1877.

444 *Silver World*, April 14, 1877.

445 Nosserman, *Many More Mountains, Vol. II*, pg. 95.

446 *William's Tourists Guide and Map of the San Juan Mines of Colorado*, pg. 16.

447 Nosserman, *Many More Mountains, Vol. II*, pg. 56.

448 Kaplan, "Colorado's Big Little Man: The Early Career of Otto Mears, 1840-1881," pg. 132.

449 Burton Smith.

450 D.A.R., *Pioneers of the San Juan Country, Vol. II*, pg. 60.

451 *Rocky Mountain News*, May 31, 1877.

452 Thompson, *The Social and Cultural History of Lake City, Colorado*, pg. 50.

453 D.A.R., *Pioneers of the San Juan Country, Vol. II*, pg. 60.

454 *Rocky Mountain News*, September 28, 1879.

455 Bell, *The Pilgrim and the Pioneer*, pg. 259.

456 Bell, *The Pilgrim and the Pioneer*, pg. 262.

457 Hall, *History of Colorado, Vol. IV*, pgs. 157-158.

458 Wright, *Tiny Hinsdale of the Silvery San Juan*, says spring of 1878.

459 Wallace, *Epitaph for an Editor*, pg. 101.

460 Wright, *Tiny Hinsdale of the Silvery San Juan*, pg. 138.

461 His full and detailed account can be found in Bell, *The Pilgrim and the Pioneer*, pgs. 223-235.

462 Wallace, *History with the Hide Off*, pg. 168.

463 Brown, *Empire of Silver*, pg. 58.

464 Irving, *Geology and Ore Deposits Near Lake City, Colorado*, pg. 71.

465 January 5, 1878.

466 Darley, *Pioneering in the San Juan,* pg. 18.
467 Smith, *Sisters in Sin,* pg. 33.
468 Nosserman, *Many More Mountains, Vol. II,* pg. 310.
469 Houston, "Lake City's Melody of the Past," pg. 161.
470 Hall, *History of Colorado,* Vol. IV, pg 158.
471 Fossett, *Colorado, Its Gold and Silver Mines,* pg. 97.
472 Wallace, *Epitaph for an Editor,* pg. 37.
473 Wallace, *Epitaph for an Editor,* pg. 37.
474 Reyher, *Silver and Sawdust, Life in the San Juans,* pg. 11.
475 See Chapter 8 of Smith, *Ouray, Chief of the Utes.*
476 Adams was born Charles Schuanbeck.
477 Smith, *Ouray, Chief of the Utes,* p. 165.
478 D.A.R. *Pioneers of the San Juan Country, Vol. II,* pg. 92.
479 Nichols, *Under the Sun at Lake City,* pg. 50.
480 Quoted in Wallace, *Epitaph for an Editor,* pg. 36.
481 Wright, *Tiny Hinsdale of the Silvery San Juan,* pgs. 104-105.
482 Wright, *Tiny Hinsdale of the Silvery San Juan,* pg. 105.
483 Bell, *The Pilgrim and the Pioneer,* pgs. 446- 447
484 There is a long article on Mears in D.A.R., *Pioneers of the San Juan Country, Vol. I,* 1942, pg 15, etc.
485 Nichols, *Under the Sun at Lake City,* pg. 50.
486 Wallace, *Epitaph for an Editor,* pg. 14.
487 D.A.R., *Pioneers of the San Juan Country, Vol II,* pg. 95. See Thompson, *The Social and Cultural History of Lake City, Colorado,* Chapter 7 for information on the many Lake City clubs.
488 Smith, *San Juan Gold,* pg. 46.
489 Fossett, *Colorado, Its Gold and Silver Mines,* pg 52.
490 Ingeroll, *Crest of the Continent,* pg. 263.
491 *Silver World,* May 22, 1880.
492 Griswold, *Colorado's Century of "Cities,"* pg. 112.
493 Wright, *Tiny Hinsdale of the Silvery San Juan,* pg. 82.
494 Thompson, *The Social and Cultural History of Lake City, Colorado,* pg. 7.
495 Nosserman, *Many More Mountains, Vol. II,* pg. 203.
496 Smith, *Sisters in Sin,* pg. 38.
497 Smith, *Sisters in Sin,* pg. 37.
498 Smith, *Sisters in Sin,* pg. 39.
499 Vandenbusche and Borneman, "The D. & R. G. Lake City Branch and a Galloping Goose," p. 29.
500 Vandenbusche, *The Gunnison Country,* pg. 15.
501 Vandenbusche and Borneman, "The D. & R. G. Lake City Branch and a Galloping Goose," p. 30.
502 Kaplan, "Colorado's Big Little Man: The Early Career of Otto Mears, 1840-1881," pg. 137.
503 Smith, *San Juan Gold,* pg. 98.
504 *Silver World,* October 15, 1881.
505 *Silver World,* January 1, 1881.
506 Wright, *Tiny Hinsdale of the Silvery San Juan,* pg. 123.
507 Hall, *History of Colorado,* Vol. IV, pgs. 160-161.
508 Wallace, *Epitaph for an Editor,* pg. 52; Burke, *A Bumpy Ride,* pg 62.
509 Smith, *San Juan Gold,* pg. 105.
510 Quoted in Nosserman, *Many More Mountains, Vol III,* Pg 190.
511 Nosserman, *Many More Mountains, Vol III,* Pg. 20.
512 Smith, *San Juan Gold,* pg. 34.
513 Nosserman, *Many More Mountains, Vol III,* Pg. 19.

514 Smith, *San Juan Gold*, pg. 34.

515 Smith, *San Juan Gold*, pg. 73.

516 Smith, *San Juan Gold*, pg. 79.

517 Smith, *San Juan Gold*, pg. 74.

518 Smith, *San Juan Gold*, pg. 75.

519 Smith, *San Juan Gold*, pg. 101.

520 Smith, *San Juan Gold*, pg. 90.

521 Not the same as the *Silver World* editor.

522 Smith, *Exploring the Historic San Juan Triangle*, pg. 101.

523 In 1901, the house was converted into Lake City's only hospital, but was dismantled for its building materials in 1923.

524 Houston, *Lake City Reflections*, pg. 95.

525 Monroe, *San Juan Silver*, pg. 191.

526 *Silver World*, April 29, 1882.

527 Wallce, *History with the Hide Off*, pages 183-186) (The Ocean Wave Bridge has been replaced by the 8 ½ Street Bridge, which is in basically the same spot and gives access to Ball Flats.

528 See also Monroe, *San Juan Silver*, pg. 191.

529 Bell, *The Pilgrim and the Pioneer*, pgs. 447-459.

530 Sammons, *Keepin' the Peace*, pg.102.

531 Thompson, *The Social and Cultural History of Lake City, Colorado, 1876-1900*, pg. 152.

532 Burton Smith.

533 *Silver World*, April 9, 1882.

534 Oldham, *Alferd, Soldier, Prospector and Cannibal*, pgs. 36-37,

535 See Houston, *Lake City Reflections* for more stories.

536 See Houston, *Lake City Reflections* pgs. 93-94.

537 See Mary Joy Martin's books mentioned in the bibliography.

538 Smith, *Song of the Hammer and Drill*, pgs. 56-77.

539 Sometimes called Hell's Half Acre.

540 Strahorn, *Gunnison and the San Juans*, pg. 79.

541 *Lake City Mining Register* January 1, 1881.

542 *Silver World*, August 13, 1881.

543 Wallace, *History with the Hide Off*, pg. 34.

544 Wallace, *History with the Hide Off*, pg. 70.

545 Kushner, *Alferd Packer, Cannibal! Victim?*, Pg. 19.

546 Wright, *Tiny Hinsdale of the Silvery San Juan*, pg. 91.

547 Thompson, *The Social and Cultural History of Lake City, Colorado, 1876-1900*, pg. 115.

548 Burke, *Ghosts of the Lake Fork*, pg. 135.

549 *Lake City Times*, June 4, 1891.

550 Nosserman, *Many More Mountains, Vol. III*, pg. 307.

551 Bancroft, *History of Colorado*, pg. 619.

552 Smith, *San Juan Gold*, pgs. 125-126.

553 Fossett, *Colorado, Its Gold and Silver Mines*, New York, 1885.

554 To this author's knowledge no one, other than the federal government, has ever "owned" the lake, although various people and government bodies have and do own the use of the water from the lake. However there evidently were people who tried to file on the lake and were not successful.

555 Crofutt, *Crofutt's Grip-Sack Guide to Colorado*, pgs. 112-113.

556 Crofutt, *Crofutt's Grip-Sack Guide to Colorado*, pg. 112.

557 Ingersoll, *Crest of the Continent*, pg. 262.

558 Ingersoll, *Crest of the Continent*, pg. 263.

559 Ingersoll, *Crest of the Continent*, pg. 263-264.

560 Wallace, *Epitaph for an Editor*, pg. 59.
561 Wallace, *Epitaph for an Editor*, pg. 49.
562 Smith, *Song of the Hammer and Drill*, pg. 27.
563 LaMassena, *Colorado's Mountain Railroads*, pg. 164.
564 Nossaman, *Many More Mountains, Vol. II*, pg. 234.
565 Henderson, *Mining in Colorado*, pg. 51.
566 *Lake City Times*, May 14, 1891.
567 Wallace, *Epitaph for an Editor*, pg. 67.
568 *Lake City Times*, January 15, 1891.
569 Griswold, *Colorado's Century of Cities*, pg. 122.
570 Houston, *Lake City Reflections*, pg. 110.
571 Reyher, *Through the Valley of the Shadow of Death*, pg. 32.
572 Wood, *I Hauled These Mountains in Here*, pg. 305.
573 Vandenbusche and Borneman, "The D. & R. G. Lake City Branch and a Galloping Goose," pg. 61.
574 Stone, *History of Colorado, Vol. I*, pg. 290.
575 Houston, "Lake City's Melody of the Past," pg. 164.
576 Houston, "Lake City's Melody of the Past," pg. 164.
577 Thompson, *The Social and Cultural History of Lake City, Colorado, 1876 to 1900*, pg. 47.
578 *Lake City Times*, April 20, 1893.
579 Houston, Lake *City Reflections*, pg. 85.
580 Womack, *Our Ladies of the Tenderloin, Colorado's Legends in Lace*, pg. 123.
581 Vinton, *Lake City and Hinsdale County, Colorado*, pg. 2.
582 Vinton, *Lake City and Hinsdale County, Colorado*, pg. 4.
583 The streets were still dirt.
584 Vinton, *Lake City and Hinsdale County, Colorado*, pg. 30.
585 Stone, *History of Colorado, Vol. I*, pg. 847.
586 Wolle, *Stampede to Timberline*, pgs. 352-353.
587 Eberhart, *Guide to the Colorado Ghost Towns and Mining Camps*, pg. 390.
588 Cross, *A Brief Review of the Geology of the San Juan Region of Southwestern Colorado*, pgs. 103-106.
589 Quoted in Wyman, Hard Rock Epic, pg. 19.
590 Houston, "Lake City's Melody of the Past," pg. 164.
591 Quoted in Wallace, *Epitaph for an Editor*, pg. 72.
592 Wallace, *Epitaph for an Editor*, pg. 97.
593 Wallace, *Epitaph for an Editor*, pg. 80.
594 Wallace, *Epitaph for an Editor*, pg. 84.
595 Henry Woods reports that Nickole was only wounded.
596 Wright, *Tiny Hinsdale of the Silvery San Juan*, pg. 125.
597 Wright, *Tiny Hinsdale of the Silvery San Juan*, pg. 126.
598 Quoted in Wallace, *Epitaph for an Editor*, pg. 89.
599 Wallace, *Epitaph for an Editor*, pg. 89.
600 Henry Woods reveals that "Old Sid" was named after Alex's brother.
601 Smith and Bezek, *On the Backs of Burros*, pg. 120.
602 Quoted in Wallace, *Epitaph for an Editor*, pg. 89.
603 Wallace, *Epitaph for an Editor*, pg. 91.
604 Houston, "Lake City's Melody of the Past," pg. 165.
605 Vickers, *Welcome Home, The Story of the Vickers Ranch*, pg. 69.
606 Burton Smith information.
607 Vandenbusche and Smith, *A Land Alone: Colorado's Western Slope*, pg. 253.
608 Burton Smith.
609 *William's Tourists Guide and Map of the San Juan Mines of Colorado*, pg. 11.
610 Wallace, *Epitaph for an Editor*, pg. 23.

611 Vandenbusche and Smith, *A Land Alone: Colorado's Western Slope*, pg. 84.

612 *William's Tourists Guide and Map of the San Juan Mines of Colorado*, pg. 4.

613 Simmons, *The San Luis Valley*, pg. 158.

614 Vandenbusche and Smith, *A Land Alone: Colorado's Western Slope*, pg. 84.

615 Nosserman, *Many More Mountains, Vol. III*, pg. 137.

616 *Denver Republican* January 1, 1882.

617 See *Colorado Rail Annual No. 14*, pg. 37, and *Trails Among the Columbine*, Sundance 1988, "The Lake City Branch."

618 *Silver World*, November 26, 1881.

619 Vandenbusche and Borneman, "The D. & R. G. Lake City Branch and a Galloping Goose," pg. 38.

620 Vandenbusche and Smith, *A Land Alone: Colorado's Western Slope*, pg. 86.

621 Burke, *Ghosts of the Lake Fork*, pg. 86.

622 Collman, "The Lake City Branch," pg. 168.

623 Vandenbusche, *The Gunnison Country*, pg. 158.

624 Nosserman, *Many More Mountains, Vol. II*, pg. 109.

625 Nichols, *Under the Sun at Lake City*, pg. 54.

626 Collman, "The Lake City Branch," pg. 180.

627 Vandenbusche and Borneman, "The D. & R. G. Lake City Branch and a Galloping Goose," pg. 4.

628 Vandenbusche, *The Gunnison Country*, pg. 159.

629 LaMassena, Colorado's Mountain Railroads, 1st Edition.

630 Vandenbusche, *The Gunnison Country*, pg. 120.

631 Another word for "Hell."

632 *Lake City Sentinel*, June 29, 1889.

633 Wright, *Tiny Hinsdale of the Silvery San Juan*, pg. 57.

634 Wilkins, *Colorado Railroads*, pg. 73; LaMassena, *Colorado's Mountain Railroads*, 1st Edition.

635 Swank, *Mountain Memories*, pg. 62.

636 Burke, *Ghosts of the Lake Fork*, pg. 91.

637 One mile to the depot.

638 Pitney, *My Lake City Railroad Memories*, pgs. 1-6.

639 Collman, "The Lake City Branch," pg. 167.

640 Burke, *Ghosts of the Lake Fork*, pg. 106.

641 Burke, *Ghosts of the Lake Fork*, pg. 108.

642 Burke, *Ghosts of the Lake Fork*, pg. 111.

643 Henry Woods.

644 Collman, "The Lake City Branch," pg. 189.

645 Wright, *Tiny Hinsdale of the Silvery San Juan*, pgs. 55-56.

646 Benson, *Pioneer Ranching in the Rockies*, pg. 32.

647 Burke, *Ghosts of the Lake Fork*, pg. 113.

648 Vandenbusche and Borneman, "The D. & R. G. Lake City Branch and a Galloping Goose," pg. 50.

649 Burke, *Ghosts of the Lake Fork*, pg. 177.

650 Pitney, *My Lake City Railroad Memories*, pgs. 8-9.

651 D.A.R., *Pioneers of the San Juan Country, Vol. II*, pg. 64.

652 Vandenbusche and Borneman, "The D. & R. G. Lake City Branch and a Galloping Goose," pg. 55.

653 Wright, *Tiny Hinsdale of the Silvery San Juan*, pgs. 50-60.

654 Sloan and Skowronski, *The Rainbow Route*, pg. 134.

655 LaMassena, Colorado's Mountain Railroads, 1st Edition.

656 Wood, *Over the Range to the Golden Gate*, pgs. 84-86.

657 Not true, but it sounds very romantic.

658 Benson, *Pioneer Ranching in the Rockies*, pg. 32.

659   Vandenbusche and Borneman, "The D. & R. G. Lake City Branch and a Galloping Goose," pg. 84.

660   Benson, *Pioneer Ranching in the Rockies*, pg. 32.

661   Vandenbusche and Borneman, "The D. & R. G. Lake City Branch and a Galloping Goose," pg. 86.

662   U. S. Census Records.

663   Livingston," Sapinero-Lake City Branch of the Denver and Rio Grande Western," Denver Westerners Roundup, XXXII, No. 2 (March-April, 1976).

664   Collman, "The Lake City Branch," pg. 190.

665   Burke, *Ghosts of the Lake Fork*, pg. 102.

666   *Silver World*, July 1882, quoted at Reyher, *Silver and Sawdust*, pg. 118.

667   Nosserman, *Many More Mountains, Vol.I*, Pg. 128.

668   *Lake City Mining Register*, January 1, 1881.

669   Nosserman, *Many More Mountains, Vol.II*, Pg. 20.

670   Smith, *Exploring the Historic San Juan Triangle*, pg. 135.

671   Nosserman, *Many More Mountains, Vol.II*, Pg. 202.

672   *Lake City Mining Register*, January 11, 1881.

673   Wolle, *Stampede to Timberline*, pg. 351.

674   Nosserman at footnote 12, *Many More Mountains*, Vol. II, pg. 96 feels it was not the same man because the Silverton smelter owner consistently used the initial "B" in his name. However this author has found several sources where the Lake City Greene used this middle initial.

675   July 27, 1878.

676   Thompson, *The Social and Cultural History of Lake City, Colorado, 1876 to 1900*, pg. 167.

677   Quoted in Griswold, *Colorado's Century of "Cities,"* pgs.143-144.

678   Nosserman, *Many More Mountains, Vol. II*, pg. 96.

679   The only other incorporated town ever in Hinsdale County was the town of Debs in the far southern part of the county in the 1900s.

680   *Lake City Mining Register*, January 1, 1881.

681   Thompson, *The Social and Cultural History of Lake City, Colorado, 1876 to 1900*, pg. 166.

682   Wolle, *Stampede to Timberline*, pgs. 353-354.

683   Newburn, *Postal History of the Colorado San Juan.*

684   Bancroft, *Unique Ghost Towns and Mountain Spots*, pg. 71.

685   Lampert, *Lake City Places*, pg. 101.

686   Wright, *Tiny Hinsdale of the Silvery San Juan*, pgs. 146-148.

687   Wolle, *Stampede to Timberline*, pg. 351.

688   Eberhart, Guide to Colorado Ghost Towns and Mining Camps, pg. 390; Wolle, *Stampede to Timberline*, Pg. 351.

689   Eberhart, Guide to Colorado Ghost Towns and Mining Camps, pg. 390; Wolle, *Stampede to Timberline*, Pg. 352.

690   Newburn, *Postal History of the Colorado San Juan.*

691   Griswold, *Colorado's Century of "Cities,"* pg. 232.

692   Lambert, *Lake City Places*, pgs. 49 & 55.

693   Felts, *Oen Edgar Noland*, pg. 21.

694   Griswold, *Colorado's Century of "Cities,"* pg. 120.

695   Kinquist, *Stony Pass*, pg. 48.

696   Newburn, *Postal History of the Colorado San Juan.*

697   Felts, *Oen Edgar Noland*, pg. 18.

698   The Wrights write that the post office at Lake Shore was servicing the mines close by, but that there was not a town, only a few other cabins. Wright, *Tiny Hinsdale of the Silvery San Juan*, pg. 47. Photos of the day show at least twenty cabins, more than many of the Hinsdale "towns."

699 Wright, *Tiny Hinsdale of the Silvery San Juan*, pg. 47. The Wrights write that Carson City was very active in the early seventies, but no other evidence of this early activity has been found.

700 Griswold, *Colorado's Century of "Cities,"* pg. 231.

701 Newburn, *Postal History of the Colorado San Juan*.

702 Rawson, *Carson Country*, pg. 1.

703 Rawson, *Carson Country*, pg. 8.

704 Rawson, *Carson Country*, pg. 9.

705 The Wrights say 1897- 1902.

706 Burton Smith reports there was also a post office on the south side of the divide on Lost Trail.

707 Rawson, *Carson Country*, pg. 18.

708 Athearn, *The Coloradans*, pg. 20.

709 Bancroft, *Unique Ghost Towns and Mountain Spots*, pg. 72.

710 Ruhoff, "Back Country Adventures in Mineral and Hinsdale Counties," pg. 117.

711 Burke, *A Bumpy Ride*, pg. 358.

712 Burton Smith feels the town was named for the founder of the Sherman Williams Paint Co., who homesteaded the area that was later occupied by the Redcloud Ranch.

713 The Wrights say 1897-1905.

714 Wright, *Tiny Hinsdale of the Silvery San Juan*, pg. 36.

715 Wright, *Tiny Hinsdale of the Silvery San Juan*, pgs. 45-46.

716 Wolle, *Stampede to Timberline*, pg. 358.

717 Wright, *Tiny Hinsdale of the Silvery San Juan* says there was no town called Burrows Park, and Newburn, *Postal History of the Colorado San Juan* states it was only the name of the post office serving Argentum.

718 Eberhart, *Guide to the Colorado Ghost Towns and Mining Camps*, pg. 394.

719 Nosserman, *Many More Mountains, Vol. I*, pg. 137.

720 Newburn, *Postal History of the Colorado San Juan*.

721 Nosserman, *Many More Mountains, Vol. II*, pg. 37.

722 Wright, *Tiny Hinsdale of the Silvery San Juan*, pg. 35, notes the Wrights lived at Whitecross for some time.

723 Ruhoff, "Back Country Adventures in Mineral and Hinsdale Counties," pg. 121.

724 Eberhart, *Guide to the Colorado Ghost Towns and Mining Camps*, pg. 394.

725 Wolle, *Stampede to Timberline*, pg. 362.

726 Wolle, *Stampede to Timberline*, pg. 362.

727 Wright, *Tiny Hinsdale of the Silvery San Juan*, pg. 45.

728 Wright, *Tiny Hinsdale of the Silvery San Juan*, pg. 46.

729 Nosserman, *Many More Mountains, Vol. I*, pg. 312.

730 Eberhart, *Guide to the Colorado Ghost Towns and Mining Camps*, pg. 394.

731 Griswold, *Colorado's Century of "Cities,"* pg. 144.

732 Nosserman, *Many More Mountains, Vol. II*, pg. 312.

733 Wright, *Tiny Hinsdale of the Silvery San Juan*, pg. 36.

734 Eberhart, *Guide to the Colorado Ghost Towns and Mining Camps*, pg. 395.

735 Ruhoff, "Back Country Adventures in Mineral and Hinsdale Counties," pg. 123.

736 Rickard, *Across the San Juan Mountains*, pg. 91.

737 Nosserman, Many More Mountains, Vol. I, pg. 153.

738 Newburn, *Postal History of the Colorado San Juan*.

739 Nosserman, *Many More Mountains, Vol. II*, pg. 305.

740 Burton Smith.

741 Eberhart, *Guide to the Colorado Ghost Towns and Mining Camps*, pg. 394.

742 Stone, *History of Colorado, Vol. 1*, pg 272.

743 Vickers, *Welcome Home, The Story of the Vickers Ranch*, pgs. 94 & 96.

744 Crofutt, *Crofutt's Grip-Sack Guide to Colorado*, pg. 112.

745 Rickard, *Across the San Juan Mountains,* pg. 88.

746 Reyher, *Silver and Sawdust, Life in the San Juans,* pg. 11.

747 Bell, *The Pilgrim and the Pioneer,* pg. 245.

748 Irving and Bancroft, *Geology and Ore Deposits Near Lake City, Colorado,* pgs. 12 & 13.

749 Irving and Bancroft, *Geology and Ore Deposits Near Lake City, Colorado,* pg. 38.

750 Irving and Bancroft, *Geology and Ore Deposits Near Lake City, Colorado,* pg. 40.

751 Irving and Bancroft, *Geology and Ore Deposits Near Lake City, Colorado,* pg. 41.

752 Irving and Bancroft, *Geology and Ore Deposits Near Lake City, Colorado,* pg. 69.

753 Strahorn, *Gunnison and the San Juan,* pgs. 82-83.

754 Strahorn, *Gunnison and the San Juan,* pg. 84.

755 Bancroft, *History of Colorado,* pg. 619.

756 Bancroft, *History of Colorado,* pg. 501, footnote 31.

757 Vickers, *Welcome Home, The Story of the Vickers Ranch,* pg. 37.

758 Morse, *A Brief History of Mining in Hinsdale County,* pg. 31.

759 *William's Tourists Guide and Map of the San Juan Mines of Colorado,* pg. 8.

760 Strahorn, *Gunnison and the San Juan,* pg. 70.

761 *William's Tourists Guide and Map of the San Juan Mines of Colorado,* pg. 8.

762 Morse, *A Brief History of Mining in Hinsdale County,* pg. 38.

763 Brown, *An Empire of Silver,* pg. 28.

764 All information on mills is from Wickerman and LeBaron, *Mine Owners and Mines of the Colorado Gold Rush,* pgs. 251-252.

765 Crofutt, *Crofutt's Grip-Sack Guide to Colorado,* pg. 112.

766 Crofutt, *Crofutt's Grip-Sack Guide to Colorado,* pg. 112.

767 Hall, *History of Colorado, Vol. 4.*

768 Morse, *A Brief History of Mining in Hinsdale County,* pg. 40.

769 Morse, *A Brief History of Mining in Hinsdale County,* pg. 68.

770 Smith, *Exploring the Historic San Juan Triangle,* pg. 133.

771 Henderson, *Mining in Colorado,* pg. 51.

772 Vinton, *Lake City and Hinsdale County, Colorado,* pg. 10.

773 Strahorn, *Gunnison and the San Juans,* pg. 71.

774 Wickerman and LeBaron, *Mine Owners and Mines of the Colorado Gold Rush,* pg. 245.

775 Strahorn, *Gunnison and the San Juans,* pg. 72.

776 Vinton, *Lake City and Hinsdale County, Colorado,* pg. 10.

777 Brown, "Mineral Zones in Whitecross," pg. 14.

778 Wickerman and LeBaron, *Mine Owners and Mines of the Colorado Gold Rush,* pg. 237.

779 Vinton, *Lake City and Hinsdale County, Colorado,* pg. 9.

780 Wright, *Tiny Hinsdale of the Silvery San Juan,* pg. 48.

781 Irving and Bancroft, *Geology and Ore Deposits Near Lake City, Colorado,* pg. 75.

782 Irving and Bancroft, *Geology and Ore Deposits Near Lake City, Colorado,* pgs. 76-77.

783 Wickerman and LeBaron, *Mine Owners and Mines of the Colorado Gold Rush,* pg. 237.

784 Irving and Bancroft, *Geology and Ore Deposits Near Lake City, Colorado,* pgs. 77-78.

785 Irving and Bancroft, *Geology and Ore Deposits Near Lake City, Colorado,* pg. 78.

786 Irving and Bancroft, *Geology and Ore Deposits Near Lake City, Colorado,* pg. 80.

787 Irving and Bancroft, *Geology and Ore Deposits Near Lake City, Colorado,* pg. 80.

788 Wright, *Tiny Hinsdale of the Silvery San Juan,* pg. 49.

789 Irving and Bancroft, *Geology and Ore Deposits Near Lake City, Colorado,* pg. 81.

790 Wickerman and LeBaron, *Mine Owners and Mines of the Colorado Gold Rush,* pg. 234.

791 Irving and Bancroft, *Geology and Ore Deposits Near Lake City, Colorado*, pg. 83.

792 Wickerman and LeBaron, *Mine Owners and Mines of the Colorado Gold Rush*, pg. 247.

793 Vinton, *Lake City and Hinsdale County, Colorado*, pg. 7.

794 Henderson, *Mining in Colorado*, pg. 51.

795 *William's Tourist Guide to the San Juans*, pg. 7.

796 Henderson, *Mining in Colorado*, pg. 51.

797 Brown, *Mineral Zones in Whitecross*, pg. 14.

798 *William's Tourist Guide to the San Juans*, pg. 7.

799 Morse, *A Brief History of Mining in Hinsdale County*, pg. 29.

800 Wolle, *Stampede to Timberline*, pg. 351.

801 Irving and Bancroft, *Geology and Ore Deposits Near Lake City, Colorado*, pgs. 85-95.

802 Muriel Wolle.

803 Wright, *Tiny Hinsdale of the Silvery San Juan*, pg. 48.

804 Wolle, *Stampede to Timberline*, pg. 344.

805 Wickerman and LeBaron, *Mine Owners and Mines of the Colorado Gold Rush*, pg. 240.

806 Fossett, *Colorado, Its Gold and Silver Mines*, pg. 517.

807 Brown, *Mineral Zones in Whitecross*, pg. 14.

808 Irving and Bancroft, *Geology and Ore Deposits Near Lake City, Colorado*, pg. 102.

809 Vinton, *Lake City and Hinsdale County, Colorado*, pg. 20.

810 Irving and Bancroft, *Geology and Ore Deposits Near Lake City, Colorado*, pg. 101.

811 Vinton, *Lake City and Hinsdale County, Colorado*, pg. 20.

812 Vickers, *Welcome Home*, pg. 126.

813 Vinton, *Lake City and Hinsdale County, Colorado*, pg. 20.

814 Vinton, *Lake City and Hinsdale County, Colorado*, pg. 13.

815 Irving and Bancroft, *Geology and Ore Deposits Near Lake City, Colorado*, pg. 116.

816 Brown, *Mineral Zones in Whitecross*, pg. 14.

817 There is some doubt that the name change was made this early.

818 Rickard, *Across the San Juan Mountains*, pgs. 84-85.

819 Morse, *A Brief History of Mining in Hinsdale County*, pg. 31.

820 D.A.R., *Pioneers of the San Juan Country, Vol. II*, pg. 87.

821 Wickerman and LeBaron, *Mine Owners and Mines of the Colorado Gold Rush*, pg. 240.

822 Wikipedia "Golden Fleece Mine."

823 Wickerman and LeBaron, *Mine Owners and Mines of the Colorado Gold Rush*, pg. 240.

824 Strahorn, *Gunnison and the San Juans*, pg. 71.

825 Rickard, *Across the San Juan Mountains*, pgs. 80-84.

826 Rickard, *Across the San Juan Mountains*, pg. 86.

827 Kaplan, *Otto Mears, Paradoxical Pathfinder*, pg. 13.

828 Irving and Bancroft, *Geology and Ore Deposits Near Lake City, Colorado*, pg. 109.

829 Irving and Bancroft, *Geology and Ore Deposits Near Lake City, Colorado*, pg. 110.

830 Henderson, *Mining in Colorado*, pg. 5.

831 Ruffner, *Reconnaissance of the Ute Country*, writes of one.

832 Vinton, *Lake City and Hinsdale County, Colorado*, pg. 17.

833 Swank, *Mountain Memories*, pg. 37.

834 Rawson, *Carson Country*, pg. 15.

835 Newburn, *Postal History of the Colorado San Juan*.

836 Brown, "Mineral Zones in Whitecross," pg. 6.

837 Henderson, *Mining in Colorado*, pg. 51.

838 Crofutt mentions that the lake is eighty feet at its deepest, but Burton Smith's father measured it at 90 feet in 1939.

839 Nora Smith

840 Burton Smith reports it was either the Contention or the Ramsey Mill.

841 *Silver World,* "A Quick Primer on Lake San Cristobal," pg. 4.

842 Alferd Packer said there were no fish in the lake, and Lt. Ruffner verified this a few months later.

843 *Tiny Hinsdale of the Silvery San Juan,* pg. 112.

844 Burton Smith.

845 *Tiny Hinsdale of the Silvery San Juan,* pg. 113.

846 Burton Smith was given this information by Tom French, Superintendent of the Creede Federal Fish Hatchery.

847 Burton Smith.

848 Nichols, *Under the Sun at Lake City,* pg. 6.

849 Nichols, *Under the Sun at Lake City,* pg. 6.

850 *Silver World,* June 2, 1877.

851 *Silver World,* June 21, 1879.

852 *Hall's History of Colorado, Vol. IV, 1895 Vol. 4,* pgs. 155-156 and 159.

853 Burton Smith.

854 Thompson, *The Social and Cultural History of Lake City, Colorado, 1876 to 1900,* pg. 111.

855 Vandenbusche, *A Land Alone: Colorado's Western Slope,* pg. 54.

856 All of Lake Shore Inn information is from Nora Smith.

857 Swank, *Mountain Memories,* pgs. 77-78.

858 Houston, *Historic Homes of Lake City, Colorado,* pg. 11.

859 Burton Smith reports some geologists feel there may be as many as five earthflows.

860 Burton Smith quoting a talk with slide expert J. W. Fandrich.

861 See J. W. Fandrich's small book, *The Slumgullion Earthflow,* available at the Lake City library.

862 Vandenbusche and Borneman, "The D.& R.G. Lake City Branch and a Galloping Goose," pg. 25.

863 Vandenbusche and Borneman, "The D.& R.G. Lake City Branch and a Galloping Goose," pg. 27.

864 Burton Smith.

865 Swank, *Mountain Memories,* pg. 80.

866 Bates, *A Quick History of Lake City, Colorado,* pg. 24.

867 Swank, *Mountain Memories,* pg. 87.

868 Burton Smith relates that Hill 71 got its name when the USGS mislabeled it as 71 Mountain which is nearer Lake San Cristobal and in the spring has a snowfield that looks like "71."

869 Swank, *Mountain Memories,* pgs. 87-88.

870 Swank, *Mountain Memories,* pg. 53.

871 Burton Smith.

872 Eberhart, *Guide to the Colorado Ghost Towns and Mining Camps,* pg. 386.

873 Burton Smith.

874 Burton Smith.

875 *Crusaders for Wildlife* and Smith, *Ouray, Chief of the Utes,* pg. 65.

876 Nichols, *Under the Sun at Lake City,* pg. 12.

877 Wallace, *Epitaph for an Editor,* pg. 93.

878 Thompson, *The Social and Cultural History of Lake city, Colorado, 1876 to 1900,* pgs. 161-162.

879 Collman, "The Lake City Branch," pg. 166.

880 Swank, *Mountain Memories,* pg. 8.

881 Griffiths, *San Juan Country,* pg. 190.

882 Burton Smith.

883 Vandenbusche, *A Land Alone: Colorado's Western Slope,* pg. 302.

INDEX